MEN OF FIRE

MEN
OF
FIRE

GRANT, FORREST, AND THE CAMPAIGN
THAT DECIDED THE CIVIL WAR

JACK HURST

BASIC
BOOKS

A Member of the Perseus Books Group

New York

Published by Basic Books
A Member of the Perseus Books Group

Text design by Cynthia Young
Set in 10-point ITC New Baskerville

Library of Congress Cataloging-in-Publication Data
has been applied for.

ISBN–10: 0-465-03184-6
ISBN–13: 978-0-465-03184-9

10 9 8 7 6 5 4 3 2 1

To Donna,
with love and admiration

ULYSSES S. GRANT. Photo courtesy of Bettmann/CORBIS.

NATHAN BEDFORD FORREST. Photo courtesy of
Bettmann/CORBIS.

CONTENTS

CONTENTS

LIST OF ILLUSTRATIONS

GLOSSARY OF PARTICIPANTS

BALDWIN, WILLIAM E.—Confederate colonel, commander of Fourteenth Mississippi Infantry and Buckner's Second Brigade; Baldwin's brigade, on loan to Pillow, led infantry out of Fort Donelson in attack of February 15.

BROWN, JOHN C.—Confederate colonel, commander of the Third Tennessee Infantry and Buckner's Third Brigade; held right wing of Confederate trenches at Fort Donelson.

BUCKNER, SIMON BOLIVAR—Confederate Brigadier general, commander of Second Division of the Army of Central Kentucky; prewar friend of Grant and public castigator of Gideon Pillow; opposed coming to Fort Donelson.

BUELL, DON CARLOS—Union brigadier general, commander of Department of the Ohio, headquartered in Louisville; career soldier; older friend and mentor of Federal general-in-chief George B. McClellan; rival of Department of the Missouri commander Halleck.

CAMPBELL, ANDREW JACKSON (JACK)—Confederate captain, Forty-eighth Tennessee Infantry, initially stationed at the Danville bridge, then briefly at Fort Henry before participating in the headlong retreat.

CHURCHILL, JAMES O.—Union first lieutenant, Eleventh Illinois Infantry, hellishly wounded in Forrest's attack on his unit's flank and rear on February 15.

DRAKE, JOSEPH—Confederate colonel, commander of Fourth Mississippi Infantry and Tilghman's Second Brigade at Fort Henry as well as a brigade in Pillow's attack at Fort Donelson.

FLOYD, JOHN B.—Brigadier general, commander of a brigade of Virginia troops and on-site commander of Fort Donelson beginning February 13; antebellum U.S. secretary of war whose apparent sympathies with seceding states resulted in Union cries of treason on his part; had feared capture from war's outset.

FOOTE, ANDREW H.—Union navy flag-officer; prewar had rigorously policed illegal slave-ships off Africa and fought Chinese in Second Opium War; commander and latter-day builder and outfitter of the revolutionary river-designed ironclad gunboats.

FORREST, NATHAN BEDFORD—Confederate lieutenant colonel of cavalry, commander of all cavalry at Fort Donelson; antebellum slave-trading magnate and Mississippi plantation owner, Memphis city councilman, and intrepid participant in many bloody civilian personal encounters.

GRANT, ULYSSES S.—Federal brigadier general, commander of Union forces around Cairo and then at Fort Henry and Fort Donelson; had glittering combat record in Mexican War; resigned from prewar army amid rumors of drunkenness; failed at several civilian enterprises; finally managed to overcome his prior reputation to get, second-hand, an infantry colonelcy and, soon afterward, commission as brigadier.

HALLECK, HENRY WAGER—Union major general, commander of Department of Missouri including western Kentucky and southern Illinois; headquartered at St. Louis; vaunted West Point graduate, military intellectual, and attorney who became rich in prewar California; precise, exacting, and difficult.

HANSON, ROGER W.—Confederate colonel, commanding Second Kentucky Infantry in Buckner's division; held extreme right of Confederate trenches at Fort Donelson; walked with a limp because of antebellum wound in duel over a woman.

HEIMAN, ADOLPHUS—Confederate colonel, commander of Tenth Tennessee Infantry, a brigade during Fort Donelson fighting, and, at times before that battle, Fort Donelson as well as Fort Henry; German immigrant; antebellum Nashville architect.

HILLYER, WILLIAM S.—Union captain, aide on Grant's staff, prewar attorney in St. Louis, where the antebellum Grant briefly had a desk in the building from which Hillyer and his partners operated.

JOHNSON, BUSHROD RUST—Confederate brigadier general; subcommander under Pillow; gave final approval for siting of Fort Henry; Ohio-born West Pointer; prewar college professor; cashiered from U. S. army for promoting smuggling scheme; unknown to his Southern friends, in youth he helped guide fugitive slaves up the Underground Railroad.

JOHNSTON, ALBERT SIDNEY—Confederate major general, commander of Confederate territory west of Alleghenies; West Pointer; longtime friend of Jefferson Davis and Leonidas Polk; antebellum secretary of war of Republic of Texas, Mexican War veteran; later commander of U. S. Second Cavalry; commanded U. S. Army's Department of the Pacific at secession.

KOUNTZ, WILLIAM J.—Abstemious Pittsburgh steamboat magnate; sent to McClellan at Cincinnati near outbreak of war by fellow prominent Pittsburgher Edwin Stanton and a Pittsburgh congressman; given charge of river transportation of troops and supplies as well as finding steamboats to be bought and converted to gunboats.

LOGAN, JOHN A. "BLACK JACK"—Union colonel, commander of Thirty-first Illinois Volunteers; prewar southern Illinois congressman very instrumental in turning his district from secession-sympathizing to rigidly unionist; had horse shot beneath him at Belmont; got nickname from color of his hair and eyes.

MCARTHUR, JOHN—Union colonel, commander of Twelfth Illinois Infantry and First Brigade, Smith's Second Division; native Scot; arrived in America as twenty-three-year-old blacksmith; rose to antebellum ownership of Excelsior Iron Works in Chicago.

MCCAUSLAND, JOHN—Confederate colonel, commander of Thirty-sixth Virginia Infantry; son of an Irish immigrant; graduated first in his class at Virginia Military Institute, where he became assistant professor of mathematics; took a cadet detachment to hanging of John Brown; served under John Floyd in West Virginia.

MCCLELLAN, GEORGE BRINTON—Union major general, general-in-chief of all Union forces; West Pointer and later instructor there; served in Mexican War and later surveyed potential railroad routes across the West; antebellum chief engineer for Illinois Central Railroad and, on brink of war, president of Ohio & Mississippi Railroad; after Fort Sumter, major general of Ohio volunteers; led campaign in western Virginia; commander of Army of Potomac in August 1861; general-in-chief from November 1.

MCCLERNAND, JOHN A.—Federal brigadier general, commanding Grant's First Division; private in Black Hawk War; antebellum newspaperman and long-term southern Illinois congressman; unionist Democrat; given his high rank by Lincoln to keep southern Illinois loyal; had horses shot under him at Belmont; endlessly and duplicitously ambitious.

MCGAVOCK, RANDAL W.—Confederate lieutenant colonel, sometime commander of Tenth Tennessee Infantry; antebellum Harvard graduate, attorney, Nashville mayor; served at both Fort Donelson and Fort Henry before the battles.

MCPHERSON, JAMES B.—Union lieutenant colonel; engineer; assigned by Halleck to Grant's staff to monitor his drinking; antebellum first in his class at West Point; supervised fortification of Alcatraz Island in San Francisco Bay.

PHELPS, SETH LEDYARD—Union lieutenant, navy; commander of timber-clad gunboat *Conestoga*; incessantly patrolled Tennessee, Ohio, and Cumberland rivers; much-trusted subordinate of Foote in construction of gunboats and mortar boats and gathering intelligence.

PILLOW, GIDEON JOHNSON—Confederate brigadier general; second in Fort Donelson command; antebellum attorney, engineer of James K. Polk's Democratic nomination for president; appointed by Polk to be major general in Mexican War, where he intrigued against commander Winfield Scott; one of Tennessee's richest men; after outbreak of war, mustered large Tennessee forces, then saw his Tennessee rank of major general reduced to brigadier when state's forces were transferred to the Confederacy.

POLK, LEONIDAS—Confederate Major General; West Pointer; resigned commission immediately after graduation and went into the Episcopal ministry; antebellum champion of doctrine that God ordained slavery; friend of Jefferson Davis and Albert Sidney Johnston; commanded in the West until Johnston arrived; violated Kentucky neutrality by seizing Columbus, Kentucky, where he then anchored Johnston's left.

PORTER, WILLIAM D. "DIRTY BILL"—Commodore, U.S. navy; skipper of the *Essex*, which sustained heavy damage at Fort Henry; scalded by bursting boiler in the battle.

RAWLINS, JOHN AARON—Union captain; Galena, Illinois, lawyer and city attorney; antebellum Democrat politician who supported Stephen A. Douglas in election of 1860; his support of Union was so strong that Grant offered him a place on his staff when Grant became brigadier general; Rawlins became Grant's closest intimate among his aides.

SMITH, CHARLES F.—West Pointer; Grant's commandant and instructor while Grant was there; career soldier; commanded at Washington for two weeks; abruptly transferred to recruiting duty before being sent west to command at Paducah, Kentucky; then put under Grant, who admired him and felt awkward giving him orders.

TILGHMAN, LLOYD—Confederate brigadier general; West Pointer, son of a Maryland congressman; resigned from army after graduation; became railroad engineer; lived in Paducah, Kentucky, for several years antebellum;

after secession, commissioned brigadier general; commanded both Fort Henry and Fort Donelson; was more interested in building winter housing than rendering the forts invulnerable.

WALKE, HENRY—Commodore, U. S. Navy; commander of gunboat *Carondelet* at Fort Henry and Fort Donelson; antebellum, career naval officer.

WALLACE, LEW—Union brigadier general; son of governor of Indiana; Grant division commander at Fort Donelson; antebellum newspaperman and member of Indiana legislature; adjutant general of Indiana after outbreak of war.

WALLACE, WILLIAM HARVEY LAMB—Union brigadier general; commanded brigade under McClernand at Fort Henry and Fort Donelson; antebellum Illinois attorney and district attorney; recruited Eleventh Illinois.

WHARTON, GABRIEL C.—Confederate colonel of Fifty-first Virginia and commander of Floyd's first brigade at Fort Donelson; antebellum graduate of Virginia Military Institute and then civil engineer in the Southwest.

Requiem

IT WAS A BATTLE of the Bulge without overcoats. Its bloody snow constituted the tip of an iceberg of misery rarely paralleled in the annals of American military history.

The struggle began with river-borne sailors getting boiled alive in the tin cans of the nation's first metal-clad navy, while their roaring cannons maimed and mangled volunteer artillerists in the gore-streaked mud of riverside earthworks. These opening salvos were followed by days of marching and floundering through ice and mud, charging and repelling with musket and bayonet, and trying to keep from dying in a fiery yet frozen hell.

For nearly a month, sleet and snow and near-zero temperatures punctuated continual rain, freezing thousands of soaked and ill-clad men who couldn't build fires at night on windswept ridges or in watery trenches because of hundreds of pitiless sharpshooters. It was war at its most surreal, the blameless dying for the mistakes of the inept, in a tragedy climaxed by perhaps the most comically shameful surrender in U.S. history. And it culminated in mass municipal exodus as thousands of residents of Nashville, the first Confederate state capital to be recaptured, panicked, rioted, and ran after their retreating army in fear of a pillaging Union horde.

The battles of Fort Henry and Fort Donelson, fought at the outset of 1862, split Dixie breast to bowel. They also yanked from obscurity two of America's most different and remarkable commanders of men: Ohio's impassive Ulysses S. Grant, the man who would ultimately win the Civil War, and Tennessee's mercurial Nathan Bedford Forrest, who would become the most uncompromising symbol of its unvanquished. Yet this platform for the two giants' first widely publicized feats held the public consciousness for only seven weeks as the war's costliest in lives, manpower, and territory. But even far bloodier Shiloh, fought amid showers of peach blossoms instead of gale-whipped sleet, could hardly match Fort Donelson in enormity of per-capita agony.

For more than three years, combatants in the war's endlessly studied eastern conflict battled to a tie. The thing was won on the backside of the

Appalachians, and the Tennessee campaign of February 1862 was the western theatre's first and profoundest blow. Although many more-venerated killing grounds were later to be consecrated, each would mark just one more valiant attempt by the Confederacy to recoup its staggering losses of Forts Henry and Donelson, the supply depots of Nashville, and the vastness bounded by southern Kentucky, northern Alabama, the Cumberland Mountains, and the Mississippi River.

The Confederates never could do it. Even more important, even with a Forrest they could not defeat the Union general whose tottering career was saved and transformed forever by this campaign.

PART I

RECONNAISSANCE

Fall–Early Winter, 1861–1862

The City of Mud

As FAR SOUTH AS ILLINOIS goes before becoming Missouri or Kentucky, Cairo squats like a furtive lookout. Behind tall dikes, the little town occupies a sliver of needle-shaped lowland separating the Ohio and Mississippi rivers. Just upstream, two substantial tributaries—the Tennessee and the Cumberland—join the Ohio.

Despite its mosquitoes and malaria and packs of night-swarming levee rats, Cairo had always been well-placed for trade, legitimate and otherwise. In January of 1862, thousands of marching feet gave the sullen, secession-sympathizing town the derisive moniker "City of Mud" as it mushroomed into a mini-metropolis, an increasingly popular confluence of buyers and sellers. Other things were coming together there, too.

Cairo's needle pointed southeasterly across Kentucky toward Nashville, the new Confederate States of America's chief supply depot west of the Appalachians. With five railroads and a wharf teeming with steamboat traffic, the Tennessee capital also boasted machine shops, foundries, an armory producing 250 rifles a week, a percussion-cap factory turning out 250,000 caps a day, a plow plant retooled to manufacture Southern sabers, and burgeoning caches of meat, ammunition, and other necessities for the recently recruited Confederate armies. Nashville provided distribution for the Confederacy's foremost iron-manufacturing region as well as for the north end of its agricultural breadbasket. Yet between Cairo and this Confederate capital lay just two unfinished and undermanned military outposts: the earthen forts Henry and Donelson just south of the Tennessee border. With Confederates in Virginia having shattered an attacking Union army at Bull Run the previous July and the war east of the Appalachians lulling toward stalemate, the focus of meaningful action was shifting westward. Now the conflict's central theatre smoldered toward explosion, and it was small wonder that the Cairo area's top two military men were focused on the direction of the needle.[1]

The older of the two men was fifty-five-year-old Andrew H. Foote, whose job it was to construct and command the gunboats of a revolutionary Federal river-borne navy. The son of a Connecticut senator, Foote had already fashioned a glittering career for himself outside the sphere of his father's influence. The senator could control the rest of his half-dozen sons "pretty well," Foote's eldest brother would remember, but the old man could no more than "guide" Andrew. Commanding a brig off the west coast of Africa earlier in his career, the headstrong son had risked the ire of Southern members of Congress by helping British Royal Navy crews pursue and search the many slave ships bound for the Americas. One hundred thousand slaves a year were being transported to the New World in the late 1840s, even though overseas importation of purchased human beings had been illegal in America since 1808. Foote proved so adept at interfering with this traffic that his ship was credited with a marked decrease in it, and in 1854 he wrote a book about his experience titled *Africa and the American Flag*.

Like his father, Senator Samuel Augustus Foote, the son was no thoroughgoing abolitionist before the war, but Andrew did nurse an antipathy toward human bondage that seems to have sprung from fervent Puritan Congregationalism. His faith was so pronounced that he required his sailors to attend religious services each Sabbath and often held the rites himself. As if interference with the international slave trade were not enough, he also had incurred the disapproval of Dixie's worldly-wise aristocratic politicians by leading a temperance movement on the seas, reducing and ultimately removing the navy's per-sailor grog ration.[2]

Foote was a man of contrasts. An associate remembered him as blackeyed, stocky yet agile, exhibiting a "sailor-like" manner "that made his company highly desirable." Along with his fervent religion he displayed great sympathy for human failings, having supported congressional banning of the punitive naval practice of flogging. But he was merciless in the face of the enemy. He believed the only way to defeat a foe was to seek out and destroy him, and even his religion hardly curbed his bloodlust once he determined that his cause was right. Five years earlier, in 1856, as a neutral observing and protecting American interests during the Second Opium War against the Chinese, Foote responded to fire on his flag by personally leading two hundred eighty-seven sailors and marines in attacks that routed thousands of entrenched Chinese.[3]

Foote's combativeness probably helped him form a bond with his otherwise unlikely co-conspirator, the Cairo army commander: a younger, less overtly political and reputedly bibulous Ulysses S. Grant. Thirty-nine years old, Grant had been sent to southern Illinois to command some twenty thousand infantry and cavalrymen who were massing there—shortly before Foote arrived to supervise completion of a fleet of metal-covered and "timber-clad" gunboats to help protect them. At a slouching five-feet-seven and 135 pounds, Grant was a quiet, rumpled little man often pictured with his mouth in a grim, tight line. A new brigadier general, he recently had had his photograph taken in uniform looking foolish in a feathered hat, his facial expression suggesting dawning recognition of the image the picture could convey. His more natural sartorial style—borrowed from the Mexican War general Zachary Taylor—ran toward informal borderline slovenliness, unbuttoned tunics with tarnished buttons, and no rank on the collar. The world soon would learn, however, that the attention Grant withheld from his clothes tended to be applied to weightier concerns.

That Grant and Foote entered into collusion would not have seemed unlikely at the time. Each man needed something from the other. Grant, realizing he had to have water-borne transportation and firepower during the road-drowning winter season, obviously saw sense in collaborating with the man in charge of the novel gunboats. He may also have come to respect Foote not just out of deference to the sailor's rank and distinguished service record, but also for his approachable manner, which resembled Grant's own. Foote needed Grant, as well. A naval officer now assigned to the army's governmental parent, the Department of War, rather than to the Department of the Navy, Foote was a military orphan, dependent on army officers not only for his power, but also for many of the men assigned to his vessels.4

* * *

It was very cold in late January 1862. Ice blocked the Mississippi River at St. Louis, impeding transport of troops to Cairo, but Grant and Foote kept busy. Grant worked from breakfast to midnight seven days a week, he reported in a letter to his sister Mary. For a man of unusually direct and succinct correspondence, he did manage to write her a lengthy letter. And he and Foote also took time for extended conversations, perhaps in part because they shared the frustration of serving the recently installed Missouri commander, Henry W. Halleck. Like his Kentucky counterpart and rival, Don Carlos Buell, and their mutual Washington superior, George B. McClellan, Halleck was intellectually brilliant and all too aware of it. He was also loath to risk his vaunted reputation without the promise of guaranteed success. For this reason Foote would come to regard Halleck as a "military imbecile."

So Foote conspired with Grant. In January, the naval veteran would come to recall, he "proposed" to the younger officer a joint operation: "that with

ANDREW HULL FOOTE

four of the boats and 6,000 troops we should ascend the Tenn. [River] and attack Fort Henry.

"The general preferred the Cumberland and Fort Donelson as the more appropriate points of attack," Foote's recollection continued, "but [Grant] yielded to my views if Genl. Halleck's assent could be obtained."[5]

Grant later implied that the idea was more his than Foote's. He claimed the plan had been on his mind for some time, but that is debatable. For months his attention, along with that of his commanders in St. Louis, had been riveted on the Confederates' Mississippi River bastion at Columbus, Kentucky, eleven miles downriver from Cairo. Foote's gaze, by contrast, had been repeatedly drawn to the lightly defended Tennessee and Cumberland rivers, about which he was kept continually informed by captains of the armed steamboats that he kept busy reconnoitering the region.

The most important thing, though, is that Foote and Grant concurred. Either route would smash the railroad link between Columbus and Confederate headquarters at Bowling Green, isolating the two wings of the South's western army, but the reasons the pair differed in their initial ideas on where to do it seem obvious. Foote naturally gravitated toward a prize that would yield the most to the navy. Attacking Fort Henry, rather than Fort Donelson, would not only flank Columbus and Bowling Green, but also would throw open the Tennessee River to gunboat incursion as far upstream as northern Alabama, delivering Richmond a staggering psychological blow. Grant, by contrast, surely envisioned a coup that would be even more consequential to the army—and buttress his recent reversal of a downward-spiraling career. He had just written sister Mary that he hoped to hold his command long enough to participate in "at least one battle," and that battle needed to be important. So in shifting his gaze from Columbus he likely did first consider attacking Fort Donelson on the Cumberland, a move that promised to give him a more visceral military victory. Such a course, like Foote's, would out-flank both Columbus and Bowling Green, but it would also threaten a Con-federate state capital and the mountains of war materiel being manufac-tured and stored there.[6]

Grant's confidence was hardly brimming, though. He plainly was not im-pressing his commander. Henry Halleck was officious, prickly, and difficult to ingratiate. He also was quick to infer incompetence in others and so ar-rogant and precise that he may already have cost himself immediate com-mand of all the Federal armies. At his home in California a few months ear-lier, Halleck had refused to accept an order to report to Washington because of a wording error in the communiqué (the writer had addressed him as "major" rather than "major general," the army's highest rank at that juncture). A corrected document was unable to arrive in time to summon him east before the job went to McClellan.[7]

Instead of command of all the Federal troops, Halleck ended up with part of the western theatre, taking over the Missouri–Illinois–western Kentucky department from flamboyant, hip-shooting John C. Fremont in mid-Novem-ber. On August 30, Fremont had made the pivotal mistake of freeing the so-called "human property" of slaveholders in his fiefdom, thereby jeopardiz-ing the tenuous loyalty that Abraham Lincoln was trying to preserve in the indispensable border states of Kentucky, Maryland, and Missouri. In contrast to the abolitionist Fremont, Halleck possessed less sympathy for slaves than for the many other people he saw as his inferiors. The fugitive bondspeople flocking to his troops for freedom and protection from their masters he re-garded as drags on his forces and impediments to his plans; he ordered them banned from his lines and left to their very limited devices—unless they were needed for manual labor.

On November 19, 1861, the day Halleck assumed command in St. Louis, Grant had asked permission to go there and familiarize his chief with Cairo's necessities and possibilities. The request met with an icy reception. Less than two weeks earlier, Grant had launched an unauthorized and bloody attack on a Confederate camp at Belmont, Missouri. Instantly controversial, the raid had exceeded orders, achieved no immediately discernible gains, and cost casualties approaching twenty percent. Halleck, to whom rashness was a cardinal sin, refused Grant's interview request and brusquely ordered the subordinate to forward his information "in writing."

Rebuffed, Grant soon wrote his father that he was "somewhat troubled lest I lose my command." Then things got worse. He acted on a St. Louis telegram from "W. H. Buel, Co." ordering him to stop a steamboat headed south and send back its Confederate prisoners. The prisoners, according to the telegram, were fraudulently claiming to be designated for exchange for captured Federals. But after Grant had complied with the order, Halleck archly wired him to ask by what authority the prisoners had been returned to St. Louis. Grant replied by sending a copy of the message he had received, only to have Halleck respond that no "W. H. Buel" was known at his headquarters and that it was "most extraordinary that you should have obeyed a telegram sent by an unknown person and not even purporting to have been given by authority." Halleck ordered the prisoners "immediately" remanded to Cairo. Grant lamely tried to absolve himself, contending that such a wire would reasonably have come from the provost marshal or from headquarters "and I do not know the employees of the former nor the staff of the latter." He added that he "never dreamed of so serious a telegraphic hoax" being perpetrated at such a "large and responsible" office as Halleck's. Later the same day, Halleck notified him that the telegraphic culprit, who had "no authority whatever," had been arrested. He added a scolding: "You will hereafter be more careful about obeying telegrams from private persons countermanding orders from these Head Quarters."[8]

*　　*　　*

Grant had problems enough at his own headquarters. His principal subordinates were all men of markedly higher previous status than himself: an Illinois congressman; a son of a governor of Indiana; and a distinguished professional soldier who had been West Point's commandant, as well as its infantry tactics instructor, when Grant was a cadet.

The ex-commandant, oddly, was the least problematic of the lot. Philadelphia-born Brigadier General Charles Ferguson Smith was a stalwart fifty-four-year-old whom Grant admired and was deferential in giving orders to—for good reason. Smith, by far the most qualified field officer in the Cairo command, was a forbidding presence who tolerated no familiarity from subordinate officers.

Smith's ability, professional stature, and willingness to accept orders from a former pupil may have been reason enough to explain Grant's warmth toward him, but Smith was also said to have been laboring to overcome a problem with which Grant was all too familiar. A prominent *New York Tribune* reporter who first became connected with Grant's staff around this time (closely enough to claim to have sat "beside" Grant "around nightly campfires") later wrote that Smith had been assigned to the western front "in disgrace" because he "sometimes drank to excess." He had been seen drunk on the streets of Washington while briefly in charge there, the newsman claimed. He added that the incident may well have cost the old soldier higher command, and Grant "was only the more zealous in his attachment now [that] the veteran was in trouble."

Whether or not the *Tribune* report was completely accurate, it is certainly true that the preceding April Smith had been transferred out of the defense of the Washington district after fewer than three weeks. He was sent, first, to recruiting duty in New York, then on to the western theatre, all of which delayed his commissioning as a brigadier general until after Grant had received his. So Smith may have had as much reason to be grateful for Grant's respect as Grant did for Smith's acceptance of his authority.[9]

Less trustworthy was Brigadier General Lew Wallace, the Indiana governor's son and highly ambitious future author of *Ben Hur*. Having been reared in proximity to power, Wallace sometimes behaved like a spoiled child. During artillery target practice in the Mexican War, a young Wallace ignored two cracker barrels that had been set up as targets and instead wheeled and fired his gun toward a flock of sheep three hundred yards off. The next day, mutton graced "nearly every mess-kettle, and compliments poured in on me in a shower," he reported in his memoirs. But a day later his commander ordered him to pay a bill presented by the slaughtered flock's Mexican owner. "I protested, but without avail," he remembered. "The shot cost me more than half a month's pay." If Wallace gave the least thought to the cost to the farmer, let alone the sheep, he neglected to mention it.

In the fall of 1861, suspicions of intrigue on the part of Wallace roused the displeasure of Grant's staff, and admirers of Smith as well. The old officer's loyalty to the Union had been questioned publicly because of his reluctance, common to professional soldiers, to make political declarations. The questions got more numerous after Smith upbraided some Wallace troops at Paducah for agitating locals by hauling down a citizen's Confederate flag. This prompted some of Wallace's men to send home reports that Smith was pro-secession.[10]

More problematic for Grant was his second in command, Brigadier General John A. McClernand. A windy, fifty-year-old Democratic congressman,

McClernand had the habit of sidestepping regular channels and communicating with Grant's superiors all the way up the chain of command to the White House. A fellow resident of Springfield, Illinois, McClernand had known Lincoln for decades and had sometimes partnered with him in court cases. Skills as an ex-newspaperman and lawyer helped the Democrat wield much national influence for the Union in Congress during the secession crisis, and Republican Lincoln made him a brigadier general to strengthen loyalty in the southern Illinois region settled largely by immigrants (such as McClernand and Lincoln himself) from below the Ohio River. Political from hat to toenails, McClernand appeared to get along with Grant early on, and Grant did the same with McClernand. This almost certainly was because McClernand thought Grant was a minor, harmless, temporary rival—and because Grant knew McClernand was a major, dangerous one.[11]

*   *   *

Grant's greatest source of anxiety during the winter of 1861–62, however, seems to have been William J. Kountz, forty-five-year-old owner of a Pennsylvania steamboat fleet. The war had blocked river commerce from the Midwest to New Orleans and idled the bulk of the steamboat industry, and McClellan had recruited Kountz and some of his boats to assist in the eastern Ohio–western Virginia theatre. A river pilot for a quarter-century and a builder and owner of steamboats for more than two decades, Kountz became McClellan's superintendent of water transportation and doubtless expected to profit from authorizing the placing of some of his own inactive boats in government service. A postwar thumbnail biography asserts that during the summer and fall of 1861 Kountz "purchased all the steamboats that were converted into gunboats, and also many other boats for transports." Due to the incompetence of Lincoln's legendarily corrupt first secretary of war, Pennsylvanian Simon Cameron, all sorts of suppliers were fleecing the government during this period. A friend would later assert that Kountz was rigidly honest, though, and McClellan clearly valued him, eventually sending him to St. Louis to organize river transportation there.[12]

Known for his abrasiveness, Kountz began stepping on toes in Cairo, asking questions without checking in at Grant's headquarters, soon after his arrival sometime in the latter half of December. Grant penned him a stiff note saying he had heard the visitor had been "making inquiries into matters pertaining to this command" and ordering him to stop "until you have reported to me and shown your authority." It turned out, however, that Kountz *had* reported—to Grant's subordinate, McClernand—and he soon began implying that Grant was participating in corruption in steamboat and other contracts.

Any such assumption was without merit. Financially honest nearly to the point of naiveté, Grant just the preceding week had followed up a *Chicago Tribune* report that there was corruption in lumber contracting in the office of his Cairo quartermaster. He soon reported that his investigation showed the newspaper's charges to be true and asked that the quartermaster be replaced. Periodically in deep need of money in the years before the war, Grant never tried to acquire it by cheating anybody. But, needing to make a favorable impression on Halleck, he was understandably leery of Kountz's clumsy probing.[13]

Even friends acknowledged that Kountz was overbearingly insistent, devoid of tact, and oblivious to military chains of command. In mid-January, Grant ordered him arrested, saying that the Pennsylvanian's "great unpopularity with river men and his wholesale denunciation of everybody connected with the Government here as thieves and cheats" had made it difficult to get crews and boats to move troops. Grant had been forced to also arrest some of the boatmen to get them to serve at all. He suggested that Kountz be assigned elsewhere, writing that the troublemaker seemed to want his position only to punish riverboat operators he disliked and to acquire government business for a craft in which he had invested. But Grant lodged no charges, saying that they would be "embarrassing to the service."[14]

Things got embarrassing anyway. In late January 1862, Grant found himself struggling to weather his most dangerous drinking controversy of the war with none of the credentials of victory that would sustain him through more clamorous episodes later.

A reputation for thirst had dogged him from the old prewar army, but it had received renewed and wider notice the previous autumn. An October evening he spent reminiscing about the Mexican War with Smith in the Paducah, Kentucky, quarters of Wallace spawned "lurid" newspaper "accounts of the meeting at my house," Wallace would later remember. "It was an orgie [sic], a beastly drunken revel by both Grant and Smith—so the story ran," Wallace went on. Wallace then offered a correction, although somewhat faintly: "There were liquors and cigars on the night in question, *and some singing* [italics added], but no intoxication or anything like a revel. Nevertheless, a charge against General Grant of habitual drunkenness arose about that time, and spread through the country."[15]

And into ominous circles. On December 17, a Galena citizen recently returned from St. Louis wrote to Grant's most influential sponsor, Illinois congressman and Lincoln intimate Elihu B. Washburne, that he had learned on "good authority that Genl Grant is drinking very hard" and suggested that Washburne write to John Rawlins, a self-described liquor-loathing Galena lawyer and Grant aide who claimed to monitor and discourage Grant's thirst. Washburne did write Rawlins, who replied with a long, impassioned letter defending Grant. Rawlins said the statement that "Genl Grant is drinking very hard" was "utterly untrue" but acknowledged there had been occasions when visits by prominent Chicagoans and others did prompt the general to down single glassfuls of champagne or, during problems with a dyspeptic stomach, two glasses a day of beer. In "no instance," Rawlins insisted, did Grant ever drink "to excess" or "enough to in the slightest" hamper his job performance.

But the rumors did not die. On December 30, abstinence fanatic William Bross of the *Chicago Tribune* wrote Secretary of War Cameron that he and associate editors at the *Tribune* had accumulated "convincing" evidence that "Gen U. S. Grant commanding at Cairo is an inebriate . . . We think it best to call your attention to this matter, rather than to attack Gen. Grant in the *Tribune*." Noting that he did not know Secretary Cameron personally, Bross gave references that included "his Excellency President Lincoln."

On January 17, the arrested Kountz—himself reputed to be fanatically abstemious—fired off a letter to brand-new Secretary of War Edwin Stanton. Like Kountz, Stanton was a prominent figure in Pittsburgh and had helped recommend the steamboatman to McClellan. Kountz told Stanton about his plight and added that "Stealing from Govt. is still going on here." The next week he went on to draft formal and inflammatory charges against Grant, alleging among other things not only that the Cairo commander had tippled with enemy officers on flag-of-truce steamboat trips to Columbus, Kentucky, but that Grant repeatedly had become so drunk around headquarters that he was "unfitted for any business." The document purported to cite specific dates and places.[16]

His friends rejected these charges as motivated by vengefulness, but Grant needed to get moving down the Tennessee River—or somewhere— while he still had an army.

Fall–Early Winter, 1861–1862

Bowling Green

At BOWLING GREEN, one hundred fifty miles east of Cairo and fifty miles north of Nashville, the Confederacy's western military commander presented a far more imposing image than the unkempt and beclouded U. S. brigadier chafing in southern Illinois.

Kentucky-born Albert Sidney Johnston was the picture of a soldier. Broad-shouldered and trim, he stood an erect six-feet-one. He had served the United States in campaigns against Mexicans, Indians, and Mormons, and at one time had been secretary of war of the independent Republic of Texas. In 1861, he dramatically rode cross-country from California, where he had commanded the U.S. Army's Department of the Pacific, to New Orleans to board a Richmond-bound train and tender his services to the Confederacy. Jefferson Davis, the gratified new chief executive, proclaimed Johnston to be worth more than ten thousand other men, but for his trouble offered him a reward of dubious value: command of Department No. 2, a position even more problematic than Grant's.

The Confederacy's—and, in September, suddenly Johnston's—sprawling Department No. 2 stretched from the Appalachian Mountains not only to the Mississippi River, but also across already-bloody Missouri, encompassing practically everything between that line and the Gulf coast. The crown jewel of this vast area was the state capital at its northern edge: blasé Nashville, whose city fathers remained preoccupied with commerce. Despite fervent appeals by fiery secessionist Governor Isham G. Harris, the city had accepted the new war with distraction. A boosterish borough, the Tennessee metropolis already had sought to become the Confederacy's capital when that designation was moved to Virginia from Montgomery, Alabama. Despite its grand ambitions, Nashville—like many river towns—stood on feet of clay: its seventeen thousand souls included, in one four-block area, the residents of no less than sixty-nine houses of prostitution.[1]

Focused on commerce, Tennessee's capital had no defenses of its own and little inclination to construct any. This was because Kentucky initially declared itself neutral in the sectional struggle, putting a buffer between Tennessee and the avowedly Union states north of the Ohio River. Then in early September 1861, just prior to Johnston's arrival west of the Alleghenies, Tennessee's need for more tangible protection became urgent. Confederate General Leonidas Polk, consulting no higher authority, sent troops pouring across Tennessee's northwest border in violation of Kentucky's neutrality. He quickly occupied the Mississippi River bluffs at Columbus, cliffs so high they were called a "Gibraltar." The Bluegrass State's unionist legislature, outraged, requested a retaliatory Federal invasion.

So Albert Sidney Johnston arrived to find Nashville naked, its buffer gone. With little realistic alternative, he ordered a Confederate advance into the rest of Kentucky, hoping to rally residents to Confederate ranks and put Union commanders on the defensive. He thus established the so-called Cumberland Line, a long but thin demarcation spreading not many more than forty thousand raw and poorly armed volunteers across three hundred miles from the Mississippi River to the Alleghenies. Polk, with sixteen thousand Confederates, settled in at Columbus, effectively blocking the Mississippi. Twenty-two thousand men under generals Simon B. Buckner and William Hardee fortified Bowling Green, an important junction of railroads running from Louisville, Kentucky, to Nashville and Memphis. North of Cumberland Gap in the less accessible eastern mountains, General Felix Zollicoffer commanded another four thousand charged with defending eastern Tennessee, especially the vital tracks over which trains to Richmond chugged up the Tennessee Valley from the Deep South.

But large Federal armies were massing across his front, and Johnston's long defense line was in jeopardy at several points. Behind his right, in Zollicoffer's rear, most East Tennesseans were stoutly unionist and threatening to try to secede from the Confederacy. The Cumberland Line's left center, around the little forts Henry and Donelson, appeared particularly sieve-like, the Tennessee and Cumberland rivers offering inviting avenues for a major Federal breach. And these waterways were most navigable at flood stage, which the rains of winter would bring.

Johnston's problems were not all geographic, either; he also had difficulties with personnel. For one thing, although Polk, Zollicoffer, and the other generals were men of considerable eminence, much of it was civilian-based.

Zollicoffer was a nearsighted journalist-turned-politician from central Tennessee who had served in Congress but had no military training. Leonidas Polk had roomed with Johnston at West Point, had graduated in the class just ahead of Jefferson Davis, and had become one of Davis's closest friends. But he had quickly left the army for the Episcopal ministry and won his prominence quoting scripture sanctioning slavery. In 1861, Polk had allowed Davis to prevail on him to become a Confederate major general and accept command of Department No. 2—until the arrival of Johnston, whom Polk recommended for the job. A third high-ranking Johnston subordinate, John B. Floyd, had been governor of Virginia and then U. S. secretary of war for four years before resigning in December 1860. He then became highly controversial—a traitor, many cried—for having ordered the transfer of guns to southern arsenals where secessionists could seize them.

Other Johnston generals did possess significant military experience, although it varied widely in quality and promise. The most seasoned of the lot, Georgia native William J. Hardee, had commanded at West Point following distinguished service in the Mexican War. He had written a highly influential military textbook, *Rifle and Light Infantry Tactics*, which many new commanders on both sides were now frantically skimming. In early 1861, Hardee had quit the U.S. army, accepted a Confederate commission, and raised an Arkansas brigade that he was leading when Johnston came west from Richmond. In the old U.S. army, he and Johnston had worked closely together in the Second Cavalry, with Johnston commanding and Hardee serving as his second subordinate behind Robert E. Lee. So Johnston knew Hardee well.

Simon Bolivar Buckner, a Kentucky-born West Pointer, had gone on to teach at his alma mater, but his nit-picking nature ultimately got him all but exiled to duty in New York Harbor. There, in 1854, seemingly providentially, he was on hand to give his friend Grant financial assistance when the Ohioan, newly resigned from the army amid rumors of excessive drinking, landed in Gotham with no means of getting home. Buckner himself quit the army in 1855, but, unlike Grant, he did so because of brighter civilian prospects: managing the lakeshore Chicago real estate of his wife's father. After the Deep South seceded, Buckner became inspector general of the secessionist Kentucky State Guard and swelled its ranks to ten to twelve thousand men. His work was so imposing that an alarmed Abraham Lincoln sent five thousand muskets for distribution to unionist Kentuckians.[2]

The most aggravating of Johnston's cadre of generals was Gideon Johnson Pillow, an energetic complainer and seeker of unilateral glory. Nearly two decades earlier, on the floor of the 1844 Democratic national convention, he had masterminded the presidential nomination of Tennessee darkhorse James K. Polk over a former president, New Yorker Martin Van Buren, in one of the most important events in antebellum politics; Polk's nomination and subsequent election constituted a smashing triumph by southern slaveholders clamoring to annex Texas and other territories in which to expand their "peculiar institution." Pillow had no military training

and negligible martial ability, but his friend Polk, worrying about the popularity of generals Zachary Taylor and Winfield Scott, appointed Pillow a general in the Mexican War. There, Pillow intrigued against his superiors and
made significant battlefield blunders. By 1861, lawyer Pillow had become
one of Tennessee's richest men and a notable Democratic kingmaker, and
he was named head of Tennessee's provisional army by the politically astute
Governor Harris. Soon Richmond accepted transfer of Pillow's Tennessee
legions into the Confederate army, but President Davis, son-in-law of
Zachary Taylor, refused to accept their commander's state rank of major
general, offering him only commission as a brigadier. Davis's mistake was in
making Pillow a general at all. While commanding Tennessee's provisional
army Pillow had unwittingly given Northern spy Allan Pinkerton a tour of
the fortifications of Memphis, and in September, after becoming a subordinate Confederate, he had pushed Polk to violate Kentucky's neutrality.[3]

The most enigmatic of Johnston's generals, despite a West Point education and service in the Seminole and Mexican wars, was Ohio-born Bushrod
Rust Johnson. He was an ex-college educator in Kentucky and Tennessee
whose distant past was unknown to virtually everybody in his adopted South.
In youth, he had helped his older brothers move fugitive slaves up the Underground Railroad. He also had been cashiered from the U. S. Army during the Mexican War for trying to bribe a superior officer to allow government transport of smuggled civilian goods. This crime occurred in a weak
moment—Johnson had received no recognition for participating in four battles, had been relegated to rigorous supply duties in the rear, and then had
been beset by an attack of yellow fever that nearly killed him—but the army
and President Polk refused him a second chance. Discharged quietly in 1847
after an eleven-year army career, he took up teaching and prospered. Personally, though, he was pathetic. His wife of six years died in the late 1850s,
leaving her husband with their only child, a mentally retarded son. The widowed professor was close-mouthed and duplicitous, knowing that his shame
remained on file in Washington and shimmered in the Mexican War memories of a handful of officers still living.[4]

*   *   *

But it was Albert Sidney Johnston himself who lay claim to the most glittering Confederate resume in the West. Regarded as one of America's handful
of premier officers, he saw his southernness so feared in early 1861 that he
was replaced as commander of the U.S. Army's Pacific District soon after being assigned. Then, in a turnabout prompted by the Lincoln administration's desperate wish to keep Kentucky in the Union, the secretary of war in

Washington wrote him that he would be given "the most important command and trust" as soon as he could arrive there—presuming, of course, that he decided to come there at all.

Johnston apparently agonized over which flag to choose—he had served the Federal one for eighteen years, after all, and his native Kentucky refused to secede—but his allegiance to Texas made up his mind. By the time the Lincoln offer arrived in California, Johnston had vanished into the southwestern desert on the first leg of his long trek to Richmond.

Taking up the vast new trans-Alleghenies burden, he soon understood the tenuousness of his position. His new superiors and their resource-strapped government hamstrung him. The white population of the remaining Union, around 19 million, was almost four times that of the Confederacy, and although all of America was overwhelmingly agrarian, more than 90 percent of its industry was clustered in the North, which turned out more than nine-tenths of its annual product in 1860. Too, the new Confederacy was anchored on the principle of states' rights, and Dixie's governors tended to think first of defending their own borders before supplying aid beyond them. With Richmond focused on the fighting on its doorstep, Johnston found himself restricted in the number of states on which he could call for direly needed reinforcements and ordered not to use most of the food and other supplies in the region he was assigned to protect; these were to be forwarded to Virginia.

Fortunately for the South during this early period, Johnston's early experience leading frontier campaigns against Indians and Mexicans had made him adept at transforming meager assets into major ones in the eyes of his opponents. While privately imploring Davis and three Confederate governors for more men and more and better arms, he published in friendly newspapers greatly inflated accounts of his troop numbers and otherwise gave such appearance of impending aggressiveness that several Federal commanders (but rarely Grant) worried for the safety of St. Louis, Cincinnati, Louisville, and Cairo.[5]

One officer Johnston was not fooling, though, was himself. He worried about the total lack of reserves not only for his center in Bowling Green, but also for his left and right. He wrote the Confederate secretary of war in Richmond on Christmas Day 1861:

> *The position of General Zollicoffer . . . holds in check the meditated invasion and [Federally] hoped-for revolt in East Tennessee; but I can neither order Zollicoffer to join me here nor withdraw any more force from Columbus without imperiling our communications toward Richmond or endangering Tennessee and the Mississippi Valley. This*

I have resolved not to do, but have chosen, on the contrary, to post my inadequate force in such a manner so as to hold the enemy in check [and] guard the frontier . . . till the winter terminates the campaign; or, if any fault in his movements is committed, or his lines become exposed . . . to attack him as opportunity offers.[6]

Militarily and personally, Johnston's psychological make-up mixed contrary tendencies: toward all-out attack and perplexing paralysis.

In California, as the secession crisis developed, he was so conflicted by his different senses of duty that he considered sitting the war out in the Golden State. His personality combined the soaring dreams, the chivalric code, and the fitful temperament of Southern aristocracy. As an angry child, he threw himself beneath the feet of horses ridden by his older brothers in a suicidal snit. As an adult he consigned his family to land-poor near-poverty by buying a six-thousand-acre Texas plantation that had no clear title, thereby indebting himself for years, getting sued, and placing his eldest son—who finally had to buy the place—at considerable hardship.

Johnston had taken command of the Texas army in 1836 at a critical time. The brand-new Lone Star Republic was seeking to preserve its just-won independence from Mexico and protect its burgeoning settler population from Native American raids, and his military talents were badly needed. Yet, he immediately allowed himself to be drawn into a duel by his disgruntled second in command, the officer whose place he had taken—and then, with the right of choosing weapons for the event, lengthened his odds of survival by picking pistols, which his opponent was known to be most adept in handling and which he himself had not used in more than a decade. Not surprisingly, he lost the duel, suffering a shot to the front of the right hip that injured a sciatic nerve as it passed through the pelvis; although the altercation was not fatal at the time, it may have led to his death later, possibly causing him to suffer unnoticed the wound that would ultimately kill him at Shiloh. With knightly flair, Johnston explained at the time that he fought the duel out of conviction that the soldiers he had been assigned to lead would not follow a coward. His bravery won the loyalty of not only the troops, but of the opponent who shed his blood.[7]

The armies of the Civil War were much larger than any previously mustered on American soil, so the military experience of prewar officers was of varying importance, but Johnston's appears crucial. Accustomed to patrolling the plains where outposts were far-flung, he had developed a loose-reined management style, giving his officers maximum discretion in how they handled their posts and fought their battles. His command atmosphere was one of genteel clubbiness, reflecting his upbringing on the upper rung of Southern society. Half-brother to a Louisiana United States senator, he had been invited in his youth to the White House, and his attainments included not only a prep-school and West Point education but long-term friendships with such people as the president of the new Confederacy.

Johnston exhibited the subtle, not-always-conscious arrogance of a plantation-rooted aristocracy. Like the rest of his class, he believed that the right of white men to rule red, brown, and black people was not just absolute, but divine. For his time and station, however, he appears to have been unusually sensitive to the feelings of other people. On his plantation, he would not whip trouble-making slaves—but he did occasionally sell them, which for them could be immeasurably worse. He was extraordinarily composed under pressure, preferring in uncomfortable situations to bear shame himself rather than inflict it on others.

Finally, there was combat. Johnston had fought his duel, participated in the Mexican War, and sent units out on self-righteous "chastisements" of Indians, but he had never commanded an army under fire. Granted, in the America of his lifetime there had been few opportunities to do that. And Johnston made such a stunning picture of a general that Jefferson Davis asserted that if he was not one the South had none. The Confederate president's judgment, though, was all too humanly fallible. Whether Albert Sidney Johnston was more than his picture remained to be seen.[8]

Soldier Reborn

Grant

Because the prewar officer corps was so small, Ulysses Grant knew most of his Confederate opponents—not just by their considerable reputations but, to widely varying degrees, personally. Simon Bolivar Buckner had been one year behind him at West Point, Bushrod Johnson three years ahead. Albert Sidney Johnston, Hardee, and Pillow all had participated in some of the same Mexican War battles that he had. The sole present foes of whom he likely had no prior personal knowledge were Polk, who had left the army when Grant was five years old, and John Floyd, who possessed no antebellum military experience or training at all.

Most of these opponents surely also knew Grant.

He had been recognized for gallantry under fire in Mexico and had competently discharged his duties as quartermaster of the Fourth Infantry. But so far the negatives of his reputation seemed to overbalance the positives. His application to West Point had been reluctant. As a youth, he had no military ambitions and only attended the military academy because his father, although a prospering tanner, did not want to pay for his son's education. The youth did come to revere the aesthetics of the Point's Hudson River grandeur, but while there, instead of studying, he preferred drawing pictures and reading novels from the campus library by James Fenimore Cooper, Washington Irving, a naval adventure author named Frederick Marryat, and, especially, Irish writer Charles Lever, who wrote several volumes about young men traveling around Europe. Probably because of this penchant, Grant was elected president of the literary society. But his dress and bearing were not as sharp as his mind. Trivial demerits, for such flaws as looking "slouchy and unmilitary" in infantry exercises, relegated him to a final standing of twenty-first in a class of thirty-nine, his best marks coming in mathematics and horsemanship.

In the latter, he surpassed even the aristocratic Southerners, who took their equine mastery for granted. He loved horses. In childhood, he had swung from their tails and played beneath their stomachs outside his father's shop. To the remonstrance of worried neighbors, his mother responded with a blithe coolness that her son inherited, saying that horses "seem to understand Ulysses."

And vice versa. Ulysses was an equestrian marvel. At two, with adult assistance, he ecstatically rode his first pony. At five, he stood on the back of a trotting horse, balancing himself with the reins. At nine, neighbors brought him horses to break and train; and at eleven he stayed on a difficult animal at a circus performance even when a monkey was thrown onto his back. Hometown folks would not have been surprised that at West Point it was "Ulys," not the Southerners, who set an academy jump record that stood for a quarter-century.[1]

Despite these triumphs, he harbored deeply buried hurts. In boyhood, his name was predictably corrupted to "useless," and he was seen by some as stupid after being sent by his father to buy a horse and forthrightly telling the seller the highest price his father had authorized him to pay. Most children quickly forget such slights, but Grant was so wounded that he remembered to record them with quiet humor fifty years later.

Such memories extended beyond boyhood. Going home for the first time after two years at West Point, he made sure to arrive in resplendent uniform and was mortified when two different local civilians lampooned his appearance; he quickly retreated to the less prideful attitude of his mother and never gloried in military finery again. Then came the first of his career's vocational disappointments. Despite his brilliance on horseback, he botched his entrée to the cavalry by a rare fit of overt anger, striking a mount at West Point.

Similarly, becoming a doting husband and father did not free him from persistent reasons for domestic concern. His wife, Julia, had been markedly less eager to marry him than he was to marry her, and when he was away from her in the army she responded only fitfully to his habitual daily letters. And Julia's family and his own, coming from opposite sides of the incendiary slavery issue, cared little for each other.[2]

Remarkably, though, this litany of discouragements, more than enough to defeat most highly sensitive men, served only to stiffen the resolve of this one. Over the years, Grant seemed to become ever more dogged and implacably committed to his struggles. Beneath the self-effacing quietude of his surface galloped the indomitable handler of horses—and, by inference, other forces larger than himself.

Despite serving as an army officer for eleven years before his antebellum resignation, Grant at the beginning of 1862 had only recently commanded troops, and he later remembered having to lose a fear of that heavy responsibility. He later wrote about passing a defining milestone on his path to military self-confidence. He claimed it occurred in Missouri during the autumn of 1861, on the brink of what might have been his initial battle as a commander.

His Twenty-First Illinois Volunteers were ordered out against a Confederate colonel named Thomas Harris near the town of Florida, Missouri. The march crossed twenty-five miles so deserted that the newly appointed colonel and his troops caught a glimpse of just two people, horsemen who galloped off as soon as they were spotted. "As we approached the brow of the hill from which it was expected we could see Harris' camp, and possibly find his men ready-formed to meet us," Grant wrote in his memoirs:

> . . . my heart kept getting higher and higher until it felt to me as though it was in my throat. I would have given anything then to be back in Illinois, but I had not the moral courage to halt and consider what to do; I kept right on. When we reached a point from which the valley below was in full view I halted. The place where Harris had encamped a few days before was still there and the marks of a recent encampment were plainly visible, but the troops were gone. My heart resumed its place. It occurred to me at once that Harris had been as much afraid of me as I had been of him. This was a view of the question I had never taken before; but it was one I never forgot afterwards.[3]

In fact, Grant had received information the day before that Harris and his men were unlikely to be encountered at Florida, but this exaggerated account perfectly captures Grant's personality. His mild modesty, self-deprecation, and discomfort with praise were described by one longtime friend, fellow West Pointer and in-law James Longstreet, as almost "girlish." The description was appropriate. These traits were legacies from his Presbyterian mother, who was once described by a friend as thinking "nothing you could do would entitle you to praise . . . you ought to praise the Lord for giving you an opportunity to do it." By 1861, her son's profound sense of disappointment in his own accomplishments and restless impulse to redeem a fruitless life had likely reinforced this mindset.

His depiction of the non-incident in Florida, Missouri, includes an important feature of Grant's essence. Describing his emotions in his memoirs, he wrote that in anticipating the possibility of a battle with Harris and his men he had not feared for his personal safety. In the Mexican War he had, he wrote, "been in all the engagements . . . that it was possible for one person to be in." But he had never been "in command." Had another officer been the colonel and himself a lieutenant colonel at Florida, he added, "I do not think I would have felt any trepidation."[4]

Almost certainly. He had always been bold in combat. Long before Florida, in the Mexican War, he had learned that anticipating battle was for him
far more harrowing than actually fighting it. According to another veteran
of the Mexican fray, it was impossible to keep Grant out of action even
though he was often assigned to support, rather than front-line positions.
Under fire he was, as one of his commanders wrote, a man "*of* fire." Fellow
Mexican veteran Longstreet later described him as so "cool, swift, and hurried" in the fray that he seemed to belong in battle. His Mexico feats included volunteering during house-to-house urban fighting at the Battle of Mon-
terrey, even though he was an officer and an adjutant, to carry to division
headquarters a message that the forwardmost brigade was running out of
ammunition. To deliver it he had to gallop down the city's embattled streets
through enemy fire at every intersection, and he did so like a rodeo per-
former or attacking Indian, one foot across his horse's back and an arm
around its neck, shielding himself with the animal's body. Afterward, he gave
all credit to the heroism of the horse, Nelly, just as, following his epic West
Point jump, he had directed the praise toward that animal, York.[5]

Still, the Mexican War taught him several lessons crucial to a commander's role. As quartermaster, he became deeply aware of the truth of the
adage that an army travels on its stomach, and he learned a great deal about
the intricacies of keeping that stomach supplied. By watching the way General Zachary Taylor led the Mexican campaign, he also learned that a commander's aggressiveness was of crucial psychological importance, both to his
own troops and to their enemies.

Taylor influenced Grant in more subtle ways, as well. The tobacco-chew-
ing Mexican War commander refused to wear a uniform, moved among his
men as if one of them, and expressed himself in words that were few, down-
to-earth, and well-chosen. He also was unflappable under both fire and
heavy responsibility, habitually making do with the resources at hand and
not demanding more. Once Taylor personally complimented Grant for refusing to stand on military ceremony, jumping into the Gulf to help some of
his men perform a task he had ordered done. Grant quickly began to emu-
late his idol.[6]

Grant's self-control and mildness of manner owed much to the twin influ-
ences of his mother and Taylor; toward the end of his life he wrote that he
never recalled having used a "profane expletive." But when he wanted to, he
was more than capable of expressing his opinions in unmistakable terms.
When Union recruits pulled down a Confederate flag at a self-styled Confederate headquarters in St. Louis in 1861, Grant was present in a semi-military
capacity. A few minutes afterward, he found himself sitting almost alone in a

streetcar when a Southern sympathizer boarded and loudly groused that "where I came from if a man dares to say a word in favor of the Union we hang him to a limb of the first tree we come to." Indulging his gift for understated and pointed expression, Grant replied that residents of St. Louis were apparently "not so intolerant," judging from the fact that "I had not seen a single rebel hung yet; nor heard of one." Then he added with iron undertone: "There are plenty of them who ought to be, however."[7]

Grant was utterly opposed to the Confederate cause, but his political views were moderate. That possibly explains the edge in his tone that day in St. Louis. Secession was extremism, the antithesis of moderation. He disdained what he saw as the South's overbearing minority insistence on making the rest of the nation—the majority—repeatedly do her bidding on the subject of slavery, a system for which he had absolutely no empathy but was resigned to as an alternative to war.

He was steeped from boyhood in consciousness of the slavery question's destructive potential. He had grown up in a town on one of the most active lines of the Underground Railroad. He had gone to school in two nearby municipalities—Ripley, Ohio, and Maysville, Kentucky—where runaway slaves were both aided and pursued with fanatic zeal. His father, a very vocal opponent of the "peculiar institution," had worked in his own youth for the slave-aiding father of abolitionist martyr John Brown. In adulthood, Jesse Grant excoriated slavery as fostering indolence and destroying work skills in the owning class. By contrast, Jesse's wife, Hannah, was staunchly loyal to the Democrats, the party espousing slavery, and her influence possibly moderated the views of their son to some extent. But although he was much less demonstrative, Ulysses exhibited some of his father's political leanings.

But he was no radical. He rejected—in fact abhorred—the idea that abolitionism should be valued above the Union itself. He had not lived in Illinois long enough to vote in 1860, but if he had, he later wrote, "pledges" (to friends, presumably) would have required him to diverge from the path of his Republican father and brothers and his own Whig background and cast his ballot for Stephen A. Douglas, the passionately unionist Illinois Democrat who tried to straddle the slavery question. But in the four-man presidential race between Douglas, John Bell of Tennessee, John C. Breckinridge of Kentucky, and Illinois Republican Abraham Lincoln, the real contest was between Breckinridge, the candidate of voters who planned to secede if they did not win, and Lincoln. Of those two, Grant preferred Lincoln.

And yet, in 1848 Grant married a daughter of slaveholders. The Dents were Missouri planters, and eventually Julia owned servants given her by her father. Grant himself briefly held title to a human being. Thirty-five-year-old

William Jones apparently ended up in his possession from the Dents while Grant was farming following his 1854 resignation from the prewar army.

When he moved to St. Louis in 1859, though, Grant filed papers freeing Jones—who was worth approximately one thousand dollars—despite the fact that Grant needed money. He never explained his motives in Jones's case, and it is possible that he required the slave to pay something for his freedom; Jones's writ of manumission says, in part, ". . . I Ulysses S Grant of the City & County of St. Louis in the State of Missouri, for divers good and valuable considerations me hereunto moving, do hereby emancipate and set free from Slavery my negro man William . . ." Whatever the "divers good and valuable considerations" might have been, Grant certainly could have gotten more from a fellow slaveholder than Jones himself would have been able to pay. But in moving to the city Grant was clearly unwilling to abandon a man whom he had worked beside in the fields to the whims of the marketplace and the uncertain mercies of a new owner.

The reaction of Julia's family to the freeing of Jones can only be conjectured. The burning issue that increasingly divided the nation had long since distanced Grant from the Dents, and he and his father-in-law frequently argued over it. Grant was no slavedriver, refusing to force slaves to work via threats of whipping and other punishment; he also paid rented slaves more than other renters did, angering the others. One family servant eventually would remember that in the hearing of some of the bondspeople, Grant declared a wish to free the Dent slaves as soon as possible. But in the antebellum South, slaves were worth more than the land they worked. Neither Grant nor the Dent servants could afford to buy that much freedom.[8]

* * *

Utterly unprepossessing to those who did not know him, Grant was less so to those who did. Medical officer John Brinton, who was assigned to Grant's staff at Cairo, recalled that in their first meeting the general "was a very short, small, rather spare man" whose "beard was a little long, very much longer than he afterwards wore it, unkempt and irregular, and of a sandy, tawny shade." His hair was the same color, "and at first glance he seemed to be a very ordinary sort of a man, indeed one below the average in most respects." But Brinton soon found that Grant's face "grew upon me. His eyes were gentle with a kind expression, and thoughtful." Although, as Brinton wrote, he "did not as a rule speak a great deal," he had a subtle sense of humor with intimates. When his family came to Cairo for an extended visit and his beloved four-year-old son greeted him at the door in the evenings by pummeling his knees in a challenge to wrestle, the general would often intone with mock solemnity—just before getting down to roll on the floor with the boy—"I do not feel like fighting, Jess, but I can't stand being hectored in this manner by a man of your size."9

The doting father was a repository of hidden riches: an officer who had not loved West Point but had learned its essentials; a soldier who had found combat irresistible and peacetime military life disastrously boring; an almost tongue-tied public speaker, an occasionally entertaining conversationalist, but an astonishingly gifted writer; and a man of such direct forthrightness that he was a bad card player—and of such high personal honor that he insisted on repaying a five-dollar debt to Longstreet at a time when Grant and his family were in dire financial straits.10

Grant adored his wife and family and was desperate to prove himself worthy of them. He had a great deal *to* prove to them, too. Despite his early promise in the Mexican War, his fortunes had declined significantly in its wake. The reason was alcohol.

His hard drinking began out of loneliness in the dull vacuum of the peacetime army, stationed between 1852 and 1854 on the Pacific coast two-thirds of a continent away from his family. According to several seemingly reliable accounts, Grant did not drink a great deal nor particularly often, but his constitution was such that he often appeared inebriated after even one drink. During the Civil War, he would explain to a fellow general at a dinner in St. Louis that he "dare[d] not touch" the goblet by his plate because "Sometimes I can drink freely without any unpleasant effect; at others I could not take even a single glass of wine." Small amounts of alcohol sometimes visibly affected him, and two or three glasses, in the words of another officer, "would make him stupid." Probably because of that, he tended to drink only in short, infrequent "sprees," but his physical makeup, which tended toward the delicate, insured that these could not go unnoticed.

Grant showed sufficient competence during his time stationed in the Oregon Territory and northern California that he was promoted from lieutenant to captain of infantry. But on one catastrophic payday in 1854, he apparently showed up at his company's pay-table too intoxicated to conduct business. When word leaked out, his commander, a martinet who had disliked him from their first meeting years earlier, reportedly gave him a choice of resigning from the army or facing military charges of drunkenness. Although associates urged Grant to stand trial because they felt the offense was trivial enough to result in acquittal, one of his lifelong friends later explained that "he would not for all the world have his wife know that he had been tried on such a charge." Instead, Grant abruptly resigned the commission that had supported his family in reasonable, if unostentatious, style.11

The Grants then slipped slowly into want. He tried truck farming and re-peatedly failed, not for lack of effort but because of the capriciousness of weather and the agricultural economy. A national financial panic in 1857 made worthless his bumper crops of oats, corn, potatoes, cabbages, and mel-ons; two days before Christmas of that year he pawned his last valuable, a gold watch, so the family would have twenty dollars with which to celebrate the holiday. In 1858, he was "attacked by ague and fever," which hung on for a year and hobbled his ability to work.

Whenever bad weather or other obstacles prevented him from other work during his farming years, he sold firewood on the street in St. Louis. There he was spotted by a thunderstruck fellow Mexican War officer who asked what in the world he was doing peddling wood. He jokingly replied with the directness and lack of artifice that was his essence: "I am solving the problem of poverty."[12]

By the time the Civil War began, Grant had been not only a farmer, but also a real estate salesman, customhouse clerk, and unsuccessful candi-date for county engineer in St. Louis, as well as a hopeful member of the teetotaling Sons of Temperance. In 1860, he hit the bottom of his career: a clerkship in the home office of his own father's leather-goods concern in the Mississippi River trading town of Galena, Illinois. The job his father provid-ed him—drawing up bills and collecting debts as well as selling goods and buying hides—saved him from destitution, and he seems to have worked de-terminedly, if not joyfully, to keep it.

During these trying years, when a true alcoholic would have almost cer-tainly reached his nadir, Grant appears not to have indulged his thirst much at all. His tendency to dabble, however, may have varied according to how far he had to travel from the warmth of his own hearth. In Galena in 1860, he is reported to have "smoked to excess" but not to have imbibed. Upriver in Wisconsin where he traveled on leather business, however, a bartender observed that his practice was to have one drink.[13]

On April 12, 1861, when the war's first shots were fired on Fort Sumter, Ulysses Grant was thirty-nine years old, working for his father, and laboring to recover from civilian financial failure and a military reputation as a drunkard. The outbreak of war suddenly offered the prospect of both. A conflict that he first assumed could not last three months gave him an unan-ticipated and seemingly fleeting second chance at the profession he might never have left but for the bottle.

As a trained former soldier, he was asked after Sumter to help the town of Galena form a volunteer company. Then, however, he rejected the offer to lead it, feeling that his experience entitled him to higher rank. The governor of Illinois finally appointed him colonel of the Twenty-first Illinois Infantry, but only after disappointments that included a two-day wait outside the office of Major General George Brinton McClellan, commander of all volunteer forces in Ohio. Grant and McClellan had encountered each other during the Mexican War and again later at Fort Vancouver, where quartermaster Grant had outfitted a McClellan-led expedition seeking a proposed railroad crossing of the Cascade Mountains. Grant now hoped McClellan would remember their acquaintance in the old army, and McClellan doubtless did—but his dominant memory may have been of how irate he had become when Grant, after arranging everything for McClellan's project, started one of his "sprees" and got drunk before the outfitting could be completed. The new major general found no time to see the ex-captain.[14]

Within weeks after his fruitless wait to see McClellan, Grant found himself commissioned a colonel and then the lofty grade above that. The new general was a man of contrasts: a quiet soul who liked to ride his horses fast; a fundamentally honest one who, perhaps because of his lengthy familiarity with the bottle, had become increasingly secretive and adept at the art of creative self-justification. His defensiveness about drinking had hardened over the years. Whereas in the old army he had allowed others to remonstrate with him about it, by 1862 he rarely allowed the subject raised around him. He thus seemed to have reached some sort of uneasy accommodation with his inner demons. His persona now combined a near-desperate desire for quick success with the steel nerve to hold out for his best chance of achieving it. The calm exterior and fidgety, explosive inner energy suggest a person perpetually itching to get away from himself and some things he had done and might do. Aching to erase seven years lost in a civilian wilderness of manifest inadequacy, he quickly became the first Union general in his theatre to focus not on covering his rear but, instead, on attacking. His restless determination to strike affected the war in the West almost immediately.[15]

4

Soldier Born

Forrest

GRANT WAS NOT the only obscure but rising figure on the western front in the late autumn of 1861, nor was he the only one destined to be remembered with awe. The other was a teetotaling Confederate cavalry officer operating around Hopkinsville, Kentucky: Lieutenant Colonel Nathan Bedford Forrest.

Grant and Forrest were, in many ways, similar. They were nearly the same age—Forrest was forty at the outset of the war, less than a year older than Grant. Both were consummate horsemen. Both were outwardly fearless, habitually restless, focused on results instead of ceremony, accustomed to making do with the resources at hand, and in need of fresh fields of endeavor. Both were also lucky, never having stopped a lethal bullet despite much exposure to gunfire. And both, like most of their fellow officers, were not above massaging the truth in recounting their deeds and motives.

But here the similarities ended. Forrest was a talented poker player, a fearlessly brilliant bluffer whose instincts at the table were the opposite of Grant's. And in contrast to Grant's external calm, the Confederate possessed a temper as quick and harsh as delta lightning.

Forrest had risen from frontier poverty to self-proclaimed millionaire status with no military education and scarcely any schooling at all—so little that he was, as a cultured subordinate would delicately put it, "indisposed to the use of the pen." So newspaper friends doubtless wrote for him early advertisements of the Memphis business he established in the early 1850s with a fast-changing succession of partners.

Forrest & Maples
SLAVE DEALERS . . .

Have constantly on hand the best selected assortment of FIELD HANDS, HOUSE SERVANTS & MECHANICS, at their Negro Mart, to be found in the city. They are daily receiving, from Virginia, Kentucky and Missouri, fresh

supplies of likely young Negroes. Negroes Sold On Commission and the highest market price is always paid for good stock. Their Jail is capable of containing Three Hundred and for comfort, neatness and safety, is the best arrayed
of any in the Union. Persons wishing to purchase, are invited to examine their
stock . . . [1]

Unlike Grant, who went on to become one of the most accomplished
memoirists in the history of American letters, Forrest's rare and labored personal correspondence reflected that the sum of his entire formal classroom
instruction totaled just six months. Yet his prose, while colorfully erratic, was
rarely mistakable in meaning. A note he wrote to a Memphis acquaintance
during the war is characteristic in both its picturesque spelling and its directness of style: "I had a small brush with the Enamy on yesterday they wair not
looking for me I taken them by Suprise they run like Suns of Biches."[2]

Other personal and cultural dissimilarities widened the gulf separating
the Ohio-born brigadier and the Memphis lieutenant colonel. Grant's laconic internalizing was probably in part a reaction to his successful, overbearing
father; Forrest's less noted sire, a blacksmith, died when the son was sixteen,
leaving the youth to assume the role of family patriarch. Grant and Forrest
were each their parents' firstborn son, but Forrest had a twin sister who died
in childbirth. While Grant was of slightly less than middling height and
breadth, Forrest was tall and athletic, and early on he was forced to use his
size and anything else at hand to protect his family from the dangers of the
frontier. Where Grant had inhabited a household separated from legalized
slavery by family philosophy and the Ohio River, Forrest spent most of his
adulthood in or near one of the epicenters of the Southern slave trade. In
the home of his garrulously political father, Grant doubtless heard many
heated complaints against the constitutional provision that accorded the
South unfair electoral advantage by granting each slave two-thirds of a vote.
Whatever youthful awareness Forrest had of politics, by contrast, was in-
evitably dominated by Tennessee's own fiery pro-slave President Andrew
Jackson, whose home sat just seventy-five miles from Forrest's birthplace and
whose White House terms spanned Forrest's late boyhood and early teens.

At six-feet-one-and-a-half and one hundred eighty pounds, Nathan Bedford Forrest was more than forty pounds heavier than Ulysses Grant and a
head taller. He was a connoisseur of weapons, horses, and dogs. Like Grant,
Forrest loved children and sometimes shed tears, but, very unlike Grant, he
also endured titanic mood swings. Carrying himself with the Jacksonian
mien of a man thrusting himself into the master class, he could be emphatically profane and flatly, lethally dangerous.

*   *   *

Had the Confederacy's western high command not been occupied with other matters that fall and early winter, it might well have sought more information on this combustible lieutenant colonel. He cut a singular figure, totally unlike the hordes of well-born twenty- or thirty-something gallants with whom the officer ranks of both sides were filling as fast as politicians could pull strings. He was, like Grant and many another officer in this new war, a political appointee, but nobody who knew him would have called him an average one.

Like Grant, Forrest must have seemed rather old to be racing horses at breakneck speeds. And he had much more to lose than most of his juniors: 3,345 acres of rich Mississippi cotton land as well as properties in Memphis, all earned by nearly three decades of furious struggle that began with his birth in a southern Tennessee log cabin. Reverses consigned his father's family to a leased hill farm in northwest Mississippi and the father to an early grave. As the eldest of eleven children—six boys who lived to adulthood and five girls who didn't—young Bedford became accustomed to eating breakfast by candle glow to be in the fields by dawn, and he followed many sunsets sitting before the hearth sewing homemade clothes and shoes for his siblings. His inventiveness and ferocious determination to succeed revealed themselves early. When an ox team he was driving balked in terror in a creek amid a developing flash flood, a teenaged Forrest grabbed the ear of one of the animals and bit off part of it, causing them to bolt forward out of danger.[3]

With his hard-won wealth at stake, it is hardly surprising that a full two months elapsed after the firing on Fort Sumter before he volunteered as a private. On June 14, six days after Tennesseans voted to leave the Union, he and his fifteen-year-old son and his youngest brother all joined a cavalry force, the Tennessee Mounted Rifles, that was forming near Memphis. A few weeks later Gideon Pillow, then still commander of Tennessee's Provisional Army, and Governor Harris, both of whom had known Forrest as a locally prominent Democrat, pulled the ex–vice president of the Memphis Jockey Club out of the ranks and made him a lieutenant colonel of cavalry. His long, catlike frame and incendiary temper made him seem created for combat.

War was, indeed, the perfect arena for his powers. His hardscrabble history had prepared him to command, for he was emphatically a man less of contemplation than of action, of split-second decisiveness, and he had risen to local note by helping, initially as a Mississippi constable, to expand the rule of law over his corner of the brawling southwestern frontier.

Law-abiding communities had become used to turning to him in times of crisis, when diplomacy no longer worked and naked force was the crying need. He was quintessentially self-reliant. As a slave-trader, he had driven bands of chained black people into Memphis from Kentucky, Mississippi, Arkansas, and perhaps as far away as Texas, acquiring much experience telling people what to do while depending on no one but himself to see that they did it.

Forrest had pulled himself out of the frontier fields onto the periphery of prominence with burning zeal, exceptional courage, excellent powers of deduction, and an intense capacity to focus. In his early twenties, he graduated from the plow to become junior partner in an aged uncle's farm supply business at Hernando, Mississippi. He then succeeded to the firm's proprietorship after the uncle died in a town-square fight—in the course of which his nephew took on three men, including the killer, and bested them with a two-shot pistol and a knife thrown him by a bystander. Soon, probably because of his fearlessness in the melee, he became town constable. He also married upward, winning the hand of Nashville Female Academy–educated Mary Ann Montgomery of Horn Lake, Mississippi. He accomplished this considerable feat by creatively overcoming the objections of her Presbyterian minister uncle. When the preacher protested, "Why, Bedford . . . you cuss and gamble, and Mary Ann is a Christian girl," the young suitor replied: "I know it, and that's just why I want her."

Early on, the young husband had to scramble for a living. He opened a stageline and a brickyard and apparently expanded the slave-trading part of his farm supply business. But when the community was late paying for his construction of a local "male academy" and he used direct and unflattering language to demand his money, the son of one of the richest slaveholders in DeSoto County challenged him to a duel. Perhaps to avoid antagonizing the local aristocracy by killing one of its own, he moved a few miles north to Memphis and plunged into slave-trading fulltime.4

Soon he was traveling throughout most of what was then the Southwest. Back home in Memphis, though, he played a significant role in saving a man from a lynch mob and, around the same time, supplying key testimony to convict the city's most prominent slave-trader of a sensational murder. The witness himself then became the city's best-known slave-yard operator, and not much later he appeared on the ballot for city council. In 1858, he received the most votes in his ward and went on to represent it over the next two years, becoming chairman of the Finance Committee. He also served as the council's spokesman for the highly important new Memphis & Charleston Railroad and for the mayor, who appears to have been a cousin.

As a large-scale slave-keeper, he was an authority on such municipal matters as jails and escapee apprehension, but mingling with lawyers and other city fathers in a droning deliberative body was not easy for a man so accustomed to taking quick, decisive, individual action. After he had worked for months with other members of a special committee to find the city a location for a new Market House, the council heeded the objections of a wealthy widow and rejected a site near her home that Forrest had recommended and on which a down payment had been made. Forrest threatened to resign if the council took the action it did and then hotly followed through, saying he planned never to serve on a special committee again. Within two months, though, he characteristically cooled and allowed himself to be appointed to other bodies.

In debate, he was forceful and unrestrained, once describing an opponent as "the worst-scared man" he "ever saw." When another member declaimed that the council had taken a cowardly action, he quickly regretted his choice of language. Forrest interjected that he was sure the member had not used the word "coward" in reference to *him*, since the speaker knew he was "a fighting man."

The citizens of his ward re-elected him in 1859 by more votes than he had received the first time, but his fellow councilmen were not so approving. The first time he resigned from the council on a sudden whim they reinstated him five weeks later, but the second time, when he quit again after they decided to go ahead with an investigation that he branded a waste of time, he was voted out even after offering to return.[5]

Around the time of his second resignation in 1860, he remained prominent enough to be one of fifteen local Democrats arranging for a mass meeting to hear secessionist firebrand William L. Yancey of South Carolina, an advocate of legally reopening the African slave trade. By the following year, though, Forrest's political fortunes had ebbed to the point that he was living not in Memphis but on his rustic, though highly productive, Mississippi plantation. There, local authorities soon indicted him for violating the law by gambling at cards. He was at a time and station of life when most people faded quietly into retirement, but he was not the kind of man who faded anywhere. He needed a new field of endeavor, one in which he could tell people what to do rather than politick them into doing it. The guns of Sumter obliged.[6]

*   *   *

Despite his lack of military training, Forrest brought to the Confederate army a wealth of individual fighting experience. In more than two decades of defending himself and others everywhere from public squares to dueling fields, he had learned to sense an enemy's vulnerabilities, physically and psychologically. He had become a master at instilling opponents and even friends with fear.

The key to victory in individual or collective combat, Forrest believed, lay in getting the psychological upper hand, intimidating foes with an appearance of crushing power. He claimed to have discovered this principle in boyhood, riding a half-broken colt past a home guarded by vicious dogs. The dogs spooked the colt, which lunged sideways to escape and hurled young Forrest into their midst. He scrambled up to run away, then found there was no need. The dogs had been so frightened by this large object suddenly thrown at them that they already had turned tail. No matter one's strength, Forrest inferred, there is always great value in attacking boldly. It was a rule he lived by in personal as well as military encounters for the rest of his life.

Forrest had given the psychology of combat so much thought that he could even detail how it worked. To a curious fellow Confederate he explained that, since most men tended to look at a battlefield with fear and revulsion, he sought to make the enemy's initial impression of it as "shocking" as he could. Rather than hold a significant force in reserve, he tried to deliver all he had in the "fiercest" way possible, so as to immediately "overawe and demoralize." Then, he said, "with unabated fury, by a constant repetition of blows" he could kill, capture, and drive the foe "with but little difficulty." He even refined it all into one homely sentence: "Get 'em skeered, then keep the skeer on 'em." [7]

His friend Sam Tate, president of the Memphis & Charleston Railroad, could not know how prescient he was when he wrote Albert Sidney Johnston in late 1861 that Forrest's regiment of cavalry was "as fine a body of men" as ever joined an army. "Give Forrest a chance," Tate urged, "and he will distinguish himself." [8]

A more profound understatement is difficult to cite.

September 4–November 7, 1861
Grant at Paducah and Belmont

THIS WAR THAT virtually nobody, North or South, had expected to last for more than a skirmish or two pushed on through summer. On July 21, 1861, in the first all-out battle, raw Confederates commanded by Joseph E. Johnston and P. G. T. Beauregard routed equally green Federals under Irvin McDowell at Bull Run creek in northern Virginia. The panicked Union rabble fled back to Washington, where full mobilization of the North began in earnest.

After Bull Run, a lull ensued in the east. Abraham Lincoln removed McDowell and, on July 27, replaced him with Major General George McClellan, who had advanced from Ohio into western Virginia and had just finished clearing relatively small Confederate forces from that important, railroad-crossed region. Little Mac, as he was called, took command of the army defending Washington. Wildly egotistical and arrogant but an excellent organizer and drillmaster, he quickly began melding McDowell's whipped mob and continually arriving new volunteers into a large, powerful strike force. The Union navy threw a blockade around Southern ports from there to Texas and started tightening a stranglehold on Dixie's access to overseas supplies.

On July 31, Lincoln appointed thirty-four brigadier generals across the northern and border states. One of the thirty-four, the ex-captain and now colonel of the Twenty-first Illinois Volunteers, was sitting in front of his tent in the village of Mexico, Missouri, when he read in a newspaper about his out-of-the-blue promotion. Grant rightly attributed this stroke of luck to a recently acquired patron, Illinois Republican congressman and Lincoln intimate Elihu B. Washburne. Washburne had met Grant while the two were helping organize Galena's company of volunteers, and the congressman, an avowed abolitionist, became determined to claim for Illinois this Ohio-born West Pointer.

It is fitting that Grant learned of his appointment through the newspapers. Since well before the outbreak of hostilities, he had pored over them, giving much thought to reports of the deepening sectional crisis. He expected the hostilities to be short-lived. On April 19, he wrote his Southern-leaning father-in-law that "The North is responding to the President's call in such a manner that the Confederates may truly quake.

I tell you there is no mistaking the feelings of the people. The Government can call into the field 75,000 troops, and ten or twenty times 75,000 if it should be necessary . . . In all this I can see but the doom of slavery [despite the fact that] Northerners do not want, nor will they want, to interfere with the institution . . . [But they] will refuse for all time to give it protection unless the Southerners shall return soon to their allegiance; and then, too, this disturbance will give such an impetus to the production of their staple—cotton—in other parts of the world that they can never recover the control of the market again for that commodity. This will reduce the value of the negroes so much that they will never be worth fighting over again.[1]

He expected "a few decisive victories" to "send the secession army howling," and the only danger then would be one that the South had feared for generations—and which its slaveholding upper class, by seceding, had brought upon itself. Rapid defeat of the Southern armies might spark a slave "revolt and cause more destruction than any Northern man except . . . the ultra-abolitionist. A Northern army may be required in the next ninety days to go South to suppress a negro insurrection."[2]

Still convinced that the Jefferson Davis government was not long for the world, in early July Grant eagerly followed orders to take his regiment across the Mississippi River into Missouri to help oppose guerrilla raids and the work of three Confederate armies. His troops spent the first month protecting railroad tracks and other facilities, but after years of under-employment, Grant found his responsibilities proliferating. At Mexico he was given leadership of two other regiments besides his own, plus a section of artillery. Then, around the time he was named a brigadier, Major General John C. Fremont arrived in St. Louis at Lincoln's behest to take command of the Western theatre, and Grant's horizons continued to expand. Soon, he was sent to Ironton, Missouri, to lead three thousand raw troops in blocking an expected advance by about the same number of Confederates under Hardee. Suddenly, in the war's second big battle, the Confederates, on August 10, again routed Federals at Wilson's Creek just south of Springfield, and Fremont hurried Grant west to the state capital, Jefferson City, to pull together another ill-disciplined and badly armed force to guard against the northward-marching victors. Within a week, Grant had managed to present a bristling defense, and the expected Confederate attack never came.

In late August, Fremont picked Grant for an assignment that dwarfed the previous ones. The Union's western commander wanted to challenge Confederate General Polk for control of the upper Mississippi Valley. Polk had twelve thousand troops in southeast Missouri moving up the west bank of the Mississippi, and the focus of both sides was the lofty river bluff at Columbus in neutral Kentucky. From the Columbus heights, artillery could rain destruction on any water-borne move downriver toward the critical Dixie cities of Memphis, Vicksburg, and New Orleans. Basing his new campaign in Cairo, Illinois, Fremont startlingly chose Grant to lead it, passing over a more senior brigadier, John Pope, who was also a West Pointer and one whose Illinois family had strong connections to both Lincoln and Governor Yates. Like Yates when the governor allowed Grant back into the army by commissioning him a colonel of volunteers, Fremont had to ignore advisers who opposed the appointment for all-too-obvious "reasons that were well known," as Fremont put it. They were the same reasons George McClellan had seemed to heed when Grant tried to see him in Cincinnati back in June.

Fremont, surely having no idea that Grant disliked both his pompous style and his abolitionism and had voted against him in 1856, later said he picked the Illinoisan not because he "considered him then a great general" but because he saw in Grant "a man of great activity and promptness in obeying orders" as well as "a man of unassuming character . . . of dogged persistence, and iron will."

Fremont, of all people, got it right. Grant had already *had* to be all those things. When he set out for Cairo at the end of August, he glanced over his shoulder as if to see what might be gaining on him. The old "reasons" had almost excluded him from this new volunteer army, turning him away time after time. Just before Governor Yates, with misgivings, finally handed him the Twenty-first Illinois, Grant had un-typically confided to an old army friend that he had lost all hope of returning to the service and, having left his father's employ, was worried about how he would support his family. At least once before, during his grim civilian middle years, he had tried to reconnect with the military by contracting himself to feed an army expedition headed across the plains; he had been turned away then, but as his spring of 1861 wore desperately into summer, a similar idea recurred. He wondered to the old friend if he might get a contract to at least *bake bread* for the army, reminding the friend of how well he, presumably in his quartermaster capacity, had baked it during the Mexican War.

To Julia, who apparently complained about his lengthening absence from home, he wrote on his way to Cairo: "You should be cheerful and try to encourage me. I have a task before me of no trifling moment and want all the encouragement possible. The safety of our country to some extent, and my reputation and that of our children, greatly depends upon my acts."[3]

*   *   *

On September 2, 1861, two days before Grant arrived in Cairo, Union soldiers implementing Fremont's new design headed toward tiny Belmont, Missouri, just across the Mississippi River from Columbus. This prompted Polk Confederates led by Pillow to rush across the Mississippi from Missouri into the neutral bluegrass.

Passing through the border town of Hickman, Pillow hurried on another twenty miles north to grab Columbus, which in addition to being a widely denominated Mississippi Gibraltar, was also the northern terminus of the Mobile & Ohio Railroad and thus a major land avenue running all the way to the Gulf of Mexico. Polk and Pillow had coveted Columbus for months.

Grant reacted immediately—and without authorization. After wiring Fremont for permission to respond to the Confederate move, he awaited a reply for only an afternoon before hurrying troops aboard hastily gathered steamboats. Before pushing off, he sent two more telegrams that afternoon. One informed Fremont that if he received no orders to the contrary in the next few hours he was going to respond to the Confederate aggression. The other, indicating how closely he had been following developments in the region, courteously informed the speaker of the Kentucky Legislature that its state's declared neutrality had been violated, that the Confederates had invaded and seized Hickman and Columbus.

Then that night, Grant and some of his men steamed forty-five miles up the Ohio from Cairo and the next morning, September 6, took the Kentucky town of Paducah, at the confluence of the Ohio and Tennessee rivers. Paducah was a far greater strategic prize than the potential fortress at Columbus. The Tennessee River, the mouth of which Paducah commanded, runs south-to-north roughly parallel to the north-south course of the Mississippi. Thus the Tennessee could float an invading army past Columbus's landside and get south of it, cutting off the Gibraltar from Confederate supplies and reinforcements and making it untenable. Without Confederate possession of Paducah, a Confederate Columbus would live on borrowed time.

Grant quickly placed guard detachments on the roads around Paducah, established the beginnings of a garrison, and, just before leaving to return to

Cairo at noon that same day, issued a flowery written-out "Proclamation, to Citizens of Paducah!" reassuring them that "I have come among you, not as an enemy, but as your friend and fellow-citizen . . . to defend and enforce the rights of all loyal citizens.

> An enemy, in rebellion against our common Government, has . . . planted its guns upon the soil of Kentucky and fired upon our flag. Hickman and Columbus are in his hands. He is moving upon your city. I am here to defend you against this enemy and to assert and maintain the authority and sovereignty of your Government and mine. I have nothing to do with opinions. I shall deal only with armed rebellion and its aiders and abetors [sic]. You can pursue your usual avocations without fear or hindrance. The strong arm of the Government is here to protect its friends, and to punish only its enemies. Whenever it is manifest that you are able to defend yourselves . . . I shall withdraw the forces under my command from your city.

Grant arrived back in Cairo a few hours later to find Fremont's belated and equivocal consent to seize the pivotal Kentucky town if Grant "felt strong enough." Fremont also gave him a sharp rebuke for telegraphing the legislators, along with a warning against "repetition of the offence" of presuming to speak for the Union army to civilian politicians. Fremont said that job was more appropriately that of "the Major General commanding the Department"—as it certainly was, at least under unhurried circumstances. But Grant had to act fast if he wanted to foil a Confederate movement that he had been informed was headed from Columbus to Paducah, and he realized the necessity of informing Kentucky legislators of the prior Confederate aggression before he acted. So he did the swiftest and yet most politically sensitive thing he could have done in the absence of timely orders from Fremont. Fremont, though, seems to have thought otherwise. He immediately took Paducah from its captor and placed it under the command of just-arrived General Charles Ferguson Smith.4

But Grant's taking of Paducah was a portentous moment in the maintaining of the Union—while the Polk–Pillow seizure of Columbus was the war's first great Confederate disaster. Kentucky's neutrality, the result of a standoff between Confederate-sympathizing Governor Beriah Magoffin and the unionist legislature, was doomed to a short life anyway by the military reality of the state's huge strategic value to both sides, but the Confederate invasion sent to the Federal side many of the Bluegrass State's fence-sitters. More important, it robbed Confederate Tennessee, gateway to the western Confederacy, of the vital buffer that, up to then, had protected its porous northern border from Federal invasion.

On September 3, Tennessee Governor Isham G. Harris, Pillow's friend and political associate, received an abrupt telegram from the Confederacy's secretary of war ordering "prompt withdrawal" of the "wholly unauthorized" incursion into Kentucky and an immediate apology to Governor Magoffin. Harris meanwhile sent his own dismayed wire to Jefferson Davis disclaiming any responsibility: "Confederate troops commanded by General Pillow landed at Hickman, Ky., last night. I regard the movement as unfortunate; calculated to injure our cause in the State. Unless absolutely necessary there, would it not be well to order their immediate withdrawal?" Harris also telegraphed Polk—"This is unfortunate, as the President and I are pledged to respect the neutrality of Kentucky. I hope they will be withdrawn instantly, unless their presence there is an absolute necessity"— as well as Magoffin: "The troops that landed at Hickman last night did so without my knowledge and consent and, I am confident, without the consent of the President. I have telegraphed to President Davis requesting their immediate withdrawal."[5]

By the time Harris sent his frantic wires, however, Grant's move on Paducah had made them passé. The harm Polk and Pillow had done was irreparable: the shield of Kentucky neutrality that had protected all of the South between the Alleghenies and the Mississippi was shattered. Polk's Columbus order was his last meaningful one as Confederate commander of the West. Albert Sidney Johnston was then just arriving to take over those reins, with Polk taking charge of the left wing. Johnston endorsed the Columbus capture and allowed Pillow to stay where he was, partly because when Johnston first heard about the move, he assumed that if Pillow was going to make such a momentous violation he had the military sense to send some of his troops on past Columbus to swiftly take Paducah and similarly vital Smithland, Kentucky, at the mouth of the Cumberland River. The Cumberland, after all, was a third water route into Dixie, running parallel to the Mississippi and the Tennessee, and it had the additional virtue of leading directly to Nashville, which sat on its west bank thirty miles south of the Tennessee border. But Pillow had contented himself with Columbus; he had stopped there and begun digging trenches. So, primarily to protect Nashville and the rest of the central South, Johnston had ordered his troops northward into Kentucky across the rest of the long Tennessee border, occupying Bowling Green and, well to the east, the hills north of Cumberland Gap.

While Johnston put on a sham show of aggressiveness and worried about the capacity of his undermanned force to back it up, Grant organized the bustling Cairo troop center and looked for openings. Columbus, twenty miles down the Mississippi, was the target Fremont had given him in first assigning him the Cairo command, and Grant fixated on it. He also fidgeted over the continuing need to do something consequential with his growing army while he had it. He was very conscious that his was a situation that could change at any time because he was perhaps the least-eminent general in his region. On September 10, just four days after taking Paducah, he asked Fremont for permission to attack Columbus, but the St. Louis departmental commander was preoccupied with another looming Federal disaster. Eighteen thousand Confederates under General Sterling Price had besieged a Union force at Lexington in western Missouri, and on September 20, the Lexington garrison finally capitulated. So Fremont, trying to restore Federal primacy on the opposite end of Missouri, had little time to worry about attacking Columbus.

Around November 1, as a White House–pressed Fremont set off with a large force in pursuit of the Lexington victors, he suddenly ordered Grant to have all his troops "ready to march at an hour's notice." This was the first of four directives Fremont's St. Louis headquarters sent Grant between then and November 3. In addition to putting his troops on standby to march, Grant was to make aggressive "demonstrations" on both sides of the Mississippi against Charleston, Missouri, and Blandville, Kentucky, both just short rides out of Cairo. These demonstrations, he was told, were to be characterized by constant activity "back and forward . . . without, however, attacking the enemy," the purpose being to prevent Confederates in the eastern part of the state from reinforcing those Fremont was going after in the west. Grant was also to send detachments westward from two places in southeastern Missouri, Bird's Point across the Mississippi River from Cairo and Commerce, which was twenty-some miles north of Cairo, in pursuit of a resourceful Confederate cavalry leader named Jeff Thompson; these detachments were then to aid other Federal units in driving Thompson out of southeast Missouri into Arkansas. On November 3, Grant received a final instruction from St. Louis: he and Smith were to make yet another demonstration—this one against mighty Columbus itself—to make certain that no reinforcements would be sent west into Missouri from there.

Again, and more spectacularly, Grant exceeded orders. He not only "demonstrated," but then, against Fremont's emphatic instructions not to bring on a battle, he attacked the Confederates' small Camp Johnston at little Belmont, a steamboat landing across the Mississippi River beneath the very brow of Columbus. To justify this disobedience, he concocted "information" that Confederates in the Missouri interior were about to be reinforced from Columbus.

His attack plan *was* at least somewhat in the spirit of what Fremont wanted, to prevent Columbus-area Confederates from reinforcing those in the

Missouri interior, but Grant's bogus intelligence was about as incorrect as it could be. Columbus commander Polk, that very day, reluctantly began complying with an Albert Sidney Johnston order to send Pillow and five thousand men marching, not westward into Missouri, but east to Clarksville, Tennessee, to strengthen the region around forts Henry and Donelson on the Tennessee and Cumberland rivers. Wary of the Federal buildup around Cairo, Polk had strongly opposed giving up any part of his Columbus force. Coincidentally or otherwise, he sent Jefferson Davis his resignation from the army on November 6, soon after receiving the order to detach Pillow. His old friend Davis turned him down.

To make his Belmont attack, Grant seized an auspicious, unforeseeable moment. That week Lincoln sacked the imperious Fremont. For the President, the Lexington surrender had been the last straw on what was becoming a haystack. It had begun piling up almost as soon as Fremont took over in St. Louis. Back on August 30, without checking with Washington, Fremont had announced he was emancipating the slaves of all active Missouri Confederates, a sweeping measure that jeopardized Lincoln's delicate campaign to hold border states in the Union. Fremont then had refused to revoke his decree, making Lincoln order him to do so. These were only the first of many abrasive oversteps.[6]

News of Fremont's firing began showing up in newspapers on November 3, casting into limbo Fremont's order to merely "demonstrate" downriver, and Grant set the Belmont plan in motion two days later, as soon as Fremont's firing was certain. Grant's manufacture of an excuse to attack differentiated him from most other Union generals on either front; the other generals usually made excuses for *not* attacking. Since Grant was by most accounts a fundamentally and perhaps even an unusually honest man, his creation of "intelligence" to justify his attack has to be attributable to his fear that he was about to lose his command.

As Grant well understood (and, indeed, had even written to his father around this time), his job as ground commander of the Union's impending move down the Mississippi was the most coveted in a district that had begun to bristle with better-connected brigadiers. His own second-in-command, the recent congressman McClernand, was an obvious eager candidate. The redoubtable Charles Ferguson Smith, whom Grant idolized, had arrived and been given the post at Grant-captured Paducah in early September, just days after Grant was assigned to Cairo. Also at Paducah, subordinate to Smith, was zealous Lew Wallace, son of an Indiana governor. And nearby in Missouri was blustery Lincoln intimate John Pope, who in 1861 had bragged to Grant about his acquaintances "with most of the prominent men" of Illinois.

Grant's on-again-off-again attachment to the bottle may also have helped produce his informational creativity in advance of the Belmont attack. Anyone with a drinking problem tends to become increasingly prone to—and talented at—telling white lies, both to others and to himself, in emergencies. And in late 1861, Grant almost surely felt a need to win positive headlines to balance negative ones. The resurfacing—in newsprint, no less—of his drinking image following the October late-night reunion jollity with General Smith at Lew Wallace's Paducah quarters, soon after Smith's arrival, may well have pushed him toward desperate and uncharacteristic measures. Congressman Washburne, the Grant sponsor whose district lay at the other end of Illinois, visited Cairo to check on Grant in October.[7]

* * *

However diverse his motives, Grant's troop transports cast off from Cairo under cover of darkness on the evening of November 6. His purpose was so hush-hush that he refused to tell even his senior subordinates where they were headed. As the steamboats and a protective vanguard of two gunboats turned down the Mississippi instead of up the Ohio, the new Federal volunteers aboard the vessels cheered, assuming they were headed toward Columbus. They welcomed the prospect of battle.

But Grant made them wait. At 11 p.m., his transports tied up on the Kentucky bank nine miles above Columbus. He had ordered Colonel John Cook at Fort Holt in Kentucky, just across the Mississippi River from Cairo, to march south toward Columbus. Smith, Grant's only confidant in the planning stages of this affair, had been requested to make the same sort of threatening move from Paducah; Grant did not even tell Smith the whole plan; he said his aim was to "menace" Belmont. On the Missouri side of the Mississippi, he had ordered Colonel Richard Oglesby to march out of Commerce, Missouri, on the trail of Jeff Thompson; unlike the instructions Grant had received from Fremont's office to drive Thompson out of southeast Missouri, Grant's orders to Oglesby were simply to "destroy" Thompson. When Grant received the final order from St. Louis, the one telling him to launch a demonstration against Columbus, though, he had sent Oglesby new instructions to turn his march southward—and to communicate with Grant "at Belmont." Out of Bird's Point, meanwhile, he sent Colonel W. H. L. Wallace and elements of his Eleventh Illinois Regiment southwest toward Charleston. There, Wallace would be between Oglesby and Grant. Halting the transports on the Kentucky bank for a few hours while all these other movements were underway obviously would add even more weight to the impression that something big was up and Grant and Smith were mounting a coordinated assault on Columbus itself.

Here on the Kentucky shore, Grant later claimed, he received a 2 a.m. message from W. H. L. Wallace. According to Grant, the message said that Confederates from the Columbus garrison were crossing the Mississippi to Belmont apparently to march west to cut off Oglesby. Later, Grant also maintained, highly questionably, that his decision to attack was made on the trip downriver:

> I had no orders which contemplated an attack by the National troops, nor did I intend anything of the kind when I started out from Cairo; but after we started I saw that the officers and men were elated at the prospect of at last having the opportunity of doing what they had volunteered to do—fight the enemies of our country. I did not see how I could maintain discipline, or retain the confidence of my command, if we should return to Cairo without an effort to do something.

The elaborate ruses by Smith and Cook worked for a while. When Polk's lookouts saw Federal vessels steaming down the Mississippi that morning, the Columbus commander cancelled Pillow's Clarksville march two hours after it had begun and rushed the ever-eager Tennessean back to Columbus. Soon, Polk sent Pillow across the river to oppose Grant while holding most of the Columbus garrison in readiness for a land assault by Cook and Smith.

Visible from the heights of Polk's fortress, the Federals disembarked upstream on the Missouri side and came across country to take Camp Johnston from the rear. About halfway there, in the middle of an eastward jut of woodland and cornfields formed by a long curve in the Mississippi, they ran into Pillow.

Already infamous among professional soldiers for having once dug a ditch on the wrong side of his trenches in Mexico, the Tennessee brigadier once again proved his military ineptitude. He set up the right of his line in a field facing woods, causing one of his men to say later that he felt like a participant in a "duel with his enemy behind a tree and he in the open field." Pillow then compounded his error by ordering some of his troops to charge the enemy in the woods. A subordinate, Colonel Thomas Freeman of the Twenty-second Tennessee Infantry, described the assault in his official report as "ill-judged and almost impossible."

Inadequately supplied with ammunition and subjected to hot and incessant fire from the protected Union troops, Pillow's men were hardly to blame for finally breaking and fleeing. Crowds of Confederates cowered in disorder behind the Mississippi's tall banks by the time Polk, watching from his bastion across the river, decided the Smith and Cook advances were just feints. He then sent reinforcements led by Mexican War veteran Frank Cheatham.

An aristocratic native of Nashville and brother of its present mayor, the profane Cheatham exhibited hard drinking and fistfighting tendencies greatly admired by his soldiers. He crossed the Mississippi unopposed by the Federal gunboats *Lexington* and *Tyler,* whose commanders feared lethal plunging fire would rain from the Columbus cannons above them. Once across the river, Cheatham and Pillow rallied Pillow's skulkers and counterattacked.

The Union troops had stopped in the Confederate camp to pillage and celebrate, assuming the battle had been won. There General McClernand, much accustomed to public speaking, indulged himself in a brief oration, along with other officers, while their men huzzahed and looted. Grant, emphatically not one of the speakers, ordered the camp set afire to regain control. Before he could fully do so, however, his men were hit so hard by the resurgent Southerners that they themselves now took a turn at fleeing. The Confederates chased them back to their boats and then shot at them from the bank as the vessels lurched away. Grant was the last man aboard; with the mooring lines already cast away, he was forced to slide his second mount of the day (his first had been shot under him) down the steep riverbank and across a makeshift gangplank in a hail of bullets. He had left behind on the battlefield, along with his dead horse, his mess chest and a gold pen. His troops' retreat was so hasty, in fact, that the Twenty-seventh Illinois, which had gotten separated from the other Federal units in the battle, was left behind. It had to be rescued by boats that, at the behest of a justifiably frantic McClernand, went back for that purpose.[8]

After making it onto the steamboat *Belle Memphis,* Grant lay down on a couch to catch his breath and perhaps contemplate his little army's close brush with total disaster. He then sprang up again to look ashore, perhaps in hopes of seeing the Twenty-seventh Illinois. Almost immediately, a Confederate musket-ball tore into the couch, passing through its head to lodge in its foot.[9]

The cornfield brawl at Belmont might have been recorded more generally as a Confederate triumph had the numbers of troops engaged more nearly resembled those later reported by Pillow: twenty-five hundred Confederates, he said, against seventy-five hundred Federals. In reality, by the time the battle ended, Pillow and Cheatham had a total of five thousand on the field against Grant's thirty-one hundred. Grant showed that he could play with figures, too, soon telling the Navy's Captain Foote that in killed, wounded, and missing he estimated his loss at no more than two hundred fifty men. In reality, both sides sustained about six hundred casualties. One hundred and twenty Union soldiers were killed, one hundred five Confederates.

Bloody and amateurish though it was, the Battle of Belmont had made up in strategic and psychological implication for all it lacked in tactical sense. Grant subsequently claimed that "the two objects for which the battle of Belmont was fought were fully accomplished. The enemy gave up all idea of detaching troops from Columbus"—and not just into Missouri; the enemy encouraged Polk to be even more reluctant to transfer any of his Columbus force anywhere. And, Grant added, "The National troops acquired a confidence in themselves at Belmont that did not desert them through the war."[10]

Belmont outraged Foote. With his river force under the direction of generals rather than his saltwater superiors in the Navy, he now had received the last slight he intended to take from the army—and especially from Grant. Grant had promised to keep Foote informed of any move entailing combat, then suddenly "forgot" to in the run-up to Belmont. At the last minute, he had ordered a Foote subordinate to command the gunboats accompanying the hush-hush mission. Foote complained to Secretary of the Navy Gideon Welles about the incident and noted that his rank of captain was equal only to that of an army lieutenant colonel. He urged that he be promoted to flag-officer to prevent further army "want of consideration" for their service branch.

Foote's sensitivity was understandable. He was working night and day on the myriad tasks of preparing the eagerly awaited ironclad fleet for water. Beginning in early October, his wooden gunboats already were doing vital reconnaissance and infantry support on the rivers. Key Foote lieutenants continually prowled the Tennessee and Cumberland, nurturing Union sentiment along the banks while gathering otherwise-inaccessible information on construction progress at forts Henry and Donelson. Seth Phelps of the *Conestoga*, most notably, suggested that these forts could be captured.

Foote and his people did not deserve to be treated like the army's stepchildren, and their status improved markedly after Belmont. Foote's flag-officer promotion arrived from Washington within the month, and Brigadier General Grant found himself dealing with the naval equivalent of a peer.[11]

6

November 8, 1861

East Tennessee Erupts

THANKS CONSIDERABLY to Grant's cowing of Polk at Columbus, the center of Johnston's Cumberland Line, and especially its vital but neglected region between the Tennessee and Cumberland rivers, would afterward be without much help from the Mississippi-bluff fortress to its left. And Johnston soon got bad news from behind his right.

Barely twenty-four hours after the Belmont donnybrook, unionists in Tennessee's Appalachian region launched the revolt long feared by Confederates: five of the nine bridges on the connected East Tennessee & Virginia and East Tennessee & Georgia railroad lines went up in clouds of smoke and pillars of fire. These two roads were vital to the Confederacy. Together they comprised the principal transportation link between the Davis government in Richmond and the fertile grain- and meat-producing areas of the west-central and Deep South that could keep it functioning.

The Confederates reacted with panicked fury.

NASHVILLE, November 12, 1861

His Excellency JEFFERSON DAVIS:
The burning of the railroad bridges in East Tennessee shows a deep-seated spirit of rebellion in that section. Union men are organizing. This rebellion must be crushed out instantly, the leaders arrested and summarily punished . . .

ISHAM G. HARRIS

Up until that point, the Tennessee governor had recommended a policy of forbearance toward his state's Union-loving mountaineers largely because their votes were necessary for his own reelection. But the unionists did not regard the Harris policy as forbearance. He had taken them out of the Union, which to them was a crime tantamount to sacrilege.

Harris's intended gentleness had failed, and it now threatened the central artery of the whole Confederacy. The two hundred thirty miles of rails of the East Tennessee & Virginia and the East Tennessee & Georgia lines crossing the Tennessee Valley were gravely damaged at both ends. Single bridges at Bristol and Greeneville in the north and three more near the southern tip, one at Cleveland and two near Chattanooga, lay wholly or partly in ashes. Only four of the trestles on the route survived, and some of these had been attacked.

Harris's alarmed response to the uprising was more than equaled by the reaction of the new Confederate secretary of war, Judah P. Benjamin. Responding swiftly, Benjamin instructed Confederate authorities in eastern Tennessee to bring all suspected bridge-burners summarily before "drum-head court-martial" and hang those found guilty "on the spot." "It would be well to leave their bodies hanging in the vicinity of the burned bridges," he added.[1]

In Greeneville—hometown of Andrew Johnson, the only United States senator from a seceded state who continued to occupy his seat—two convicted bridge burners soon swung from an oak tree beside the railroad tracks, their bodies left to entertain passengers aboard the cars. Trains were ordered to slow as they passed, and some of the riders reportedly exploited the opportunity and used the corpses for shooting practice. After two days, the remains were in such a state of abuse and decomposition that they had to be removed.

Several other men were condemned to death; a few had their sentences commuted. Those arrested for traitorous activity included a Johnson son-in-law, Judge David T. Patterson, but Knoxville authorities complained that Patterson, Sevier County state senator Samuel Pickens, "and other ringleaders of the same class" had "so managed as not to be found in arms." Johnson's other son-in-law, Dan Stover, was in hiding. He ultimately would be found to have helped plot the torching of the bridges in support of a planned Federal invasion of East Tennessee.

Benjamin instructed his East Tennessee commanders to take Patterson, Pickens, and the others to Tuscaloosa, Alabama, as prisoners of war. On November 14, Brigadier General W. H. Carroll rushed to Knoxville from Memphis with two Confederate regiments and declared martial law in the city, sending his troops on a house-to-house weapons search. Civilian movement in both Knoxville and Chattanooga was restricted, and Confederate troops and their local allies assaulted and dispersed camps of unionists in more than a dozen counties. They started rounding up hundreds of people and shipping them south to prison. Others were conscripted into the Confederate army and sent to regions where they could be better trusted.

By November 25, relieved Confederate authorities began to think the tide of revolt had crested and the immediate danger past.[2]

The first year of formal hostilities began winding down. But the closing days of 1861 would be marked by an obscure yet ominous engagement.

7

December 28, 1861

Forrest at Sacramento

O N THE THRESHOLD of 1862, the Civil War's get-serious year, the conflict got its baptism in the fire of Nathan Bedford Forrest. His first wartime battle was small, more of a glorified skirmish, but to anyone paying attention it raised eyebrows. Operating in a new arena known to reduce even some peacetime ruffians to quavering cowardice, he showed himself fully as formidable as he had been on the Mississippi backroads and the rowdy streets of Memphis.

By this time, half a year into his military career, Forrest already had begun to exhibit a genius for crafty military trickery. In late July of 1861, as soon as he received his commission, he had gone to Kentucky for recruits and arms. He hauled five hundred Colt revolvers (bought with his own money) out of Louisville under the nose of the suspicious unionist Home Guard, carting them out of town in a farm wagon and bagged up as potatoes. Then, he and a company of ninety Kentucky recruits, being escorted on the first leg of their initial army journey by a host of well-wishing civilians, headed for Clarksville below the Tennessee-Kentucky border. Informed that two companies of Home Guards were waiting to stop him fifteen miles ahead at Munfordville, Forrest drew up not only his recruits but also their civilian friends beside some railroad tracks running into Munfordville to be viewed by passengers on the next train. When he reached Munfordville, most of the unionists had fled in fear of his seeming horde, and he scattered the remaining few with a charge by his enlistees.[1]

Like Grant, Forrest had come to this war to fight and ached to do it. Sent in October to Fort Donelson, Forrest went on to Hopkinsville, having requested the transfer to be of more meaningful use. Following Grant's initiative-seizing assault at Belmont, Albert Sidney Johnston at Bowling Green increasingly needed information on the gathering Federal force in western Kentucky, and Forrest busied himself reconnoitering for the Hopkinsville headquarters of Brigadier General Lloyd Tilghman.

He ranged far afield of Hopkinsville. On November 19, following an eight-hour, all-night, thirty-two-mile ride to Canton, Kentucky, on the Cumberland River north of Fort Donelson, he ambushed the Federal gunboat *Conestoga* with only some cavalry and one small cannon. The *Conestoga* ultimately withdrew from the fusillade-filled stalemate, but Forrest had shown that his cavalry would attack even gunboats. In early December—"weary of the routine of camp service and of short tours of scouting duty," his authorized biography reports—he took four hundred fifty troopers on a twelve-day reconnaissance all the way to the Ohio River near Henderson. This foray included an incident notable for its ignorance—or disregard—of military propriety regarding civilians. Forrest forgot his general respect for religion and retaliated for the kidnapping of some secessionist-sympathizing Kentuckians by grabbing ten Unionist Baptist ministers. He held eight of them, while sending two to recover the Confederate sympathizers.[2]

But it was December 28 before he and his men had their first fight with Union soldiers. He was leading three hundred members of his regiment on the third day of another prolonged reconnaissance when residents of the town of Rumsey, twenty miles south of the Ohio River at Owensboro, reported a Union force of five hundred mounted troops heading south just ahead. Forrest hurried his men forward. A mile north of the hamlet of Sacramento, his advance riders overtook and surprised the Federals, who turned out to number, by their own count, one hundred sixty-eight. The Federals' mere presence seemed to trigger Forrest's mercurial temper, and he grabbed a rifle and fired at them, then bolted ahead with such speed that he outran most of his column. The Federals fell back to a hill, formed a battle line just over its crest, and began shooting. Forrest ordered his lead troopers to hold their fire for the first eighty of the two hundred yards remaining, then commanded them to deliver three rounds—only to discover that most of his force had yet to arrive. He pulled back to re-form, and the movement looked enough like a preparation to retreat that the Federals launched a charge of their own. They tried "to flank our left," his official report would recall, and Forrest responded by dismounting several men "to act as sharpshooters." Then he ordered his own flanking attacks to both right and left as he personally led a mounted assault on the Federal center.

The flank strikes were slowed by dense undergrowth, but the tactic worked nonetheless. When the Union troopers detected them, they briefly withstood the central charge, then broke. A Federal report said forty-five of the Union horsemen had "repelled the charge . . . resisted the whole body of the enemy for ten minutes and . . . would have repulsed them, but at this critical moment some dastard unknown shouted 'Retreat to Sacramento!'"

The Federals rushed to comply with this anonymous order and then, with Forrest in all-out pursuit, neglected to stop at Sacramento. In the village, the Confederates "commenced a promiscuous saber slaughter of their rear," Forrest wrote from Hopkinsville two days later, and a Federal report acknowledged that the retreat entailed "some loss." In what would become a Forrest hallmark, he had his men "keep the skeer on 'em," pushing the Union retirement "at full speed" for two miles beyond Sacramento. During the chase, Federal captains Bacon and Burges "were run through with saber thrusts," Forrest's report said, while a third captain, Davis, was thrown from his horse and surrendered. When Bacon and Davis fell, their riderless mounts collided and went down at the foot of a small rise just as Forrest himself came along in pursuit at a wild gallop. His own horse became entangled with those on the ground and went down, hurling him twenty feet beyond.[3]

According to Forrest's report of the battle, the "bleeding" Union wounded littered the retreat route for two miles; he ambitiously claimed that the enemy dead numbered sixty-five, with another thirty-five made unfit for combat. The language and details of the report make clear how hungry the new lieutenant colonel was for battle. Forrest wrote, for example, that the Federal troopers, deprived of their fallen officers,

> . . . threw down their arms and depended alone on the speed of their horses. Those of my men whose horses were able to keep up found no difficulty in piercing through every one they came up with, but as my horses were run down while theirs were much fresher, I deemed it best to call off the chase, for such it had become, leaving many wounded men hanging to their saddles to prevent their falling off their horses. Returning, we found their dead and wounded in every direction.[4]

Forrest did not describe his own role in the fight except to write that Captain Davis had surrendered "as my prisoner." But in forwarding the report to the Bowling Green headquarters of Albert Sidney Johnston, Brigadier General Charles Clark added that Forrest's report of the "dashing affair at Sacramento" was "a modest recital of one of the most brilliant and successful cavalry engagements" of the young war. Recommending Forrest to his superiors, Clark added that he himself had been "assured by officers and men that throughout the entire engagement [Forrest] was conspicuous for the most daring courage; always in advance of his command. He was at one time engaged in a hand-to-hand conflict with 4 of the enemy, 3 of whom he killed, dismounting and making a prisoner of the fourth." Clark also claimed to have learned from independent sources that Forrest's count of the Federal killed and wounded was "not overestimated," while the Confederate dead numbered just two.[5]

Forrest's men were as impressed as Clark was, but they were also considerably daunted. Major D. C. Kelley, a Methodist minister-turned-soldier, later wrote that Forrest's "passion" in his early battles ran so hot "that he was almost equally as dangerous to friend or foe." At Sacramento, Kelley, for the first time, saw combat transform his commander. "[W]hen he rode up to me in the thick of the action, I could scarcely believe him to be the man I had known for several months," the major later remembered. "His face flushed till it bore a striking resemblance to a painted Indian warrior's, and his eyes, usually mild in their expression, were blazing with the intense glare of a panther's springing upon its prey."[6]

Kelley had glimpsed his commander's essence. It could be terrifying.

8

January 19, 1862

Mill Springs, Kentucky

WITH SCANT EMPATHY from a nonchalant Southern populace, Albert Sidney Johnston waited gloomily for the Federal hammer to fall: at Columbus or Bowling Green, around Cumberland Gap, at the Tennessee or Cumberland rivers on little forts Henry or Donelson, or at some simultaneous combination of two or more of these. On New Year's Day 1862, it began its descent. Brigadier General George H. Thomas's five thousand Union troops at Lebanon, Kentucky, set out to march in a cold rain soon laced with ice. Central Kentucky commander Don Carlos Buell finally had turned the troops loose toward Cumberland Gap.

"We were really going towards the enemy," drummer boy William Bircher of the Second Minnesota marveled.

They were not doing it quickly, though. The sleet and rain of this day had set in long-term. Even though the first two-thirds of the trek was made over turnpike, their six hundred wagons averaged just four miles a day for more than two weeks. The doubled teams lurched along under whips and curses in deep mud and freezing water on roads turned wretched. Their ultimate goal, many hoped, was Knoxville, halfway down the Tennessee Valley.

The specter of East Tennessee had haunted Abraham Lincoln for months. That area of hills and mountains was a long knife of Union-loving territory lodged in the Confederacy's vitals all the way to north Georgia. When the central and western grand divisions of Tennessee voted overwhelmingly in June to leave the Union, residents of the state's eastern third elected to stay in by a margin of 32,923 to 14,780. The section's most popular newspaper, until its suppression by the Confederates in October 1861, was the *Knoxville Whig* of publisher-editor William G. "Parson" Brownlow, a poison-penned Methodist minister whose favorite printed description of the Confederacy was that it was "hell-born and hell-bound." The *Whig* was a daily Bible for hardy, insular mountaineers, whose hilly farmsteads could neither support nor afford slave labor. These tenacious people hated slavery—

not out of sympathy for the slave but from deep resentment of the political dominance of Tennessee politics by the slaves' aristocratic owners. Two thousand hill men who had hardly been out of their own counties before defied the new Confederacy and hired guides to lead them up foot trails through mountain passes into Kentucky to enlist in the Federal army.[1]

Lincoln wanted to give this knife in the Confederate stomach a wrenching twist. He knew that if the area's loyalist flame were ignited by the arrival of Federal troops, the result would cripple Confederate forces in front of Washington by severing Richmond's rail lifeline to the Deep South. He also believed capturing East Tennessee would make the region a cancer in the middle of Dixie and foster uprisings of Union-loyal elements all across the Confederacy. So the November bridge burnings had been plotted in Kentucky and Washington as well as East Tennessee. A Reverend William B. Carter had sneaked out of the region in late September with a scheme to torch the railroad bridges in coordination with an army advance into East Tennessee. Carter first approached Federal officers in Kentucky and expatriate Andrew Johnson, the eloquent East Tennessean who had derided secession and continued to serve in the U.S. Senate. Carter then was sent to the top of the chain of command to confer with Lincoln and Army of the Potomac commander McClellan at the White House. They gave him a secret payment of at least twenty-five hundred dollars to bring his plan to fruition, and Lincoln issued orders for the army in Kentucky to invade East Tennessee. On November 8, the bridge arsonists kept their end of the bargain, even cutting telegraph wires across the region, but the army did not invade. The Federal commander in Kentucky at the time, Brigadier General William T. Sherman, underwent a crisis of confidence in the face of Albert Sidney Johnston's phony bellicosity and halted an early November move by General Thomas toward Cumberland Gap. The resulting harsh Confederate crackdown on East Tennessee's loyalists with hangings and imprisonments, the latter including venerable "Parson" Brownlow himself, added a pall of guilt to Lincoln's East Tennessee anxiety. Sherman, shattered, asked to be replaced and quickly was, with highly regarded but balky career officer Don Carlos Buell. Lincoln pushed more desperately for a drive on Knoxville, and finally, after protesting repeatedly and with reason about the miserable mountain roads and extreme supply difficulties, Buell, on December 29, gave Thomas the New Year's Day go-ahead.

But he had held Thomas back so long that his deep reservations about the roads were more than justified. Such thoroughfares as existed through the mountains at all were only marginally usable in good weather, and in mid-winter they were creeks of clay. It took Thomas's column seventeen days to travel the sixty-five miles to little Logan's Crossroads, the junction with the road leading eleven miles south to General Felix Zollicoffer's Confederate base at Mill Springs. This was the farthest south a Federal force had been allowed to go, though, and Thomas was due some of the credit for the achievement.[2]

For two months, Thomas had been the man in the middle, a position with which he was familiar from the war's outset. A native Virginian and a West Point–trained career officer in the antebellum army, he already had braved the rage of sisters who, because of his decision to stay with the Union, were destined never to speak to him again. Now he was torn between the exasperation of Lincoln, McClellan, Andrew Johnson, and the many others pleading the desperate cause of the eastern Tennessee unionists and, on the other side, the mulish and aloof Buell, rival of new Missouri/Western Kentucky commander Halleck for the dubious title of McClellan of the West. Arrogantly insecure, focused on preparing to fight rather than fighting, Buell was no more disposed to offer battle than his eastern commander and even more impervious to the political necessity, at this point, of doing it. He had left Washington for his new assignment two months earlier espousing the Lincoln–McClellan idea that the East Tennesseans had to be rescued quickly, but he became quietly insubordinate on reaching Kentucky. Five days after Thomas moved out of Lebanon toward Mill Springs, Buell conveyed to Lincoln his conviction that the railroad stretching south from Louisville to Nashville, although less direct, offered the easiest route to freeing the East Tennesseans.[3]

"I have no fear of their being crushed," he blithely wrote McClellan.

The president, professing distress and disappointment at Buell's revelation, quickly replied with intelligence and compassion:

> I would rather have a point on the railroad south of Cumberland Gap than Nashville—first, because it cuts a great artery of the enemy's communication, which Nashville does not; and, secondly, because it is in the midst of loyal people, which Nashville is not . . . [M]y distress is that our friends in East Tennessee are being hanged and driven to despair, and even now I fear are thinking of taking rebel arms for the sake of personal protection. In this we lose the most valuable stake we have in the South.[4]

Thomas had been volunteering for months to try to take the more direct route, through the gaps and passes along the Eastern Kentucky–East Tennessee border.

Even now, it seemed a chance worth taking. As Lincoln had noted, this march would be unlike Federal operations in many other parts of the South because it would be made through remote non-slaveholding, hill-country counties where the majority of local sentiment was rabidly unionist. And, if successful, it would cut that vital stretch of Confederate railway between Dixie's supply-laden interior and the northern Virginia theatre on which most of Washington was fixated.

By mid-January, however, the weather had deteriorated to the point that Thomas himself questioned the wisdom of the march. He remained resolved, though, to do what he had come to do: destroy, capture, or at least chase out of eastern Kentucky the few thousand Confederates under Felix Zollicoffer who comprised the right wing of Albert Sidney Johnston's long, tenuous defense line. That brought Thomas, on January 17, to this road junction at the farm of a family named Logan, where he had to await four of his eight-and-a-half regiments that had fallen behind on roads plowed into frigid swamps by passage of his lead units.

With Thomas at Logan's were the Tenth Indiana, Ninth Ohio, and Second Minnesota infantry regiments, and the First Kentucky Cavalry, plus Battery C of the First Ohio Light Artillery. Just eight miles down the road at Somerset, there were two more brigades of Union troops under General Albin Schoepf. But as the rain continued and rivers rose, Thomas feared isolation from Somerset, and he ordered Schoepf to hurry out a brigade of temporary reinforcements until his straggling units could catch up. Schoepf sent the so-called Tennessee Brigade, comprised predominantly of the escaped East Tennesseans who were eager to march homeward. Their commander was Brigadier General Samuel P. Carter, brother of the Reverend William B. Carter who was a principal author of the bridge-burning plot.

When the Tennessee brigade—the First and Second Tennessee plus the Twelfth Kentucky—arrived at Logan's that evening, its soldiers had to bivouac hungry and at the mercy of the elements, their tents and rations having been left behind in wagons halted by the rising waters of Fishing Creek. The men had had to cross the flooding stream on foot just to get to Logan's at all.

"Here we remained through the day and night of the 18th, exposed to the excessive rains without shelter," reported the Twelfth Kentucky's Colonel William Hoskins.[5]

Earlier that day, Thomas had sent two of his lagging units, the Fourteenth Ohio and the Tenth Kentucky, off with a wagon train and one day's rations to capture a large Confederate forage party reported to be camped six miles from Logan's. Normally prudent, Thomas had let himself get separated from his four lagging regiments near a significant force of the enemy and then had neglected to command his men to entrench. But he may have committed some of these seeming errors intentionally.

Thomas originally planned to attack the Confederates' left flank at Beech Grove, across the flooded Cumberland from Mill Springs, so as to separate them from the best places to re-cross the river while Schoepf assaulted them frontally. But Schoepf, a half-Polish Austrian who had fought in Europe, dissented and proposed an alternative scheme to draw the Confederates into the open. Thomas, who had battled Seminoles in Florida and Comanches in Texas, liked the trickery idea enough to forward it to Buell. Although he never said so in a subsequent report, Thomas apparently hoped to provide a target inviting enough to lure the Confederates out of the Beech Grove trenches. Entrenching his own men would hardly have done the trick.

To insure that his encampment would have adequate warning of an attack, though, Thomas did order the positioning of what amounted to three successive picket lines: the First Kentucky Cavalry two miles down the Mill Springs road; some Indiana infantrymen three-quarters of a mile closer in; and, finally, still a mile from Thomas's main camp, the camps of the infantry pickets, Companies I and K of the Tenth Indiana Volunteers.[6]

*   *   *

At Beech Grove, new Confederate wing commander George B. Crittenden—youngest son of unionist U.S. Senator John J. Crittenden of Kentucky and brother of Federal Brigadier General Thomas L. Crittenden—knew he was in precarious straits. A few weeks earlier, in early December, Zollicoffer had crossed most of his men over the Cumberland to Beech Grove from Mill Springs—one day before receiving a letter from Johnston in Bowling Green ordering him not to. Here, the river made a horseshoe bend to the south, and Zollicoffer thought his force needed to be inside the horseshoe. "The river protects our rear and flanks," he wrote Johnston on December 10. He did not see that, as Johnston soon emphasized to Crittenden in Knoxville, he "has the enemy in front and the river behind." That, of course, risked doom. The rains having made the river unfordable, Zollicoffer had trapped himself.[7]

On December 13, just four days after Zollicoffer's errant crossing of the river, Crittenden was assigned command over eastern Kentucky—and over the hapless Zollicoffer. Crittenden quickly ordered Zollicoffer to re-cross to Mill Springs, but, on arriving there to take command himself, Crittenden found Zollicoffer still at Beech Grove with only two flat-boats and a "small stern-wheel steamboat," the *Noble Ellis*, "unsuited for the transportation of horses" or artillery. Crittenden ordered the building of larger craft, but he had hardly given the command when, on January 17, cavalry scouts reported Thomas "moving across my front on the road . . . towards Somerset, with the intention of uniting with the Somerset force and attacking Beech Grove." The next day, as Thomas perhaps intended when he sent two of his lagging

regiments in pursuit of the Confederate forage party, Crittenden's infor-
mants discovered not only that Thomas was camping at Logan's but also that
he was awaiting the arrival of "re-enforcement" by troops from his rear as
well as others from Somerset. "Crittenden was also informed by cavalry
scouts that Fishing Creek between Somerset and Logan's was flooding "and
would prevent . . . passage by any infantry force."

Knowing he had to act fast, Crittenden reacted with boldness, or maybe
panic. Contrary to all wishes and expectations of his departmental commander, he notified Johnston that, "threatened by a superior force of the enemy
in front and finding it impossible to cross the river, I have to make the fight
on the ground I now occupy." Johnston had not wanted him to make a fight
at all.[8]

Then Crittenden found that not only was he unable to retreat across the
river to Mill Springs because of lack of boats, he could not even fight on the
ground he occupied. Beech Grove was unfit to resist a determined attack.
With no engineering help available to him, Zollicoffer had selected a site
commanded by surrounding heights and one from which artillery could not
work well against advancing infantry.

Crittenden called a hurried conference of his senior officers on Friday
evening, the 17th, and proposed to beat Thomas to the attack. A majority of
the senior officers apparently agreed, although talk in the camp of the Nineteenth Tennessee on Saturday, as the men readied their weapons and other
gear, had it that Zollicoffer and the Nineteenth's commander, Colonel D. H.
Cummings, had opposed the plan. Saturday evening, having learned by then
that Thomas was separated from the units in his rear and also, Crittenden
hoped, from Schoepf by Fishing Creek, the Confederate commander called
another council of war. At this meeting "it was determined, without dissent,
to march out and attack the enemy . . . the next morning." That meant they
had to depart Beech Grove at once, and they did. At midnight, Crittenden
got his whole force moving northward into a "night . . . dark and cold," with
bitter winds driving sleet and rain in the soldiers' faces. They were on the
road to Logan's taking Thomas's bait, if that was what it was.

Zollicoffer's brigade—independent cavalry under Captains Saunders and
Bledsoe, then the Fifteenth Mississippi, Nineteenth, Twentieth, and Twenty-
Fifth Tennessee infantries, and four cannon under Captain Rutledge—took
the lead. They were followed by the Seventeenth, Twenty-Eighth, and Twenty-Ninth Tennessee plus two cannon commanded by Captain McClung, all of
which comprised another brigade under Brigadier General W. H. Carroll.
Behind these toiled the reserve, the Sixteenth Alabama plus cavalry battalions commanded by lieutenant-colonels Branner and McClellan.[9]

The rain-drowned road was more like a canal; in places, the mud and water were more than a foot deep. It took Crittenden's little army six hours to wade the nine miles to where Thomas's cavalry pickets waited. Not only were the Confederates weary by the time they began arriving, but the forward units were three miles ahead of the rear ones.

Around 6:30 a.m. on January 19, shortly after dawn, Confederate cavalry drove mounted pickets of U.S. First Kentucky Cavalry back a quarter-mile to a log house just left of the road, where they met a hot fire. The road continued straight northwestward over small hills and swales for nearly a mile, then forked into a Y at an intersection with the so-called "old Mill Springs Road." The latter angled off due north while its newer, parallel successor continued northwestward a quarter-mile or so to the left; both forks led toward the camps of the Federal regiments. Between the Confederates and the Y were two low, round ridges divided by the road into two fields. At the first ridge's foot stood another log house that soon became a bloody Confederate hospital.

The battle along the Mill Springs road just south of the forks would be simple but signal, a three-and-one-half-hour slugfest revealing weaknesses that would dog Confederates in the West for the rest of the war. The worst involved weaponry. Despite efforts by Governor Harris to collect workable guns from civilians the previous fall, many of the Tennessee Confederates were armed with aged flintlock muskets yet to be converted to percussion-caps and thus requiring priming powder that was difficult to keep dry. And some of the men in Carroll's brigade were recruits so raw that they had been assigned to the unit just a day earlier and knew almost nothing of drills and commands.[10]

But they could fight. A company of skirmishers from the Fifteenth Mississippi moved to the left of the road and, amid hot fire, drove pickets of the Tenth Indiana out of another log cabin and adjoining woods at the foot of the second ridge. The Mississippians then crossed the road to rejoin their regiment, while behind them, staying on and to the left of the road, came the Nineteenth Tennessee driving straight ahead, double-quicking across the field and into the woods. There they met and drove backward the main body of the Tenth Indiana. The Confederate attack almost reached the forks of the road and came near overrunning the horses of the Federal cavalrymen, who were desperately fighting on foot there at the Indianans' right rear.

Thomas, roused from his headquarters bed, reached the field about the time his Second Brigade commander, M. D. Manson, sent in the Fourth Kentucky to reinforce the reeling Tenth Indiana. The Hoosiers, commanded by

Lieutenant Colonel William Kise, had been "thinned and mutilated," but they had stemmed the Confederate tide alone for almost an hour. The Fourth Kentucky now steadied the Union left by opening a "deadly fire" into the ranks of the Fifteenth Mississippi.[11]

The Kentucky Federals then charged out of the trees into the hill-crowned field east of the road. Broken by a fence bordering the "old Mill Springs" fork—the right arm of the Y—and then a creek bed running nearly parallel to the fence, this field hosted a struggle that "became very warm," reported Colonel Speed Fry of the Federal Fourth Kentucky Infantry. The Confederates used the creek bed for cover to move their troops onto the Fourth Kentucky's right flank, which had been left naked when the Tenth Indiana fell back under the assault by the Fifteenth Mississippi and the Nineteenth Tennessee. The Mississippians now rose out of the depression just enough to deliver galling fire at close range, and Colonel Fry thought the Southerners' use of the stream bed so unfair that he rashly climbed onto the fence, "denounced them as dastards, and defied them to stand up on their feet and come forward like men," according to a postwar account. Fry did not stay on the fence long. Having first ordered his men past it, he now commanded them to retreat behind it for cover. There they weathered two charges by the Mississippians, who came forward, he reported, with "bayonets fixed and their large cane knives unsheathed."[12]

The day, which had dawned soggy and sullen, had become further clouded by gunsmoke that "was beaten back by the rain and, settling on the ground, increased the gloom," according to a member of the Confederate Nineteenth Tennessee. When the Fifteenth Mississippi encountered the Kentucky Federals, Lieutenant Colonel Edward C. Walthall apparently remembered a warning by Crittenden in the council of war the night before. Because many of the Confederates wore blue uniforms at this early stage of the war, Crittenden had noted the danger of firing into friendly forces. To prevent this, the Southerners adopted an unfortunate password: "Kentucky." Walthall's skirmishers now reported that they thought the troops in front of them were the Confederate Twentieth Tennessee, which had been following them but presently were being deployed to the right. Walthall had his men lie down while he went to a high point and shouted to his front: "What troops are those?"

"Kentucky," somebody shouted back.

"Who *are* you?" Walthall yelled, apparently wanting a unit number.

The reply he got was the same as before, so he ordered the unfurling of a Confederate flag. The banner immediately received a volley, which riddled its folds and put twenty balls in the body of an accompanying lieutenant.[13]

Zollicoffer, probably also mindful of Crittenden's friendly fire admoni-
tion, soon rode up to Colonel Cummings of the Nineteenth Tennessee and
ordered him to have his men stop firing. He then moved off to the right of
the road and unwittingly approached Colonel Fry of the Federal Fourth
Kentucky, who had ridden up the side of the ridge to reconnoiter on his
unit's right. Zollicoffer was so close that the two men's knees touched, but
he was also near-sighted and clad in a white raincoat that hid his uniform.
He told Fry: "We must not fire on our own men. Those"—waving toward his
left—"are our men." Fry agreed and was moving back toward his regiment to
comply when a Zollicoffer aide rode out of the woods. Seeing that Fry was a
Federal, the aide fired, hitting Fry's horse with a shot that also slightly struck
the colonel himself. Fry spurred his wounded animal away and fired a pistol
back toward Zollicoffer. Some of the men of the Fourth Kentucky fired, too.
Zollicoffer was struck by a ball from a pistol and two more from muskets,
one of the shots striking his heart. He died immediately, perhaps in the process of realizing his mistake. The Nineteenth Tennessee, having been ordered not to fire, had to endure a dismaying fusillade from the Fourth
Kentucky.[14]

The Mississippians under Walthall, unhampered by any no-fire order,
charged and nearly broke Fry's right. Then Thomas sent the Tenth Indiana
back to retake the position it had first occupied to the right of Fry. News of
Zollicoffer's death spread fast, and in the interval in which the Nineteenth
Tennessee stopped firing, the Confederate drive stalled. A subsequent general advance by Carroll's supporting brigade could not regain the Confederate momentum. The fight was hardest along the fence row where for a full
hour, according to Crittenden, the Fifteenth Mississippi tried to drive between Kise's Hoosiers and Fry's Kentuckians. By the time the Tenth Indiana
got back to the fence on its return to the field, it found "many of the enemy
. . . lingering" there. Kise later wrote that these were "bayoneted by my men
between the rails."

To reinforce Kise and Fry, who now were almost out of ammunition,
Thomas ordered up the Second Minnesota and the so-called Bully Dutchmen of the Ninth Ohio, who already had seen action in western Virginia.
The Dutchmen went in on the Federal right, while the Minnesotans took
over for Kise and Fry. The Second Minnesota's right ended up "about 10
feet from the enemy" at the fence, where the fighting was virtually hand-to-
hand. Confederates and Federals "pok[ed] their guns through the same
fence," reported the Ninth Ohio's Colonel Robert McCook. The Minnesotans and Mississippians repeatedly assaulted each other for control of
the fence, but the Ninth Ohio's charge on the Union right stopped the

Confederate flanking attempt, and the Southerners "retired in good order to some rail piles, hastily thrown together, the point from which they had advanced upon the Fourth Kentucky," McCook wrote.[15]

On the other end of his line, Thomas had sent Samuel P. Carter's Tennessee Brigade to smother a bid by the Confederate Twentieth Tennessee to turn the Union left. With both their wings overlapped and the enemy's center reinforced, the Confederates began to give ground, getting beaten by not only superior generalship but by luck and greater firepower. Carroll's regiments reinforced the Fifteenth Mississippi and the Nineteenth, Twentieth, and Twenty-fifth Tennessee and vainly tried to dam the rising Federal tide, but under the Union counterattack the Twenty-eighth Tennessee, backing up the Confederate center, "broke and fled in confusion from the field," Carroll later reported. The Twenty-ninth Tennessee, behind the Twenty-eighth, likewise "fell back in considerable disorder and could not be induced to face the enemy again." Carroll later indicated in his battle report that he hardly blamed either unit: "The repulse of the regiments of my command that gave way in confusion during the battle is attributed, in a great measure, to the inefficient and worthless character of their arms, being old flint-lock muskets and country rifles, nearly half of which would not fire at all . . . I saw numbers of men walking deliberately away from the field of action for no other reason than [that] their guns were wholly useless."[16]

A member of the Nineteenth Tennessee wrote that he saw "two or three of the boys break their guns over the fence after several attempts to fire them." In the Twentieth Tennessee, another soldier recalled that "one-third of the arms of the Confederates" were "useless," and many that did work operated so poorly in the rain that they were able to be fired no more than a dozen times throughout the battle.[17]

With Crittenden's counterattack foiled, his lead units, the Fifteenth Mississippi and Nineteenth Tennessee, fell back in the face of a mid-morning Federal counterthrust. Official tallies showed that the Mississippians had lost forty-four killed, one hundred fifty-three wounded, and twenty-nine missing. The Twentieth Tennessee, which in trying to turn the right of the Fourth Kentucky, had run into enfilading fire from Carter's Federal Tennessee Brigade, lost thirty-three killed, fifty-nine wounded, and eighteen missing. The Nineteenth Tennessee's respective totals were ten, twenty-two, and two, similar to those of the Twenty-fifth and Seventeenth Tennessee, the other Confederate units most consistently engaged.[18]

The Southerners now streamed from the field. A retreat to Beech Grove was ordered, but "it did not take much ordering," W. J. McMurray of the Twentieth Tennessee would remember. W. J. Worsham of the Nineteenth recalled that during the battle he "picked up a Yankee overcoat and put it on in the cold rain," only to remove it and throw it over the wet ground for a mortally wounded comrade to die on as "the whole line" gave way. Men left the battlefield "in wild confusion and disorder." Worsham remembered trying to help the wounded as much as possible in the fear-filled rush to avoid capture. He helped carry Charley Clemenson of the Nineteenth's Company E in a blanket into the yard of the cabin used as a field hospital, but by then fellow Confederates "were hurrying by as rapidly as they could, the road and the woods . . . full" of comrades "in hot haste to be gone . . .

"Poor Charley was dying when we laid him down. We can never forget the sad anxious expression of his face as we left him . . . dying alone, deserted by all whom he thought were friends, left on the cold ground with naught but the cold rain to wash the sweat of death from his brow."[19]

*　*　*

The Confederates retreated back down the Mill Springs road. It had taken them six hours to travel it before dawn, but they now made better time, leaving behind one mired cannon and an appalling litter of haversacks. The Federals pursued, but with a deliberateness that would come to be regarded as characteristic of Thomas in this war. The heavy mud was one reason for their measured pace. Another was that many of them, having entered the fight without breakfast, continually stopped to rifle the discarded Confederate packs and sample the contents: bacon as well as cornmeal ground by the facility for which Mill Springs was named. It was late afternoon before Thomas's lead elements reached Beech Grove and started shelling its fortifications.

Almost as soon as night fell, Crittenden began ferrying his men across the Cumberland on what was virtually their sole conveyance, the small steamboat *Noble Ellis*. He managed to get the men out, but that was all. Next morning, the Fourteenth Ohio and Tenth Kentucky moved forward to lead an assault and found Beech Grove deserted. At the ferry crossing below the bluff, they discovered a crush of eleven artillery pieces, more than one hundred fifty wagons, and a thousand horses and mules. Even the steep road up the far bank was strewn with baggage, and the *Noble Ellis* had been set afire and sunk.

"General, why didn't you send in a demand for surrender last night?" Colonel Fry asked Thomas, noting all the evidence of Confederate panic.

The Union commander looked up, hesitated, and then admitted a mental lapse. "Hang it, Fry," he said. "I never once thought of it."[20]

On the Cumberland's opposite bank began the hardest march the Nineteenth Tennessee's Worsham "experienced during the four years of war."

McMurray of the Twentieth recalled "a long journey, hitherto unparalleled," through the "rough, barren, and unfriendly country" of the Cumberland Mountains. The first night, they stopped a mile southwest of Monticello, Kentucky, pitching no tent "for we had none; neither had we blankets on which to lie . . . Having had nothing to eat all day long, we lay down with empty stomachs to dream of the plenty we had left in camp. The next morning we had issued to us an ear of corn to each man (as if we were horses) to parch for breakfast" over "fires which were very poor for want of [dry] wood."

Worsham wrote that they lived on this parched corn "almost the entire ten days" of their frantic straggle from Mill Springs to Gainesboro, Tennessee.[21]

Many miles west at Bowling Green, the Confederate western high command recognized Logan's Crossroads and the flight from Mill Springs for what they truly constituted: disaster. Johnston's first intimations of it, because of the remote area's scant communications, were from accounts in newspapers from Louisville. After reading them, he wrote Richmond:

"If my right is thus broken as stated, East Tennessee is wide open to invasion—or, if the plan of the enemy be a combined movement upon Nashville, it is in jeopardy . . ."[22]

9

January, 1862

False Starts and a Real One

Except for Thomas's excited marchers heading off to hunt down Zollicoffer in eastern Kentucky, the new year came to the rest of what was left of the United States beneath a pall of reproachful urgency.

From the White House to statehouses, newspaper offices, Grant's Cairo headquarters, and wherever expatriate U.S. Senator Andrew Johnson waited in mounting frustration to accompany troops invading his home state, there throbbed a profound consciousness that time was being lost, that each passing day gave the Richmond government longer life and a stronger claim to legitimacy. Yet the North, which so obviously dominated the Confederacy in every area from manufacturing to manpower, floundered like a muscle-bound giant. In the East, the superb organizer George B. McClellan, elevated to command of all the Union armies on November 1, already had begun to display the liver of a chicken, repeatedly shrinking from risking his legions in battle. From McClellan in Washington as well as from his western subcommanders Don Carlos Buell in Louisville and Henry Halleck in St. Louis came a single, continuing, disheartening refrain: Not ready yet. Something substantial needed to begin happening fast, and little seemed to be.

The western war was particularly problematic because Buell and Halleck were having as little as possible to do with each other. Halleck preoccupied himself with cleaning up the Confederate opposition as well as Fremont-spawned corruption in Missouri, which made up most of the business end of his department. Buell, meanwhile, organized and drilled his swelling ranks of new volunteers and fended off Lincoln's, McClellan's, and Andrew Johnson's unhappy calls for the liberation of East Tennessee. Buell disappointed them mightily by saying he preferred liberating Bowling Green and Nashville first, then excused his lack of progress in even that direction by adding that until he was ready to move he wanted to do nothing to put the Confederates on their guard.

Halleck and Buell, and thus the Union, had a deeper problem, too. The positions of the two subordinate generals pitted them against each other. Their departments bordered in western Kentucky at the Cumberland River, so neither man could take much large-scale action east of the Mississippi, where Lincoln's Republicans increasingly demanded it, without help from the other. Rank and personal ties complicated their situation further. Halleck's major-general stars made him superior to Brigadier General Buell, but Buell was the close, older friend and role model of General-in-Chief McClellan, a relationship Buell counted on to protect him from Halleck. Buell and Halleck did not even open a dialogue until McClellan came down with typhoid fever, and Lincoln seized the opportunity—in New Year's Eve telegrams to both generals—to press them to cooperate. The President suggested to Halleck that he support Buell's much-awaited advance against Bowling Green with "a simultaneous movement . . . on Columbus" to prevent enemy reinforcement of Buell's front. Buell and Halleck then began reciting litanies of reasons why they were unready to move, meanwhile trying to coerce or wheedle the support and subordination of each other.

Halleck made sure, though, that he could not be accused of wholly disregarding presidential orders. On January 6—after complaining to Buell that he was busy in southwest Missouri, had received no information whatever about Buell's Bowling Green plan, and thought its basic concept unwise—he ordered Grant to "make a demonstration in force" into western Kentucky to threaten Columbus. Grant was to make his movement as confusing to the enemy as possible by telling everybody, including newspapermen, that his target was Dover, the little town adjacent to Fort Donelson on the Cumberland, and that no less than seventy-five thousand troops would be marching to take it.

Grant despised diversions. They ran counter to his nature. Like any other bluff, a diversion was without substance, not really amounting to anything, and triviality offended Grant's essence. That trait, as well as a jaundiced view of Buell's inactivity, is perhaps reflected in Grant's dry references to the Halleck-ordered expedition in his *Personal Memoirs*. He had been ordered to do it at all, he wrote, because it was "supposed, that Buell was about to make some move against the enemy."

With Grant's Halleck-ordered announcement of a Dover campaign, Cairo's dreary St. Charles Hotel suddenly swarmed with reporters drawn by the expectation that something significant was finally about to happen. The press, at that time, was a niche industry being propelled into wide popularity and importance by the intense interest, North and South, in war news. The men who showed up in Cairo in January included three representing New York dailies—Albert Richardson of the *Tribune*, Richard T. Colburn of the *World*, and Franc Wilkie of the *Times*—along with Charles Coffin of the

Boston *Journal.* Wilkie wrote that Cairo's inhabitants now found themselves confronted by "newspaper men at every step: they block up the approaches to headquarters . . . they are constantly demanding passes, horses, saddles, blankets, news, copies of official papers, a look into private correspondence, and things whose use and extent are only appreciated by omniscience."

Soon after Halleck supplanted Fremont in St. Louis, the new chief had simplified his department's command structure by placing the Paducah garrison of Brigadier General Charles F. Smith under Grant at Cairo, a logical move since Smith's command had to be supplied through Cairo, anyway. But it required Grant to issue orders to his admired former West Point commandant and instructor, which Grant found awkward. With respectful deference, he now sent Smith orders to head south from Paducah toward Fort Henry while Grant himself accompanied McClernand's six thousand men toward Mayfield, Kentucky, halfway between Fort Henry and Columbus. It turned into more than a week of forays willy-nilly, sodden sallies made, Grant wrote, in "very bad" weather on roads that were "intolerable." They required "splashing through the mud, snow and rain, the men suffering very much." But, he reflected, "the object of the expedition was accomplished"; at least, the Confederates had moved no troops eastward from Columbus, and on the other side of the state Buell subordinate Thomas triumphed at Logan's Crossroads.[1]

But Thomas's victory at Logan's did not occur until January 19, and the mountains in which it happened were so remote that news required a day or two to filter out. And Thomas's activities were so far away as to easily appear unconnected to Grant's. Grant's diversion, intended to mystify Johnston at Bowling Green, was viewed as insignificant and all but idiotic by the impatient press. "If you want to be disgusted, just come out here," Bostonian Coffin wrote privately to his longtime friend, U.S. Senator Henry Wilson of Massachusetts in mid-January. "Last week you were told that a grand expedition of 75,000 men were moving from here. The dispatches were dictated by General Grant himself." But then, Coffin complained,

> Grant only moved with about *14,000* including the force at Paducah.
>
> They have been traveling up and down in the mud between here and Mayfield [Kentucky]. I was out yesterday and found them scattered like sheep in a pasture. The advance was within six or seven miles of Columbus. Infantry regiments were miles from any support. They were scattered . . . and this in the face of *25,000* rebels at Columbus. If Polk had known of their condition he could have picked them all up as a chicken eats corn. What Grant intended to do no one knows. But to cap the climax Grant returned . . . last night and the troops are all on the way back. They will all be in tonight.

Informing the senator that the letter could be used "any way you please for it is the truth," Coffin went on to write that the Union's western front was "in a deplorable condition." He reported that Halleck, the department commander, had "not once left St. Louis" nor "visited one of his divisions"—which needed supervision: there "is a looseness of discipline unparalleled." The newsman added that their fellow New Englander, naval Flag-Officer Foote,

> *is all most in despair.*
>
> *He came to my room last night and we had a long talk . . . He feels that he has been [bad]ly used. The gunboats are nearly ready, but he says that it will be useless to shell Columbus without the army cooperates. I do not believe you will see anything done in the West this winter. Buell is still in Louisville seventy-five miles from his army, and there are no signs of any movement there. Commodore Foot[e] says that the rebels are strengthening their works every day; that they are becoming very formidable.* [2]

Coffin was a perceptive and usually accurate journalist—a rarity at the time—but his prediction could not have been more wrong. On the other hand, neither Grant, who returned from his soggy diversionary canters to encounter Kountz's appalling charges, nor even Halleck could have foretold the impending future when Coffin wrote his letter. The year's first month would reach its final days before the St. Louis commander suddenly faced the apparent necessity of attacking, not just feinting, toward Nashville.

On January 29, McClellan wired both Halleck and Buell that the enemy on their connected front appeared about to proliferate: the vaunted Confederate General P. G. T. Beauregard, hero of Fort Sumter and Bull Run, was rumored headed from Virginia to the west with fifteen regiments. Uncharacteristically, Halleck leapt to react. That very day, January 29, he sent Foote notification that as soon as he learned the status of one of the roads to Fort Henry he would order the move for which the naval officer and Grant had been pushing. It seems significant that this careful i-dotter and t-crosser did not also immediately inform Grant of his abrupt change in plan. He likely had trouble bringing himself to personally favor his pushy subordinate with this order that Grant had so avidly—and, in Halleck's view, so impertinently—come to St. Louis to request in person not a week earlier. Perhaps Halleck wanted and expected Grant to hear the order from Foote, thereby being put in his place. Whatever he meant, Halleck told only the naval officer to "have everything ready."

The next day, January 30, as Halleck continued to write and issue go-ahead orders, Buell blithely replied to "My Dear Friend" McClellan with

Don Carlos Buell

another vapid telegram promising more of the same. It said only that Buell had received the Beauregard heads-up and would "try to write to-night at length about matters here." Then, having no idea of Halleck's sudden activity, he busied himself composing a substantial wire to the St. Louis commander to apply more pressure to get Halleck to bow to Buell's orders whenever Buell decided to move against Bowling Green. He asked for a "prompt" strike by Halleck's troops against the Cumberland and Tennessee river railroad bridges connecting Johnston in Bowling Green with Polk in

Columbus—followed by a naval run up the Tennessee all the way into northern Alabama. With typical condescension, the Louisville chief added that the railroad bridges should be comparatively easy to seize and were "well worth the risk of losing one or two" of the gunboats whose construction and outfitting had cost Foote so much energy and worry.[3]

Thus Buell stayed elbow-deep in correspondence while Halleck un-typically got men moving. Halleck's quick response to McClellan's Beauregard hearsay indicates that he was anxious to get ahead of not just Beauregard but Buell—so anxious, in fact, that he left himself no time to replace the scruffy Cairo commander in whom he had exhibited so little confidence. Sometime that same day, January 30, Halleck wired McClellan that in response to the Beauregard news Grant and Foote would be ordered to "immediately reduce and hold Fort Henry . . . and to cut the railroad," the very things Buell requested that day that Halleck be "prompt" about doing when Buell chose the moment. Halleck, having chosen the moment himself, wired Buell that the order had been given "already."[4]

The reaction from Louisville was swift and ominously diffident. Plainly taken aback, Buell blinked, wiring a one-sentence demand for particulars as to "plan and force and the time, &c." Halleck replied on that day, still January 30, with an almost audible laugh up his sleeve. He reiterated that an "immediate" attack already had been ordered and added that the force was "about 15,000," with reinforcements to follow as soon as possible. The assault time would be passed along to Buell as soon as it was determined.

Buell, emphatically one-upped, began to retreat—and to snipe at Halleck's unilateral act. "Do you consider active cooperation essential to your success," he wired Halleck on January 31, pointedly adding, "because in that case it would be necessary for each to know what the other has to do . . . It would be several days before I could actively engage the enemy . . ." Halleck's response this time was cool and superior, that of a major general to a brigadier. "Cooperation at present not essential . . ." he wrote. "Write me your plans and I will try to assist you."[5]

The back-and-forth with Buell, though, would become scarcely a footnote to the order Halleck finally sent on January 30 to his least-appreciated subordinate. In it, the renowned military author penned some of the most important words of his career.

"Brig. Gen. U. S. Grant, Cairo, Ill.," the terse telegram said. "Make your preparations to take and hold Fort Henry. I will send you written instructions by mail."[6]

PART II

FORT HENRY

10

February 3–5, 1862

Grant and Foote

O<small>N THE LATE AFTERNOON</small> of February 3, under a leaden sky drizzling sleet, the first of a fleet of thirteen steamboats pushed off from Cairo's dreary wharves into the icy, churning current of the Ohio River.

Each of the high, double-decked vessels was crowned with twin black majestic smokestacks that magnified the boats' stature—even riding as low in the water as they rode this evening. Loaded to the rails, they teemed with blue-clad Federal volunteers carrying rifles and three days' rations, their cartridge-boxes sagging with forty rounds of ammunition. As before the Belmont fight and, indeed, as almost always in an army, none of them knew where they were headed, for once again General Grant had decreed secrecy that kept even division commanders ignorant of the destination. So it was with an anxious joy that these members of McClernand's division, the first of two crammed transport-loads of an army that would total twenty-three regiments and more than fifteen thousand men, departed the cheerless City of Mud and slipped into a dismal dusk. They were headed upstream toward Paducah, forty-five miles east.

Grant had left Cairo the day before for the little Kentucky town that his energy and foresight had grabbed for the Union back in September. Before setting off, he told McClernand to get the boarding of troops done as expeditiously as possible, and at Paducah, in the company of his old friend and mentor General Smith, he waited for them to arrive. Foote's four ironclads—*Essex, Carondelet, Cincinnati,* and *St. Louis*—nosed in around noon February 3, and the flag-officer himself, worrying up to the last minute with procuring enough army-assigned crews to man them, arrived with the wooden gunboats *Tyler, Conestoga,* and *Lexington* in the evening. The troop-burdened transports were held up by the heavy Ohio current, which had gained further strength from cold rains that seemed to have set in for the winter, and by the time the troops began arriving after dark, the commanders had become concerned.

Grant waved them into the mouth of the Tennessee and pointed them south toward Fort Henry.[1]

By now, new volunteers unfamiliar with war's capricious peril had begun to make its acquaintance. When the transport *Chancellor* moved out from the Cairo wharves that afternoon to make room for the filling of another vessel, Matthew Wallace, a young officer in the Fourth Illinois Cavalry, lost his balance and plunged into the Ohio. The next day Wallace's older brother, a colonel just elevated from leadership of the Eleventh Illinois Infantry to command McClernand's Second Brigade, wrote his wife, Ann:

> *It was a dark cold day and everything was covered in sleet . . . He was passing along the guard* [rail] *and slipped. He put out his hand against one of the swinging beams . . . —it gave way and he lost his balance and fell overboard forward of the* [paddle-] *wheel and passed under the wheel, and although he had his saber, carbine and pistol on and his overcoat, he struck out and swam some distance toward the shore, but the load was too much for him and he sank before assistance reached him.*[2]

The sadness surrounding his brother's freak death was likely compounded for Colonel W. H. L. Wallace because the cavalry's boat trip had been scheduled to be a short one. Thirteen miles south of Paducah, the mounted troops were to go ashore and trek the rest of the way to Fort Henry cross-country. General Halleck had ordered it, obviously to clear the west-bank roads to Henry of any Confederate resistance. Also, transport steamers were in such short supply that taking even the infantry would require two trips: Smith's Second Division embarking from Paducah after MClernand's had been landed at the destination.[3]

It was a huge undertaking that impressed bystanders. Soon after the Illinois Wallaces' family tragedy, Indiana Brigadier General Lew Wallace, no relation, watched from the Paducah riverbank as the protective vanguard of seven gunboats—four of them the "black, creeping, menacing, ugly" ironclads—turned into the Tennessee from the Ohio and steamed sluggishly southward leading "a long line of transports in convoy, each loaded to the guards with the First Division . . ."[4]

Watching the gunboats pass, even the zealous Grant had to be considering that the odds of a quick Fort Henry victory looked longer now. Hardly more than a week earlier, during the western Kentucky diversionary feints, General Smith had accompanied a gunboat reconnaissance to Henry. He reported great vulnerability on the part of both the Tennessee facility and a half-fortified commanding bluff overlooking it from the river's other—Kentucky—side. "Two ironclad gunboats would make short work of [them]," Smith had

asserted then. Since then, though, Smith had received more troubling information. On January 30, he wrote Grant that a "very intelligent" resident of
Hickman, Kentucky, who claimed to be a Union man, had escaped Confederate authorities and, in conversations overheard aboard a train near Fort Henry, had learned that the Henry defenders now numbered six thousand. The
Kentuckian also heard fellow passengers say that the Federal movement in
the area had been detected and that the Confederates "believed it meant an
attack on Fort Henry, hence the reinforcement . . . I have information from
Columbus fully confirming the reinforcement of Fort Henry and adding that
the enemy is prepared to throw in that direction at short notice a force of
15,000." To ensure that Grant got this new information before leaving Cairo,
Smith had telegraphed its essentials the same day.[5]

Similar intelligence kept arriving. On January 31, Navy Lieutenant Seth
Phelps returned from another Henry foray on the *Conestoga* and offered a final pre-attack assessment. Phelps reported to Foote the likelihood that Confederates had heavily mined the river around an island just north of Fort
Henry to prevent Federal boats from getting close enough to the fort to attack. Phelps said he had inquired about the condition of the roads connecting Fort Henry with both Fort Donelson and the town of Dover on the Cumberland a dozen miles away, the route Confederate reinforcements from
Bowling Green would have to take to reach Fort Henry cross-country. He
learned, he wrote, that their surfaces were hard enough, but the country
through which they ran was rough, dotted with hills.

"There is evidently a large force at Fort Henry," the young naval officer
added in closing. "[T]he report everywhere is that an attack is anticipated by
the rebels and that they are prepared to defend the post at all hazards."[6]

Grant did not blink. His bent was to focus on doing the job, not on weigh-
ing its degree of difficulty. So he concentrated on working the plan Halleck
had provided. His superior had given him minutely detailed instructions,
pointedly allowing him minimum discretion. The First Division would land
on the river's east bank north of the fort and block reinforcement or retreat
via the twin roads to Fort Donelson and Dover. Two brigades of the Second
Division under Smith, meanwhile, were to capture less-finished but more imposing Fort Heiman on the west bluff. When Heiman was taken and the investment of Henry complete, Smith's third brigade was to cross the river
nearer Henry and lead the rest of Smith's division, as well as all of McClernand's, in an all-out assault.[7]

McClernand's men arrived four miles north of the fort on the afternoon
of February 4. Grant wanted to get them closer, past flood-swollen Panther
Creek, so he decided to test the range of the Confederate guns. Boarding
the *Essex*, he ordered Captain W. D. Porter to move up south of the creek

WILLIAM DAVID PORTER

and draw Confederate fire. The first several shots "fell much short of us," Grant later remembered, and he accordingly decided to bring McClernand's men to the south side of the creek to give them an easier overland route for their assault. Porter was about to withdraw the *Essex* when a shell from a Confederate rifled cannon passed over the boat and fell far beyond it. A second zeroed in. "[It] passed very near where Captain Porter and I were standing, struck the deck near the stern, penetrated and passed through the cabin and so out into the river," Grant wrote. "We immediately turned back, and the troops were debarked [north of] the mouth of the creek." *Essex* second mate James Laning would recall that the shot Grant described barely missed the general and Porter, passing "over the spar-deck among the officers, through the officers' quarters . . . commander's pantry and cabin." It caused, "however, no damage, except breaking some of the captain's dishes and cutting the feet from a pair of his socks, which happened to be hanging over the back of a chair in his cabin."[8]

That night, north of Panther Creek, McClernand's men camped on the hills overlooking the river. With their own eyes they now could see the prize: Fort Henry and its Confederate flag.

"I am very tired to-night," Colonel W. H. L. Wallace wrote Ann Wallace that evening. "I haven't got used to my new responsibilities as commander of a brigade in the field and feel, of course, a great deal of anxiety about details. I trust, however, that all may, with the will of God, work for the best . . . My quarters to-night are in a negro cabin, with my brigade bivouacked on the hills about me."

McClernand, exercising flowery skills likely developed in his newspaper years, soon wrote that the fires of their bivouac—which he cunningly named Camp Halleck—lined "the crest and down the slopes of lofty hills and in the valley toward the river" and "together with the many transports and gunboats which had come up and formed the foreground, exhibited a grand and imposing spectacle." It did not go unnoted. McClernand himself reported that the sight was studied by enemy scouts on the other side of the river.[9]

With some eight thousand Federal troops now on the east bank of the Tennessee, the transports turned back to Paducah to bring up Smith's division. Accompanying the empty transports on board the *New Uncle Sam*, Grant wrote Julia that his "anxiety will be great to-night being at Paducah whilst my forces are almost within cannon range of the enemy, and that too in inferior numbers." On February 5, he returned with Smith. Then he wrote her again, saying that the next day would bring "the tug of war." "I do not know accurately" the number of Confederates at Fort Henry, Grant acknowledged, but he estimated that it was "probably 10,000 men." Characteristically, he remained upbeat. "I am . . . in good spirits yet," he wrote in conclusion, "feeling confidence in the success of our enterprise."

The effort's first combat casualties occurred that day, much of which was required to ferry in Smith's men and put most of them ashore on the Tennessee's west bank. On the east side, McClernand probed southward. He chased away Confederate pickets a mile and a half from the fort, and about 10 a.m. First Brigade commander Richard Oglesby pushed forward infantry and cavalry. Oglesby's Illinoisans soon discovered Confederate cavalry lurking about their flanks and rear. The Confederate horsemen charged, apparently trying to cut off some of the Union cavalry from the infantry-supported main body, and a ten-minute firefight ensued, killing one man on each side and wounding several. The arrival of the main body dispersed the attackers, and the Federals took trophies of firearms and sabers.[10]

Sometime during that day, February 5, Federal scouts found more than two dozen women gathered in a farmhouse in the area, a decidedly suspicious circumstance. Under interrogation, one of the women let drop that

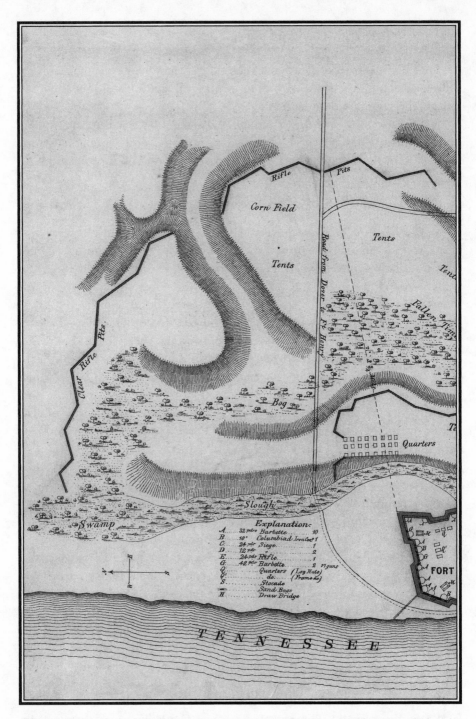

Explanation:

A.	32 pdrs Barbette	10
B.	10" Columbiad Iron	1
C.	24 pdr Siege	1
D.	12 pdr	2
E.	24 pdr Rifle	1
G.	42 pdr Barbette	2 7guns
Q.	Quarters (Log Huts)	
	do. (Frame &c)	
S.	Stocade	
	Sand Bags	
H.	Draw Bridge	

PLAN OF FORT HENRY AND ITS OUTWORKS. Lieutenant Colonel James B. McPherson, sent by Halleck to spy on Grant, supervised the drawing of this map showing Fort Henry surrounded by its huts and tents, with most of its rifle pits and armament facing north or northeast. Telegraph Road leads eastward toward Fort Donelson just north of the fort, while the longer

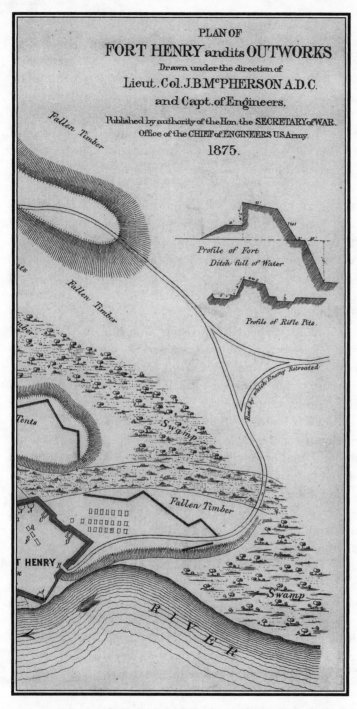

Ridge Road to Dover angles off toward the south. (This map, and those on pages 178 and 190, were originally published in the *Atlas to Accompany the Official Records of the Union and Confederate Armies* [1891–1895], and are reprinted here, courtesy Library of Congress.)

her husband was a Confederate captain inside Fort Henry. The interrogator took it upon himself to impart information of his own. "By tomorrow night, madam, there will be no Fort Henry," he said. "Our gunboats will dispose of it." The woman snapped back a defiant and revealing rejoinder: "Not a bit of it. They will be blown up before they get past the island." Under threat of imprisonment in a Federal army guard-house, the woman finally broke and told of "torpedo" mines that had been laid in the channels around Panther Island.

The woman's story corroborated the earlier information of *Conestoga* commander Phelps, and Foote sent the *Conestoga* and another timber-clad, the *Tyler*, to the west channel, through which the next day's gunboat assault would advance. As the sailors fished around for mines, they saw two Confederate steamboats, the *Dunbar* and the *Lynn Boyd*, approach the fort laden with troops. The Federal vessels fired a few shells at the fort and at the steamboats, which withdrew.[11]

That evening, with Smith's troops still arriving, Grant finalized details of the attack. Troops still were coming in at 10 p.m., and because Grant doubted that the latecomers could get into position any earlier than late morning, he set 11 a.m., February 6, as starting time for the assault on both land and water. He would have preferred to wait until the 7th, he soon wrote, but he felt time was of the essence because both Halleck and local sources were warning that Confederate numbers inside Fort Henry were growing fast.

Grant met with Foote that evening to coordinate their attacks. The naval veteran suggested that his gunboats start toward the fort an hour later than the army to allow the soldiers more time to surround it before the assault began. Grant refused. Possibly he had in mind the latest scouting reports from McClernand's command, which estimated that Henry already contained anywhere from the six thousand Confederates that Smith had reported on January 30 to as many as twenty thousand. With that many defenders, the battle might not end by dark. Seeming to provide for the possibility of a two-day fight, Grant ordered that the infantry move "with two days' rations of bread and meat in their haversacks." A protracted affair that would draw more Confederate reinforcements and alarm Halleck could best be avoided by getting both the army and the gunboats going as soon as possible. If the navy did some softening up of the garrison before the army arrived, so much the better. So, whether he truly believed it or not, Grant told Foote he was confident his infantrymen could reach their assigned places on schedule.

Foote's outward self-confidence, bolstered by his staunch religious faith, was at least as brimming as Grant's and more outspoken. He had spent some of this afternoon preaching a sermon to his sailors, exhorting them to trust in God in the coming battle. Now, when Grant rejected his proposal to vary the pre-attack jump-off times, Foote showed his trust not only in the Almighty but in himself and the as-yet-untested ironclads. He may well also have been miffed that Grant refused his advice as to the starting time. "I shall take [Fort Henry] before you get there with your forces," he said.[12]

*   *   *

The friendship the two men ultimately achieved was hard-won.

Foote had arrived in Cairo in mid-September and was officially assured by the St. Louis office of then–theatre commander Fremont that "the fleet of transport steamers shall be under your exclusive control and direction." The Fremont order added grandly that "No obstacle of any kind is to prevent your moving with part or the whole of your fleet, whenever in your discretion it may be necessary."

Good military commanders zealously guard their turfs, expecting to be held accountable for them, and Foote soon found himself bumping boundaries with a "general at Cairo" who goes unnamed in some of Foote's correspondence but is specifically identified as Grant at other times. Some of the unidentified references may have been to Cairo garrison chief McClernand, but more likely denoted the district commander.

Grant's general's star was still fairly new, so he was not much accustomed to enjoying the prerogatives of command. He may therefore have been doubly protective of even their slightest privileges—especially since he knew he was surrounded by men interested in taking them from him. He disliked, for instance, having subordinates ride ahead of him when traveling with his staff. Foote's naval rank at that time, captain, was equivalent only to the army's lieutenant colonel, and the newcomer found that both Grant and whoever any other unnamed "general at Cairo" may have been were plainly disinclined to take orders from a lieutenant colonel, especially the naval equivalent of one.

When Foote went to Cairo in late October to acquire a wharfboat on which to store gunboat arms, ammunition, and other materiel, he appears to have taken for granted that Grant would have to give it to him. He arrived armed with not only Fremont's all-encompassing order but also his own obvious seniority in age and experience, as well as a bluff and hearty manner. He quickly found the younger, smaller, and wirier Grant to be no pushover. Foote soon wrote the assistant secretary of the Navy complaining that "the brigadier-general" at Cairo refused to accommodate him unless he received "a positive order from General Fremont" himself, not just some generic pronouncement carried around in Foote's wallet. To Foote's dismay, Grant refused to take any orders whatsoever from the navy. Despite

Fremont's blanket decree that Foote would have the authority to move any part or all of his fleet at his own discretion, Foote reported that "the general at Cairo says he will keep [all or any one of Foote's boats] if *the whole Navy* direct them to move." Foote began to bombard his Washington superiors with requests for promotion to flag-officer, a naval rank corresponding to the army's major general.[13]

Foote's repeated pleas finally bore fruit after Grant attacked Belmont on November 7 without informing Foote beforehand, which he earlier had promised to do. Grant claimed he simply "forgot," and Foote was embarrassed and outraged to be in St. Louis when the battle occurred.

"I deeply regret the withholding of this information from me, as I ought not only to have been informed, in order that I might have commanded the gunboats, but it was a want of consideration toward the Navy . . . ," he wrote Navy Secretary Welles. He complained that the army's officers showed, "from want of experience, no appreciation of our wants," and added

> *it may be readily seen the importance of the naval officer commanding, whoever he may be, of having the appointment and rank of flag-officer for the safety and efficiency of the gunboats, by giving him immunity from the orders of brigadier-general down to lieutenant-colonel, who are inexperienced in naval matters . . . For these reasons the department will appreciate my position and see that I can not much longer serve effectively unless rank is given me corresponding to my command and its responsibilities.*[14]

Foote's promotion arrived within the month—the first dispatch in which he signed himself "Flag Officer" is dated November 24—and Grant's communications speedily became more deferential. On December 13, Grant wrote Foote "respectfully ask[ing]," rather than ordering, "your cooperation with the gunboats" in connection with a rumored Confederate intention to attack points near Cairo. Less than a week later, Foote wrote Halleck that Grant had agreed to give shore accommodations to new recruits for the flotilla "until I can distribute them among the boats."[15]

Fighting headaches, literally and figuratively, Foote was a deep-water navy man landlocked in an army desert, trying to complete the construction, arming, and manning of a fleet of untried armored river boats and equally revolutionary auxiliary craft carrying shell-lobbing mortars. The already-high tension had grown over the course of the fall. There were increasing appearances by Confederate gunboats on the lower Mississippi as well as on the Tennessee, and reports of more of these craft being built along both. Plus there was the looming onset of flood season, which would give the Federals their best opportunity to ascend the Tennessee and the Cumberland in boats. The infantry would have no viable transportation alternative, most roads becoming corridors of mud. So Foote *had* to have his boats ready in time not only to guard the vessels that would move the troops but to lead those troops' attacks on riverside forts. Up to November 24 the army had shown little understanding of his difficulties, but now the landlocked seaman was suddenly equivalent to a major general, carrying a supplemental document to that effect signed by President Lincoln himself. Grant now had to realize that there were more reasons to cooperate than not to.

But Lincoln's decision to replace Fremont with Halleck in September surely also helped bring Grant and Foote closer. Grant and Foote were rare specimens at this stage of the war, officers who wanted to fight and itched to move against an enemy who they sensed was not ready to meet them. Over the course of the winter, both men may well have come to recognize their warrior kinship. Certainly, they both were experiencing the same kind of difficulties with their haughty and cautious new chief.

In some ways, Foote's relationship with Halleck was as tense as Grant's. Halleck harbored deep doubts about the value of Foote's gunboats and mortar boats—the concept of an inland armada, after all, was utterly untried in world history—and Foote found the West Point–trained new St. Louis commander nowhere near as respectful of him and his mission as the civilian-turned-general Fremont had been. Three days after Christmas, Foote wrote the assistant navy secretary that, despite the fact that few sailors were to be had in the states of the Midwest, Halleck still would not allow him to use army personnel to man the nearly finished ironclads, which "I had the authority to do from General Fremont." As a result, after "We had all things in comparative good condition . . . Now we are thrown back again for want of men. I see no other way for us to organize effectively but to have 1,000 men sent us from the east immediately . . .

"I know General Halleck's difficulties," he added with a touch of political wariness, "and find no fault with him or his course, except that he seems to question my judgment about navy matters, of which, of course, he can know but little, and I, of course, must know vastly more than he does."[16]

* * *

All this brought Grant and Foote to the evening of February 5, 1862. The two gathered with Grant's division commanders, McClernand and Smith, on the Foote flagship *Cincinnati* to watch Lieutenant Phelps and men from the *Conestoga* bring on deck a "torpedo" mine found in their sweep around Panther Island. Five-and-a-half feet long, it was a metal cylinder pointed on each end and filled with seventy-five pounds of gunpowder. As one of the sailors investigated the weapon, it suddenly made a fizzing sound. The senior officers scattered immediately. Smith and McClernand dropped prone while Grant and Foote dashed for the ladder to an upper deck, the vessel-savvy Foote arriving there first. Lower-ranking sailors laughed at their leaders' reflexive fright; one later wrote that McClernand's and Smith's face-down dive to the deck looked as if they believed that "the hour for evening prayer had arrived." Foote, doubtless trying to recover the appearance of equanimity appropriate to the commander of the fleet, needled Grant.

"General, why this haste?" he inquired.

Grant, whose performance under fire had always been as steady as any man's ever, was no doubt as embarrassed by the incident as Foote and almost certainly did not appreciate Foote's directing more attention to it. His reply exhibited an iron edge that reflected the competitive nature of even their cooperation.

"That the navy might not get ahead of us," he said.[17]

The Gunboats

Rodgers and Foote—and Kountz

T HE GRANT–FOOTE PLAN for a combined assault on Fort Henry was not just revolutionary, it was experimental. The confrontation the two men had so persistently sought permission to launch would be the first in America, and possibly in the world, in which steam-powered armored watercraft teamed with infantry to challenge earthen, river-bank fortifications—or anything else.[1]

The construction and arming of Foote's ironclads had been finished fewer than three weeks before the ships began moving upriver from Cairo to begin the attack. They were not quite the first metal-plated ships, but they were the first to be armored for offensive, rather than defensive, purposes. For centuries, navies worldwide had shared the belief that ships could not challenge fortresses.

History's first ironclad vessel, the *Gloire*, was christened barely two years earlier, in 1859. The French government had commissioned the *Gloire* in response to new military technology that had been developed during the Crimean War. Rifled cannons and especially their shells—artillery projectiles filled with explosives that could be fired farther and with much greater accuracy—had begun to wreak havoc on the kind of wooden-hulled warships that had ruled the waves for millennia. Military craft suddenly had to become floating fortresses to remain viable against the escalating advances in firepower; iron plating, itself a recent invention, was found able to accomplish the transformation.

The first metal-protected Union gunboat in America, the *St. Louis*, was, like her sister river-borne craft, inland-constructed under the auspices of the army rather than the navy. This fact may explain why the invention of the inland gunboats and their early exploits on western rivers have received short shrift in the annals of either service branch—the army tends not to be much interested in navy feats, and the navy is hardly eager to glorify naval achievements accomplished under army supervision. But the Civil War's western gunboats went to work before any others in the hemisphere and were arguably more innovative than the saltwater ones. In contrast to seagoing ironclads, which were constructed more completely of metal, those plying the rivers had to be lighter to move across shallower depths. So ironclads built for use on the Mississippi and its tributaries were made mostly of wood and then partially, and pretty thinly, coated with iron.

Ironclad construction was initiated in North America by the Confederates soon after secession. The Confederate government sought to neutralize the Union's overwhelming dominance in the number of wooden vessels on America's coasts and rivers by fielding a craft capable of destroying them. When Tennessee seceded in June, its officials swiftly set to work on two metal-protected rams at Memphis. Federals felt compelled to keep pace, and the *St. Louis* hit water a month before the Union navy's more famous *Monitor*, first riding the Mississippi's currents in late autumn of 1861. The *St. Louis* had been preceded a few months earlier by "timber-clad" armed steamboats requested in May by McClellan, then commanding the Department of the Ohio. Built to help protect the massing Federal troops at Cairo, the timber-clads were so called because they were "armored" with thick oak planking, which could defend their crews from small-arms fire but not much else.

Inland production of ironclads, as well as the timber-clads, began under Commodore John Rodgers, who was sent west on loan from the navy. Rodgers had supervised the initial construction or conversion—from existing steamboats—of all but two of Foote's gunboats. It was an enormous and thankless task.

"I found in the West only river steamers, with their high pressure boilers on deck, with all their steam connections entirely exposed, and with three-story houses of thin white pine erected on their hulls," Rodgers wrote on September 7, 1861. "Steamboats were not well suited to become warships," Rodgers thought, but, facing the reality "that the Government wanted gunboats immediately," he energetically went about finding the most viable freshwater candidates available, vessels that were "sound and above the average strength." He then supervised all the changes that had to be made to them. Extra timbers and beams were added to allow them to bear the weight of cannons. Their thin exterior planking was removed and replaced with oak five inches thick. Their boilers, which had been on deck, were dropped into the hold to make them less vulnerable to enemy fire, and the connecting steam pipes were similarly lowered. Rodgers also appointed officers, established pay scales, opened centers to try to enlist crewmen, and contracted for everything from gun carriages and anchors, bought uniforms and bedding—in short, Rodgers oversaw every aspect of a huge undertaking. "At last we are afloat," he recalled in September, referring to the just-launched three timber-clads that were the first gunboats to ride water. "[S]poken of con-temptuously at first, our estimated value and efficiency rose every hour . . . [E]ach boat is estimated worth 5,000 soldiers, and no service is thought too arduous for our zeal or too dangerous for our powers." [2]

His boats were built for utility, not beauty, and that was particularly true of the ironclads.

They were 175 feet long, with the metal plating running most of the way down each side to protect the vital machinery within. Each craft measured more than fifty-one feet across at its widest point and boasted thirteen guns; the three largest presented nine- and ten-inch muzzles, which faced the front through bows coated in two-and-a-half inches of metal. Each ship's side mounted four smaller weapons, and the stern had two more.

These riverine ironclads were popularly dubbed "turtles"—not just be-cause they were so wide and flat-looking, but also because they were slow. Designed to travel a maximum of nine miles an hour, they were unable to achieve nearly that against high-water currents like that of the Tennessee in flood season.[3]

Commodore Rodgers started construction and got it into various stages on most of the western theatre's early ironclads, but he lasted only long enough in his position to finish the three timber-clads—*Tyler, Lexington,* and *Conestoga.* Throughout his five-month tenure, Rodgers had to run a gauntlet of politics. Soon after coming west in May, his presence prompted an unhap-py letter from a Pennsylvania congressman to Secretary of War Simon Cameron. The representative indignantly informed the secretary that Rodgers's job already had been given to another person as well as to, in the congressman's view, a more appropriate one: William J. Kountz.

"[A]n old sea captain," Representative James K. Moorhead wrote of Rodgers, " . . . can . . . know nothing of rivers and river steamboats."[4]

*   *   *

Kountz, though, did. Born in Ohio fifty miles from Pittsburgh, he had navi-gated the Ohio and Mississippi rivers since age ten. Basing his operations in the burgeoning Steel City, he had piloted, captained, built, bought, and sold steamboats from the mid–1840s onward, and at the war's outset he owned and captained the *City of Memphis,* one of the larger and finer craft of its day.

Soon after Fort Sumter's surrender, Kountz traveled to the Cincinnati of-fice of McClellan, who had just re-entered the army from civilian life to take command of the Army of the Ohio. This was about the same time Grant spent his fruitless two days outside McClellan's office in quest of a commis-sion, but Kountz had better connections. A McClellan letter of the period says Kountz was "sent out to me by . . . Secretary of War" Cameron, and a Kountz letter around the same time indicates that his journey to see McClellan was also made on the advice of his nationally prominent fellow Pittsburgher, Washington attorney (and ex-Buchanan administration attorney general) Edwin Stanton. And by the time of their interview, Kountz and McClellan almost certainly already knew each other—at least by reputation. Kountz had worked in 1858–59 as freight agent for the Illinois Central Railroad at its southern terminus, commercially crucial New Orleans, when McClellan was the Illinois Central's chief engineer and vice president. Their 1861 meeting went well; according to a later, flattering account, Kountz "volunteered his services without compensation to take charge of the river transportation," and McClellan accepted them.[5]

Kountz probably made his generous offer because he was under-employed. Dixie's secession had shut down river ferriage of Midwestern goods into the South and vice versa, and steamboat proprietors faced bankruptcy. Kountz probably wanted to get some of his boats into government employment, which would provide reliable income.

So paralyzed was the shipping industry, in fact, that Commodore Rodgers was able to buy the *Conestoga*, the *Lexington*, and the *Tyler* in the early summer of 1861 for a bargain price of $62,000, two-thirds of what they had cost to build. But when Rodgers requisitioned the funds, he was quickly informed that he could only purchase boats with the assistance of Captain Kountz, McClellan's director of river transportation. In his letter of protest, Pennsylvania representative Moorhead sounds eager to wield influence for one of his district's more prominent and powerful businessmen. He wrote the secretary of war that he was "greatly surprised" to hear that the naval officer was in Cincinnati "buying and arranging for steamboats" and was, in fact, at that moment headed for Moorhead's—and Kountz's—home city, Pittsburgh, on the same mission. Moorhead contended, correctly, that the navy lacked authority on the western rivers, that "the Western [army] command had been given to General McClellan," and that the navy had sent Rodgers west only to arrange to place cannon on steamboats acquired by the army, not to acquire the steamboats. "I am now astonished to find that he claims to have charge of the entire movements on the water," the congressman wrote.

> General McClellan had consulted with Captain Kountz, one of our best and most efficient river men, and notified him that he would require his services in this branch, and when about to give him an order to purchase and prepare boats for transportation, to the chagrin of both, Captain Rodgers steps in with his commission or authority from the Navy. Please give this your early attention and inform me of the result.[6]

Secretary Cameron apparently did give the congressman's complaint quick action. Two weeks after Moorhead wrote Cameron, the latter's fellow cabinet member, Navy Secretary Gideon Welles, sent Rodgers a telegram of rebuke. It emphasized that all military activities on the western rivers "are under the direction and control of the Army" and that Rodgers was "not authorized to make requisitions except for armament and crew." Kountz continued his work with McClellan while advising Rodgers. Later that summer, a Kountz-commanded transportation fleet was mentioned in official correspondence as assisting McClellan's campaign in western Virginia, and a Kountz postwar thumbnail biography claims that during his army stint he "purchased all the steamboats that were converted into gunboats, and also many other boats for transports." Rodgers seems, in fact, to have come to value him.[7]

But McClellan's successful reclaiming of western Virginia that summer soon got "Little Mac" sent east as heir apparent, then heir, to aged Winfield Scott as commander of all the Union armies in the fall. Rodgers and Kountz were sent to General Fremont in St. Louis, where Rodgers was quickly shelved. The commodore would not authorize Fremont's buying and armoring of a particularly expensive wrecker boat, a heavy steamer that in peacetime had been used to drag grounded vessels and other craft off "snags" in the rivers. Since Rodgers's brother-in-law was U.S. Quartermaster General Montgomery Meigs, who already had criticized Fremont's erratic finances, Fremont preferred somebody—probably anybody—else. A bitter Rodgers was replaced by Andrew Foote.[8]

*   *   *

Even before his arrest by Grant, Kountz's accusatory manner had got him into trouble. When ordered to St. Louis by McClellan in the late autumn, he made the mistake of trespassing on the fiefdom of Congressman Frank Blair, a St. Louis Democrat, without first consulting Blair. The congressman was reputed to have done more than any other man to keep the border state of Missouri in the Union in 1861. For that, Lincoln revered him, and, according to a Kountz letter written around that time, Blair got Kountz's assignment temporarily suspended in favor of another man, whom Kountz claimed to have already "exposed for robbing the Gov[ernment]."[9]

Kountz was reinstated when Halleck supplanted Fremont in November. The new St. Louis commander felt strongly—and, in the middle of a war between two parts of the same nation, naively—that civilian politics had no place in army matters. To him, the case would have been clear: Kountz had been appointed by the army chain of command—specifically, by

Quartermaster General Meigs at the request of McClellan—while Blair was merely a congressman, however powerful.

Grant, trying that autumn to coordinate myriad supply arrangements associated with both the raising of the largest armies America had ever seen and proportionate greed on the part of the nation's businessmen, had requested a new quartermaster.

A few weeks after Halleck's assumption of command in mid-November, Kountz started turning up at Cairo, where he swiftly found an ally in McClernand, commander of the Cairo garrison in Grant's district. Acting more like a congressman than a general, McClernand welcomed Kountz's investigations without first informing Grant. McClernand must have been aware that the inquiries might help undermine his immediate superior and possibly get the district command for himself. Perhaps he also wished to deflect attention from some connection he may have had with acting Cairo quartermaster (and brother of the Illinois secretary of state) R. B. Hatch, who soon would be dismissed on corruption charges.[10]

Grant reprimanded Kountz for barging into his district and poking his nose into sensitive matters without first reporting to district headquarters, but soon, apprised that Kountz had first checked in with McClernand, he met jointly with McClernand and Kountz and tried to work with the boatman. Grant certainly knew that there was plenty of corruption at Cairo that needed investigating because he had been battling it himself. The atmosphere there and elsewhere was tense with newspaper charges that the government was being overcharged for army timber, bread, forage, and other supplies by rapacious civilian contractors. Grant, in late December, sometimes stressing that contracts had been made without his knowledge, was trying to resolve these problems.

At the same time, thanks to McClernand, Kountz's Cairo position became more official. The political general wrote Halleck's quartermaster that Kountz "can render valuable service to the Government if he is placed in charge of river transportation at this port." This endorsement had to have been a godsend to Kountz, whose persistent ignoring of military commanders' jurisdictions and high-handed bossing of their civilian employees had relegated him to on-again-off-again duty in St. Louis, even after removal of the objections of Congressman Blair. In Washington, U.S. Quartermaster General Meigs, an early Kountz ally, was becoming more equivocal as complaints mounted, continuing to endorse Kountz's aims but warning that his quarrelsomeness with military officers, unchecked, could get him "dismissed from the service." In St. Louis, Halleck's quartermaster, possibly glad to get Kountz out of his own hair, took the opportunity offered by McClernand's letter requesting that Kountz be assigned to Cairo; in late December, the

JOHN A. MCCLERNAND

assignment was made. Then McClernand quickly reported that the boatman "seems to be doing a good job" as chief of river transport and "in addition has offered to take over the job of post quartermaster."

Grant was not enthusiastic. The incessantly pushy steamboat captain was yet another harassing vexation at a time when Grant was trying to hang onto his command and get it moving down the Mississippi. Perhaps he sensed that Kountz's unannounced but eventually acknowledged ambition was to put all transport on the western rivers under a single authority: his own. He may well have sensed something more sinister—that Kountz, unwittingly or otherwise, was becoming a tool of McClernand's ambition to supplant his commander. Grant's adjutant and confidant, John Rawlins, had despised McClernand since the aftermath of the Belmont battle, when the ex-congressman sidestepped the chain of command to write a report of the battle to McClellan in Washington and received a congratulatory letter from Lincoln, who sent no such letter to Grant. McClernand had tried to take credit for anything worthwhile that happened at Belmont, and Rawlins despised him for it. "God damn it, it's insubordination!" Rawlins shouted to other staff members. Mimicking McClernand's printed self-praise, he went on: "McClernand says—. McClernand did—. After his great victory McClernand—. The bastard! The damned, slinking, Judas bastard!"

Whatever he thought, Grant, in marked contrast to Rawlins, kept his composure. He wrote Halleck's office in late December sighing that Kountz "knows but little of Military etiquette and I am afraid will never learn," but he continued to try to work with the troublemaker. Lack of etiquette, though, was not Kountz's only problem. He exhibited scant recognition that Grant was preparing to fight a war rather than run a profit-making peacetime business. At one point, the steamboat boss proposed saving on fuel by proper planning that would allow the use of slower supply vessels in non-emergency situations, apparently not recognizing that in war zones non-emergencies can become emergencies overnight. Kountz also highly aggravated the steamboat crews that Grant relied on to transport men and supplies. The men were already unhappy with government pay that was well below pre-war levels and Kountz, whom even a friend described as "ex[c]ited and abrupt in his manner," only made matters worse.[11]

On January 14, Grant complained to St. Louis that the steamboat tycoon, "from his great unpopularity with river men, and his wholesale denunciation of everybody connected with the Government here as thieves and cheats[,] was entirely unable to get crews for the necessary boats. I was compelled to order that boatmen, if they declined serving voluntarily, should be put aboard the boats and be made to serve as prisoners . . . He seems to have desired to be placed on duty here for no other purpose than to wreak his revenge upon some river men who [sic] he dislikes, and to get into the service of Government a boat in which he has an interest." Kountz had become such a pest that to avoid him Grant moved his maps, papers, and other work upstairs from his office in a Cairo bank building into Julia's sitting room.

Two days before he wrote the Kountz-denouncing letter to St. Louis, in the midst of managing the series of Halleck-ordered troop movements across western Kentucky in support of Buell, Grant rebuked Kountz for terminating the government service of a particular transport steamboat and thereby interfering with his work. For Grant, Kountz's dismissal of this steamboat seems to have been the last straw. He reinstated the boat and on January 14 ordered an aide, Lieutenant William S. Hillyer, to "arrest" Kountz and confine him to the St. Charles Hotel until the steamboat tycoon could be assigned elsewhere. Grant installed another civilian, G. W. Graham, as head of river transportation and lodged no charge against Kountz, nominally for "the good of the service," but maybe also to reduce the number of

Cairo disturbances that had to be reported to Halleck's office. Kountz, furious, immediately started telling all who would listen that G. W. Graham was corrupt and Grant a corrupt drunk.[12]

Within the week, he made his accusations formal in a document he fired off to Halleck's headquarters in St. Louis:

Charges and specifications preferred against Ulysses S. Grant, Brigadier General Commanding District of South East Missouri [now District of Cairo]

CHARGE 1ST
Drunkenness while on duty, in violation of the Forty-fifth Act of First Section of the Articles of War, regulating the United States Army.

SPECIFICATION 1ST
In this, that the said Ulysses S. Grant Brigadier General, and commanding at the post of Cairo, in the State of Illinois, the same being in the District of Southeast Missouri, heretofore to-wit: On or about the sixth day of December 1861, and while on duty; accompanying a 'flag of truce' from Cairo Ill. to Columbus, Ky the same being on a Government steamboat on the Mississippi River, between Cairo Ill and Columbus, Ky. did then and there while so on duty become, of his own voluntary act, beastly drunk, insomuch that the said Ulysses S. Grant, was then and there, from the said cause, incapacitated for any business Contrary to the rules and regulations for the Army of the United States.

SPECIFICATION 2ND
In this, that the said Ulysses S. Grant Brigadier General commanding &c, on the day and year, at the place last aforesaid, being on duty with a 'Flag of Truce' sent from the Union Government forces, at Cairo Ill, to the Rebel forces at Columbus, Ky, did then and there, and while with men who were in rebellion against the Government of the United States, by the use of intoxicating liquors, drank in the presence of, and with said rebels, become beastly drunk, and by reason thereof, incapacitated for duty, contrary to the rules and articles of the Army of the United States.

SPECIFICATION 3RD
In this, that the said Ulysses S. Grant at the time and place stated in the first Specification, and while on duty as a United States officer, to wit, as Brigadier General in the United States army, become intoxicated contrary to the rules and articles for the United States Army.

SPECIFICATION 4TH
In this that on the 7th day of December 1861 and on divers days since said day, the said Ulysses S. Grant, Brigadier General &c, at the city of Cairo Ill. and

while on duty as Commanding General of the District of Southeast Missouri, the same including Cairo Ill. did become and was then and there intoxicated to drunkenness, and was then and there guilty of drunkenness, contrary to the rules and regulations of the United States Army.

CHARGE 2ND
Conduct unbecoming an Officer and a Gentleman

SPECIFICATION 1ST
In this, that the said Ulysses S. Grant, heretofore, to wit: on or about the sixth day of December 1861, at Cairo, Illinois and on divers days and times since said day, has been repeatedly and often openly drunk, and so much intoxicated as to be unfitted for any business, thereby setting an evil example to the officers and soldiers under his command.

I, William J. Kountz, prefer the above charges and specifications against Ulysses S. Grant, and ask that a Court Martial be convened to try the same. [13]

It is impossible to know whether Kountz saw firsthand the acts alleged in his official charges. He seems to have been in and out of Cairo before becoming permanently assigned there in the latter half of December, and the way the allegations are written gives little indication of personal knowledge, raising suspicion that, at least in part, they were hearsay. It seems odd and likely more than coincidence that McClernand chose December 17, just as he and Kountz were becoming more closely associated, to write a substantial letter introducing himself to Halleck, the man who could remove Grant and replace him with McClernand. It may also be significant that Kountz, apprising Pennsylvania congressman Moorhead of the charges he was filing against Grant, added: "I have been supported by Genl. McClernand who is a very worthy indestryous & good man but his hands has been tied."

It seems unlikely that Grant was guilty of everything that the Kountz document accuses him of. The strongest guarantee of Grant's sobriety was always the presence of Julia, and she was with him in Cairo on December 6–7 and most of the rest of the time, until he departed for Fort Henry.

That said, it is possible that Kountz simply smelled alcohol on Grant, heard that the general had a convivial glass of something with one of his many visitors, and had another such glass aboard a flag-of-truce boat and that each time it appeared to affect him. Such might well have constituted "beastly" drunkenness to Kountz, whom a later Pittsburgh account described as a fanatical total abstainer who could not "tolerate a drinking man in his presence." Or perhaps, as claimed by correspondence from other Cairo visitors during this period, on one or more of those occasions it was true.[14]

To February 3
Grant, Halleck, and Fate

SEVEN AND A HALF months before the Union transports shoved off for Fort Henry, one of American history's most unimaginable reversals of individual destiny had begun to come to pass. Inexplicably, Grant's abysmal run of luck had turned.

In June of 1861, the first colonel appointed to command the Twenty-first Illinois Regiment could not handle the job, and at nearly the last minute Governor Yates had overcome personal reservations and commissioned Grant to do it. In August, Congressman Washburne of Illinois, because he wanted as many Illinois generals as he could get, got Grant appointed brigadier. In September, Fremont, looking for someone to carry out orders swiftly and without question, passed over several much more prominent subordinates and gave Grant on-the-ground command of the massing movement to clear the Mississippi. In November, the interval between Fremont's removal and Halleck's arrival allowed Grant to disobey orders and make his bloody attack on Belmont without reprimand or worse.

True, Grant had made his luck. He did so with an innate, nervous impulse to be always moving, as well as an indefatigability that was not to be denied. Both traits were all the more extraordinary because they had been not in the least cowed by seven previous years that would have broken and finished many another man. But Grant had been just as driven and determined during his hard civilian years as he was in his bright new military ones, so although he can be credited with supplying the huge intestinal wherewithal needed to capitalize on the luck that finally came, the luck itself arrived from outside himself, as if on a wave of the tide of history. That wave dislodged from obscurity a man who at almost forty had finally failed himself into a job working for his father—but now the long-ebbing tide had turned and was gathering momentum of historic proportions. In the space of just seven more years night-and-day different from his past ones, it would sweep this enigmatically steely little man into the White House.

But until almost the end, such a result never would be a foregone conclusion. His improbably good fortune would, in fact, threaten time after time to evaporate into abject disappointment and shame. And never would his luck be as dodgy and near running out as it would from the latter part of January into mid-February 1862. In those weeks, its continued flow would seem a near miracle, the likelihood of its being dammed and dried up all but certain. His most dangerous enemy would not even be an enemy. It would be his commander, Henry Halleck.

On January 20, Grant had written Halleck requesting permission to come to department headquarters in St. Louis for a meeting with his chief. It was his third such request, following others on November 20 and January 6. The preceding ones had been brusquely turned down, but this time, although Halleck's reply would be remembered by Grant as "not gracious," consent was given.

Halleck had known about Grant's drinking since California, and Halleck may have feared that the unimpressive subordinate only wanted to get to St. Louis for recreational purposes. But Grant had come on business: to disclose findings of the latest Smith gunboat reconnaissance to Fort Henry and to ask Halleck's permission to go down the Tennessee to make the capture Smith had thought would be easy. Halleck, though, had no interest in having a friendly talk with his Cairo commander. He had been receiving continual reports from Cairo casting doubt on not only Grant's character but his ability. And so when he arrived in St. Louis on the evening of January 23, Grant found himself, as he later recalled in his *Personal Memoirs,* "received with so little cordiality that I perhaps stated the object of my visit with less clearness than I might have done. I had not uttered many sentences before I was cut short as if my plan was preposterous." Halleck refused to look at Grant's maps, coolly asked him if his errand had to do with needs of his command, and then informed him that strategy and tactics were "the business of the General commanding the department"—in other words, of Halleck only.

"When he wishes to consult you on that subject," he icily added before unceremoniously walking out, "he will notify you."

"I returned to Cairo very much crestfallen," Grant wrote.[1]

And no doubt shaken. Henry Wager Halleck was daunting. A New York farmer's son, he had long since left the fields for higher ground. Now, at fifty-six, he appeared professorial with a visage a bit toad-like: five-feet-nine and stocky, with prominent forehead and bulging, intimidating, almost contemptuous eyes that watered in hay season. He was also flintily difficult for all but his few intimates to deal with: hemorrhoidal, precise, and continually stressed by the enlarging authority that he craved and believed his due. Along with Albert Sidney Johnston and Robert E. Lee, Halleck was numbered among America's most respected military minds, and Grant, overawed by his commander's "gigantic intellect," professed to believe him one of the "greatest men of the age."

By most contemporary measurements, he was. While Grant had spent his Pacific Coast military stint on a personal spiral downward, Halleck capitalized handsomely on his. Assigned the military position of secretary of state to the territorial governor of California, Halleck acquired valuable land and mineral rights and finally left the army in 1854 after helping to form one of the territory's most lucrative early law firms. His California enterprises led Pittsburgh lawyer Edwin Stanton, briefly attorney-general in the Buchanan administration and soon to replace Simon Cameron as Lincoln's secretary of war, to view Halleck as "totally destitute of principle" and "probably the greatest scoundrel and most bare-faced villain in America." Whatever he was, by 1861 his single-minded shrewdness had reaped personal assets worth a fabulous $500,000.

How far determination had taken Halleck from the confining plow handles of his youth was measured by his marriage to a granddaughter of Alexander Hamilton, and his egotism reflected the height of his social climb. A review he published of another writer's work in California in the 1850s said, for example, "we most sincerely regret this chapter was ever written or published. It is so replete with errors"; he went on to describe the author of the unfortunate paragraph as having "not a single characteristic as qualification of a historian."

While still in the army, he had followed a teaching interlude at West Point by writing his influential volume on military strategy, *Elements of Military Art and Science.* Rather than a creation of Halleck himself, his book was more a translation of the precepts of Swiss military historian Baron Henri Jomini, a general who served under Napoleon and whose early–nineteenth-century literary works had made him the preeminent delineator and exponent of Napoleonic strategy, the most influential military thinking of the era. Studied extensively at West Point, Jomini used the campaigns of Napoleon to present warfare as a chess game of positions turned and taken rather than enemies pursued and bloodied. For Jomini, war was geometry—an antiseptic enterprise carried out by professional soldiers along "interior lines" of communication and supply and in a near-vacuum of minimum civilian contact, damage, and interference.

Like Jomini, Halleck believed wars were best won by outmaneuvering opponents and forcing them to retreat, not whipping them in battles. In his own book, he referred to warfare as a "contest" whose most important features were extensive preparation, ability to evade attack and loss, and rapt focus on capturing map points, not destroying armies. Halleck was, in short, everything Grant was not: rich, intellectual, and unencumbered by the bottle—as well as elitist, arrogant, crafty, and not very eager to fight.[2]

*   *   *

But Halleck did not dismiss Grant from their uncordial interview because he found the idea of an attack on Fort Henry "preposterous," as Grant put it. What Halleck considered preposterous was that an underling, especially such an unimpressive one as Grant, should presume to advise Henry Halleck about anything.

Halleck did not disapprove of attacking southward along the Tennessee and Cumberland rivers. He had been considering that very strategy for at least a month. In late December, Brigadier General William T. Sherman, who had been added to Halleck's staff after suffering a nervous collapse as Buell's predecessor in Louisville, saw his new boss point to a map of the Kentucky front one evening at the Planter's House in St. Louis. Halleck asked his chief of staff and longtime best friend, Brigadier General George W. Cullum, to trace the Confederate western defense line with a pencil. Cullum drew a mark from Columbus on the Mississippi River eastward through Bowling Green and beyond. The vaunted instructor then asked a second question whose answer was elementary to any military student of Jomini and Halleck: "Now where is the proper place to break it?"

"Naturally, the center," he was answered.

Halleck took up the pencil himself and drew a line north-south through the midpoint of the horizontal one. This vertical mark passed through Fort Henry.

"That's the true line of operations," he announced.[3]

At the time of Grant's visit, though, Halleck felt no urgent need to commit to an *immediate* assault on Fort Henry, although events were beginning to nudge him in that direction. Recovering in mid-January from a ubiquitous scourge of Civil War soldiers, the measles, Halleck was mulling a Fort Henry campaign for perhaps mid-February, when his current Missouri operations would be concluded. For weeks, Buell in Louisville had been suggesting to McClellan that Halleck be *ordered* to begin a diversionary movement up the Tennessee and Cumberland rivers to support Buell's designs on Bowling Green and Nashville. Halleck had learned only lately of the Buell–McClellan plan and had been fending them off with his unfinished trans-Mississippi business. Despite their pressure, he knew that at that time he did not have to do anything. War Order No. 1, Lincoln's desperate attempt to require all Union commanding generals to begin forward movements by Washington's birthday, was not issued until January 27, so even that did not demand action before February 22. In the meantime, Halleck hoped to coax support out of the balky Buell for a *Halleck*-led offensive, rather than supply aid for a Buell-bossed operation.4

There was another reason for waiting, too, and to Halleck's mind it was compelling. Although Halleck was already planning an attack on Fort Henry, he had no intention of allowing Grant to lead it. Halleck regarded the Henry operation as entirely his own, but in his intellectual view of strategy and tactics, armchair generalship was entirely appropriate to his position of intellectual superiority. A field commander was just an instrument for use on the ground. The Kountz allegations, both the new formal ones and the boatman's many purported findings of corruption on the Cairo scene, seemed to indicate just how imperfect the particular instrument in Cairo was. The grounds for dissatisfaction with Grant were proliferating. They doubtless began with the tone-setting rashness of Grant's highly controversial attack on Belmont just before Halleck arrived in St. Louis. This was followed closely by Grant's bald-faced initial underestimates of his Belmont casualties. Since then the number of seeming sins had mounted. There was Grant's failure to question the bogus "Buel" telegram of instructions; the various newspaper allegations of Cairo supply fraud; and a less-public litany of additional similar charges coming from Kountz and others. Finally, there was Grant's continuing impatient tendency to try to push not just the enemy but—as when he took Paducah without orders, similarly assailed Belmont, and repeatedly pressed for the move against Fort Henry—his own commanders.

The Cairo brigadier appeared sloppy in his actions as well as his dress, both of which surely rankled Halleck's perfectionism. In many of his communications, including the one in which he replied to Halleck's rebuke in the "Buel" fiasco, Grant failed even to spell his commander's name correctly, rendering it as "Hallack." That undoubtedly offended a man who a few months earlier initially refused to accept a Washington invitation to return to active military eminence because the letter inadvertently addressed him as "Major." But most alarming of all to the St. Louis commander would have been Grant's eager, almost hungry, approach to fighting. Halleck's philosophy of war left little room for the aggressive spirit that was Grant's military essence. Halleck's influential book on strategy ritualistically rushed through the advantages of an offensive in the most perfunctory prose:

It is waged on a foreign soil, and therefore spares the country of the attacking force; it augments its own resources at the same time that it diminishes those of the enemy; it adds to the moral courage of its own army, while it disheartens opponents . . . Regarded simply as the initiative of movements, the offensive is almost always the preferable one, as it enables the general to choose his lines for moving and concentrating his masses on the decisive point.

But then, even in attempting to tout the offensive, Halleck revealed his habitually defensive mindset. "The first and most important rule of war," he wrote with sudden seeming passion, "is, to keep your forces as much concentrated as possible. This will not only prevent misfortune, but secure victory."

Preventing misfortune was at least as important to Halleck as securing victory, and, no matter the expressed opinions of Smith and Foote and especially Grant that Fort Henry would be a quick and easy conquest, potential misfortune lurked menacingly in any attack up the Tennessee River. Halleck's Jominian view stressed that an attacking force must be overwhelming. He believed that no less than sixty thousand Federal soldiers, almost four times as many as Grant had, were needed to safely invade the Henry–Donelson area. Halleck's distrust of Grant only multiplied his anxiety about the dearth of Federal troops.

For his part, Grant felt this distrust, and it made him ever more eager for battle. The cloud of doubt that had again risen over his abilities following the party at Lew Wallace's the previous autumn had now turned pitch black, threatening a downpour that could wash away his life-changing field command. He had been forced to quit the army as a captain just seven years earlier to dodge the shame of a charge of excessive drinking, and the Kountz document now working its way up the chain of command was far more damning than any allegation Grant could have faced in 1854. He desperately needed to do something that might finally give him and his family a secure future.

Halleck's concerns about Grant pushed *him*, at the same time, toward letting Grant do as little as possible. His own reputation large and long made, Halleck shrank from losing it on the kind of colossal mistake that seemed all too probable in assailing an out-of-the-way fort with too few troops commanded by an impulsive and sloppy field general.[5]

Halleck may also have already heard, following Kountz's January 14 arrest, preliminary rumblings of the drunkenness charges, because in the latter half of January the St. Louis commander's search for a Grant replacement as commander of a looming field operation, which had begun in December, became more fevered. On January 24, little more than hours after Grant's visit to St. Louis and two days before the Kountz document arrived at Halleck's headquarters, Halleck had asked McClellan to coax

HENRY W. HALLECK

aging Brigadier General Ethan Allen Hitchcock out of retirement. Halleck wanted Hitchcock in Grant's place and hoped to lure him to it with a promotion to major general.[6]

* * *

So while Halleck badly wanted to delay the Fort Henry operation for a few weeks, Grant, in the wake of the St. Louis interview, surely felt even greater urgency to get it—or something—started as quickly as possible. Halleck's low opinion had been made unquestionably evident, and Grant had to have suspected that he was running out of time to redeem himself.

His response to his problem was singularly typical. He not only refused to give up on the proposed offensive, he became more insistent on it. Less than a week after the painful meeting with his superior—and one day after issuance of War Order No. 1—Grant and Foote, united by mutual aggressiveness, sent Halleck their twin telegrams renewing the request to attack, Foote's asserting that Grant "and myself are of the opinion" that Fort Henry could be taken by four gunboats and enough troops to hold it once captured. The next day, January 29, Grant followed with a longer one sounding a Foote refrain: if Henry was not taken immediately, the Confederacy would "materially strengthen" it along with Fort Heiman and Fort Donelson.7 Then, in its least likely and most crucial manifestation in all of Grant's life, his newfound luck again fell into the breach. That day, the 29th, was the one on which Halleck received and snatched up McClellan's report of the Beauregard rumor—and acted on it with such uncharacteristic speed. Unknown of course to Grant, Halleck's sudden order to him to attack Fort Henry was a bold bid to steal a march on Buell in their battle for supremacy in Federal western command. The Thomas victory at Logan's Crossroads in Buell's department had just been hailed as the war's first great Union victory, and that, coupled with McClellan's deep and longstanding admiration of Buell, threatened to make Major General Halleck in St. Louis a handmaiden to Brigadier General Buell in Louisville. Halleck swiftly needed a more resounding victory than Buell's.8

So Halleck chose to live for at least a few more days with his ever-deepening reservations about Grant—and hold in abeyance the inflammatory Kountz allegations that had arrived on his desk on January 26. In his campaign for a Grant replacement, they could be the ace in the hole.

His first response to Kountz's document was to sidestep. He immediately returned the charges to Cairo and referred them to Grant himself, adding the notation that they had not been "sent through the proper channel." Whether this was intended as a warning to the unloved brigadier, a hopeful ploy to induce him to repeat his action of 1854 and resign in the face of impending shame (the vaunted but outranked Smith, after all, was just upriver at Paducah in position to take over until Hitchcock arrived), or just a stall for time while Halleck mulled the problem, is impossible to know.

Whatever Halleck's intention, Grant again displayed his steel nerve. Handling the charges as if they constituted just a routine matter having nothing to do with himself, he asked that Kountz furnish him with an extra copy so that his headquarters could retain one while forwarding the other to St. Louis. Then he endorsed his copy on January 29 to show that it had come through his headquarters and sent it on. But that same day, January 29, he followed up his and Foote's telegrams of the day before with another reminding Halleck that the Confederates must not be given time to reinforce Fort Henry. It was a desperate bid to get going and outflank his looming personal disaster with an attack up the Tennessee River.

And then destiny intervened. That very day, with the wheels of the Hitchcock appointment still grinding, Halleck decided he had no more time if he wanted to outmaneuver Buell and capitalize on Fort Henry's weakness. So he reacted to McClellan's Beauregard report by authorizing the attack Grant and Foote had urged. The St. Louis commander again indicated his lack of trust in Grant, though. He immediately telegraphed Foote the news that he would order the move as soon as he received information on the condition of a land route to Henry, but he allowed another day to pass before he informed Grant.9

So an accident of fate allowed Grant to remain in charge of the Fort Henry–bound troop transports casting off from Paducah, the last point from which the expedition could be conveniently stopped and its commander snatched back to Cairo. Halleck hedged his bet, though. Along for the ride was a new Halleck-assigned engineer, Lieutenant Colonel James B. McPherson, whose presence was a direct result of the multiplying Cairo reports of which the Kountz

JAMES B. McPHERSON

document was the most recent and most official. McPherson later would tell physician Brinton that his mission was to check on "General Grant's habits."

"It is said that he is drinking terribly and is in every way inefficient," McPherson explained.10

Grant left behind in Cairo as little evidence of the Kountz matter and other Halleck dissatisfactions as possible. He took along every document that had passed between his and Halleck's headquarters—so much material that Halleck chief of staff Cullum, sent to run the Cairo office in Grant's absence, would complain to his commander that not "even a file of your orders, which I daily want for reference," remained. On the troop transports bound for Fort Henry, staff members saw their chief appear uneasy, continually looking back over his shoulder until the convoy steamed southward up the Tennessee River beyond Paducah. Only then did he relax. Although he had taken leave of Cairo with a nasty cold, he slapped aide John Rawlins on the shoulder almost giddily.

"Now we seem to be safe, beyond recall," he said. "We will succeed, Rawlins; we must succeed."11

They had to.

Fort Henry to Late Morning of February 6

The Confederates

Over the outer and inner works of Fort Henry, whose walls and flag were so distantly visible to the Federals in McClernand's camps, February 6 dawned with welcome clearing of a sky whose bottom had fallen out in overnight downpours. The torrents had so heightened the rage of the already-swollen river at the facility's front that waves now filled surrounding lowland behind it, lapping at the edge of the higher ground on which its outer trenches ran like rivulets with the rain. The place's Confederate commanders had begun to comprehend that payment had come due on their seasons of indecision, delay, and neglect.

For three days the men commanded by West Point–trained Brigadier General Lloyd Tilghman, longtime Paducah resident and son of a Maryland congressman, had watched with mounting concern as the sky behind Panther Island blackened with smoke from gunboats and transports. Then they saw Foote and Grant reconnoitering and landing load after load of infantry.

Their alarm was justified. Rather than the ten thousand men that Grant estimated him to have, Tilghman led a Henry garrison of effectives numbering about one-fourth of that: elements of the Tenth, Forty-Eighth, and Fifty-First Tennessee, Twenty-Seventh Alabama, Fourth Mississippi, and Fifteenth Arkansas, along with a so-called Alabama Battalion, an Alabama cavalry battalion, a spy company, another battalion of cavalry, and Captain Jesse Taylor's seventy-five heavy artillerymen. Only one-third of these troops—approximately eight hundred men—were "at all disciplined or well armed," Tilghman himself soon wrote.

By morning of February 6, Tilghman knew he had erred a day earlier in wiring superiors that with reinforcements he had "a glorious chance to overwhelm the enemy." The Federal force was too large. Besides, no reinforcements had come.[1]

*   *   *

Tilghman had taken command of both forts, Henry and Donelson, in late November, and from the outset his leadership was testy and erratic. He would report later that he had been nearly "broken down by incessant work" since the previous June in forming and drilling two brigades at nearby Hopkinsville, Kentucky. He added that he was hardly able, on December 15, to take on the formation and training of a third brigade and at the same time complete the defenses of the state-line forts on the Tennessee and Cumberland rivers.

Fort Henry was a low Confederate priority—a fact reflected in the small size of its garrison and the fact that Tilghman was assigned to command both it and Fort Donelson while also drilling new troops. Earlier, when Tennessee's troops were still her own rather than the Confederacy's, provisional commander Pillow had been so intent on defending the Mississippi River that he wrote a Nashville railroad engineer that he saw "no present danger" along the Tennessee because there was "nothing of military importance to be gained by ascending" it.

Pillow was, of course, wrong. Columbus, Kentucky, where even then he had wanted to locate the South's Gibraltar, would be outflanked and doomed by a movement up the Tennessee—and loss of the critical railroad bridges connecting Middle and West Tennessee could isolate Confederate regions and armies. Too, there were the major iron-producing area between the rivers and the fact that the Tennessee River was the quickest potential Federal route to strike western Alabama, eastern Mississippi, and the vital east-west Memphis & Charleston Railroad.[2]

Tilghman seems to have spent more time trying to train, equip, and build winter housing for his Fort Henry troops than he did strengthening their position. His most serious errors involved lack of work on Fort Heiman, the high-rising but only lightly fortified ridge across the Tennessee that overlooked and potentially protected Fort Henry. Not having transferred his headquarters from Donelson to Henry until January 15, Tilghman apparently delayed approving the plan for the Fort Heiman defenses until it was too late to build them. Meanwhile, a few hundred slaves brought in from northern Alabama to do much of the kind of labor needed at Heiman were idled, and the Henry garrison worked on building winter huts for themselves.[3]

But Tilghman was not to blame for the fort's most glaring deficiency: its location. That was largely the fault of Tennessee's attorney general, Daniel S. Donelson, a sixty-year-old West Pointer (and nephew of Andrew Jackson) who had little engineering experience and had been out of the army nearly

four decades. He was speaker of the lower house of the Tennessee legislature in the summer of 1861 when Tennessee Governor Harris, ever politically aware, asked Donelson to help choose suitable positions for defense of
the state as near the border of then-neutral Kentucky as feasible. With reservations, Donelson approved a fort site on the Cumberland picked by civil
engineer Adna Anderson of the Edgefield & Kentucky Railroad and assistant Wilbur Foster, a surveyor who had become a private in the First Tennessee Infantry. But Donelson rejected Anderson's choice of a position on
the Tennessee near the mouth of Standing Stone Creek. Asserting that
there was no good place for a defensive facility on the Tennessee's east side,
he finally settled on another point due west of the one on the Cumberland,
despite the fact that it sat on ground lower than the river's normal winter
flood stage.

On June 9, 1861, Attorney General Donelson's site selection then received final approval from another, younger West Pointer: Bushrod Johnson,
the native Northerner whose hidden past included abolition activism and
military disgrace. Johnson apparently shrank from overruling a high state official and possibly complicating his hopes for promotion in Tennessee's provisional, not-yet-Confederate army. Whatever his motives, Johnson approved
Donelson's Tennessee River site, which was quickly named Fort Henry after
new Confederate Senator Gustavus A. Henry of Clarksville. A more defensi-
ble facility on the Cumberland, on which construction was already underway, was christened Fort Donelson after the aging attorney general himself.
Work began shortly afterward on Fort Henry. It was garrisoned by the Tenth
Tennessee Regiment of Irishmen under Colonel Adolphus Heiman, a Prus-
sian-born Mexican War hero and prominent Nashville architect.4

Except for Daniel Donelson and Bushrod Johnson, no Confederate professed to like Fort Henry. Artillerist Jesse Taylor, a former member of the
U.S. Navy who arrived there in September, was "convinced by a glance at its
surroundings that extraordinarily bad judgment, or worse, had selected the
site . . . I found it placed on the east bank of the river in a bottom commanded by high hills rising on either side of the river and within good rifle
range." He reported his assessment to state military authorities at Nashville
and was told that Henry's selection had been made by "competent engineers" focused on its capacity to supply, and receive support from, Fort
Donelson.

Taylor looked closer. He noticed a watermark high on a tree, then more of
them. He reported that his "investigation convinced me that we had a more
dangerous force to contend with than the Federals—namely, the river itself."
Residents of the area told him that the fort's location "was not only subject to
overflow, but that the highest point within it would be, in an ordinary

February rise, at least two feet under water." He conveyed this information to Nashville, too, but was curtly informed that Tennessee's troops were now under the command of Richmond and he should send his report to General Polk at Columbus. When he did that, he was referred to commander Albert Sidney Johnston, who then—quickly—sent engineer Jeremy Gilmer, a Confederate major, to examine the problem.[5]

Gilmer noted more difficulties. His initial inspection of the fort in early November found that it was dangerously overlooked by the heights across the river; enemy artillery placed there could easily kill or rout any Fort Henry garrison. Because the state line dips suddenly southward with the river beside Fort Henry, the west shore was in Kentucky, but the Bluegrass State's formerly prized neutrality had become history in September.

A local engineer officer was sent across the river to lay out another facility on the west bank's imposing hill. It was named Fort Heiman after the Tenth Tennessee's commander, and a large contingent of Alabama slaves was expected to be sent to do the construction work in late November. The slaves did not come until January 1, though, and they arrived in nowhere near the numbers promised; they had to be supplemented with soldiers. By the time Gilmer arrived for a second inspection at the end of January, Tilghman was trying to make up for lost time. According to Gilmer, Tilghman and his engineers were throwing up fortifications at both sites "so rapidly that when I reached the fort they were far advanced." Rifle pits surrounded both installations. Fort Heiman, though, did not possess artillery powerful enough to be effective at long-range against gunboats or troops on the east side of the river.[6]

*　　*　　*

On February 3, with the Union invasion expected daily, Gilmer inspected Fort Henry's defenses a second time. What he found could hardly have been heartening. Tilghman had troops laboring "day and night" sandbagging a temporary above-ground magazine made necessary by the river, which was rising with the continual winter rains. Flooding had threatened to drown the underground magazine and foul the ammunition. But at least Confederate pickets were reporting no sight of the Federals yet, and on February 4 Gilmer and Tilghman rode to Fort Donelson to make a similar inspection there. Around noon they heard "heavy firing" from Fort Henry that continued for half an hour, and at 4 p.m. a courier arrived from Heiman at Henry saying Federals were landing "in strong force" at Bailey's Ferry three to four miles downstream. Tilghman persuaded Gilmer to remain with him, and the two departed Donelson again for Henry.[7]

For the Henry garrison, the period of Tilghman's absence had been increasingly nerve-wracking. For two days they had observed, and sometimes skirmished with, Federal troops trying to reconnoiter along their flanks. They watched as the gunboats and transports kept landing more and more troops in their sight but beyond their cannons' reach. When any of the Union vessels ventured nearer, the Confederates fired at them—and ducked, noting that "some of their shells fell a quarter of a mile beyond the fort, showing a range superior to our own," as Colonel Heiman of the Tenth Tennessee would report.

Heiman, in charge in his commander's absence, positioned a light battery and a detachment of Fourth Mississippi infantrymen north of the fort at the Dover road, and it was this detachment that at 4:30 a.m. on February 4 spotted a signal rocket fired by a picket located farther out, at Bailey's Landing. The fort answered with a rocket of its own, and the picket then fired three more to signify the approach of three Federal gunboats. Heiman hurried a courier toward Tilghman at Donelson and ordered the fort's waterside guns—which included a ten-inch columbiad, a rifled twenty-four-pounder, and eight thirty-two-pounders—manned and loaded with shot. He also sent upriver and out of danger five steamboats that had been serving the garrison. Two of the boats, the *Dunbar* and the *Lynn Boyd*, were dispatched farther south to bring forward two "skeleton regiments," the Forty-eighth and Fifty-first Tennessee, totaling about four hundred men, who had been guarding the Danville railroad bridge.

Shortly after dawn on February 4, pickets on both sides of the river reported the approach of a large fleet. In the fort, Heiman could see "the smoke from several gunboats" rising over Panther Island. He sent small mounted detachments northward along both banks to try to find out what this all meant, whether the Federals were landing infantry. Most of Forrest's cavalry was still in western Kentucky, but the single company of it at Henry was assigned to cover roads leading to the fort from Bailey's Ferry. Heiman ordered two companies of the Fourth Mississippi Infantry and part of a battery into rifle pits covering the approach of the Dover Road three-quarters of a mile east of the fort, while two companies of the Alabama infantry battalion were sent to trenches further to the northeast covering the road to Bailey's Landing. Additional men were dispatched to sink a dozen torpedoes in the river on the west side of Panther Island, the route attacking gunboats could be expected to use to stay out of sight of the fort's gunners as long as possible. Lack of "powder and time," though, prevented the anchoring of any of the devices in the main channel.

Sometime past 9 a.m., the gunboats began shelling the Bailey's Landing pickets out of their quarters. Heiman's mounted scout parties soon returned to report troops being unloaded on the east bank. Heiman sent off another courier to Tilghman and continued the work he and his commander had been supervising on the walls—and trying to keep the water out of the fort.

"The lower magazine had already 2 feet of water in it," he would recall later.

Throughout the morning, the troops at Fort Henry watched and waited for the inevitable. Around noon, five gunboats showed themselves in the river's main channel nearly two miles off, out of range of all of the fort's guns except the twenty-four-pounder rifle and the ten-inch columbiad. The Confederates were reluctant to use the columbiad because it had exhibited such frightening recoil in trial firings that it, in Heiman's word, "disarranged" itself.

Then, at about 1 p.m., the gunboats opened fire. The shells rained into, around, and beyond Henry. The fort responded with both its rifled gun and the columbiad until, "on the third or fourth fire," the columbiad broke one of its clamps, causing Heiman to fear that the recoil from another shot might turn it over. He ordered it silenced, but the rifled gun continued its work "in quick succession."

The gunboats' fire continued and even increased as they drew nearer, their thirty-two-pounders opening up. After a half-hour, though, this trial round of conflict between gunboats and a river fort ended abruptly. The boats withdrew downriver beyond the cover of Panther Island, and Heiman surveyed the damage. He found that none of the Federal shells fired into the fort had exploded, and only one man had been wounded. But he detected no cause for optimism. He ordered the troops on the heights across the river to be ready to move to Fort Henry "at a moment's warning" and dispatched another message to Tilghman at Donelson "that the enemy was landing a large force and additional transports were arriving. At five o'clock," he added in his report, "I sent another courier, with an escort, to the general . . . requesting his orders, or, what I desired more, his presence, and cautioned him not to come without a strong escort and by the upper road, believing that the enemy already had pickets on the main Dover road."

As daylight faded, Heiman sent two companies of his Tenth Tennessee and a rifled six-pounder cannon to beef up the Dover road outposts. Only at 5 p.m., when he had sent his third or fourth courier to Tilghman, did he think of sending word to Polk seventy-five miles away at Columbus. To Johnston, ninety-five miles distant at Bowling Green, he dispatched no message at all.[8]

*   *   *

Down at the Danville bridge, Confederate Captain Andrew Jackson (Jack) Campbell and his company of the Forty-eighth Tennessee had been camped between the river and a marsh since January 23, with "no straw or anything else to keep our hides out of the mud, which was plentiful . . . The weather [was] . . . very wet and there [was] . . . a great deal of sickness in the regiment." Campbell's men, gathered from rural Maury County in central Tennessee, had been sworn into state service December 12, put on a train to Nashville almost immediately, and inducted into the Confederate ranks on December 16.

Jack Campbell's military service had been brief and already marred by sadness and privation. While still at the Camp Maury mustering facility three miles north of Nashville, Campbell learned that his mother had fallen deathly ill, apparently from exposure to cold weather while dyeing jeans for his military uniform at an open-air kettle a couple of weeks earlier. He caught a train home to the little Fountain Creek community and managed to arrive before she "passed from time to eternity." A locally respected former justice of the peace who himself had battled sickliness since his mid-teens, Campbell had worked in the fields alongside his slaves partly for his health's sake. He was approaching his twenty-eighth birthday when he left his bereaved home to return to the regiment. "Under the circumstances, it [was] the hardest parting I had ever made," he wrote in his diary. "The old negroes who had nursed me in infancy seemed to be much affected."

On January 19, Campbell and the Forty-eighth had received their first marching orders. They trooped to the state capital to draw arms—"principally flint-lock muskets with but few bayonets, which caused much grumbling among the privates"—then were taken by steamboat to Clarksville. Three days later, the unit boarded a train for a forty-mile ride to the hamlet of Danville, where its members found only two Confederate companies and what was apparently the town's sole storekeeper already having "packed up his goods to save them from the Federals." On February 4, Campbell heard "the report of every cannon" in Heiman's half-hour exchange with the Union gunboats, and after dark the regiment got the order "to repair to Fort Henry at once . . .

> We embarked about ten o'clock, leaving our wagons and mules (which we had just received) . . . and several privates. We left a good many sick, who were in the Danville Hotel, which had been converted to a hospital as a military necessity. We arrived at Fort Henry a short time before day (Feb. 5th), without any sleep—the boat being so crowded. The night was very cold, and after a weary time we got the boat unloaded. Blundering about in the dark we turned into the quarters of the 10th Tenn. Reg't. At daybreak we carried our baggage out to the land side of the fort and stuck down in the mud; wood hard to get and nothing to eat.[9]

*   *   *

Just before midnight of February 4, Tilghman and Gilmer arrived back from
Fort Donelson escorted by three companies of the Ninth Tennessee Cavalry
battalion under Lieutenant Colonel George Gantt. On the morning of the
5th, Tilghman faced quick, hard choices. Reasoning that muddy roads
would prevent Grant's troops from getting artillery up the Fort Heiman
ridge, he moved the already-alerted Twenty-seventh Alabama and Fifteenth
Arkansas from Heiman to the east side of the river, leaving behind only
three companies of cavalry. Even with these additional troops, he was unable
to fill all of Fort Henry's rifle pits, so he distributed his men in the ones
nearest the fort and left the surrounding and enfilading hills undefended.
The fewer than one hundred artillerists remaining inside the walls were
drilled on handling the installation's guns.

Probably shortly after noon, Tilghman learned of the late-morning skirmish of Captain Milner's Confederate cavalry with the McClernand mounted reconnoitering party. One Confederate and one Federal had been killed
by the time Milner's men drove the Union horsemen back onto supporting
infantry and then fell back. Possibly fearing these Federals were the vanguard of an impending infantry assault, Tilghman gathered battalions of five
companies each of the Tenth Tennessee and Fourth Mississippi infantries
and, along with fifty cavalrymen, led them to the skirmish site. By the time
they arrived, the Union force had gone, and by late afternoon Tilghman returned to the fort after reinforcing the infantry companies in the trenches
covering the Bailey's Ferry road.

Toward evening of the 5th, the Thirtieth and Fiftieth Tennessee infantry
at Fort Donelson, about seven hundred fifty men with two cannons, were ordered west to Kirkman's Furnace halfway out the Dover road toward Fort
Henry. Their purpose was to give the Henry troops a small reserve for use in
the battle that was all too obviously imminent.[10]

After dark, it began to rain. Actually, it began to pour. Jack Campbell and
the men of the Forty-eighth Tennessee already had endured their sleepless
night on the steamboat from Danville, which had been followed by an event-
ful day: a late-morning deployment into line of battle to repel an assault that
never came, then the series of incoming shells fired by the gunboats. The
latter did no damage, Campbell reported in his diary, but they made an impression: "This was my first view of an exploding shell, which rendered me
very sensible of my unhealthy location." Well into the afternoon, with "no
further prospect of a fight presenting itself," the men of the Forty-eighth
were allowed to prepare a tardy mid-day meal, and the coming of darkness
sent them "turn[ing] in early, being worn out with loss of rest and sleep." It

was to be an interrupted slumber. The soldiers had hardly gotten comfort-
able before, around 8 p.m., "the long roll was beat" and they "jumped into
our clothes and turned out in the rain. It proved a false alarm."

By morning of the 6th, the seasonal rise of the river had been augmented
by the night's torrents. The Tennessee was flooding dangerously as overwhelming numbers of Federals visibly prepared a land-and-water assault that
appeared ready to begin at any moment. With the raging river now pummeling Henry's parapets and the surrounding backwaters widening across what
had been dry land, Tilghman realized that Fort Henry had no chance.

"I argued thus," he wrote soon afterward. "Fort Donelson might possibly
be held, if properly re-enforced, even if Fort Henry should fall; but the re-
verse of this proposition was not true. The force at Henry was necessary to
aid Fort Donelson."

To that end, he pulled his infantrymen out of their water-logged trenches
and ordered Colonel Heiman and all the troops except Taylor's artillerymen
further from the fort, onto the lower road toward Fort Donelson.

When this directive came, Jack Campbell and the men of the Forty-eighth
were concerning themselves with the mid-day meal: "Some had just eat their
dinners, some had just prepared theirs, and others were cooking." Tilghman's order, as communicated to Campbell's unit, was "to withdraw from
the range of the fleet and prepare to meet the land forces." They hurried to
the intersection of the southernmost Fort Donelson road, where they were
halted, out of shooting range of the boats.

Tilghman's aim was to have his little band of artillerymen inside the walls
buy the infantry time to escape. Planning to join the retreat himself at the
last moment, he waited grimly for the Federals' metal-covered boats to
round Panther Island again and enter the optimal range of his guns.[11]

That did not take long. Heavy plumes of black smoke began rising downriver, and at 11 a.m., one by one, seven gunboats emerged from behind the
island. Two miles downstream from the Fort, they formed their line of battle,
the ominously black ironclads in front.[12]

The waiting was over.

February 6, Late Morning
Attack

Soon after arriving on the east bank of the Tennessee on the morning of February 4, McClernand had sent a battery and two infantry regiments to seize the southbound road to Fort Henry where it crossed Panther Creek. Around dusk on the 5th, his men were rejoined by the bulk of his mounted troops, the Fourth Illinois Cavalry, arriving from their laborious journey overland, and later that night McClernand received final orders from Grant regarding the attack: " . . . move at 11 o'clock a.m. tomorrow . . . and take position on the roads from Fort Henry, Fort Donelson, and Dover. It will be the special duty of this command to prevent all re-enforcements to Fort Henry or escapes from it." Grant assigned Smith the potentially harder job of taking the higher ridge fortifications across the river.

Then came the torrential overnight downpour. McClernand's men—"without tents and ill prepared for exposure," McClernand reported—were soaked and shivering on the morning of the 6th as they faced the daunting tramp to cut off Fort Henry. The short time Foote's gunboats needed to take up their attack positions in the river was nowhere near sufficient for the soldiers to have to march to theirs, crossing flooded creeks and in some places even cutting new roads through marshy lowland. McClernand later wrote that the distance by river was half the length of the land route. A man in ranks later recalled that the infantry's struggles were multiplied by the accompanying light artillery. Every time its pieces sank in the mire, the infantrymen had to lay down their rifles, divest themselves of their packs, and push the guns out.

The First Division had covered four miles and was approaching the northernmost of the two roads from Henry to Fort Donelson—the shorter so-called Telegraph Road that the Confederates had cut through the woods to string communication wire between the forts—when, as McClernand would report, "the firing of our gunboats . . . [was] distinctly heard by my men."

His Federals were still two miles from Henry.[1]

*   *   *

The night's deluge had made a miserable prelude not only for Grant's soldiers, but also for Foote's crewmen. They had to keep their vessels' steam
power up and both anchors down to prevent being swept downstream by the
rising current and its heavy, dangerous burden of driftwood, fence rails, lumber, and large uprooted trees, their destructive power multiplied by the
force of a flood further swollen by the night's torrents. For the sailors, however, the downpour also would prove advantageous. Commander Henry
Walke of the gunboat *Carondelet* later recalled that when the 6th "dawned
mild and cheering, with a light breeze sufficient to clear away the smoke"
from shells and the gunboats' smokestacks, the men aboard the boats "saw a
large number of white objects which through the fog looked like polar bears
coming down the stream."

These were the "torpedo" mines laboriously laid by Confederates around
Panther Island. Mostly undiscovered by Phelps's crews on the 5th, they had
been dislodged by the rising water. The raging river current, or maybe just
inferior construction, had caused them to leak, fouling their explosive
charges, but Foote's sailors could not know that at the time. Had the torpedoes remained undisturbed by the river or been loosed by it before dawn,
"some of them would surely have exploded near or under our vessels,"
Walke would write. He added that his men, whose zeal had been subdued
somewhat by their night-long, rain-pelted effort to prevent the current from
dragging *Carondelet* downstream, viewed the dislodging of the torpedoes "as
providential and a presage of victory."[2]

They were hardly cocky, though. When Foote, at 10:20 a.m., gave the order for the gunboats to make their final preparations for battle, then at
10:50 directed them to begin steaming from the river moorings beside Mc-
Clernand's camp to their pre-attack positions behind the cover of the island,
the sailors seemed to realize that what they were about to attempt was unprecedented and momentous. Never in naval history had ironclad gunboats
attacked a riverbank fortress.

Against the river's fierce current, the slow gunboats were even slower, and
Foote was in no hurry in any case, knowing that the infantrymen faced
formidable obstacles of water and mud in reaching their assault position.

"As we slowly passed up this narrow stream," Walke wrote, "not a sound
could be heard nor a moving object seen in the dense woods which over-
hung the dark and swollen river. The gun-crews of the *Carondelet* stood silent
at their posts, impressed with the serious and important character of the service before them. About noon the fort and the Confederate flag came sud-

denly into view, the barracks, the new earthworks, and the great guns well manned."

Fort Henry proper, covering three acres, sat at the end of a straight mile and a quarter run of the Tennessee south of Panther. The sailors could see the river already inundating two of the lower guns along the installation's five-sided, eight-foot, earthen parapet, part of which boasted a thickness of fourteen feet. Outside the wall, water virtually islanded the place. Federal accounts of that morning make no mention of the fort's moat, doubtless because it had vanished beneath the flood. The river's rise had made a shallow lake between the parapet and the line of rifle pits several hundred yards north along the river, as well as other trenches to the east on the Fort Donelson roads.

In silence, the gunboats rounded Panther Island and sluggishly steamed to positions that put the four ironclads—*Cincinnati, Carondelet, Essex,* and *St. Louis*—a half-mile in front of the more vulnerable timber-clads *Conestoga, Lexington,* and *Tyler.*

Watching the fort grow nearer across the turbulent water, many a crewman must have remembered Foote's words as he inspected the gunboats one by one beginning the previous afternoon. Aboard each, he offered his customary prayer and addressed officers and crew on how to act once the firing began. "It is particularly necessary that all should keep cool," his instructions had run. "Do not attempt rapid firing, but take deliberate aim. Rapid firing wastes ammunition, heats the guns, throws away shot in their wild range, and encourages the enemy with a fire which proves to be ineffectual." With New England thrift and deep consciousness of the thousand little details with which he and his predecessor, Commodore Rodgers, had had to grapple to get this fleet built and fitted out, he also admonished the gunners to remember that each shot fired would "cost the government about eight dollars.

"Get the worth of your money," he added.[3]

A naval contemporary would recall that Foote "had more of the bulldog than any man I ever knew . . . [W]hen the fighting came . . . he was in his element—he liked it." But he went into it spiritually prepared. He later would remember rising on the morning of the 6th having "agonized" throughout the night "in prayer for victory." When his gunboat commanders came aboard the *Cincinnati* around 10 a.m. for final instructions, he had given each some encouraging words, a handshake, and another prayer for the protection of God.[4]

Settling into position four abreast south of Panther Island, the ironclads began moving toward the fort. The infantry was not to be seen on either side of the river, as Foote had warned Grant it would not be. But Foote's blood was up. He decided to do what he also had told Grant: he would take Fort Henry on his own. At 12:30 p.m. by his own watch, *Cincinnati* availed herself of her flagship status and broke the hush, launching the first shell at Fort Henry from a mile away. On the Tennessee's west bank, men of Smith's division, near enough to the river to hear, if not see, as they struggled to reach Fort Heiman, cheered so loudly at the blast that they could be heard a half-mile away.

The battle was on.[5]

*   *   *

Following *Cincinnati's* lead, the bow guns of *Carondelet, St. Louis,* and *Essex* opened up. *Conestoga, Lexington,* and *Tyler,* ordered to hang back because of their inferior armor, hugged the river's east bank and lobbed longer-range shells. For a time, the gunboats did all the firing. The fort's weapons stayed silent until the Federals moved a hundred or so yards closer, which they did at a snail's pace, laboring against the current. For millennia, success at naval warfare had depended on bringing maximum firepower onto targets from ranges at which there was the least chance of missing, and although—as the Confederates already had discovered—the boats' guns well outranged those of the fort, Foote trusted in the age-old conventional wisdom and steamed straight for Henry's walls.

Because *Cincinnati* flew the banner of the flag-officer, it attracted the most Confederate fire. One shot struck the pilothouse with such force that Foote himself had the wind knocked out of him for several minutes. But he kept coming, and the damage incurred to both the enemy and to Foote's own vessels was daunting. Captain Walke on *Carondelet* watched shots from the boats tear holes in Henry's parapet and throw earth "in great heaps over the enemy's guns," but he also saw Confederate shells strike the sides of the gunboats and break and scatter the iron-plating "as if it had been putty." The Federal boats greatly overmatched the Confederate firepower, and their job was simplified by the unexpected absence of opposing shells from Fort Heiman on the heights across the river. But the fort's fire was devastatingly accurate. It penetrated the armored openings around the muzzles of the cannons and drew blood in ghastly fashion.[6]

Porter's ill-starred *Essex,* seemingly fated for three days to bear the brunt of Foote's burden at Henry, saw its nine-inch guns fire seventy-two shots before, around 1:15 p.m., a Henry shell came through a gun-opening and took off the head of Acting Master's Mate S. B. Brittan, whose brains spattered the man beside him. The shell went on to strike the middle boiler, and steam

HENRY WALKE

and scalding water spewed wildly. Porter himself was badly burned before he threw himself out another gun-opening, where Seaman John Walker, hanging onto the side of the boat, caught his commander by the waist and kept him from plummeting into the surging, coffee-colored river. James Laning, saved by having been ordered aft just moments earlier, turned to see "a crowd of men rushing" after him. Told that an enemy shell had blown away the steam-pipe, he ran astern and looked out a porthole to see many of his fellow crewmen trying to keep from drowning in the surging current. Aboard ship, "many others were writhing in their last agony.

As soon as the scalding steam would admit, the forward gun-deck was explored. The pilots, who were both in the pilot-house, were scalded to death. Marshall Ford, who was steering when the explosion took place, was found at

LEW WALLACE

his post at the wheel, standing erect, his left hand holding the spoke and his right hand grasping the signal-bell rope. A seaman named James Coffey, who was shot-man to the No. 2 gun, was on his knees, in the act of taking a shell from the box to be passed to the loader. The escaping steam and hot water had struck him square in the face . . . 7

Out of control, *Essex* drifted downstream until it was thrown a line and towed out of range by a Federal tugboat whose crew had been viewing the conflict and blowing a whistle every time a Union shot appeared telling.

The rest of the gunboats kept moving and firing. They had closed to within six hundred yards of the fort's walls and had had to lower their guns' elevation from seven degrees to three. Foote's *Cincinnati* had her smokestacks and "after-cabin . . . completely riddled." One crewman had been killed and nine more wounded, and the Confederate fire had put two of her guns out of action. From the deck of the *Carondelet*, Walke saw one Confederate shell strike *Cincinnati* with "the effect . . . of a thunder-bolt, ripping her side-timbers and scattering the splinters all over the vessel. She did not slacken her speed."

Carondelet herself was struck by thirty-two shots that smashed her chimneys, rear cabin, and all of her lifeboats. Early on, she had fallen out of her place in the line of ironclads when her pilot, Daniel Weaver, rang the wrong bell in the engine-room, then found that the boat's bell lines had somehow gotten reversed. Figuring out the problem, Weaver rang the other bell and *Carondelet*, which had backed up about half her length, moved back into line. Because of the formation, the officer over her starboard gun could not bring it to bear on the fort and asked for permission to shoot at a couple of steamboats that were visible fleeing from Henry heading upriver. He got clearance and sent a shell through the upper cabin of one of these. The target was later discovered to be a hospital vessel whose flag was out of sight, but the shot hurt no one.

Of all the ironclads, *St. Louis* was luckiest, taking seven hits and suffering no casualties. The timber-clads were untouched by Confederate fire.[8]

Ashore, the Union infantrymen could only hear the din and wonder what it meant. McClernand's troops, accompanied by Grant, were still battling not Confederates but mud that was often half a leg deep and sometimes submerged in floodwaters. Their comrades on the west bank were no better informed on the progress of the battle, although they felt its effects. When the gunboats got between Smith's men and the fort, some of the Confederate shells from "over-elevated" guns "sailed roaring and screaming into the tree-tops" above them, "darkening the air with fragments of limbs," Lew Wallace would remember. He would add that "the effect was to energize everybody on the march."

The mingled firing of the boats and the fort, Wallace recalled, was "an almost unintermittent thunder." It was not only "indescribably awful" but rife with frustrating suspense."[W]e could see nothing of the fight on the river. [T]o us hastening through the woods, it was all smoke, sound, and fury. The most we could assure ourselves was that somebody was getting hurt." [9]

Assailed and Assailants, Early Afternoon

DESPITE THE ACCURACY of the Confederate gunners, the situation inside the fort was deteriorating quickly.

The first fire from the front line of gunboats as they came four abreast in mid-river above Panther Island was "one broad and leaping sheet of flame," artillerist Jesse Taylor would remember. Men of both sides recalled that initially the fire of the fort seemed more accurate than that of the gunboats. But after the *Essex* was struck and disabled, a series of dismaying critical accidents befell the defenders. Their longest-range and most deadly weapon, the rifled twenty-four-pounder, blew up, killing or wounding every man serving it. Around the same time, the ten-inch columbiad's priming wire became stuck in the vent and rendered it useless. Federal shells blasted Henry's earthen walls with such force that they dislodged piles of dirt, throwing them over some of the Confederate guns and gunners. The remaining cannoneers "became very much discouraged when they saw the two heavy guns disabled, [and most of] the enemy's boats apparently uninjured and still drawing nearer and nearer," Gilmer reported. "Some of them even ceased to work the 32-pounder guns, under the belief that such shot were too light to produce any effect upon the iron-clad sides of the enemy's boats."[1]

Some of the gunboats, firing too high, rained destruction behind Fort Henry in the area where Tilghman had sent the entire garrison, except the artillerymen. "Our regiment being in the rear, shells fell around us very thick for a while," recalled Jack Campbell of the Forty-eighth Tennessee. Because of the gunboat fire the infantrymen of Lieutenant Colonel McGavock's Tenth Tennessee "moved our position from place to place," eventually reaching the intersection of the Fort Donelson road and the longer, more southern route leading to Dover. This intersection was guarded by several pieces of Confederate light artillery, and the infantrymen began to assemble around these guns. Cavalry then hurried in with word that Union infantry were a half-mile away and "approaching in large force." The Confederates dug in on both sides of the cannons, and McGavock sent a messenger into the fort to tell Heiman he was about to be confronted with a large enemy force. He asked for instructions.[2]

Inside Henry, things were only getting worse, with "the gunboats nearing all the time, their point-blank range telling fearfully upon the fort," Heiman later wrote. At 1:10 p.m., only four of the fort's guns were still operating—which, Tilghman claimed, was just as well, since so many of his gunners were "so completely broken down . . . [that] I could not well have worked a greater number." At 1:30 p.m., Tilghman tore off his coat, ran to a thirty-two-pounder cannon, and began firing it himself. He later wrote that he delivered two shots on the *Cincinnati*, "which had the effect to check a movement intended to enfilade the only guns now left to me." But Tilghman and his men could only delay the inevitable. Engineer Gilmer told Heiman that it was "evident the fort could not hold out much longer" and asked Heiman, as second in command, to prevail on Tilghman to surrender. Further resistance could only cost more lives, he argued. Heiman agreed with Gilmer's assessment but refused to approach Tilghman. He said the decision was Tilghman's to make without interference.

Other officers, including Gilmer, then decided not to be so deferential. They took it upon themselves to suggest surrender to Tilghman. "I shall not give up the work," the general answered. Tilghman was well aware that the fort was doomed, but he had strategic reasons to hold out as long as possible. "Every moment, I knew, was of vast importance to those retreating [to] Fort Donelson," he later explained in his report, "and I declined, hoping to find men enough at hand to continue a while longer the fire now so destructive to the enemy."

Tilghman then told his concerned subordinates that he had not "yet" lost a lot of men, then asked why so many of their guns were not firing. According to Heiman, the other officers replied "that several of the men were killed, many wounded, and all the rest exhausted, and that we had no men to relieve them." Tilghman ordered fifty infantrymen sent in from the units outside the walls to help the weary cannoneers, but so few personnel were left that nobody could be found to carry the message. Heiman decided to take it himself and hurried out of the fort's disintegrating walls.[3]

Tilghman finally gave in, but not everybody knew it at first. Colonel Milton Haynes, chief of Tennessee's artillery corps, was helping work one of the last serviceable guns when he heard someone shout, "Cease firing!" He swiftly countermanded the order, assuming it was bogus, but a moment later, at 1:50 p.m., he was aiming his gun to fire it again when a nearby cannoneer yelled, "Look, someone has raised a white flag!" Haynes, certain that the act was unauthorized "as such an order ought to have been given through me as chief of artillery," commanded the gunner to go tear it down and shoot the

man responsible. But as the gunner quickly discovered, it was Tilghman himself waving the flag from the parapet. Upon hearing this news, Haynes hurried to Tilghman to verify the white flag and was quickly assured of its au-
thenticity.

Tilghman later described his flag-waving as an "experiment," a bid for a
truce period during which he hoped to buy yet a little more time for the retreat to Fort Donelson. Tilghman explained to Haynes that the garrison now
hardly had enough able-bodied people to man two guns. But the white flag
did not have its intended effect: it was apparently obscured by the battle
smoke, and the gunboats' barrage continued. Tilghman then leaped back
down from the parapet and "continued the fire" from the two guns "for five
minutes" before finally acceding to the requests of his subordinates that he
give up the fight.

Haynes, perhaps still angry that he had not been consulted, refused to be
part of the surrender. Despite the fact that he was "chief of artillery" and had
been supervising much of the handling of the guns, he suddenly claimed he
was there only as consultant to Tilghman. He shook hands with the general
and hurried from the fort.[4]

Tilghman quickly ordered Captain Taylor to haul down the Confederate
flag from a listing, shell-blasted flagstaff. The captain recruited an orderly
sergeant to help and climbed with the noncom to a viewpoint he later described as "exciting and striking.

> At our feet the fort with her few remaining guns was sullenly hurling . . . harm-
> less shot against the sides of the gunboats, which, now apparently within two
> hundred yards of the fort, were in perfect security and with the coolness and
> precision of target practice sweeping the entire fort; to the north and west, on
> both sides of the river, were hosts of "blue coats," anxious and interested spec-
> tators, while to the east the feeble forces of the Confederacy could be seen
> making their weary way toward Donelson.
>
> On the morning of the attack, we were sure that the February rise of the
> Tennessee had come; when the action began, the lower part of the fort was al-
> ready flooded, and when the colors were hauled down, the water was waist-
> deep there . . . [5]

Heiman had yet to reach his infantrymen when the firing ceased, and he
turned and rushed back to Tilghman "for further orders." But Heiman had
not been inside the fort when the colors came down, Tilghman explained,
and was therefore not included in the surrender. Tilghman ordered him to
get out at once and lead the march to Donelson.

That trek was already well underway. The messenger whom McGavock had sent into the fort to find Heiman had returned with news of the surrender, and McGavock had started the column hurrying eastward. Soon the procession was joined by Haynes, who after leaving the fort had walked along the river until he found a stable. There, he appropriated a horse with neither saddle nor bridle. "[M]ounting him," he later wrote, "I rode by the fort and passed up the bank of the river and swam the sheet of backwater a mile above the fort." Soon afterward, he caught up with the Confederate column.[6]

* * *

Aboard *Cincinnati*, Foote saw Fort Henry's flag descend, but he did not see it come completely down. Suspecting treachery, he ordered the boats to cease fire and waited. Then he saw two Confederate officers in a small boat leaving the fort, which now had become so awash in the rising river that it might as well have been a sinking ship. A quarter-mile of water "running like a mill-race" lay between its foundering walls and its outer trench line. Approaching the flagship, the two Confederate officers—acting adjutant W. L. McConnico and captain of engineers Charles Hayden—hailed the vessel and announced that General Tilghman wished to speak to Flag-Officer Foote.

Suddenly the crew of the *Cincinnati* understood the visit's significance. The sailors burst forth with a cheer so uproarious that Foote himself "had to run among them & knock them on the head to restore order." Even a doctor joined in. "The surgeon hollered and howled & I told him that he ought to be ashamed of himself."

Foote swiftly dispatched Commander Stembel of *Cincinnati* and Lieutenant Phelps of *Conestoga* in a cutter to enter the fort, raise the Union flag, and tell Tilghman that Foote would meet him aboard the gunboat. The Stars and Stripes soon fluttered from Henry's flagstaff, and Stembel brought Tilghman to the flagship. Phelps stayed behind inside the fort to establish Federal authority.[7]

Foote later informed a friend that Tilghman arrived aboard *Cincinnati* in a shattered state. Perhaps the Confederate commander was regretting his heat-of-the-moment decision to stick by the Henry guns rather than retreat with the troops to Donelson as he originally planned. According to the secondhand Foote account, Tilghman wrung his hands and despaired over his reputation, which he described as "gone forever."

"General, there is no reason that you should feel thus," responded Foote, who knew nothing of his foe's prior plan. "More than two-thirds of your [guns are] disabled, while I have lost less than one-third of mine. To continue the action would only involve a needless sacrifice of life, and, under the circumstances, you have done right in surrendering. I shall always be ready to testify that you defended your post like a brave man."[8]

Foote then noted that his dinner was nearly ready, invited Tilghman to share it, and they went together into the cabin to Foote's table. Behind them on deck they left at least one reporter. Although the tight security Grant had established surrounding the onset of the campaign had forced several reporters "to display some agility in overtaking" the expedition, representatives of the New York Times, the New York Tribune, the St. Louis Republican, and at least one Chicago paper had managed to catch up. When a Chicago reporter aboard Cincinnati asked Tilghman how he spelled his name, the general, probably still smarting from his sense of shame, arrogantly responded that he did "not desire to have my name appear in this matter in any newspaper connection whatever. If General Grant sees fit to use it in his official dispatches, I have no objection, Sir; but I do not wish to have it in the newspapers."[9]

Tilghman's demand was swiftly and memorably rejected. Perhaps in reaction to Tilghman's brusqueness toward the press, or perhaps merely expressing his own partisan glee at the Federal triumph, one of the newsmen quoted Tilghman—by name—as cavalierly telling Foote that he was "glad to surrender to so gallant an officer as you." The journalist then went on to quote Foote as boorishly replying: "You do perfectly right, sir, in surrendering, but you should have blown my boat out of the water before I would have surrendered to you." The story is almost certainly untrue: Commander Walke of Carondelet later claimed to have been standing near the captive and captor and wrote that he heard nothing of the sort, adding that Foote "was too much of a gentleman to say anything calculated to wound the feelings of an officer who had defended his post with signal courage and fidelity." In his own report, Tilghman described Foote's behavior as "graceful." Like Tilghman, Foote complimented his foe in his report to Navy Secretary Welles. Fort Henry, he wrote, "was defended with the most determined gallantry by General Tilghman, worthy of a better cause."

*   *   *

As the surrender took place aboard the Cincinnati, Smith's men across the river had to guess at what was happening. The west bank commander and Lew Wallace were riding alongside each other amidst their muddy, struggling infantrymen when, according to Wallace's recollection much later, Smith suddenly noticed that the firing had stopped. Then a courier from the advance unit rode back with news that Fort Heiman had been evacuated. It was undefended.

"How do you know?" Smith asked.

"I have been in," the soldier said.

"The devil!" Smith replied.

Smith then ordered Wallace ahead and up the ridge to take possession of the empty installation. Wallace rode onto the hill, over an earthen wall, and soon found himself confronted by a large, circular tent. Dismounting, he looked inside and, from a table piled with papers, persuaded himself he was in Colonel Heiman's erstwhile headquarters. In an adjoining open-sided second tent, he found a still-warm kettle containing a large hunk of nicely cooked pork, a pot of coffee, a pone of cornbread, and a mess-chest of condiments. The seeming feast had apparently been prepared by the cavalrymen who were the last Confederate tenants after the infantry's withdrawal the day before.

Wallace took possession and invited his commander to join him in a meal. Before they ate, though, they looked around the rest of the facility and found that, "though unfinished, a stiff fight could have been made from it." Across the east side of the parapet, "within easy cannon range," stretched the river and, in the flood of its other side, Fort Henry. They saw the Stars and Stripes waving from Henry's sinking "stump of a flag-staff," the half-drowned parapets, and, "a few hundred yards off . . . the four black gunboats which had done the chore of conquest."

Then they returned to the pork.

"The absence of Colonel Heiman was never more sincerely regretted," Wallace's recollection of their dinner gallantly closed. "Out of a small contribution foraged from General Smith's right pistol-holster we drank the excellent German's health."[10]

*   *   *

By the time of the meeting on the *Cincinnati*, the retreat of the Confederate infantry had turned into a mad dash. Ordered to take the southernmost route eastward, the Dover road not yet reached by McClernand's men, "we had to go through one of the Ten[nessee] River bottoms which was full of mud and water," Lieutenant Colonel McGavock remembered in his diary. "The horses drawing the artillery were very indifferent. They fell and floundered and the wheels went down over the hubs in the mire. I ordered the drivers to take the horses out, spike the guns, and leave them."

While Colonel Heiman was still at the fort, McGavock had taken command of the column and was consequently near its front. At its other end

scrambled the Forty-eighth Tennessee, along with the Fifty-first Tennessee
and the Fifteenth Arkansas, and the view from the rear differed considerably
from McGavock's. Captain Jack Campbell saw the mired guns and took them
to have been "disgracefully abandoned . . . at the first creek" by "cannoneers
[who] cut out the horses and fled, pursuing a course well calculated to cre-
ate a panic." The prevailing mood got further stressed as the retreat encountered many more obstacles, the first being the creeks: "Crossing the streams,
which were very much swollen from recent rains, caus[ed] some confusion
in our retreating columns."[11]

Some of the mounted units, having the means to flee faster, did—at both
ends of the ragged procession.

"Gantt's [Ninth Tennessee] Cavalry acted most shamefully and disgracefully," McGavock recalled in his diary. "Instead of remaining in the rear to
protect the infantry, they rushed by us, some without their hats and . . . all
evidently panic stricken. I got in front of them and endeavored to stop them,
but my efforts were to no avail. On, on they went, and I lost sight of them entirely." According to Jack Campbell, Gantt's cavalry never took up a rearguard position. It "was . . . in front and some Ala. cavalry near the rear,"
Campbell's diary reports.

Campbell's delicate health had been severely challenged by nearly two
weeks of cold rains since the Forty-eighth arrived on the banks of the Tennessee and was further tried by two days of sleep deprivation in moving from
Danville to Fort Henry. Campbell and four other members of his company,
along with a minister named Gillam from another company, had fallen behind their regiment because they were unwell. They caught up, however,
when the rest of the unit, learning that the Union cavalry was on their heels,
halted and formed a line of battle on a steep hillside. The nervous officers
then decided not to wait for the Federals to arrive and instead took up the
retreat again. At that point, the Alabama cavalry, which Campbell said
should have been acting as rearguard, began deserting its post in similar
fashion to Gantt's.

Col. Hughes of Ala., (the only field officer I saw after the retreat began) rode
up to the Ala. cavalry and commanded them for God's sake to halt and protect
the infantry. By riding along with them for fifty yards and pleading with them,
he finally halted them. In a few minutes the enemy's cavalry came up and fired
upon our rear. The Ala. cavalry, after firing, came tearing by as though a thousand of the enemy were upon them, running over some of our men.

My comrades and myself, being behind the regiment, broke down, and
knowing that if we remained in the road the [Federal] cavalry would be certain
to kill us or take us prisoners, went up a hollow into a gorge on the side of the

hill and lay down to rest. By this time some eighteen of us had gotten together, all of the number having their arms. As we lay there we could hear distinctly the beating of drums at Ft. Henry, which we afterwards were told was seven miles away.[12]

The absence of the skedaddled Alabama horsemen was quickly felt. Sometime during the first half of the retreat, Heiman overtook McGavock and other officers leading the withdrawal; Heiman reported it occurred three miles from Henry, but Campbell never saw him. Wherever it was, Heiman told McGavock and the others with the lead units that the rear of the column had been attacked by Union cavalry. Portions of the Fifteenth Arkansas and the Alabama battalion had returned the Federal fire "handsomely," he added, but not before an Arkansas major and an Alabama captain were surrounded and captured. Heiman wrote that he was forced to draw up "the whole force in line of battle" but that, a half-hour later, enough of a semblance of order had been restored for the column to move on again. Heiman reported that they continued to be hounded with diminishing vigor until sunset. [13]

Their pursuers were members of an element of the Fourth Illinois Cavalry. The Illinoisans reported charging the rear of the Confederate column for the first time when it was still exiting Henry's outer defense lines. They then chased the Confederate troops "several miles and until nightfall and, successively overtaking [its] rear guards of cavalry and infantry, quickly dispersed them," McClernand reported. He added that the Federals killed one Confederate, captured thirty-eight, and recovered six abandoned guns along with "a large number of different kinds of small-arms, knapsacks, blankets, animals; in short, anything calculated to impede [their] flight . . ."[14]

Victors and Vanquished, February 6

Late Afternoon and Evening

INSIDE FORT HENRY'S WALLS, some of the Federals got their first look at a fresh battlefield. Its destruction would represent hardly a drop in the buckets of blood soon to hemorrhage in the western theatre, but the sight was nonetheless sobering.

"Although the officers and crews of the gun-boats gave three hearty cheers [at the surrender]," wrote *Carondelet* Commander Walke, "the first inside view of the fort sufficed to suppress every feeling of exultation." They saw a Confederate surgeon laboring "with his coat off to relieve and save the wounded . . . [O]n every side the blood of the dead and wounded was intermingled with the earth and their instruments of war. Their largest gun . . . was dismounted and filled with earth; the carriage of another was broken to pieces and two dead men lay near it, almost covered with heaps of earth; a rifled gun had burst, throwing its mangled gunners into the water."

The Seventh Iowa's Colonel J. G. Lauman wrote that "the killed in the Fort" were "torn all to pieces," and surgeon John Brinton, who did not arrive until the next day, found Henry still a "dreadful sight" of overthrown cannon, "some with their muzzles pointing in the air, their carriages . . . broken and stained with blood. Here and there, too, were masses of human flesh and hair adhering to the broken timbers" that, with interlaced hickory lathing, had held the earthen walls in place. Colonel W. H. L. Wallace wrote Ann Wallace that the effect of the gunboat fire on the fortifications had been "terrible. Guns dismantled, earthworks torn up and the evidence of carnage meet the eye on every hand."

W. H. L. Wallace's Second Brigade had still been "some three or four miles out, on the march, when the cannonading ceased," Wallace informed Ann. "It . . . was tremendous . . . The enemy seemed to have been seized with a panic, and the whole body . . . left, leaving one artillery company in the fort." Similarly, when Lauman's Iowans and Hoosiers arrived, they "found the enemy had run away and left everything behind. The bread baking in the ovens and meat cooking. We should have bag'd the whole force."[1]

Grant was embarrassed that they had not done so—and that the gunboats had won what there was of this fight on their own. Grant did not even reach the fort until after 3 p.m., at least a half-hour after the surrender, at which time the facility was turned over to him by Foote's people. The riverine navy was of course under the overall command of the army, so the victory ultimately could be counted as Grant's, but Foote had fulfilled his pre-fight prediction that the gunboats would take Henry before the troops reached the battlefield.

That afternoon and evening, the unkempt little man in the blue brigadier general's coat tallied the captured and the casualties—ninety-four prisoners, a small but indefinite number of Confederates killed, and sixteen wounded or missing. Foote would report to Secretary of the Navy Gideon Welles that in addition to Tilghman and his staff he had captured sixty or seventy men in the fort and another sixty sick Confederates on a hospital boat. Grant reported a Federal total killed, wounded, or missing of about forty, most of them scalded on the *Essex*. This approximation may, like his earlier drastic downplaying of his losses at Belmont, have been intentionally low, or perhaps it was based on incomplete figures. Tilghman later wrote that the next morning he, as a captive, heard "the total casualties of the enemy . . . stated in my presence . . . to be 73 . . . ."

Whatever the exact sum, it was not enough to give Grant pause. He had seen much higher numbers at Belmont and in Mexico, and he had work to do. Immediately after arriving at the fort, he began dispatching a flurry of telegrams, letters, and orders. Unlike most commanders, he tended to write out—rather than dictate or delegate—his communications, committing them to paper in succinct, straightforward terms marred only by haphazard spelling.[2]

His first telegram was to his commander, and it hinted at the apprehension that had surely infected him in the face of Halleck's obvious disdain and the Kountz charges that now had been piled atop it. Grant still had not personally led his army into battle in a way that could guarantee him a future.

"Fort Henry is ours," he began the wire to Halleck. Mentioning that the fort had surrendered to Foote's gunboats before the infantry could arrive, he hurried on to lines that must have given his cautious commander a momentary shiver: " . . . I shall take and destroy Fort Donaldso[n] [sic] on the eighth and return to Fort Henry with the forces employed unless it looks feasible to occupy that place with a small force that could retreat easily to the main body. I shall regard it more in the light of an advance grand guard than as a permanent post."

Taking and destroying Fort Donelson would fulfill Grant's compelling need to stamp his own name, rather than Foote's, on a noteworthy military victory. The rest of the sentence—the implied promise to return swiftly to Fort Henry—might have been intended to mollify the deep defensive instincts in Halleck, but the offhand attitude of the entire dispatch indicates how itchy Grant remained to prove himself and how increased pressure only increased the aggressiveness of his nature. Union commanders knew almost nothing about Fort Donelson (even how to spell it) at the time. In contrast to Fort Henry, which the gunboats had regularly scouted beforehand, Donelson had been less accessible to river-borne reconnaissance. The Confederates had sunk chain-linked trees in the Cumberland more than a mile north of it, blocking the channel.[3]

*   *   *

While Grant was writing to his commander, the vanquished Confederate troops were still floundering fearfully eastward. Lieutenant Colonel McGavock of the Tenth Tennessee confided to his diary that the erstwhile garrison was "fortunate" to have taken the southernmost and considerably longer route to Dover, "for if we had gone the regular Dover road we would have been cut to pieces . . . We marched at least twenty miles over very bad roads—and high creeks. In crossing some of the creeks the men had to go four abreast and hold each other up . . . with their cartridge boxes hung on their muskets to keep them dry."

Obviously referring to the rabble-like behavior of the cavalry, McGavock added that members of his regiment "never broke lines during their long march" and were not to blame for the abundant evidence of panic in their wake. To the contrary, "they picked up many [small arms] left by others and brought them safely to Ft Donelson. Some of them had as many as half doz [small arms], some swords, and some overcoats, etc." He said they "reached Ft Donelson about 12 oc at night."[4]

These comparatively organized elements, though, seem to have been just members of the Tenth Tennessee. McGavock's regiment was both preceded and followed by many other Confederates who no longer stood on the ceremony of unit designation.

One of the many disorderly groups, Captain Jack Campbell of the Forty-eighth Tennessee and his fellow stragglers, ventured cautiously from their hiding place in the hillside gorge after dark. Finding the Federal cavalry gone, they "struck in a southerly direction and steered our course by the moon . . . [W]e traveled awhile and rested awhile, listening for the enemy—

drinking water from puddle holes in the road." Eventually, they encountered two runaway slaves "who at first aroused our suspicion that the enemy's advance guard was upon us." The Confederates pressed the slaves into
service, though, and were led by them "to a tavern ten miles from Ft. Henry." There they met a Confederate Major Clark and twenty men of the
Twenty-first Tennessee.

> We were very hungry and wished to get something to eat, but the Major insist-
> ed that if we waited to have something cooked we would be in danger, so we
> moved on, thinking ourselves able to resist a formidable attack . . . Two horses
> which were in the crowd put some of the sick men across a deep creek. We ar-
> rived within three miles of Ft. Donelson about one o'clock. Here Parson
> Gillam and I stopped, he being the only one of my crowd that remained with
> me. We lay down upon the Parson's blanket and covered [themselves] with my
> shawl, with our feet to the fire.

Throughout the night's tramp they had "passed several men sick, lying by
the roadside, but we could do nothing for them." Rising at dawn, still having
eaten nothing and walking on "sore feet and stiffened limbs," Campbell and
the reverend "wended our way slowly toward Ft. Donelson," which they managed to reach about 8 a.m. There they learned that Colonel Heiman had
caught up with the column "after we left the road" and that most of the men
had gotten to Donelson by 10 p.m. the previous evening, "nearly all wet to
their armpits." Despite contentions to the contrary in the reports of higher
officers, there appeared to Campbell to have been little system in the manner in which many of the Henry Confederates reached Donelson's safe
haven. As he put it:

"Scattering men from all the regiments outstripped all and went in without
any order, some two on a horse."5 To many, including higher-ups, scattering
and saving oneself without maintaining any order appeared preferable to capitulation. From Fort Donelson, a Confederate officer soon would write Tennessee's Governor Harris that "the blame attached to Tilghman is surrendering instead of leaving the flag flying and running with his men. The infantry
made their way with but little loss, to this place." Thinking better of the previous sentence, he added: "I mean but little loss of men—they lost all their
tents, clothing, blankets, etc., also all their Field Artillery, seven pieces." 6

Fort Henry's infantry had escaped Foote's ironclads, but the fire-breath-
ing river monsters had been so terrifying that the fugitives seemed little
ashamed of their panic. Breathing hard, they threw themselves down in Fort
Donelson's trenches and tried to recover their balance.

17

After-Battle Observations

AFTER FORT HENRY'S FALL, Grant made his headquarters on the steamboat *Tigress*, and there Confederate artillery Captain Jesse Taylor first saw the Federal expeditionary commander.

Taylor, formerly of the U.S. Navy, had been enjoying the company of two former messmates, the Foote gunboat commanders Shirk and Gwin, inside Henry's walls that first evening, and it may have been because of that association that he soon found himself in Grant's presence on the *Tigress*. The general struck Taylor as "a modest, amiable, kind-hearted but resolute man"—especially after what could have become an ugly incident. A Union officer came in complaining that he had been unable to find any documents in the captured fort having to do with Confederate troop strengths, and Taylor told him not to waste his time, that he himself had destroyed all papers having to do with that subject. The Federal officer became angry and threatened Taylor with punishment, but Grant mildly cut the officer off in mid-tirade.

"I would be very much surprised and mortified," Grant said, "if one of *my* subordinate officers should allow information which he could destroy to fall into the hands of the enemy."

But Grant apparently had little time for socializing. Mostly he seems to have worked at his desk. He had to dash off the wire to Halleck, then begin making plans for moving much of his army overland to Fort Donelson with just a single day to make all the necessary preparations. He also had to compose a much more substantial letter to Halleck's office and explain why he had not captured the Henry garrison. He was unable to schedule the attack before 11 a.m., he noted, because the last of his troops did not arrive until nearly midnight of the 5th. He would have preferred to delay the assault until the 7th so as to have Henry surrounded beforehand, he wrote, but information from Halleck, as well as from local sources, that Henry was being rapidly reinforced led him to think it was "imperatively necessary that the fort should be carried to-day." Rather oddly, he added that even if he had been able to surround the fort, "I do not now believe the result would have been any more satisfactory." He went on to repeat what he had already wired to Halleck—that he would take Fort Donelson on the 8th—and after two more paragraphs, he closed with a surely heartfelt sentiment: "Hoping that what has been done will meet the approval of the major-general commanding the department."

As usual, his last letter of the evening before blowing out his lantern was a brief note to his most frequent correspondent. Its terseness hints at more than weariness. Late into that victorious night, the punch Foote had beaten him to still smarted.

> *Fort Henry, Ten.*
> *Feb.y 6th 1862.*
>
> *Dear Julia,*
>
> *Fort Henry is taken and I am not hurt. This is news enough for to-night. I have been writing until my fingers are tired and therefore you must excuse haste and a bad pen.*
>
> *I have written to you every day so far and you cant expect long letters.*
>
> *Kiss the children for me.*
>
> *Ulys.[1]*

* * *

Grant was not the only nominally victorious Federal commander who was on edge that night. He was also not the only one who indicated it in an after-battle letter to his wife. Flag-Officer Foote was more forthcoming to Caroline Foote, though, than Grant was to Julia. Rushing back to Cairo aboard the crippled *Cincinnati* to overhaul it and the *Essex* and attend to myriad other tasks, Foote shared troubling truths with Caroline that concerned not just the hastily assembled, army-supplied crews of his undermanned ironclads but also the quality of construction of the vessels themselves.

"I never again will go out and fight half prepared," he told her. "Men were not exercised [in the duties they had to perform aboard his boats] & perfectly green. The rifle shots hissed like snakes. Tilghman, well he would have cut us all to pieces had his best rifle not burst & his 128-pounder [not] stopped in the vent." [2]

His battered ironclads had won the Henry laurels, but Foote had no time to rest on them. He had to leave for Cairo as soon as he finished the dinner with Tilghman. In addition to readying the two ironclads for combat again as quickly as possible, he had to rush completion of mortar-boats that President Lincoln, Assistant Secretary of War Thomas A. Scott, and most of the rest of the political and military establishments had been harrying him to finish. After Fort Henry, Foote himself was far more interested in their future role than he had been before. Having breasted the sting of Tilghman's cannoneers as he attacked head-on with guns that could only try to blast apart the walls of their fort, he saw the value of mortars that could lob shells over and inside those walls, injuring and killing the enemy gunners from above and behind, rather than simply trying to batter his way through many feet of earth and rock to get at them. Battering, he now saw, had nearly resulted in the defeat of his fleet by fewer than one hundred Confederate artillerymen. Half of the four ironclads he took into the battle had been put out of further action for weeks.

Tilghman, too, had noticed. In a report dated February 12, the captive Henry commander would note proudly that the fort's guns had disabled Foote's flagship [to such a degree that she had to be taken north. Confederate shells had passed clean through both her and *Essex*, smashing an *Essex* boiler and "completely riddl[ing]" the outer works of *Cincinnati.*

> The weak points in all their vessels were known to us, and the cool precision of our firing developed them, showing conclusively that this class of boats, though formidable, cannot stand the test of even 32-pounders, much less the 24-caliber rifled shot or that of the 10-inch columbiad. It should be remembered that these results were principally from no heavier metal than the ordinary 32-pounders, using solid shot, fired at point-blank, giving the vessels all the advantages of their peculiar structures, with planes meeting this fire at angles of 45 degrees. The immense area forming what may be called the roof is in every respect vulnerable to either a plunging fire from even 32-pounders, or a curved line of fire from heavy guns. In the latter case, shell should be used in preference to shot.

In Tilghman's opinion, Fort Henry had succumbed not so much to the gunboats as to predestined doom. Had he been reinforced with enough troops to man the outer works, "I might have made good the land defense on the east bank," he wrote. Dutifully, though, he refused to question why the reinforcements never came, "for I have entire confidence in the judgment of my commanding general."

Naming no names, he placed the primary responsibility where it belonged: on Daniel Donelson and Bushrod Johnson, who had selected and given final approval to the abysmal site. Had Halleck, Grant, and Foote only waited a few more days to attack, Tilghman noted, "with the river rising, one-third of the entire fortifications (already affected by it) would have been washed away, while the remaining portion of the works would have been [made] untenable by . . . the depth of water over the whole interior . . . "3

Donelson and Johnson might as well have laid out a fish pond.

18

Forrest, Early February

Hopkinsville

W<small>HEN</small> H<small>ENRY FELL</small>, Forrest and most of his Third Tennessee Cavalry were thirty-five crow-flight miles to the northeast at Hopkinsville, Kentucky. Scouting Buell's right flank, Forrest was trying to help Johnston's perplexed Bowling Green headquarters discern the aims of the Federal brain trust.

Commanding at Hopkinsville was Brigadier General Charles Clark, the officer who had so highly praised Forrest's conduct and courage during the bloody stampede of Federal cavalry at the village of Sacramento. A transplanted Ohioan who had taught school and then won election to the legislature in prewar Mississippi, Clark was a fellow Delta plantation owner and, like as not, a former customer of Forrest's slave business. He hailed from Bolivar County, just south of where Forrest had his 3,300 acres.[1]

As soon as he was pulled from the ranks and appointed lieutenant colonel back in July 1861, Forrest had begun spending large sums of personal money on weapons and other equipment for his regiment, which had come to Kentucky from Memphis with a wagon-train of supplies driven by some of his slaves. The procession halted first at Dover as construction was starting on the fort just north of that little hill town, but in November, needing better forage, Forrest moved to the more rolling terrain around Hopkinsville. There, cold weather arrived, and he housed himself and his men in semi-permanent "good floored tents and good beds," reflecting the age-old wisdom that winter was no time for major military operations.[2]

In his Hopkinsville tent slept not only his son, Private Willie Forrest, age fifteen, but also, in keeping with a widespread custom among officers of both armies at the time, his thirty-five-year-old wife. The former Mary Ann Montgomery claimed kinship to Revolutionary War general Richard Montgomery, a hero killed in a George Washington–ordered assault on Quebec in 1775. Born, like her husband, in Middle Tennessee, Mary Ann had seen her mother widowed early, but the daughter managed to attend a Nashville finishing school. As niece and early ward of a prominent minister, she remained faithful to her uncle's Cumberland Presbyterian denomination throughout the numerous violent episodes of her husband's tumultuous career.

By February of 1862, Forrest and his wife had passed the sixteenth anniversary of a marriage that had seen good times and hard ones, riches accumulated through the buying and selling of land and humanity, as well as the 1854 death of their second child. Six-year-old Fanny Forrest had been felled by dysentery from one of the many Memphis fevers. Fanny, born three years after their wedding, was the Forrests' second and final child. It is impossible to know if Mary Ann was unable to have more children or just did not want to, and how her husband (whose mother had had eleven by her first husband and more by the second) might have felt about this.[3]

Forrest's slave-buying entailed a lot of time away from home, which may well have put strains on the marriage. Perhaps other things did, too. A New York newspaper's sensational 1864 dispatch from Knoxville, Tennessee, would claim that the hated Confederate "butcher," by then infamous, had had a black mistress named Catharine by whom he fathered two children and whose standing with her master caused "domestic jars" in his home. There is only the most indirect possible evidence to support this overtly hostile claim. Memphis records show that the first slave Forrest bought individually, rather than in company with one of his several partners, was a seventeen-year-old young woman named Catharine, whom he purchased along with her four-month-old son. Whether this Catharine and the one in the New York newspaper story were one and the same seems unknowable, but if Forrest had indeed had a slave mistress the fact would hardly have been remarkable for a man of his position in the antebellum South.[4]

Whatever the truth of the New York newspaper claim, Forrest and women seem to have found each other interesting. Another Confederate general would come to note that Forrest was "very bright and entertaining" around them. His wit, much like the man himself, seems to have been edgy, plain-spoken, and strongly based in reality rather than frivolous whimsy. When an Alabama matron once inquired why his beard was black but his hair was turning gray, he answered that it might be because he tended to use his brains a little more than his jaws. But his fellow general noted that the courtesy and respect he showed women was marked, and that his most "careful" deference was reserved for Mary Ann. One of his staff officers described her as a "quiet, refined, Christian woman" who "could control him with a word" even amid his most towering rages. He had a marked reverence for piety and claimed to believe that her prayers and those of his mother had brought him unscathed through his many violent encounters.[5]

When news of Fort Henry's fall reached the Forrests' winter quarters, their conversation likely was pensive. Forrest and Mary Ann must each have sensed that his near future would hold more and greater violence than he had ever known. Like most of his fellow Confederates, he must also have been given pause by reports of the ironclads' swift and seemingly overwhelming triumph at Fort Henry. He knew a little about gunboats already. He and his cavalry had sought to ambush the Federal timber-clad *Conestoga* in November with negligible results. And the *Conestoga* had been protected only by thick wood; the ironclads were, well, *iron*clad.

Whatever Forrest thought that night, he was *un*like most of his Confederate superiors in the West (and, although he could not have known it, more like the Federal brigadier down at Fort Henry) in one all-important respect. He was not afraid.

Hungering for Victory
Grant and Halleck

IN THE WAKE of Foote's capture of Fort Henry, Grant's apparent problem—to stay in command long enough to personally win a victory that might
keep him there—remained. Despite his supervisory role in this successful
strike up the Tennessee River, he had done his reputation few favors in it.

His non-performance was not all his fault, and not just because rains had
flooded the countryside and made the attempt to surround the place so
strenuous and slow. By the time his men reached the fort it was already surrendered because, as the Seventh Iowa's commander noted in a letter
home, nobody had stayed around to defend it except Tilghman's handful of
artillerymen. Tilghman's decision that his cause was hopeless and that the
Confederates' fight between the rivers would have to be made at Donelson
was so last-minute that journalists who arrived at the scene on the heels of
McClernand's infantry thought the two or three thousand Confederate enlisted men had made up their minds to flee without Tilghman's permission.
The case for that view was circumstantial, but persuasive. As Jack Campbell
of the Forty-eighth Tennessee reported in his diary, the harried defenders
had been preparing and eating their mid-day meal when Foote suddenly assailed them. The hot food, cooking utensils, and other personal effects they
left behind made it appear that in the face of the fire of Foote's guns, and
the waters of the flooding river that threatened to isolate and inundate their
trenches, the Confederate infantrymen had left too suddenly and chaotical-
ly to have been participating in an organized withdrawal. According to the
New York Herald, they had left behind wall tents

> . . . all standing in complete order, with the camp-fires still blazing, the copper
> pots of stew for dinner boiling over them, and half-made biscuits in the pans
> beside them. Inside the tents everything was just as they had left it—pistols,
> shotguns, muskets, bowie knives, books, clothing, tables partially set for din-
> ner, letters half-opened, cards thrown down in the middle of a game . . .

It looked as though the men were out at guard mounting, expecting to return in ten minutes . . . [1]

The Confederate stampede relieved Grant's troops of some of the fault for not getting through the mud and flood north of Henry in time to capture the garrison. Grant tried to make the most of this point, even adding to his February 6 dispatch to Halleck's headquarters his expressed conjecture that the Confederates might have departed the previous evening, even though he surely saw—in the uneaten lunches, if nothing else— that most, if not all, had done no such thing. He obviously sensed that he needed to give his commander no more information damaging to himself than was absolutely necessary.

So he moved quickly to more positive matters, notifying Halleck on February 7 that the "amount of property left at Fort Henry is much larger than expected." To McClernand, he suggested not only that an officer be appointed to collect that property and "the large amount of ammunition picked up in the camps around Fort Henry and Fort Heiman," but also that horse or mule teams be sent to haul off the "abandoned wagons and plunder."

Reports in both the *Philadelphia Inquirer* and the *Cincinnati Gazette and Commercial* that Henry's little garrison had simply skedaddled in the face of the approach of Federal infantry helped prompt newspaper criticism of the army's failure to capture such a timorous foe. The correspondent for the *St. Louis Democrat*, whose editions were doubtless devoured at Halleck's headquarters in the Missouri city, wrote that "The general comment on the fight at this place is marked by much complaint of General Grant."[2]

Almost certainly, Grant's sense of personal failure at Fort Henry helped prompt his hasty dispatch to Halleck announcing that he intended to take Fort Donelson two days later. This plan significantly expanded the one he and Foote had originally proposed. On January 28, Grant had asked Halleck only for permission to "establish and hold a large camp" at Fort Henry. Suddenly given the go-ahead, he informed Halleck on January 31 that he would take Smith and McClernand along and assign one or the other "to command [at Henry] after my return." His initial wish to return quickly to Cairo from Fort Henry likely indicates three things at once. First, he may not have wanted Halleck to use his absence on the Tennessee River as reason to hand the command of the important Cairo district to someone else. Also, his mind may still have been on his months-long preoccupation with finding a way to attack the "Gibraltar" at Columbus, in which case he would have been reluctant to mire himself in a backwater operation on the Tennessee and give Halleck an opening to assign someone else to that bigger job. And he perhaps assumed that he could not be criticized by Halleck for handing over the proposed Fort Henry camp to a subordinate as venerable and trusted as Smith or as eminent as the voluble ex-congressman.

Halleck had never ordered Grant to attack Fort Donelson; he had not even hinted at such an idea to his subordinate. The St. Louis commander was indeed mulling a Donelson expedition, but on its leader's identity he was keeping his options open in the hope that Ethan Allen Hitchcock or somebody else could be rushed into command of the campaign before it moved past Henry. Halleck had wired his Louisville rival, Buell, on January 30 that he had ordered an immediate "advance of our troops on Fort Henry and Dover"—when actually he had ordered them only to Fort Henry—and three days later he went on to inform Buell that his plan was "to take and occupy Fort Henry and Dover (Donelson), and, if possible, cut the railroad from Columbus to Bowling Green." Both of these communications were probably more for effect in his escalating war of military one-upmanship with Buell than they were intended as aggressiveness against the Confederates.

In imagining any attack on Donelson, Halleck was overriding his own cautious essence. Almost certainly, he was not envisioning the capture of both forts at one blow. One of his foremost military precepts was that any move must be made with utmost deliberateness and only after methodical preparation. Another was that such a move must be made in overwhelming numbers. A full-scale attack in the region of the rivers "should not be attempted with . . . less than 60,000 men," he had written McClellan on January 20.

But in the first week of February, after having been able to scrape together only seventeen thousand troops, Halleck found himself with a subordinate not only suddenly in possession of Fort Henry but apparently on the heels of a fleeing enemy. The situation, he doubtless realized, was appallingly dangerous. The subordinate was none other than the reckless assailer of Belmont, the quiet but relentless "man of fire" whose defining trait, besides fondness for drink and none-too-meticulous administration, was that he could not be kept out of battles.[3]

*   *   *

By the time Halleck received Grant's February 6 notice that he intended to move against Fort Donelson on February 8, the St. Louis commander had to be wondering if the initiative he had seized in Union chain-of-command politics a few days earlier had led him to overstep and mount the threshold of personal disaster. Having hijacked the driver's seat in the western theatre, he began to fear that his road led off a cliff.

Part of his problem was the vacuum of leadership above him. General-in-Chief McClellan seems to have been wary of the renown of the nation's preeminent military scholar, a man whose intellectual powers were so recognized that he was beginning to be called "Old Brains." For an arrogant and dashing young molder of armies, McClellan had taken a markedly tentative tone toward both of the top commanders of his forces in the central South. He appeared unwilling to give direct orders not only to Buell, his longtime friend and military role model, but also to Halleck, an obvious rival for leadership of the Union armies. "Little Mac" also could not bring himself to force his two subordinates to cooperate. His diffidence had let Buell renege on the invasion of East Tennessee throughout the fall and early winter and now hampered Halleck's campaign between the Tennessee and Cumberland rivers.

Of course, Halleck had all but asked for some of this trouble. Having not let Buell know of his Fort Henry attack until it was being launched, he had assumed that Buell would have to supply some of the troops invading along the Tennessee and the Cumberland and thus dramatically swell their numbers. But Buell balked. Now Halleck found himself just as unable as McClellan to bend Buell to his will, and conditions were becoming frightening. A force under Halleck's ultimate command was on its own and in danger of being cut off deep in enemy territory, with a Confederate counterattack expected from east, west, or both.

The potential for dysfunction in McClellan's dual command structure in the Kentucky-Tennessee theatre had manifested itself. Buell, McClellan's choice for the theatre's heavy lifting, was outranked by Halleck. The only way Buell could achieve ascendancy in the Union West was for McClellan, who outranked both of them, to directly order Halleck to do Buell's bidding—which McClellan shrank from doing. And Halleck's seniority over Buell was moot because McClellan stood between it and its power to command.

Territorial obstructions, too, had been built into the Federal western command system. The whole state of Tennessee had been assigned to Buell months ago in expectation that he would invade East Tennessee to rescue that area's suffering Unionists. Buell had refused, and because of his habitual deliberateness and understandable fear of getting trapped behind Confederate lines, he still held not a square foot of the Volunteer State. In ordering the attack on Fort Henry, Halleck had sent Grant into territory that was Buell's. Now he felt he and Grant desperately needed help there, and he abruptly dropped the imperious, condescending tone he had used during the preceding week when telling Buell he already had ordered Grant to attack Fort Henry and that Buell's cooperation was not essential.

"Can't you make a diversion in our favor by threatening Bowling Green?" Halleck begged Buell in a wire on February 5.

Now came Buell's turn to be imperious. Although he had begged for a month for precisely the kind of movement Halleck had made, he had wanted it done on his own schedule and at his own bidding.

"My position does not admit of diversion," he icily responded to Halleck on the same day, February 5. He then added condescendingly: "My moves must be real ones." He wrote that although he planned to move "at once" toward Bowling Green, his progress would be slow since he was advancing via the Louisville & Nashville Railroad, which had to be repaired as he went. He estimated that it would "probably be twelve days before I can be in front of Bowling Green." In other words, Halleck could twist in the wind.

Halleck's well-known brains were stronger than his nerve. He became desperate. Earlier this same day, February 5, he had wired McClellan that the naval bombardment of Fort Henry had begun (this was the preliminary, mostly range-finding work of Foote's gunners), and now he followed that message with another reporting intelligence that ten thousand Confederates had "left Bowling Green by railroad to re-enforce Fort Henry.

"Can't you send me some infantry regiments from Ohio?" he beseeched. "Answer."

McClellan, too, feared a Tennessee River disaster. That evening he wired Buell asking, but not ordering, him to "assist Halleck if possible" by making a move toward Bowling Green. At the same time—7 p.m. on February 5, as Grant was mulling his final orders for the Fort Henry attack—McClellan wired Halleck that he had "suggested" to Buell that a demonstration be made on Bowling Green and that any Ohio troops would have to come from Buell, but only if "absolutely necessary."

At midnight, Buell stonily replied to McClellan that the Confederates were so strongly fortified at Bowling Green that "no demonstration . . . is practicable," but added that he would send Halleck a brigade. He then wired Halleck that he would send the brigade "if you find that you absolutely require it; otherwise I have use for it." Probably to underscore how little information Halleck had given him regarding this operation into what was nominally Buell territory, he asked for clarification as to whether Halleck's troops were moving just up the Tennessee River or up not just the Tennessee but also up the Cumberland, toward Fort Donelson. He then took another sniping shot: "You must not fail."

Halleck hardly needed reminding that failure was not an option. It was still February 5 when he wired Assistant Secretary of War Thomas A. Scott, who was visiting Indianapolis, to demand immediate shipment of "all the infantry regiments at Cairo you can possibly send me there, in order to re-enforce the column now moving up the Tennessee River." In the wire to Scott he repeated the report that ten thousand Confederates were being railroaded from Bowling Green to Fort Henry. The next morning, February 6, as Grant and Foote made final preparations for their attack, Halleck telegraphed McClellan that Fort Henry had been "largely re-enforced," this time adding that the enemy aid was coming not only from Bowling Green but from Columbus, and adding that the Confederates "intend to make a desperate stand" at Henry. Warning that "Unless I get more forces I may fail to take it," he added lamely that even if his Fort Henry effort failed, it at least surely would help facilitate a much-awaited forward movement by Buell. Continuing to crawfish, he seemed to put any incipient blame for his unilateral action on the general-in-chief's transmission of the Beauregard rumor a week earlier: "I was not ready to move, but deemed [it] best to anticipate the arrival of Beauregard's forces."

By February 6, McClellan, too, had become agitated. In response to Halleck's bombardment of telegrams, he dashed off two more to Buell. Quoting Halleck's report of Henry's reinforcement from both Bowling Green and Columbus, he brought up one of Buell's excuses and wrote that "If road so bad in your front, had we not better throw all available force on Forts Henry and Donelson?" In the second telegram, McClellan went on to urge Buell to take charge of the force on the rivers: "If it becomes necessary to detach largely from your command to support Grant, ought you not to go in person? Reply, and if yes, I will inform Halleck."

In the meantime, still on February 6, McClellan received another wire from Halleck, who now appeared convinced that he had sent far too few men down the Tennessee. In an obvious attempt to lay groundwork for later blaming a defeat at Henry on the lack of support given by McClellan and Buell, he wrote that if he could just be given another ten thousand troops, he would "take Fort Henry, cut the enemy's line, and paralyze Columbus." From there, he soared off into a scenario that he must have known was unlikely in any immediate sense: "Give me 25,000 and I will threaten Nashville and cut off railroad communication, so as to force the enemy to abandon Bowling Green without a battle."

Hours after Foote had handed the surrendered fort to Grant and steamed back toward Cairo to refit his ironclads and shepherd final construction of the mortar boats, McClellan and Halleck still had no idea that the victory had been won. At 7 p.m. of that day, the general-in-chief wired Halleck assurance that Buell "will assist you" and suggested "a sudden dash on Columbus" if Buell found he could send additional troops. The Louisville commander wired McClellan still griping that the Henry foray, "right in its strategical bearing, but commenced by General Halleck without appreciation—preparative or concert—has now become of vast magnitude." Buell added, though, that he himself had begun thinking of moving the bulk of his operation to the Henry–Donelson front even before McClellan had telegraphed that suggestion. With the excessive wariness that was habitual with him, though, he said such a move was "hazardous," since it had "to be made in the face of 50,000, if not 60,000" Confederates around Bowling Green—figures that more than doubled the number of Confederates actually in the Bowling Green vicinity. As to whether he would actually decide to make the move, Buell added, he "would answer definitely in the morning." His detractors, the number of which was proliferating in Washington and elsewhere, were not to be blamed for wondering if Buell could be persuaded to do anything that even appeared aggressive, let alone fight.

All day February 6, knowing nothing of Henry's fall, Buell and Halleck dithered back and forth, Buell pompously pondering and Halleck wringing his hands. Halleck, likely worrying that what he was telegraphing was true, claimed the Confederates were using the railroad to concentrate at Henry, that Beauregard was there "but without his troops," and that Federal bombardment of the fort was continuing. Finally Buell gave in, wiring that he would send a brigade by water to junction with Grant. By 6:30 p.m., Buell had thought more about the "vast magnitude" of the importance of success in Halleck's drive southward and perhaps envisioning blame that might fall on him if he did nothing. He wired that he was sending eight more regiments in addition to the brigade, but they were brand-new volunteers not yet organized above the regiment level. Halleck, apparently hoping to counter the reported Bowling Green reinforcement of Fort Henry and head it off before it arrived, jumpily wired back that Buell should send his detached troops not to Fort Henry but up the Cumberland to "land near Dover and operate on either side, as may be required." Buell replied typically and, in this case, understandably. "Is not the enemy in possession of the route across [to Fort Henry] from Dover?" he asked. "Please describe Grant's position and the enemy's."

Fortunately for the Federals, Fort Henry had already surrendered, and this feverish back-and-forth among McClellan, Halleck, and Buell proved to be of little consequence. But it reveals the fears, egos, and political maneuvering that surrounded the Fort Henry expedition. The bickering also discloses that every higher level of the command structure took for granted that the expedition's leader was a nonentity not long for his position. In that regard, a McClellan-to-Halleck wire at 7 p.m. the day of the victory included an ominous line. It indicated that McClellan, too, had been pondering the qualifications of the onetime unit quartermaster who now had immediate charge of the vital operation on the Tennessee River. Having just hours earlier urged Buell to take personal command there, McClellan now replied to Halleck's own recommendation for a more qualified field commander.

"I will push Hitchcock's case," he wrote.[4]

Consequences

February 7, Into the Heart of Dixie

WHILE GRANT GATHERED up plunder at Fort Henry, and his superiors considered candidates to replace him, Foote's men were ripping Dixie open to her bowels. The high water that had so hampered Grant's infantry was being ridden by the navy to the southern border of Tennessee and beyond.

In keeping with pre-battle orders issued by Foote, almost as soon as the fort surrendered, three Federal gunboats—*Conestoga, Tyler,* and *Lexington,* a timber-clad flotilla division under the overall command of Lieutenant Commander Seth Phelps—had raced upriver. Their first stop, some twenty miles south, was the critical Danville railroad bridge, a twelve-hundred-foot span linking the Confederate army's western headquarters at Bowling Green with not only Memphis to the southwest but with a line running north to Polk's fortress at Columbus. The timber-clads had been detailed by Foote for this duty because they were much faster than the ironclads, and the slowest of the three, the *Tyler,* was left at Danville long enough to destroy some track. This cut off Polk at Columbus from Albert Sidney Johnston's center at Bowling Green and made it more difficult for either Confederate general to counterattack Grant at Fort Henry.

But the aim was for the timber-clads to quickly begin wreaking much more havoc, and they did. The *Conestoga* and the *Lexington* sped on upriver into the dusk of February 6 pursuing several Confederate transport steamboats. After a five-hour chase, the Confederates burned three of the fugitive craft. Loaded with submarine mines and a variety of ammunition, one of the three exploded with such a concussion that, although a thousand yards away, it shattered skylights, blew open doors, broke locks, and loosened upper decks in the pursuing vessels.

"The whole river for half a mile around about was completely 'beaten up' by the falling fragments and the shower of shot, grape, balls, &c," Commander Phelps reported. "The house of a reported Union man was blown to pieces, and it was suspected there was design in [exploding] the rebel [boat]s [in front of] the doomed house."

By nightfall of the next day, February 7, the timber-clads had pushed nearly to the Tennessee–Mississippi border and had captured a Confederate steamer, the *Eastport*, at a Hardin County landing called Cerro Gordo. The *Eastport* was halfway into the process of being converted to a first-class gunboat, and to guard it the *Tyler*, which by now had caught up with her sister boats, again was left behind.[1]

The *Conestoga* and *Lexington* kept going. Just across the Mississippi line they captured two more steamboats. The Federal sailors passed another important railroad town, Eastport, Mississippi, soon after dawn on the 8th and continued upstream to Florence, Alabama. There they found three more Confederate-torched steamers in flames. The Union crews boarded the doomed vessels and managed to save "considerable quantities of supplies marked 'Fort Henry,'" Phelps wrote.

As the Federal naval officer later recorded in his report, the townspeople of Florence implored him to "quiet the fears of their wives and daughters . . . that they should not be molested and, secondly, praying that I would not destroy their railroad bridge." Phelps offered reassurance: "As for the first, I told them that we were neither ruffians nor savages and that we were there to protect them from violence and to enforce the law." He also promised he would not destroy the bridge because "it could possess, so far as I saw, no military importance," only connecting the town of Florence with the Memphis & Charleston Railroad on the river's opposite side.

On February 10, Phelps reported to Foote that his men had captured three steamboats, including the half-finished gunboat, and had forced the Confederates to burn six others "loaded with supplies."

He added information that might have chagrined Confederate leaders even more than loss of the booty. Two of the Tennessee counties the crews invaded were ones whose citizens had voted to remain in the Union the previous June, and their sympathies showed.[2]

> We have been met with the most gratifying proofs of loyalty everywhere across Tennessee . . . Men, women, and children several times gathered in crowds of hundreds, shouted their welcome, and hailed their national flag with an enthusiasm there was no mistaking. It was genuine and heartfelt. These people braved everything to go to the river bank where a sight of their flag might once more be enjoyed, and they have experienced, as they related, every possible form of persecution. Tears flowed freely down the cheeks of men as well as of women . . . This display of feeling and sense of gladness at our success and the hopes it created in the breasts of so many people in the heart of the

Confederacy astonished us not a little . . . I was assured at Savannah [Tennessee] that of the several hundred [Confederate] troops there, more than one half, had we gone to the attack in time, would have hailed us as deliverers and gladly enlisted with the national force. In Tennessee the people generally in their enthusiasm braved secessionists and spoke their views freely, but in Mississippi and Alabama what was said was guarded . . . There were, it is true, whole communities who on our approach fled to the woods, but these were where there was less of the loyal element and where the fleeing steamers in advance had spread tales of our coming with fire-brands, burning, destroying, ravishing, and plundering.[3]

Abraham Lincoln was convinced that in the war's first year, especially in East Tennessee but also in other regions across upper Dixie, there was much devoted Union feeling, and Phelps's report lends credence to Lincoln's conviction.

Secessionist elements, dismayed that Phelps had gotten into position to make such a report at all, tried to put the best face on it. A week or so after the cruise, the *Nashville Weekly Patriot* seized on the false but widely reported Foote retort to Tilghman at the Henry capitulation that Tilghman would have had to blow the gunboats out of the water before Foote ever would have surrendered to the Confederates. From this boorish incident, the *Patriot* said, "we may learn . . . with what we have to contend." The only alternatives, the newspaper said, were "VICTORY OR DEATH."

The *Patriot* also tried to comfort its readers. After Phelps's boats reached Florence, it reported, the town's citizens "raised two companies" on the spot, one of infantry and the other of artillery, and both quickly left town on a special train to try to overtake the invaders. The fast timber-clads had already departed, however, and this time they were headed back to Fort Henry and Cairo *with*, rather than against, the Tennessee's hard current. The Florence recruits returned home the night of the day they left—too little, too late.[4]

February 7–10

Grant and "The Crisis of the War in the West"

On FEBRUARY 7, *New York Herald* reporter Albert Richardson told Grant he had wrapped up his Fort Henry reporting and was heading back to Cairo. Grant tried to stop him.

"Wait a day or so," the general advised.

Richardson asked why.

"I am going over to attack Fort Donelson tomorrow," Grant said.

Richardson, possibly taken aback, asked if the general knew the strength of Donelson. Federal officers possessed so little knowledge of the Cumberland River fort that a few weeks earlier Smith had referred to it as "Fort Gavock or Fort MacGavock or something else," confusing its name with that of its post commander at the time, Randal McGavock. Grant persistently spelled it Donaldson, and Halleck often referred to it with no name other than that of its adjacent town: "Dover."

Grant replied with an equivocal affirmative to Richardson's question on whether he knew Donelson's strength. "Not exactly," he said, "but I think we can take it. At all events, we can try."[1]

Seemingly offhand, his response seems less an indication of overconfidence than recognition of widening possibilities that now desperately needed to be taken advantage of. The enemy had been easily pushed into headlong retreat—the day Grant talked to Richardson he was busy writing orders for the recovery of artillery, abandoned wagons, and "plunder" in the wake of the Confederate stampede. Grant's instinct was to pursue and destroy him before he recovered psychological equilibrium. Of course he had his personal reasons, as well. Ever since embarking down the Tennessee, he doubtless had felt two things at once: more leeway to use his discretion and, with every passing hour, his increasing need of a personal battlefield triumph to save the bright new military career that Halleck, with or without the Kountz charges, might suddenly shelve or sweep away. Even now, crews were attempting to run a telegraph line from Paducah to Fort Henry to hook Halleck up to him again, but there would be no such line to Fort Donelson. Grant was not a man to be directly insubordinate, but the capture of Paducah and the assault on Belmont already showed that in the face of a chance to fight he could take a very creative approach to orders. Now he had ever more pressing reasons to do it.[2]

Grant's exchange with Richardson raises an important question, however: Why would the normally discreet Grant volunteer sensitive military information to a reporter? Most generals of the time, especially the other West Pointers with whom Grant was then dealing—Smith and Halleck close at hand and, from much longer range, Buell and McClellan—despised the nosy newsmen and had as little to do with them as possible. Smith and Buell were career army men who had no military use for civilians of any kind, and Halleck and McClellan had left the army to become rich and even more loftily egotistical than they had been as antebellum officers. All four thought civilian politics and such attendant agents as journalists should have no influence on military operations.

By contrast, Grant's upbringing under his father's antislavery views and his mother's extraordinary religious piety, buttressed by his own years of financial struggle as a civilian after leaving the army, had made him humble. He was democratic by nature; his background led him to regard most people, even journalists, as acceptable acquaintances until they proved otherwise. And the years he spent as a civilian in Missouri and Illinois in the tumultuously political run-up to the war had, no doubt, heightened his consciousness of the force of public opinion. Richardson and his newspaper could help influence it.

Some favorable public notice could help bolster his flailing career. Grant quite possibly—and correctly—sensed that some newspapers (such as the *St. Louis Democrat* of that very date) would criticize him for his lack of participation in the capture of Fort Henry. Surely he also wondered if the Kountz charges were about to become headlines. When threatened, Grant's impulse was always to attack, never to withdraw into a shell. So he courted Richardson, rather than avoided him.

Grant knew that he must have a battlefield victory or capture of his own very soon, and he may have reasoned that he should get as many journalists as possible on hand to trumpet it. And if he lost . . . well, he could not lose. As he had told Rawlins on the Henry expedition's first day, they had to succeed.

*   *   *

But Grant quickly found that attacking Fort Donelson on February 8 was impossibly ambitious. First, he had had to concern himself with a multitude of other things, and most of them indicated that the attack he had promised so offhandedly would not be nearly as easy as he initially supposed.

On the day that he talked to Richardson, he obeyed a Halleck order to send a second mission upriver to destroy trestles of the railroad bridge at Danville. Track at this bridge had already been damaged by the crew of the *Tyler* the day before, but infantrymen Grant sent on a transport steamer to follow up and complete the destruction found that Confederate infantry had reoccupied the bridge soon after the *Tyler* headed south. The Confederates had driven away the Federal infantry on the steamer. Destroying the trestles would irreparably sever the vital link between the Confederates' Bowling Green and Columbus armies and block the quickest route Columbus troops could take to launch a Polk counterattack on Henry, of which Halleck was demonstrably and increasingly frightened. When the repelled steamer returned, Grant sent a gunboat to chase the Confederates away from the bridge and finish disabling it.[3]

That same day, February 7, Grant sent his cavalry on a reconnaissance that reached within a mile of Donelson and drove back Confederate pickets. That produced, however, "no definite information . . . of the number of the enemy" inside the fort, Grant reported to General Cullum back at Cairo. In this report to Cullum, and thereby Halleck, Grant did, however, mention having heard intelligence gleaned from a captured Confederate that the troops who escaped Fort Henry had fallen back on Fort Donelson, and he surmised that any reinforcements originally intended for Henry also would be sent to Donelson. This may have been a bit disingenuous. He had also heard from the Confederate POW—but did *not* report to Halleck—that Donelson was defended by more cannon than Fort Henry and that no less than *fifteen thousand* troops originally bound for Henry had been sent to Donelson. He kept the latter information to himself, it is to be assumed, because he did not want to risk further activating the nervousness of his St. Louis commander. By now Halleck, receiving minimal cooperation from Buell, indicated in a February 8 dispatch to Grant that, rather than attacking Fort Donelson, he was totally focused on holding Fort Henry.

"Shovels and picks will be sent you to strengthen Fort Henry," the February 8 message said. "The [Fort Henry] guns should be . . . arranged so as to resist an attack by land . . . Some of the guns from Fort Holt [in Kentucky, just across the Ohio River from Cairo] will be sent up. Re-enforcements will reach you daily. Hold on to Fort Henry at all hazards."[4]

Like most West Pointers—except for the top-of-their-class people, engineers such as Halleck, whose business was mainly the construction of fortifications—Grant hated trench-digging. This was not because the Point's mid- and lower classmen were lazy, but rather because it offended their allegiance to offensive, rather than defensive, warfare. They believed that digging trenches made soldiers feel their officers thought the troops were inferior to the foe, thus undermining morale. This attitude was especially Grant's, fitting as it did into his constitutional impulse to be ever moving forward.

Also, Grant knew he could not afford the luxury of digging in. He was in the middle of enemy territory and, at least theoretically, a target for counterattack at any moment from either flank in superior numbers. What he needed to do was hold the initiative, not entrench and get pinned down. Halleck, doubtless, assumed that at Henry the Federal force had at least the protection of a fort, but this particular fort, now more than one-third under water, offered questionable refuge.

Grant also strongly suspected that his danger from one of his two flanks, the western one, was minor at worst. Having for months studied Polk at Columbus and met the Confederate general in the floating flag-of-truce encounters on the Mississippi, Grant sensed that the Episcopal prelate was unlikely to emerge willingly from behind the guns of his fortress. This hunch was supported by hard evidence. Although a neophyte, Grant was already thorough in at least one administrative aspect of generalship—rapt attention to intelligence-gathering—and his spies had been telling him that Polk's Columbus force was being continually weakened by replacement of crack troops with green volunteers.[5]

Thus, Grant felt the route of likeliest Confederate reinforcement between the rivers was from Bowling Green to Fort Donelson, and it was obvious to him that he needed to get to Donelson before the bulk of those Confederate reinforcements did. With Kountz's formal charges by now back on Halleck's desk, the brigadier between the rivers must have also felt a need to give his superiors as little time as possible to ponder what to do with him. And the prospect the "man of fire" feared least was combat.

The day after Grant sent his reconnaissance mission to Fort Donelson, February 8, was the date on which he had promised Halleck to "take" Donelson. The skies, which had cleared the day of the battle, were again pouring rain, preventing troops from moving overland with baggage or artillery on miry roads. That day he reported to Cullum and Halleck that conditions were so dismally soggy that "all my troops will be kept busily engaged in saving what we now have from the rapidly rising waters."

Well, not quite all his troops. That day, Grant personally accompanied another cavalry reconnaissance cross-country to the vicinity of the Cumberland River fort, then swiftly began revising his plan. Before leaving, he had confided to General Smith that he might "move tomorrow," February 9, against Donelson, depending on the results of the reconnaissance. But by day's end, after seeing the fort for himself for the first time, he had come to realize that capturing it would be a larger job than anybody had supposed up to then.

Grant did not report what he saw on this trip; the last thing he needed to do was to further exercise Halleck. Grant did not even write about it in letters home. This was partly, no doubt, because his family was so proud of him that his letters sometimes ended up in newspapers but also because Grant's fidgety essence was to remain positive—almost desperately, as if he knew it would do him no psychological good to look over his shoulder. The solution was to advance as soon as possible. That would put distance between himself and all that lurked in the rear.

But what he had to have seen at Donelson was a fort that was no Henry. It sat on an imposing hill rising more than one hundred feet above the narrow Cumberland River, unlike the facility sunk in the wide Tennessee's swirl and mud. He also had to have seen that the Confederate presence at Donelson was proliferating, that the defenders were laying out long lines of trenches on ridges fronting the fort, and that the routes to get at these trenches from Fort Henry ran through rough, wooded country bristling with the threat of ambush. What he had seen, in sum, was that Fort Donelson was not at all just the outpost that it had been presumed to be.

Taking it would demand artillery and gunboats, and both of these would require more time to move. The gunboats that had not already been sent back to Cairo would need to steam all the way back down the Tennessee to the Ohio and then back up the Cumberland.

Yet it all had to be done quickly to give the Confederates as little time as possible to further reinforce, further entrench, and to prepare ambushes along the approach routes. With rain continuing and creeks still flooded, Grant's first job, while the gunboats were being transferred, was to get his men and guns across a low, marshy area stretching about three miles beyond the Tennessee's east banks. "We are perfectly locked in by high water and bad roads and prevented from acting offensively as I should like to do," he had reported to General Cullum at Cairo on the 8th.[6]

As the rain continued, he had plenty of other problems to contend with, some having to do with his half-disciplined volunteer soldiers. He admonished brigade commander Colonel John Cook regarding two to three hundred men of the Seventh and Fiftieth Illinois who had been "out today robbing and plundering most disgracefully." He asked Colonel Cook for the names of the officers in charge and announced that they would be recommended for immediate dismissal without trial and the enlisted men punished.

"In an enemy's country, where so much more could be done by a manly and humane policy to advance the cause which we all have so deeply at heart, it is astonishing that men can be found so wanton as to destroy, pillage, and burn indiscriminately, without inquiry," read an order issued in Grant's name and signed by John Rawlins. It announced that brigade, regiment, and company commanders must be responsible for the behavior of their units.

Grant also issued orders that all regimental-level officers must "immediately take up quarters with [their] commands and not board on steamers, as the general commanding regrets to see has been done. No officer will be allowed to go aboard any steamers except where his duty carries him." Obviously, a lot of officers had been spending much time on steamboats to evade the foul weather, while lower-level soldiers were left to sleep and eat in the wet, the chill, and the mud. These orders illustrate Grant's unusual understanding of volunteers. His time outside the army had imparted intense awareness that these were not career soldiers inured to old-army discipline but, rather, mostly rough-and-tumble farm boys who had left home to fight for their country and expected to go back to their plows and cows when the war ended. Grant believed in being firm with them but very fair—and holding their officers to higher standards.

After four days of waiting impatiently, under mounting tension, to be able to move, he very un-typically exploded. On February 10, he fired off a highly uncharacteristic written outburst to his powerful congressional sponsor, Representative Elihu B. Washburne of Illinois, with whom of all people he normally would have been expected to take a more respectful tone; the one he used likely reflected his personal strain as well as admiration and concern for his most valued subordinate. The outward provocation for this sudden release of pent-up energy, which included a very untypical oath, was congressional foot-dragging in the confirmation of Charles F. Smith as brigadier general.

The delay, Grant probably knew, likely resulted from intriguing by Smith subordinates such as Lew Wallace or rivals such as McClernand.

"For Gods sake get the Senate to reconsider Gen Smiths confirmation," Grant exhorted Washburne in an abrupt two-line communication. "There is no doubt of his loyalty and efficiency. We can't spare him now."[7]

The grasping McClernand had already been an intentional source of Grant embarrassment at Fort Henry, dubbing his pre-battle bivouac "Camp Halleck." Now he continued to display a tendency to be as well-supplied with ink as he was long-winded. A report to Grant of the First Division's performance in the battle—dated February 10 and seemingly aimed at newspaper publication—boasted that McClernand's men had been the first infantry to get inside the fort's walls (as if that had mattered). He then delivered another backhanded slap at his commander. Re-emphasizing the identity of

Henry's actual captor, he issued an "order" that the battered installation be renamed "Fort Foote"; he also wrote an ingratiatingly congratulatory note to the flag-officer.

McClernand almost certainly was feeling his oats, perhaps in expectation of impending publication of the Kountz charges. The very day of the Fort Henry battle he had written ingratiatingly to Illinois Governor Yates and promised to present the governor with a captured Confederate cannon. On February 8, he had written his fellow Springfield resident Lincoln to highly exaggerate the First Division's role in the fighting.

No fool, Grant had been dealing carefully with McClernand. During the initial days of their Cairo association, McClernand still held a congressional seat as well as his brigadier general's rank. After the Belmont fight, despite McClernand's participation in celebratory speechmaking in the Confederate camp when he should have been stopping the looting and revelry, Grant had praised the congressman's bravery under fire. This praise was obviously justi-fied—McClernand had horseflesh shot from under him at Belmont, as had Grant—but the kind words may have been intended to induce McClernand to call the battle the success that Grant maintained it was. Now, with McCler-nand's relationship with Kountz having become more apparent, and with such slaps as the "Camp Halleck" and "Fort Foote" insults being openly ad-ministered, Grant was developing a less comradely view of the man Grant aide Rawlins had wrathfully termed a "slinking Judas bastard."[8]

*　　*　　*

McClernand had no chance of supplanting Grant. Until a few months be-fore, he had represented the civilian establishment that in Halleck's view had no place in military counsels, and Halleck disliked him intensely. But Halleck did like, indeed craved, several other provisional Grant successors. He was plainly frightened to be entrusting this critical moment in his own career to Grant, and he continued on February 8 to push McClellan and the secretary of war for the appointment of sixty-four-year-old General Hitch-cock to Grant's position.

"Brigadier Generals Sherman, Pope, Grant, Curtis, Hurlbut, Sigel, Pren-tiss, and McClernand, all in this department, are [ranked as] of the same date, and each unwilling to serve under the other," he wired the secretary, making a claim that was not true. "If Brig. Gen. E. A. Hitchcock could be made major-general of volunteers and assigned to this department it would satisfy all and reconcile all differences. If it can be done there should be no delay, as an experienced officer of high rank is wanted immediately on the

Tennessee [River] line."9 Grant had been ordered to dig in at Fort Henry, but who knew what else he might do? Likely prompted by his own growing desperation and Buell's intractability and obvious disinclination to do anything helpful, Halleck suddenly beseeched McClellan for command of the whole theatre—which McClellan swiftly refused. Then, seemingly in deepening fear of disaster on the Cumberland, Halleck told McClellan he himself would go down to Fort Henry. The same day, February 8, he retracted his earlier offer to Buell to take command there. McClellan had liked that suggestion enough that he had approached Buell about it, and Buell, as usual, was pondering it. Now Halleck withdrew the offer, noting that Sherman, whom he was in the process of sending to take command in Paducah, was senior to Buell—and thus more entitled to Grant's job. Halleck again asked for Hitchcock, but said that "if General Hitchcock cannot be appointed" the job could be handled by Sherman, whose "health is greatly improved." He referred, of course, to Sherman's shattering crisis of confidence in Kentucky in mid–1861 that had prompted reports he was insane.

On February 9, Halleck enjoyed a brief triumphant moment, and he shared it with his longtime and closest friend, General Cullum at Cairo. After instructing Cullum to send more supplies to Paducah for shipment down the Tennessee and informing him that two more regiments—the First Nebraska and the Second Iowa—were on their way there, Halleck added gleefully: "McClellan gives hopes of adopting my plan entire, by sending a part of Buell's army to the Cumberland. If so, look out for lively times. The gunboats should be prepared for the Cumberland with all possible dispatch. *Hitchcock is appointed.*"

The question now was whether the Hitchcock appointment had occurred in time for the aging general to reach the front before Grant could attack Donelson.

To try to forestall calamity in the meantime, Halleck hurried off reinforcements to Grant, some eight thousand or more. He also echoed Grant's calls for Foote's gunboats to be sent down the Tennessee and then up the Cumberland for a joint assault on Donelson. But there was a hitch on the naval front. Foote was maintaining to Cullum at Cairo that he could not send the boats up the Cumberland until they had undergone extensive repairs from their Henry battering.

Halleck and Buell and McClellan wrung their hands, worrying about the prospect of attacks on Grant or Paducah or Cairo from Columbus—where the predictable Polk was rumored to have been joined by the more aggressive Beauregard. There was also the obvious threat from Bowling Green.

On February 10, Halleck wired McClellan:

It is said that Beauregard is preparing to move from Columbus either on Paduc-
ah or Fort Henry. Do send me more troops. It is the crisis of the war in the West .
. . An immense number of boats have been collected, and the whole Bowling
Green force can come down in a day, attack Grant in the rear, and return to
Nashville before Buell can get half way there. The bridges are all destroyed and
the roads rendered impassable . . . We are certainly in peril.

He then returned to a favorite theme.

"Telegraph to General Hitchcock officially, informing him of his appointment, and assign him to duty in this department."[10]

*   *   *

Grant did not press for the reinforcements Halleck was sending him, but he
knew about the efforts to get them. There was no way, though, that he could
have known much about the quickening effort to replace him. The campaign against him now had gone well past Halleck's office in St. Louis.

Two days after the Henry victory, it reached the Washington desk of Secretary of War Stanton—in the form of the most scandalous allegations yet.
Stanton, who in addition to having been an intimate of army commander
McClellan was one of the early sponsors who sent Kountz to McClellan in
1861, found in his February 8 mail a letter from Kountz, and a new list of
"Charges against Brigadier Genl U.S. Grant." They numbered nine in all and
enlarged in sensational detail on the cryptic "Conduct unbecoming an Officer and a Gentleman" mentioned in the earlier document. The latest list
read:

CHARGE FIRST
Visiting Captain G. W. Graham Head Quarters on the Wharf Boat at this place
and drinking liquor publicly while the sale and use of liquor was prohibited by
the Provost Martial [sic] by the order of the commanding General U. S. Grant
thus setting a bad example to his officers and men

CHARGE SECOND
For drinking with traitors and enemies to the Federal Government, while under a Flag of Truce, becoming drunk and incapable of attending to business: to
the disgrace of the United States Army

CHARGE THIRD
For occupying the cooks room on a Government Steamer while under a Flag
of Truce, and vomiting all over the floor—(cause drunkenness) conduct unbecoming a gentleman or an Officer

CHARGE FOURTH

For getting drunk at the St Charles Hotel and loosing [sic] his sword and uniform; and behaving in a manner disgraceful to the United States Army

CHARGE FIFTH

For receiving on board of a Government Steamer bearing a Flag of Truce, a Harlot who had been sent to Capt G. W. Graham on a pretence [sic] of being passed South, said Harlot got drunk during this trip, drinking with the Officers and was not sent South, but returned to the Hotel where General U. S. Grant visited her private room: No[.] 5 publicly, conduct disgraceful to an Officer in the United States Army.

CHARGE SIXTH

Visiting a Negro Ball in company with his Aids, QuarterMaster, and Capt Graham, There drinking a large amount of Champaigne [sic] wine, and becoming drunk, conduct unbecoming a commanding General, to the injury and disgrace of the United States Army

CHARGE SEVENTH

For retaining men on his Staff who have been repeatedly drunk in his presence, disgraceful to his high position

CHARGE EIGHTH

Getting so drunk that he had to go upstairs on all fours, conduct not becoming a man

CHARGE NINTH

For playing Cards for money while he was a disbursing agent (disbursing secret service money) [11]

These allegations' vivid detail suggests that they could have had some root in reality, but their over-the-top, cartoon-ish quality—the losing of uniform and sword, the crawling up stairs, the vomiting—sound as if they could as easily have originated in the minds of idle soldiers bored with Cairo and ascribing to their commanding officer behavior that was all too prevalent in their own camps.

Grant almost certainly did not know about this new set of charges, which although accompanied by a Kountz letter, carried no accuser's signature. He knew all too much, however, about the earlier ones Kountz signed, regarding which there had been nothing but ominous silence ever since he left Cairo. He needed to get to Fort Donelson.

Digesting Disaster
The Confederates, February 7–8

CAPTAIN JACK CAMPBELL of the Forty-Eighth Tennessee had been at Fort Donelson for no more than three hours on February 7 when Grant's initial cavalry reconnaissance prompted "an alarm . . . that the enemy were advancing upon us." Still recovering from the arduous retreat from Fort Henry,

> . . . all the forces were formed and marched out in order of battle. The excitement temporarily relieved us of all soreness and stiffness. There we were— without tents, cooking utensels [sic] or clothes—sick and worn out by exposure, excitement and hard service—hourly expecting an attack by an overwhelming force by land and water. We borrowed a few iron pans to cook in, and to sleep we piled about as best we could, some having to sleep in open air, without anything to cover with . . . On the 8th we were again alarmed by the pickets coming in and reporting a large body of the enemy near by . . .[1]

* * *

Confederate morale following the ignominious Henry disaster was wretched, and high officers suffered from it along with enlisted men—especially officers high enough in rank to know for certain how little notice the high command had given Fort Henry from the beginning. The Tenth Tennessee's Lieutenant Colonel McGavock confided to his diary:

> I always knew we would be defeated [at Fort Henry] whenever the enemy came in force I so expressed myself frequently to Gov Harris, the Military Board at Nashville and even to Gen A S Johnston, who I went to see expressly on the subject at Bowling Green. The authorities, both state and Confederate, are to blame for this disaster to our army, for Col A Heiman, the Commandant of the

post four months before the surrender, informed them of the weakness of the position in an able and elaborate report. He constantly urged the necessity of strengthening the post, but no attention was given to it. Indeed, they seemed to regard the defenses of the two rivers as not very important.

McGavock added thought-provoking lines disclosing that officers of the forts between the rivers had urgently appealed for aid from the western Confederate high command in the weeks preceding the battle. They also indicated that the Confederates might have had a well-placed friend close to high-ranking Federals.

> About three weeks ago, a letter addressed to General Tilghman was received and contents immediately telegraphed by Col Heiman to Gen Polk, Gen Johnston, and Gov Harris . . . This letter was written by a gentleman in Paducah and sent by his son who had it sewed up in the lining of his boot. He stated that Gen Smith would start on a certain day up the two rivers with 60,000 men with the gun boats and the federals expected to make a junction with Gen Buel at Nashville on the 22nd of Feb. Gen Tilghman had every confidence in the correctness of the statements in this letter, and he again sent dispatches to the proper authorities and asked for reinforcements. But no help came.[2]

This message to Johnston from Heiman repeated the exact number of troops Halleck initially claimed was required to attack the rivers. It also outlined the one-two punch McClellan was trying to get Buell and Halleck to deliver, and it dates the attack around the time Halleck had been planning to launch it until he received McClellan's message about Beauregard heading west from Richmond. But the surreptitious Paducah letter was hardly the only evidence of such Federal planning. Even Northern newspapers were carrying stories that an attack up the Tennessee and Cumberland was in the offing. All such talk seems only to have riveted Johnston's focus more single-mindedly on Buell, the highly respected foe in his front. The Confederate commander seemed to regard a rivers campaign, even after it began, as an attempt to divert him from Buell.

Hindsight teaches that Johnston should at least have ordered Polk, the forts' nominal overall commander, to move more troops toward the rivers. But Polk, after Belmont, likely would have complied with such an order only after protracted protest, and following Fort Henry's fall there was no longer time for argument.

*   *   *

While Captain Campbell tried to scare up food and shelter at Fort Donelson and Lieutenant Colonel McGavock gnashed teeth over the abandonment of Fort Henry, Albert Sidney Johnston dealt with the fact that his Tennessee River defenses were breached and gushing gunboats.

Less than three weeks after his right flank had dissolved at Logan's Crossroads, the Confederate western commander found his center isolated from his left, and with scarcely more warning. On February 4, Tilghman had telegraphed Johnston to ask for two regiments and "all the help you can [send], light battery included." Early February 5, the Fort Henry commander had vowed to "hold my position to the last" but requested speedy and ample reinforcement. A half-day later, he wired that if reinforcements were "sent strongly and quickly, we have a glorious chance to overwhelm the enemy"; he even specified that the reinforcing units be sent "to Danville, where transports will be ready" to rush them to Fort Henry. Yet just hours after Johnston received this last message on the morning of the 6th—and belatedly ordered reinforcing regiments sent from Nashville and Tuscumbia, Alabama—he learned Tilghman had surrendered.[3]

The Henry debacle was only minimally Tilghman's fault, and hardly all Johnston's. The western commander's requests to Richmond and to the governors of Tennessee, Alabama, and Mississippi for slaves and troops to build and man fortifications at Nashville and along his line north of it had produced few of either. The Davis administration was focusing almost exclusively on its eastern front, and many of the troops for whom arms were available, as well as most of the best weapons, had been sent to northern Virginia.

Also, much of Dixie's wealthy planter class, previously vociferous in its calls for secession to protect slavery, proved miserly in furnishing labor to support the institution's military defenders. Most self-styled aristocrats had refused to pull their human "property" from the fields during harvest season and lend it to the strapped Confederacy. Businessmen and other noncombatants were blasé and similarly unhelpful. When Johnston sent Major Jeremy Gilmer to Nashville to direct the raising of earthworks there, the engineer found himself laughed at and so derided as "Johnston's dirt-digger" that he abandoned the project.

On January 22, three days after the Logan's Crossroads debacle, Johnston had written Confederate Adjutant General Samuel Cooper in a tone reflecting his desperate straits and the apparent lack of concern of his government and most Southerners:

The enemy . . . may be content to hold our force fast in their position on the Potomac for the remainder of the winter; but to suppose, with the facilities of

movement by water which the well-filled rivers of the Ohio, Cumberland, and Ten-
nessee give for active operations, that they will suspend them in Tennessee and
Kentucky during the winter months, is a delusion.

All the resources of the Confederacy are now needed for the defense of
Tennessee.[4]

Johnston's January 22 warning was proved prescient at Fort Henry on
February 6. With Foote's gunboats steaming toward Mississippi and Alabama
on February 7, Johnston met with General William J. Hardee, commanding
at Bowling Green, and Fort Sumter/Bull Run hero Beauregard, who finally
had arrived from Manassas. Beauregard had come to Bowling Green directly
from a pep-talk he gave the Tennessee Legislature at Nashville. He was accompanied by just his staff—and not one of the fifteen reinforcing regiments feared by Halleck. In fact, he was still so unwell from a throat operation undergone prior to his departure from Virginia that he conferred with
Hardee and Johnston at the Covington House from a sickbed.

By now Beauregard had learned that matters in the West were not as
Richmond had led him to believe. Instead of the sixty to eighty thousand
men that he had understood Johnston commanded (because of the inflated numbers Johnston had given the press), the now-smashed Line of the
Cumberland numbered from end to interrupted end less than fifty thousand troops, ill-trained and badly-armed: Hardee's fourteen thousand at
Bowling Green, more than one-fourth of whom were too ill for duty; eight
thousand under Pillow at Clarksville; fifty-five hundred at Fort Donelson
under just-promoted Brigadier General Bushrod Johnson; and seventeen
thousand with Polk at Columbus. Across the Mississippi in Arkansas, General Earl Van Dorn commanded another twenty thousand that were not immediately available.

So, Beauregard learned, Johnston's Kentucky force of some forty-five
thousand was severely outnumbered. Against it were arrayed Grant's seventeen thousand at Fort Henry, three or so thousand guarding Cairo, and sixty
thousand effectives under Buell in central Kentucky—eighty thousand in all.
Another thirty thousand led by Halleck and his subordinate brigadier John
Pope were scattered across Missouri and western Kentucky.[5]

In his February 7 meeting with Johnston and Hardee, Beauregard apparently suggested evacuation and concentration, although how stoutly he
pushed it is disputed. The three generals agreed that they were teetering on
disaster's edge. Thanks to the Logan's Crossroads stampede, Bowling
Green's extensive fortifications could now be flanked on the right by virtually any sizable Federal force that cared to do it. They already *were* flanked on
the left by the Federal capture of Fort Henry.

Beauregard and Johnston apparently disagreed, though, on how to respond. Beauregard later claimed that he advocated falling back to Fort Donelson and striking Grant before Grant could be reinforced by Halleck or Buell. Johnston, however, remained curiously passive. Ambivalent about concentration, he wholeheartedly endorsed evacuation, about which he apparently had been brooding since learning of the defeat at Logan's Crossroads. Colonel Edward Munford, Johnston's aide-de-camp, later remembered being called into Johnston's office several days before Fort Henry's fall and being informed by the general that a vast retreat appeared inevitable. "With—or without—a battle, general?" Munford asked.

"Oh, without a battle," Johnston replied. "They will never come here [to fortified Bowling Green] to fight me."

Munford then noted all the downsides of evacuating. Kentucky's provisional Confederate government, as well as its senators and representatives in the Confederate Congress, would be deprived of protection and have to flee southward. So would the governor and legislature of Tennessee. The next topographically and strategically viable position for the Bowling Green army to dig in was south, maybe so far south of Nashville that Tennessee, too, would be abandoned. "Two states, general!" Munford moaned. The effect on Johnston's personal reputation, he pointed out, would be "serious."

"All I require to rectify that is to get in a position where I can fight a battle," Johnston replied.

But Johnston did not plan to fight this battle anywhere near where he was. Behind him, Tennessee was almost totally unfortified, Federal gunboats were cruising the Tennessee River, and north of where the Tennessee turned eastward and made its great curve across northern Alabama, there was no natural barrier sufficient to stop the onrush of Federal ground troops sure to follow the twin victories of Logan's Crossroads and Fort Henry. According to one of his regimental commanders, Colonel Frank Schaller of the Twenty-Second Mississippi, the Confederates had not yet lost Fort Henry when Johnston studied a map of the Tennessee River with some subordinates and, putting his finger down on an obscure little place called Shiloh Church near Tennessee's southern border, announced: "Here the great battle of the Southwest will be fought."[6]

Johnston's statement reflected neither genius nor clairvoyance. A look at maps had convinced intelligent commanders on both sides that the next critical point on the Tennessee River south of Fort Henry was in the area Johnston had pointed to. A few days before the Henry expedition, General Smith in Paducah had assessed the panoply of opportunity that a Henry victory would produce and pointed to Corinth, Mississippi, twenty miles south of Shiloh Church, as the next great battle site. The Corinth-Shiloh area was all but obvious because Corinth was a hub of the Memphis & Charleston, the east–west rail line that the Confederate western armies had to hold at all costs. The Union gunboat sally up the Tennessee River had not only penetrated Deep Dixie, it underscored the Federal ability to capitalize on Henry's fall by using the river to take troops practically overnight to Corinth's doorstep, flanking forts from Columbus to Memphis and imperiling the whole northern half of the western Confederacy.

So Johnston had already decided on a gigantic retreat plan before calling the Covington House conference. If the all-out attack on Grant that Beauregard advocated were to fail, Johnston understandably felt, the Bowling Green army could be crushed between Grant and the troops of Buell, who— now that Johnston had foes on both flanks racing to get behind him and cut him off—would come driving down the Louisville & Nashville Railroad.

Beauregard apparently backed down in the face of objections. He and Hardee signed a summarized account of the Covington House meeting in which all three generals concurred on a vast, risky strategy that recognized the reality that the South's principal western army had been cut in half. They agreed that (1) Fort Donelson, weak to start with and now flanked by Grant and vulnerable to gunboat attack up the Cumberland, could not be held. And (2) because the Federals now had possession of the Tennessee River and the vital railroad bridge crossing it at Danville, the Polk and Hardee wings of Johnston's army "must henceforth act independently of each other until they can again be brought together." In the likely event that the retreating Bowling Green wing would be forced to fall back from all-but-unfortified Nashville, the document said, Hardee's next logical defensive position would be at Stevenson, Alabama, on the far side of the Tennessee River along the Memphis & Charleston near Chattanooga, protecting the crucial grain belt in the East Tennessee valley. For Polk, Grand Junction, Tennessee, on the Memphis & Charleston near Memphis—or even Mississippi sites as far south as Grenada or Jackson—were proposed.[7]

Johnston's actions from this point on may seem schizophrenic, but from his vantage point they surely seemed logical. He had no way of knowing that Halleck and Buell would not cooperate, thus weakening and delaying the Federal advance. Columbus was now flanked, and the Fort Henry capture invited a back-door assault on the Kentucky fortress by Grant and others, while the broken Danville bridge prevented Confederate reinforcement from Bowling Green. Johnston's fears were valid ones: in fact, McClellan had himself suggested such a move on February 7, and its potential had been discussed in Northern newspapers.

Whatever the Federal plan was, the moment demanded utmost decisiveness on the part of the commander who had the authority to enforce his will on all Confederate forces in his region. "Johnston had . . . supreme command over all [Confederate] troops that could possibly be brought to bear upon one point," Grant later wrote, "while the forces similarly situated on the National side, divided into independent commands, could not be brought into harmonious action except by orders from Washington."[8]

Johnston, however, did not exercise the kind of authority over his subordinates that Grant believed he had. When the Confederate commander had assumed his position back in September, he assigned the Tennessee and Cumberland river forts to Polk. Now Polk, who already had tried to resign when Johnston abortively ordered Pillow from Columbus to Clarksville just before the Belmont fight, was too strapped and concerned with his own front to pay enough attention to anything else. Prior to Grant's jump-off to Fort Henry, Polk had believed the Union buildup around Cairo was preparation for a direct attack on Columbus. Now, with Grant behind him at Henry, that threat had become only a little less direct and even more daunting. Plus, Johnston was the tactful gentleman, and Polk was his longtime friend.[9]

Perhaps thinking he was aiding Columbus and the river forts as well as protecting the army at Bowling Green from Buell's rightward sidle, Johnston began sending reinforcements into the Fort Donelson vicinity despite having concurred with Beauregard and Hardee that the fort could not be held. A couple of thousand troops from Hopkinsville—including Forrest's—were sent to Clarksville along with several thousand more from Russellville, the seat of Kentucky's rump Confederate government.

On February 7, Johnston ordered Pillow's Clarksville force into Donelson itself. Johnston instructed Pillow to assume the command there from Bushrod Johnson, who had replaced the captured Tilghman only the day before. Twenty-five years later Pillow would write that Johnston ordered him face-to-face at Bowling Green to "do all that was possible" to protect the rear of the Bowling Green force by defending Donelson until "it was no longer possible to hold that place," after which he was to "evacuate the position and march the army by way of Charlotte [Tennessee] to Nashville."[10]

Personnel now became a pressing problem. Pillow, who never could be trusted to follow orders, had been a continual thorn in the side of anybody with authority over him all the way to Jefferson Davis. He most recently had left Columbus and had gone home complaining of mistreatment by Polk, which was why he now was assigned to Clarksville. There he had begun calling for more troops to be put under his command at Donelson. John Floyd, the explosive yet vacillating ex–U.S. secretary of war only recently sent west, was counseling just the opposite. Perhaps mindful of his embarrassment at getting nearly trapped behind a river in western Virginia, Floyd believed the forces gathering at this Tennessee fort on the far bank of an even larger river would be better positioned at Cumberland City beside the track of the Memphis, Clarksville & Louisville Railroad. There they, along with his own brigade of veterans of minor eastern combat, could be swiftly shifted to safety at Nashville or elsewhere. West Pointer Simon Bolivar Buckner, commanding crack Kentucky troops, agreed with Floyd and may well have been the Floyd plan's originator. But, as with so many other Confederate endeavors on the western front, Floyd or Buckner came up with their scenario too late. Union activity on the roads from Henry to Donelson had increased alarmingly, and on February 12, Johnston wrote an order directing Floyd to go to the river fort and assume command.[11]

Why, though, did Johnston not take command at Donelson himself? Instead of simply ordering Hardee to retreat from Bowling Green, he chose to stay in Bowling Green and oversee that movement himself. Hardee, a career soldier and former West Point commandant, would seem fully capable of conducting the retreat on his own; after all, he had even authored a just-published book of tactics studied by most commanders North and South (except Grant, who had barely skimmed it, and Forrest, who may never have heard of it). Too, Hardee had been third in command under Johnston in the old U.S. Second Cavalry and at least once during that time had been left in supervision of the force when both Johnston and the unit's second officer, Robert E. Lee, were absent. Yet now, rather than insure Fort Donelson's crucial defense by going to the river fort himself ("if only for a single day," as he was begged by Floyd on February 8), Johnston elected to give all his personal attention to supervising Hardee. Like Polk at Columbus, Johnston appeared to suffer from myopia, unable to take his eyes off the threat in his immediate front.[12]

The Confederate commander's inner conflict as to how to proceed is illustrated by his later explanation to Jefferson Davis that he thought he should simultaneously retreat and "fight for Nashville at Donelson." From a letter Johnston wrote to Richmond on February 8, it seems plain that he had no intention of protecting the Tennessee capital long-term.

Operations against Fort Donelson, on the Cumberland, are about to be commenced, and that work will soon be attacked [he wrote]. *The slight resistance at Fort Henry indicates that the best open earthworks are not reliable to meet a vigorous attack of iron-clad gunboats, and although* [Fort Donelson is] *now supported by a considerable force, I think the gunboats of the enemy will probably take Fort Donelson without the necessity of employing their land force in co-operation, as seems to have been done at Fort Henry.*

So Johnston hoped only to delay Foote's ugly river monsters until the Bowling Green force could be gotten south of the Cumberland and the Tennessee capital's mountains of military materiel hauled deeper into Dixie. Federal possession of Fort Henry outflanked not only Columbus but Nashville, and unless Grant were quickly met and destroyed, Fort Henry's fall doomed any attempt to hold onto the Tennessee capital longer than the few days that might permit removal of some of its enormous supply caches.[13]

By now, Johnston was not seeing even his own front very clearly. For months he had kept Union generals in Kentucky off-balance with his initial pushing of his Cumberland Line north of the Tennessee border and his planted newspaper reports of exaggerated Confederate strength. One highly notable Federal, Sherman, had become so anxiety-ridden and despondent back in November that he requested reassignment and thought of suicide. Now, though, Johnston was himself nonplussed, unsure of the locations and aims of the dispersed forces of Sherman's successor, Buell.

Buell's right flank, or at least part of it, was thought to be a little west of Bowling Green toward the Cumberland River. It was reported by Forrest's cavalry to be moving even further that way, toward Russellville and maybe Clarksville. Johnston worried about its intended destination, and the threat of that force to the Fort Donelson area was what first prompted Johnston to send Floyd and Buckner, with eight thousand men, to Russellville. Then, on February 7, Floyd was ordered south to Clarksville to guard the railroad line from Bowling Green.

"He must judge from after-information whether he shall march straight upon the enemy, now reported at South Carrollton, or wait for further developments of his intention," Johnston wrote in early February, as if Floyd, with no military experience except his recent stint as U.S. secretary of war, were capable of making such a judgment. "It is sufficient to say, he must get the best information of the movements of the enemy . . . and beat them at the earliest opportunity," Johnston added.[14]

Then Foote's decimation of Fort Henry seemed to show how old-fashioned Johnston's mode of soldiering had become. Gunboats were so new to warfare and the Henry triumph so overwhelming that Johnston, with no firsthand knowledge of the forts on the Tennessee and Cumberland, and almost certainly not realizing that Donelson's location higher on the riverbank would make it much less vulnerable to ironclad guns, took for granted that the Cumberland River facility would share Henry's fate.

The gunboats' reduction of Henry on February 6 appeared to make his planned retreat pressingly imperative, and Hardee and Beauregard agreed in the meeting on February 7. In the February 8 letter to Richmond, Johnston said he had to get the Bowling Green army across the Cumberland at

Nashville as soon as possible because "Should Fort Donelson be taken . . . the probability of having the ferriage of this army intercepted by the gunboats of the enemy admits of no delay in making the movement." With so much concern directed at the gunboats, Johnston possibly assumed that, regardless of the boats' accompanying land troops, Confederate forces sent to Donelson could be retrieved by simply moving them away from the Cumberland. That same day, Floyd wrote him from Clarksville that he had "ordered the large supplies of pork and other Government stores at this point to be sent to Nashville and deposited far enough from the river to be safe."[15]

Johnston's indecisiveness is perhaps most glaring, though, in his choice and handling of subordinates. Six months in, he still appears to have given little thought to their personalities and talents—other than, possibly, those of Hardee. He almost certainly knew Hardee well enough to be aware that that general did not enjoy great responsibility. Hardee tended to prefer a high subordinate position from which he could second-guess those in command. By contrast, both of the two men Johnston ended up putting in charge of Fort Donelson, Pillow and then Floyd, had extensive supervisory experience in military or civilian positions. Unlike Johnston himself, both already had led men under fire in this war, and Johnston would write that the two were "popular" and "among the best officers of my command."[16]

Surely he knew better. He had been in Mexico, so he had to have heard of Pillow's wrongly placed ditch and the Tennessean's problems with superiors that resulted in a controversial board of inquiry. Johnston also knew of Pillow's recent insubordinate quarrels with Polk, and he must have heard that Floyd's most notable military action was hardly a positive. It had occurred the previous September in western Virginia, where Floyd made the twin mistakes of raising troops in competition with ex-Governor Henry Wise and then ordering Wise to reinforce him in a position that Wise warned against taking in the first place. Pinned down and attacked in a bend of the Gauley River at Carnifex Ferry, Floyd's hapless unfortunates managed to escape only on a foot-bridge in the dark after Wise ignored the reinforcement order.[17]

But the Confederacy's western commander entrusted Fort Donelson, the primary defense of Nashville, and at least a third of his effective troop strength east of the Mississippi River to two of his least experienced and/or trustworthy brigadiers. But they were southern gentlemen and in the past had been Johnston's seniors. He had served in the old army under Secretary of War Floyd, had named a Utah camp after him during the Mormon campaign, and in some ways, if only subconsciously, perhaps still viewed him as a superior. Similarly, Pillow had been a major general in Mexico when Johnston was a colonel. Pillow also was the prominent intimate of a deceased president and the wielder of substantial political power in the central and western regions of the most important state Johnston was charged with defending. Pillow and Floyd thus were stalwarts of a southern political establishment with which Johnston had identified all his life. Under his plantation-master style of casually delegating hands-on labor, they were eminently entitled to the tasks he gave them.

A further explanation for Johnston's choice of the Donelson commanders, as well as his slow reaction to Henry's peril, may lurk in the wings, unmentioned at the time out of military courtesy. In Henry Halleck and Don Carlos Buell, Johnston faced two of the most respected military men in the Federal army. At Bowling Green, Johnston himself opposed the closest of the two, Buell, while at Columbus he had Polk, his own predecessor in the Confederacy's western high command, defending against Halleck. By contrast, the man these comparative giants had sent against the forts on the Tennessee and Cumberland appeared Lilliputian, a prewar captain self-exiled to civilian obscurity under an alcoholic cloud. Surely the Federal brain trust would never choose a Ulysses Grant to command a position it considered the most critical on the western front. A larger attack must be aimed at Columbus or Bowling Green.

Floyd and Pillow could deal with a Grant.[18]

*　　*　　*

For a few days after Fort Henry's fall, artilleryman Jesse Taylor and several of his fellow Confederate prisoners of war were lodged on the same steamer with Grant, where they and the officers of their captors ate at the same messtable. Taylor later recalled that he and his comrades were "treated with every courtesy" despite what could have become an ugly incident.

One evening, two young Confederate officers found the means to get drunk. This particular evening, Grant, obviously busy with his preparations to move against Fort Donelson, did not sit down to eat with them. In his absence, the inebriated young Confederates became "vociferous," discussing "politics, military men and movements, etc.," apparently denigrating Yankees in general, Union soldiers in particular, and the questionable intelligence of Federal generals. While they raved, Grant came in unobserved, sat down, and ate. He appeared to take no notice of them, but when the apprentice drunkards rose to leave, they were met at the door by a detail of Federal soldiers and conducted to the guard-house.

Taylor promptly visited them and, after apparently being beseeched by the offenders, interceded with Grant, "carrying with me regrets, explanations, and apologies," Taylor later recalled. Taylor possibly had no idea how close to the general's bones this episode had to be cutting. Grant could have taken offense at the captives' remarks, but he just smiled. He told Taylor that he had had the two locked up partly for their own safety, fearing they might run afoul of some of his own officers in the same artificially bellicose condition. He said he did not believe the offenders knew he was in their hearing at dinner and added that they would be let out of the guard-house as soon as they sobered up.

He kept his word.[19]

Casting the Die

Grant, February 10–12

A FULL FOUR DAYS after Fort Henry's fall, Grant and Halleck both still agonized about Fort Donelson. Grant itched to get there as swiftly as men, materiel, and gunboats could be gathered. Halleck, out of a defensive instinct that included the wish to minimize his odds of disaster by changing field commanders, hoped just to hold Fort Henry.

Halleck had notified Grant that picks and shovels were on the way to dig in at Henry, but he had never specifically ordered Grant to stay there. He certainly had never ordered Grant to attack Fort Donelson. He had never even reacted to Grant's assertion that he *intended* to attack Fort Donelson. Halleck *had*, however, told *Buell* that Grant was going to attack the Confederate fort on the Cumberland, probably because he was sure Grant was going to do what he said he was going to do unless given positive orders to the contrary.

Why Halleck never flatly ordered Grant either to attack or not to is puzzling. Perhaps he could not fully decide. Even though a Grant attack on Donelson would risk getting cut off and defeated, thus injuring Halleck's reputation, there was no guarantee that Grant *would* get cut off and defeated, and his aggressiveness would maintain the initiative for Halleck against Buell in their battle for ascendancy in Federal western command. And, never having ordered Grant to attack, Halleck could always disavow a defeat.

Halleck did—twice—send Grant odd instructions urging a foray *past* Donelson.

One of the many telegrams that left Halleck's headquarters on February 10 contained a reiteration of a mystifying directive that the St. Louis commander had initially sent on February 8.

The February 8 wire had promised Grant quick reinforcements and the picks and shovels with which to dig in. It also ordered Grant to press into service "slaves of secessionists in the vicinity" to improve the Henry fortifications. Halleck had followed these with two very strange sentences:

"If possible, destroy the bridge at Clarksville. It is of vital importance, and should be attempted at all hazards." On February 10, Halleck reiterated this instruction: "If possible, destroy the bridge at Clarksville. Run any risk to accomplish this."

What map was the St. Louis commander reading? The transport-protecting gunboats were gone, and to reach Clarksville by water, even gunboats faced a daunting run up the narrow Cumberland past frowning Fort Donelson cannons. And to get to Clarksville other than by boat, a bridge-destruction party would have to travel at least twelve miles to reach the Cumberland somewhere near Dover, cross the river wherever unguarded boats or rafts could be found, then trek thirty more miles across more Confederate territory and conquer whatever defenders the Confederates had stationed around Clarksville.[1]

The same day that he sent the second wire, February 10, Halleck clarified himself somewhat—to history, if not to Grant—with further telegrams. He ordered Cullum at Cairo to induce Foote "if possible" to send at least two gunboats up the Cumberland because "I am straining every nerve to send troops to Dover and Clarksville." He also fired off a telegram directed to "General GRANT or Flag-Officer FOOTE: Push the gunboats up the river to cut the railroad bridges. Troops to sustain the gunboats can follow in transports."[2]

As soon as Grant received the first of these messages, he telegraphed a two-line reply reporting that "no negroes" remained "in this part of the country to work on fortifications." Rather than ask questions, he simply added that "Every effort will be put forth to have Clarksville within a few days." But to "have" Clarksville, rather than to just cut the railroad bridge there, he first would have to "have" Fort Donelson; that was the only way Federal boats could get up the Cumberland to that northern Tennessee town.

The oblique wires regarding Clarksville were the sole indications Halleck ever sent Grant that he perhaps approved of the move on Fort Donelson; specifically, though, he still had said not a word to Grant, yea nor nay, concerning it. Grant refused to let that bother him, at least outwardly. On February 9, he wrote Mary Grant in the tone of jaunty, self-effacing, restrained pride that he often employed in letters home.

> DEAR SISTER,
> I take my pen in hand "away down in Dixie" to let you know that I am still alive and well. What the next few days may bring forth however I cant tell you. I intend to keep the ball moving as lively as possible and have only been detained here from the fact that the Tennessee is very high and has been raising ever since we have been

*here[,] overflowing the back land making it necessary to bridge it
before we could move. —Before you receive this, you will hear . . . of
Fort Donaldson being attacked— . . . You have no conception of the
amount of labor I have to perform. An army of men all helpless
looking to the commanding officer for every supply. Your plain brother
however has, as yet, no reason to feel himself unequal to the task and
fully believes that he will carry on a successful campaign against our
rebel enemy—The scare and fright of the rebels up here is beyond
conception. Twenty three miles above here some were drowned in their
haste to retreat thinking us such Vandals that neither life nor property
would be respected. G. J. Pillow commands at Fort Donaldson. I hope
to give him a tug before you receive this.*

U. S. G.3

The day after writing Mary, he wrote to nudge Foote, saying that he was
"waiting very patiently for the gunboats—to go around on the Cumberland
whilst I march my land forces across to make a simultaneous attack upon
Fort Donaldson. I feel that there should be no delay in this matter and yet I
do not feel justified in going without some of your gunboats to co-operate.
Can you not send two boats from Cairo immediately up the Cumberland?"4

The veteran naval officer—overworked with finishing and fitting out the
gunboats and supervising experimental trials of the mortar rafts while escorting troops on feints and skirmishes, let alone his capture of Fort
Henry—was being prodded toward the Cumberland by Halleck, too. He was
also being annoyed by Assistant Secretary of War Thomas A. Scott, who now
was visiting Cairo. In a wire of February 8, as if Foote had nothing else to do,
Scott had congenially demanded "a statement in detail of all your gunboats,
their equipment and force now on them; also a statement setting forth the
additional force and equipment that you need, and the same regarding the
[mortar rafts]—I will run over to Cairo on Monday [i.e., February 10]—If
you will have those statements prepared, we can talk the whole subject over
so that I can get a thorough understanding of the matter. Please answer."

With deep misgivings, Foote yielded to the entreaties of Grant and Halleck that he get moving toward Fort Donelson, writing Grant that he would
try to "be ready to start tomorrow evening [February 12] with two Boats" that
would "move slowly," adding that he himself was "very busy with Secretary
Scott" and might not be able to leave Cairo until a day later. There was another problem he did not mention: Foote did not relish the prospect of taking on the high riverside batteries at Fort Donelson so soon after Fort Henry.
Like Tilghman, he knew that his seemingly easy victory at Henry was far
luckier than it appeared to the casual eye. However fearsome the scene

appeared to the arriving Federal infantry, the damage Foote had done to Henry was, in fact, fairly minimal—he had caused few Confederate casualties while sustaining grave damage to the ironclads. The mortar boats were not ready yet, and he still did not have even enough personnel to adequately man the gunboats. For such men as he was able to get, he had had to rely heavily on the army, and it was not supplying enough of them.

Grant was ready to do whatever it took to get gunboats to the Cumberland as soon as possible. His February 10 letter to Foote offered to make up any deficiency in Foote's manpower with an army artillery company "to serve on the gunboats temporarily." On February 11, Foote wrote Navy Secretary Welles, a friend since boyhood:

> *I leave again to-night with the Louisville, Pittsburg, and St. Louis for the Cumberland River, to cooperate with the army in the attack on Fort Donelson. I go reluctantly, as we are very short of men, and transferring men from vessel to vessel, as we have to do, is having a very demoralizing effect on them; 28 ran off to-day, hearing that they were again to be sent out of their vessels—I shall do all in my power to render the gunboats effective in the fight, although they are not properly manned, but I must go, as General Halleck wishes it. If we could wait ten days, and I had men, I would go with eight mortar boats and six armored boats and conquer.*[5]

Grant, too, worried about Halleck's wishes. Despite his lighthearted tone with his sister, Halleck's silence regarding the advance on Fort Donelson appears to have affected him. On the afternoon of the 10th, he did something he had never done before and would never do again. He convened at his headquarters on the steamboat *New Uncle Sam* what would be the only opinion-inviting council of war of his career. Present for the novel event were such obvious principals as Smith, McClernand, and Lew Wallace, as well as a few others. The question for discussion, Grant announced to the gathering, was whether to move immediately against Fort Donelson to try to get there ahead of the expected Confederate reinforcements from Bowling Green or to wait for the Union reinforcements Halleck was promising. Grant looked first to his old West Point commandant and mentor, Smith.

"There is every reason why we should move without the loss of a day," the crusty veteran said.

Grant then turned to McClernand—and quickly regretted it. Instead of offering his views off the cuff, the Illinois politician pompously acted as if he were on the floor of Congress. He read aloud to the group of officers a prepared speech in which he, too, advocated marching at once, but presumed to instruct Grant in minute specifics as to what he should do along the route and on arrival. (The day before, McClernand had sent Grant a letter giving his detailed recommendations on how, and in what order, Grant's army should travel the two roads to Fort Donelson, and the remarks he read to the gathering may have been the same letter.) The performance "could hardly fail to be offensive to a superior officer," Lew Wallace remembered.

Wallace also recalled that both Grant and Smith "grew restive" before Mc-Clernand ended his lengthy presentation. The second McClernand stopped reading, Grant turned and nodded abruptly to Wallace, who agreed in a single sentence that the attack should launch as soon as possible. The rest of the officers followed suit just as swiftly, but Wallace remembered thinking that none of their replies, from Smith's on down, made much difference; Grant had already made up his mind. He likely had. But he probably also wanted to get everybody—perhaps McClernand, especially—on record as favoring the attack, in case of future trouble about it from Halleck.[6]

Besides the obvious need to beat as many Confederate forces to Fort Donelson as possible, another reason he wished to move quickly undoubtedly had to do with the man reported to be in command of the place. Grant had nothing but contempt for Pillow, whom he had repeatedly denigrated in letters home.

"I had known General Pillow in Mexico," he would later write, "and judged that with any force, no matter how small, I could march up to within gunshot of any intrenchments he was given to hold. I said this to the officers of my staff at the time."[7]

On February 10, the day of the council of war, Grant issued marching orders for the 12th. But by the afternoon of the 11th the roads had dried enough that he ordered McClernand to take his division five miles out, past the mud of the river bottom to higher ground, in the hope of preventing jammed traffic the next day. Grant's instructions on the conduct of the march resembled the suggestions he had received in the letter from McClernand, possibly indicating his continuing wariness of the ex-congressman's friendships in high places. McClernand's First Division would precede Smith's Second, two brigades taking the Ridge Road and one brigade the Telegraph Road, with Smith following on the Ridge Road.

Suddenly on February 11, Grant's fifteen thousand attackers became twenty-three thousand. Transports arrived at Henry with the first reinforcements sent by Halleck: six regiments under Nebraska Colonel John M. Thayer. Grant ordered them back aboard their boats to be steamed back down the Tennessee and up the Cumberland, escorted from Cairo to Dover by the gunboats making the same journey. He assumed it would be easier to get them to Donelson by boat rather than on wet roads already plowed by his First and Second Divisions.[8]

On February 12, Smith's and McClernand's men poured across the two roads to Dover under a warm, spring-like sun. The heat of this beautiful day and the rugged hills they had to climb challenged the discipline of some of the volunteer units, and strewn blankets and overcoats soon lined their wake.

To resist these hardy Midwesterners more effectively than Fort Henry, Fort Donelson would have to have, at minimum, more men, more fight, and a harder-fisted cavalry commander.

It would have all three.

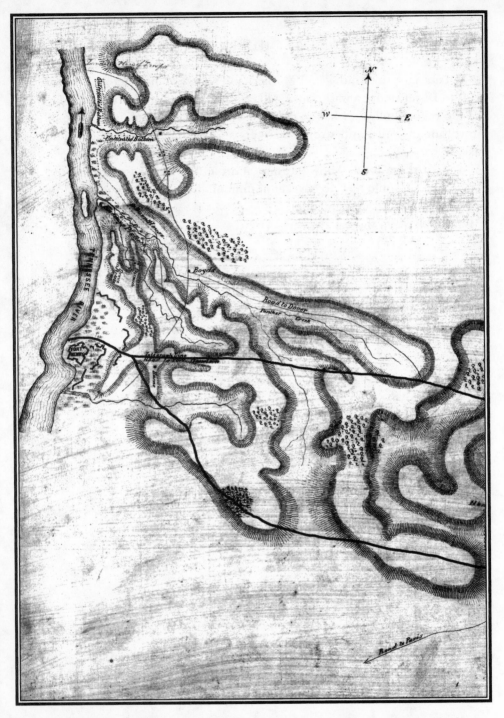

FROM FORT HENRY TO FORT DONELSON. Another map drawn under the supervision of McPherson, an accomplished engineer who graduated first in his class at West Point, shows the whole of the two roads—Telegraph to the north and Ridge below it—on which the Federals advanced on Fort Donelson and Dover, and the topography they traversed.

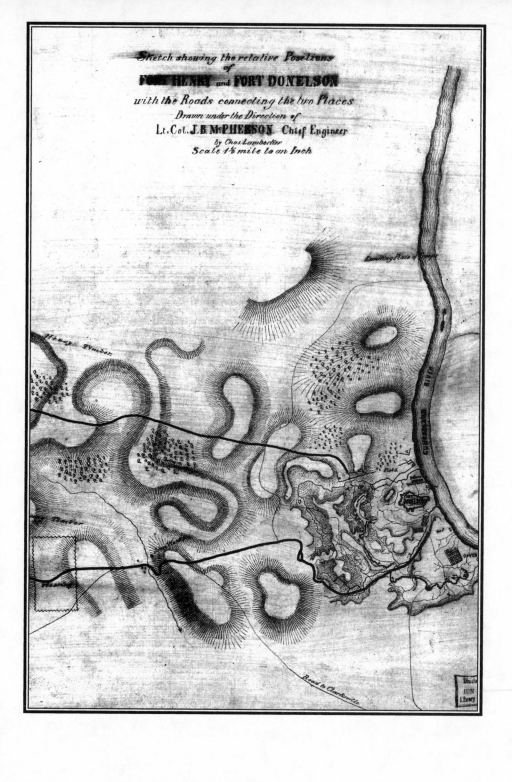

Sketch showing the relative Positions
of
FORT HENRY and FORT DONELSON
with the Roads connecting the two Places
Drawn under the Direction of
Lt. Col. J.B. McPHERSON, Chief Engineer
by Chas. Lambecker
Scale 1⅝ mile to an Inch

Road to Clarksville

PART III

"BATTLE FOR NASHVILLE": FORT DONELSON

Wednesday, February 12, Grant

Getting There

THE SHORTER OF the two direct routes to the Cumberland River fortress was twelve miles, the other fourteen. Sergeant F. F. Kiner of the Fourteenth Iowa estimated the distance of his own unit's trek at fifteen and informed his diary that he and his comrades rested several times. "As we had not been used to marching," Kiner explained, "we got tired easily." Fortunately, the day was "beautiful and warm" and they were traveling light: "We took with us nothing but our blankets and haversacks, three days' rations of crackers and boiled pork; our muskets and cartridge boxes . . . [F]orty rounds of cartridges completed our loads."[1]

The Federal troops did not expect to be out long. They were, after all, trailing an enemy that had fled pell-mell from them less than a week earlier. Lew Wallace, left behind in command of a 2,500-man garrison at Fort Henry, noted in a letter home that among the departing marchers, "Overcoats were an encumbrance." Many of the troops—"thousands," Wallace would later write—neglected to take even the blankets that the Fourteenth Iowa did. They "marched from Fort Henry as to a summer fête, leaving coats, blankets, and knapsacks behind them in camp." Grant later recalled that they simply threw them away on the road, another manifestation of the difficulties of managing an army whose enlisted men and officers were virtually all new volunteers unaccustomed to regular-army discipline. Because the Fort Henry expedition's transportation had been steamboat-borne, there were just four wagons per regiment, so the Donelson-bound troops moved without tents and baggage as well.[2]

Kiner's Fourteenth Iowa was part of the Smith-led Second Division, which did not have the five-mile head start of McClernand's First. Grant's fifteen thousand attackers clambered over rough, rolling, and sparsely settled country on the parallel roads—Telegraph to the north and Ridge below it— that had been cut a few months earlier by the Confederate Tilghman to

connect Donelson with Henry. By mid-day, McClernand's forward units were
within two miles of the Donelson defenses.

Suddenly they encountered Confederate cavalry—"strongly supported,"
as McClernand would report. The Southerners immediately menaced the
right side of McClernand's advance and readied an assault on the head of
his column. A detachment of Second Illinois Cavalry was sent forward to
drive the Confederates back, and although official Federal reports gave
these enemy troopers scant credit, their resistance was enough to halt the
Union march and give pause to Colonel Richard Oglesby, commanding Mc-
Clernand's First Brigade. Oglesby felt constrained to bring up and deploy
three infantry regiments—the Thirtieth, Eighth, and Eighteenth Illinois—in
line of battle, plus cavalry on both flanks. He identified the enemy in his report as "a large body" of horsemen "under Colonel Forrest."

"Colonel Forrest"—it is notable that Oglesby mentioned him by name,
since no Federal had ever appeared to deem the name of Lieutenant
Colonel Gantt, the Confederate cavalry commander at Fort Henry, worth remembering. Oglesby surely took note of Forrest because the Confederate
horsemen, who numbered no more than thirteen hundred, swiftly showed
themselves to be a harder-hitting lot than the skedaddlers of Fort Henry.

When Forrest encountered the Federal vanguard, a company of the Second Illinois Cavalry, in late morning, he immediately dismounted three of
his companies and sent them forward to fight as infantry, positioning them
along the crest of a hill paralleling the Ridge Road. It was an unusual move:
cavalry, at the time, was regarded as exclusively horse soldiery, performing
only work doable from the saddle, but Forrest either did not know this or, in
the likely event that he did know, did not care. This must have been what
prompted Oglesby's description of Forrest's force as cavalry "strongly supported," meaning by infantry. No Confederate infantry was present.

The first skirmish of the Battle of Fort Donelson was a brief but sharp
clash. The Confederate and Union cavalrymen charged each other. The
Confederates drove back their Union counterparts, but McClernand reported that the Union horsemen managed to hold the Southerners' "support in
check" until the Thirtieth Illinois Infantry arrived. The Confederate resistance was strong enough that McClernand himself came up to have a look.
To push past the attackers, he ordered Oglesby to "move to the right of the
Ridge Road through some old fields" to a longer-established thoroughfare—
apparently one called the Pinery Road—leading westward from Dover toward the Tennessee River. The Confederates sidled with them, however.
With too few numbers to make a head-on challenge, Forrest's men tried "in
large force to gain the rear" of Oglesby's right. The Confederates again
charged the Federal cavalry in what McClernand termed "a vigorous and

determined attack," but suddenly their quarry moved aside. Previously hidden men of the Eighth Illinois rose from the ground with leveled muskets. The infantrymen delivered "strong fire" into the Confederates, after which Oglesby turned artillery on them. Oglesby then watched as, after one cannon shot, the outnumbered Confederates "fled in confusion from the field."

But Forrest had either debuted impressively in the consciousness of commanders on both sides or, more likely, enlarged the reputation he had already established at Sacramento and elsewhere across western Kentucky. General Buckner, temporarily in charge at Donelson, reported that the Tennessee colonel's "heavy skirmishing" of the morning was conducted "with his usual gallantry."[3]

*   *   *

Donelson would be the first of the two battlefields on which Grant would directly face Forrest. But the Memphis citizen-soldier and the lightly regarded Union brigadier, although rooted in vastly different geographies and philosophies, were tenuously linked.

The connection was a Kentucky town that epitomized the wide and bitter gulf between two Americas. Maysville was a steamboat stop on the Ohio River, the Red Sea separating slaves in the central South from the world of freedom they so desperately imagined. Maysville's location had long made it a flashpoint of Southern outrage against law-breaking abolitionist plots to spirit blacks out of bondage and ferry them nine miles downriver to one of the North's staunchest stations of the Underground Railroad: Ripley, Ohio.[4]

Grant received some of his teenaged schooling in both Ripley and Maysville in the late 1830s, when the rivalry between clandestine abolitionists and ebullient slave-catchers was beginning to roil the sentiments of both towns. His slavery-hating father had emigrated from the Kentucky town decades earlier, refusing to live anywhere that sanctioned human bondage and especially the Caucasian leisure it exemplified. Jesse Grant had left an older half-brother at Maysville, though, and young Ulysses lived with his uncle while attending school there for one winter term.[5]

Forrest almost certainly had been in Maysville, too, but even if he had never set foot in the place he had by the outbreak of the Civil War acquired a memorable connection to it. A sometime associate in his wide-ranging slave business, Maysville resident James McMillan, was gruesomely murdered in Memphis in 1857 by Isaac Bolton, then the Tennessee city's foremost slave-trader. According to lurid testimony in proceedings in which Forrest was a pivotal witness, Bolton claimed McMillan had sold him a free black who later won back his freedom in court, thus requiring a refund of the purchase money. Such sales, although illegal, were so common that blacks even in the antebellum North were never completely safe unless they emigrated to Canada. The only unusual feature of the Memphis occurrence was that the sold man managed to reclaim his freedom.[6]

The case's abhorrent details exemplify some of the incendiary sources of the antagonism that fueled civil war. After the free black had been re-liberated, McMillan and a partner brought a small group of slaves into Memphis and lodged them for several days in Forrest's facilities. During the visit, Bolton lured the Kentuckian to his own slave-yard on the pretense of doing business, then shot him twice and cursed him as he writhed on the floor in a pool of blood. McMillan was taken to Forrest's house, where he died a few hours after telling the story of the attack to Forrest himself.

The 1858 trial was so sensational that its venue was changed from Memphis to Covington, Tennessee. There Forrest testified that over their four-year acquaintance McMillan had been a guest in his home "a month in all." He said McMillan was "a middle-sized, delicate, spare man" who "at the time of his death . . . was trading for a man named Hill in Kentucky" and "both of them were down with eight or ten negroes . . . They put their negroes in my [slave-]yard. McMillan remarked to me that Bolton wanted to buy a boy for him . . . He asked me what I would do if it was me. I advised him to take one [to Bolton's establishment]. He said Bolton wanted to buy the boy for his wife. I was not much acquainted with Bolton."

Forrest testified that McMillan left the Forrest residence around 9 a.m. with the slave, "Mr. Ridgeway's negro boy," to go to Bolton's slave-yard. A little later, he said, he was on a downtown street corner near the Planter's Bank, a half-mile from Bolton's, when he heard about the shooting and hurried there. By the time he arrived, McMillan had been taken to the Forrest home, where Forrest arrived in time to help undress him. The Kentuckian was found to have two wounds, "one in each hip running different directions." The *Memphis Appeal* quoted Forrest as saying McMillan asked for his "candid" opinion as to his condition; "I said he would die, he said he knew it."

After requesting Forrest's help in making some financial arrangements for his wife, McMillan told Forrest the story of his fatal encounter. He said he had arrived at Bolton's that morning with the slave and that Bolton's temper almost immediately flared. He called McMillan "a d—d rascal" who "had sold him a free negro" and demanded restitution. "He said, pay, you G-d d—d rascal, or I will kill you." McMillan first told Bolton that Bolton's brother Wash, who at the time handled the family's slave business in Lexington, Kentucky, "knew all about the free negro"—apparently meaning that Wash Bolton had decided to risk the illegal transaction on the assumption that the abducted black would not be able to get adequate legal representation. Now,

under threat of death from Wash's brother, McMillan said he had no resources on which to write a check in Memphis but would go to Forrest's,
consult his partner Hill, "and try to fix it up." At that point a Bolton employee, who also was present, departed into a back room, apparently hoping to
induce McMillan to follow him farther away from the street. When McMillan
did not go, Bolton drew a pistol and fired three times, his second and third
shots hitting McMillan. The Bolton associate then returned to the room,
and Bolton drew a bowie knife and tossed it onto the floor beside McMillan.

"There is the d—d son of a b—'s knife," Bolton told the employee.

One of the bullets had passed around McMillan's hip into his groin. In
great pain, he asked for water and other comfort and was denied both. "You
have killed me," he told Bolton.

"You d—d son of a b—!" Bolton replied. "You ought to have been killed
twenty years ago."[7]

Bolton never was convicted but reputedly spent huge sums on defense at-
torneys, was financially ruined by this outlay and the sensational publicity,
and was supplanted as the foremost practitioner of their unsavory trade by
Forrest himself. Between the crime and the trial, Forrest also had helped his
city's civil authorities face down a lynch mob to save another murderer, a
gambler named Dan Able. Two months after the Bolton trial, the city's newly
ascendant slave merchant was elected to its board of aldermen.[8]

Thus Maysville, Kentucky, had been a benchmark in the prewar careers of
both Forrest and Grant. Maysville had given a boyhood Grant a feel for the
tension of life in a society resting uncomfortably on a minority in chains.
Some two decades later, the murder of a Maysville citizen helped push Forrest toward the forefront of that same high-strung social order.

The profane vigor of his testimony against Bolton exhibited a hallmark of
Forrest's life: an offhand and surpassing fearlessness of men and their pro-
prieties. When a neighboring farmer's ox destroyed fences and crops on his
family's tenanted land on the northern Mississippi frontier, a teenaged Forrest repeatedly warned the neighbor, then shot the offending animal dead
and ultimately put bullet holes in the clothes of its owner when he appeared, gun in hand, to retaliate. When four men accosted his aged uncle
and business partner a few years later on the public square of Hernando,
Mississippi, he took them on single-handedly, wounding two with a two-ball
pistol and routing the others with a bowie-knife thrown him by a bystander.

Forrest seemed able to instantly divine what he wanted in life and then to
go after it with single-minded intrepidity. In September 1845, just months
following the Hernando melee, he married into the noted Montgomery
family after encountering the carriage of eighteen-year-old Mary Ann and
her widowed mother stuck in a creek ford. He had used his shoulder to help

their slave extract the mired wheel and then asked permission to call at their home, where he menaced other suitors—including a ministerial student—from their porch.9

When he cantered into Donelson a decade and a half later, the fort's other defenders must have sensed that this tall, gray-eyed horseman would be no George Gantt.

*   *   *

While Oglesby's men parried the futile thrusts of Forrest's far inferior force, McClernand's and Smith's divisions arrived and deployed, paralleling the Confederate lines through woods that in several places were so thick that colonels could not see from one end of their regiments to the other. Grant, partly from luck and partly from his own discernment, had, as he had predicted, been able to march to the very foot of the defenders' hastily dug rifle pits on ridges a quarter to three-fourths of a mile west of the banks of the Cumberland.

Grant had ordered McClernand's division to take position in front of the Confederate left near Dover, while Smith's men invested the Confederate right just west of the fort proper. By good fortune or intelligence, this pitted Smith, Grant's most experienced subordinate, against the Confederates' best wing commander, Buckner, while McClernand faced his fellow politico, Pillow, on the Union right. McClernand quickly found that his end of the Federal line had to keep stretching toward the river to cover critical southward roads down which the Confederate garrison could escape to Nashville, seventy-five miles away.10

Most of the Union troops were still approaching along the two roads when, in early afternoon, they heard firing from Commander Walke's *Carondelet*. It was a signal requested by Grant, at McClernand's suggestion, to apprise both the Federals and the Confederates of the arrival of the vaunted gunboats. "The object . . . was to take possession of the river as soon as possible, to engage the enemy's attention by making formidable demonstrations before the fort, and to prevent it from being reinforced," Walke later recalled.11

Walke's initial demonstration turned out to be less "formidable" than Grant had hoped for. The *Carondelet* was accompanied only by the transport *Alps*, which had towed it most of the way to Donelson against the flooding river's swift current. Grant had expected the timber-clads *Lexington* and *Tyler*, too, returning from their run into Alabama under the *Conestoga*'s Lieutenant Phelps. But Phelps, ordered by Foote to return to Cairo with his raid booty, refused to release any of his vessels to Walke. Walke regarded the rebuff as insubordinate but was unable to coax a similar attitude from Foote, who highly valued Phelps. So Walke proceeded to Donelson virtually alone, and Grant had to ask Halleck to send Foote with more gunboats.[12]

The fort's river batteries were arranged in two tiers dug into the side of a hill rising about a hundred feet above the river, one row thirty feet above the risen water line and the second thirty or so feet above the first. The upper emplacement boasted two thirty-two-pounder naval guns and a one-hundred-twenty-eight-pounder rifled gun, while the lower held eight thirty-two-pounder seacoast cannon and a ten-inch columbiad. Both levels were protected by parapets sixteen to ten feet thick from base to crest. Walke thought the "black rows of heavy guns" pointed at *Carondelet* looked like "the dismal-looking sepulchers cut in the rocky cliffs near Jerusalem" in the Middle East, except "more repulsive."

On the summit of the hill sat the central fortress itself, earthen walls six feet or more in height surrounding fifteen acres. Outside this bastion were stretched lengthening lines of rifle pits fronted by logs overpiled with dirt. These ran along mostly wooded, westerly facing ridgelines helping to enclose a hundred-acre quadrangle bounded by Hickman Creek on the north, the Cumberland River on the east, and Lick Creek, a backwater of the Cumberland to the south. Winter rains had flooded all these streams well out of their banks, which helped protect the fort's defenders from exterior attack.

The center of the quadrangle, though, was cut by the curling gorge of a third swollen tributary, Indian Creek. Separating the fifteen-acre inner fortress from Dover a mile and a half upriver to the south, this stream made it difficult for the fort's commanders to reach their headquarters in the town.[13]

Dover was the seat of Stewart County. With the arrival of so many reinforcements to Donelson, it was now a burgeoning Confederate supply depot, but the place remained hardly more than a hamlet. Its unprepossessing public square was flanked by a few stores and a couple of inns clinging to a knobby ridge, with a few roads and lanes meandering off down valleys and across other ridges toward the Tennessee River to the west and Cumberland City, Clarksville, and Nashville on various compass gradations to the east and south. Northern war correspondent Charles Coffin would eventually remember it as a "straggling village" comprising "perhaps five hundred" residents and "a half-dozen decent dwellings." A minor junction of Cumberland River steamboats and wagon traffic between Paris and Clarksville, to Lew Wallace's skeptical gaze Dover was a locality "unknown to fame, meager in population, architecturally poor. There was a court-house in the place, and (the) tavern. . . double-storied, unpainted . . . with windows of eight-by-ten glass, which, if the panes may be likened to eyes, were both squint and cataractous. Looking

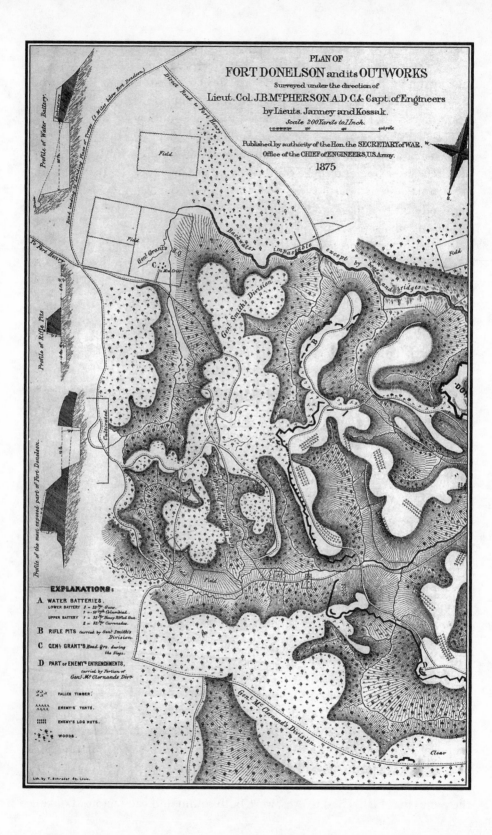

PLAN OF
FORT DONELSON and its OUTWORKS
Surveyed under the direction of
Lieut. Col. J.B.McPHERSON A.D.C.& Capt. of Engineers
by Lieuts. Janney and Kossak.
Scale 200 Yards to 1 Inch.
Published by authority of the Hon. the SECRETARY of WAR.
Office of the CHIEF of ENGINEERS, U.S. Army.
1875

EXPLANATIONS:
A WATER BATTERIES.
   LOWER BATTERY 8 = 32 Pdr Guns.
                  1 = 10 inch Columbiad.
   UPPER BATTERY 1 = 32 Pdr Heavy Rifled Gun.
                  2 = 32 Pdr Carronades.
B RIFLE PITS carried by Genl Smith's Division.
C Genl GRANT'S Head Qrs. during the Siege.
D PART of ENEMY'S ENTRENCHMENTS, carried by Portion of Genl McClernands Divn.

       FALLEN TIMBER.
       ENEMY'S TENTS.
       ENEMY'S LOG HUTS.
       WOODS.

Lith. by T. Schrader St. Louis.

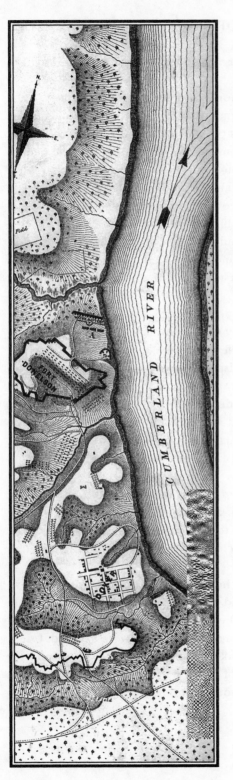

FORT DONELSON AND DOVER OVERVIEW. This third McPherson-supervised map shows the expanse Grant's troops had to cover: two miles of Confederate trenches running from Hickman Creek northwest of the fort to the roads leading out of Dover toward Nashville. Because Smith and McClernand's troops were unable to do it alone, Wallace was brought from Fort Henry and given command of reinforcements from Cairo.

through them gave the street outside the appearance of a sedgy slough of yellow backwater."[14]

Grant's men had begun sidling north and south along the face of the Confederate entrenchments. McClernand spread his troops across a long, high ridge parallel to the lower hills on which ran the Confederate outer lines. Federal sharpshooters found commanding sites from which to bedevil the feverishly entrenching Confederates, but the trees were so thick in most places that the Union artillery could find few unobstructed lanes of fire. The Confederates had used the smaller trees to form their abatis, cutting a profusion of them about chest-high and felling them outward. Left partially connected at their trunks so that they could not be pulled downhill and out of the way by gangs of attacking infantrymen, they would prove, in the words of Federal Lieutenant Colonel McPherson, "a most difficult obstacle to get over."[15]

McClernand ordered Captain Jasper Dresser's battery of Illinois Light Artillery to the front to fire at enemy tents behind the center of the Confederate line, three-quarters of a mile across the Indian Creek valley. Expending twenty-one shells, Dresser dispersed some Confederates drawn up in line of battle and saw them strike the tents. Colonel William R. Morrison and the First Division's Third Brigade, which in the early afternoon had moved so eagerly toward a reported enemy camp in the center that the men "cast away knapsacks, overcoats, and every inconvenience to . . . speedy advance," found the reported camp deserted, with only "a few camp fires" still burning.[16]

McClernand kept pushing rightward toward the river, and by evening the First Division's vanguard had reached and crossed the Forge Road leading out of Dover toward Charlotte. Near the other—northwestern—end of the lengthening Federal line, Smith was covering the Confederate right. There the Fourteenth Iowa took its place.

"We arrived to within a mile of the Fort a little before dark and . . . formed line of battle, stacked arms and laid down to sleep for the night within good common shot range from the rebel works," Sergeant Kiner soon would write. "Notwithstanding the danger to which we were exposed, I slept very soundly, with one-half of my blanket under me and the other half over me, and my head resting on a chunk of rotten wood for a pillow."[17]

Grant was closing in. On what, he could not be sure.

Through February 12, Donelson's Leaders

A Very Mixed Bag

Fᴇᴅᴇʀᴀʟ ᴄᴀᴠᴀʟʀʏ and scouts had appeared in ominously growing numbers around Dover and its adjacent fort on Tuesday, February 11. Forrest had arrived the previous evening. General Clark had been ordered to abandon Hopkinsville, and the cavalryman, after covering Clark's retreat to Clarksville, was detached to Pillow, who directed Forrest to hurry to Fort Donelson. Riding cross-country to reach the Cumberland's east bank on February 10, Forrest finished ferrying his men and horses across to Dover the following morning. That afternoon, directed to take a three-hundred–man detachment on a reconnaissance, he ran into Union cavalry three miles out. Forrest's official account of the ensuing incident perhaps reflects his long-standing vocation—salesman—and his predisposition not to underplay anything having to do with himself. Estimating the number of enemy at about double his own, he reported engaging in a brief firefight and then pushing them back six miles, "mortally" wounding "several" and capturing a prisoner.[1]

When Forrest returned to Confederate lines that evening, post commander Pillow ordered him to take charge of all of Donelson's mounted troops. These included his own Third Tennessee, of course, plus three Kentucky companies and Gantt's Ninth Tennessee Battalion. The assignment was one of Pillow's better military moves, but, as with many others, it likely stemmed from reasons other than brilliance. Besides Gantt, titular leader of Fort Henry's panicked troopers, Forrest was the only other cavalry colonel present and the ranking one in seniority. As a prominent Tennessee Democrat, Pillow was also probably well enough acquainted with the Memphis ex-alderman to know he would not countenance the sort of behavior displayed by Gantt's cavalry in the withdrawal from Fort Henry. Too, Pillow almost certainly knew Gantt, who hailed from Pillow's home county, but whether Pillow was competent enough to judge Gantt's competence is questionable.[2]

*   *   *

The man who appointed Forrest chief of Donelson's mounted troops was, in his very different way, almost as extraordinary as the appointee. Brigadier General Gideon Johnson Pillow personified what Forrest had worked all his antebellum life to become: rich and, of even more consequence, important. One of Tennessee's wealthiest men, Pillow was master of a baronial plantation in Maury County, his state's lesser equivalent of Kentucky's horse country. He also possessed vast lands in Arkansas and hundreds of African Americans, some of whom he may well have purchased at Forrest's Memphis slave-yard. His energy and organizational skill had been most famously revealed in his engineering of the unlikely presidential nomination of James K. Polk, and he himself had contended for a U.S. Senate seat in 1857.

Pillow was markedly less able as a soldier, however, despite being generally brave. He was also arrogant, vain, spiteful, insubordinate, intolerant of insubordination by officers under him, and perpetually hungry for public notice.

When ordered to Dover from Clarksville on the 9th, Pillow had only been back in the active army for a week. He had resigned at Columbus six weeks earlier only after arranging to have loyal subordinates petition Jefferson Davis to order him back to duty. When Secretary of War Benjamin asked for an explanation of his resignation, Pillow complained that Polk had been tardy in reinforcing him in the Belmont battle and then had denied him any authority at Columbus. Pillow also derided Polk for exhibiting fits of temper and lack of attention to duty. In his own turn, Polk wrote Benjamin that ever since he had been made superior to Pillow at Memphis (after Davis's refusal to make Pillow a Confederate major general), Pillow had displayed "petty jealousies" and indulged in "disingenuous criticism" while "conducting himself generally as towards a rival to be undermined and supplanted rather than towards a brother officer in the commission of the Government."[3]

Polk and Pillow were both mediocre soldiers at best. The former was almost as ponderous and archly independent as the latter was bunglingly dashing and vainglorious. But at least Pillow, unlike his otherwise-occupied superiors, had been highly concerned as early as mid-December about the peril to the Confederacy lying between the Tennessee and Cumberland rivers. Pillow's views, as usual, were self-serving—he was angling to be put in charge of the region whose perils he trumpeted—but Johnston had few other generals available. Johnston also claimed to have a "high opinion" of Pillow's military ability, which hardly credits his own. However, crisis now approached calamity. With Federal aggressiveness running rampant along the two rivers that

Pillow had warned about, Johnston may well have done the little required to persuade him to reconsider his request for retirement.

Pillow withdrew his resignation on February 2 and went back to serve not Polk at Columbus but, rather, Johnston at Bowling Green. From there he was sent to Clarksville with assurance that Charles Clark's Mississippi brigade was on its way from Hopkinsville and would make up the core of the Clarksville command. With typical verve, Pillow swiftly inspected the town and asked for more guns and troops. He went on to inform Johnston that if Fort Donelson fell, Clarksville could offer little resistance, its defensive works being unfinished and "not one" of its heavy guns ready to fire. Johnston dispatched a battery and two divisions, Floyd's and Buckner's, from Russellville. Overnight, Pillow converted Clarksville into an efficient forwarding center for men and supplies.4

But, as usual with Pillow, there were problems. The place he began forwarding the men and supplies to, without the permission of headquarters, was Fort Donelson; Buckner's large division—of five thousand men—was put on transports and sent there as soon as it arrived. Floyd, the ranking officer in the area, had been ordered to Clarksville to guard the railroad, and once he arrived he would supplant Pillow as the Clarksville commander. Likely for that reason, Pillow hastened to tell Johnston that he himself could go on the offensive against Grant from Fort Donelson as soon as Clark's Mississippians joined him. But Clark, a fellow Mexican War veteran, took his time getting down the road from Hopkinsville, then clashed with Pillow and refused to accept his orders. Johnston had to intervene on Pillow's behalf, by which time it was too late for a Pillow offensive.

The offensive probably would not have worked in any case. At least in theory, Grant *was* vulnerable from Pillow's direction immediately after Fort Henry's fall, sitting as he was in the rain backed up against the flooded Tennessee with his gunboats gone upriver and down. But the drowned roads that prevented him from attacking Fort Donelson on the 8th probably would have kept Pillow from attacking *him*, too.5

Pillow got himself assigned to Donelson on the 9th and arrived there the next day. He found a "field work of very contracted dimensions . . . constructed by the garrison to protect the battery" but "commanded by the [surrounding] hills" and generally "open to the fire of artillery from every direction." Its downriver-aimed gun emplacements boasted only a handful of thirty-two-pounder cannon, too few men to man them, and little firing experience among those few. The mood prevailing among the garrison at large seemed to reflect their defenses' vulnerability. "Deep gloom was hanging over the command," Pillow would report: "The troops were greatly

depressed and demoralized by the circumstances attending the surrender of
Fort Henry and the manner of retiring from that place."

He first lent his zeal to preparing for Foote's dreaded ironclads. He quickly located two heavier guns, a ten-inch columbiad and a rifled thirty-two-
pounder, and had them hauled to the riverside batteries and mounted. He
fattened the thin battery corps by adding to it a light artillery company and
ordering more ammunition from Nashville. Then, turning to the fort's land
side, he had Gilmer, the Johnston engineering aide who had escaped Fort
Henry, hurriedly lay out a lengthy line of outer rifle pits along the first row
of ridges ringing the river defenses. These lines, approaching three miles in
length (too long to be defended by fewer than many thousand men), took in
both the fort and the town of Dover, near whose principal wharf burgeoning
supplies of rations and ammunition were being steamed in and stockpiled.
The deep gorge of surging, swollen Indian Creek interrupted the proposed
trench lines between the Confederates' right and right center and, to defend this natural breach, cannon were clustered on heights overlooking
each side of the stream. Gilmer had to mark off the trenches with such
haste, though, that in some places the diggers were exposed to surrounding
hills that bristled with perilous sniper sites.[6]

"We are making herculean efforts to strengthen our parapets—making
narrow embrasures with sand bags," Gilmer wrote headquarters at Bowling
Green.[7]

And Pillow was putting as many men as possible behind them. His most
notable and high-handed acquisition was Buckner's Second Division, Army
of Central Kentucky, which along with Floyd's Virginians had only been ordered by Johnston from Russellville to Clarksville. Pillow took advantage of
the fact that Buckner himself was not with his division when it arrived at
Clarksville; he was still at Russellville, worrying over a report he had received
from Kentucky, said to have originated with an aide to Buell, that the "expedition up the Cumberland and Tennessee [is] chiefly a diversion." If that
turned out to be true, his division was almost sure to be more needed well
east of Clarksville.

Buckner's attention had been shifting eastward anyway, and for good reason. An appointment to reorganize and command the shattered Department of East Tennessee was on its way to him from Richmond, and on
February 9 he was alarmed to receive another Kentucky report that seemed
to confirm that the Federal move at Fort Henry was designed to draw Confederate attentions away from a heavier blow to follow in the very area to
which Richmond was in the process of assigning him. Confederate sympathizers in Lexington had sent an apparently purloined dispatch with frightening news that Buckner quickly passed on in a wire to Johnston at Bowling

Green: "900 wagons are being loaded with guns, army stores, &c., at Lexington, and sent to London, Ky . . . movement into East Tennessee [is] to be made with large force through London."

This telegram to Johnston added a final sentence indicating Buckner's dawning realization that Pillow had grabbed his division:

"All our troops here have gone on to Donelson by boats."[8]

*   *   *

The last thing Buckner wanted was to have his men serving anywhere under Pillow, and for not just proprietary reasons. His own doubtless included some of the same personal ones that Pillow had for wanting Buckner's well-drilled unit—and especially Buckner himself—under him. The two men despised each other.

Their mutual detestation dated back to 1857, just after Pillow's U.S. Senate ambitions were wrecked by the machinations of fellow Democrat Andrew Johnson, who loathed Pillow and his aristocratic airs. Buckner, a prosperous civilian businessman at the time, was in Nashville shopping for a Southern home to which to move from Chicago. While there, he decided at Pillow's expense to publicly display his dogmatic penchant for standing up for whatever he viewed as right. Reared to "do your duty in whatever field it may lie and never forget that you are a gentleman," Buckner sometimes followed this paternal injunction to extremes, even in affairs in which he was not personally involved.

A West Pointer and admirer of Mexican War hero Winfield Scott, Buckner had taken offense at published claims Pillow made during the Senate campaign about his services in the Mexican War. So, soon after Johnson defeated Pillow for the Senate seat, Buckner wrote the first of three devastating articles in the *Nashville Republican Banner* reviewing Pillow's self-glorifications. Buckner accused Pillow of taking credit for actions of General Scott—including victories Scott had won by employing measures that Pillow had earlier criticized. Buckner used military transcripts and caustic humor to snare Pillow in repeated falsehoods. The *Banner* pieces also re-publicized a highly embarrassing episode in which Pillow had apparently ordered aides to take as his personal souvenirs two captured Mexican cannon belonging to the U.S. government—and then, when caught, blamed the aides.

In one of the articles, Buckner compared Pillow to Shakespeare's comic Falstaff. He also quoted the editor of the *New Orleans Delta*, publisher of some wartime letters in praise of Pillow that also had been prompted by Pillow, as saying he had erased from these letters such language as "plunged in" and "wade waist-deep in mud and water" because, in Buckner's acid prose,

"the reputation of Gen. Pillow as a military engineer had previously 'got entangled among some ditches' in the public estimation." He was referring, of
course, to Pillow's notorious entrenching lapse.

The attacks were doubly humiliating for Pillow because Buckner and the
Banner, noting that they could not now be accused of "any purpose to influence that contest," had not published the articles until after Pillow already
had suffered the Senate loss. The pieces were signed merely "Citizen," but
Buckner notified Pillow that he was their author, a fact that became well-
known in the community. Nashville politician Randal McGavock wrote in his
journal after the first appeared that he expected Pillow to challenge Buckner
to a duel. Pillow, for whatever reason, did not.[9]

The bad blood between Pillow and Buckner manifested itself as soon as
they encountered each other at Fort Donelson. Buckner was carrying orders
from Floyd directing Pillow to release Buckner's and Floyd's troops from
Donelson and send them twenty miles south to Cumberland City nearer
Nashville on the Cumberland River. Floyd, probably with much help from
the more experienced Buckner, had developed a plan to operate from Cumberland City against Grant's right flank as he marched against Fort Donelson
from Fort Henry—while Pillow held Donelson with a much smaller force.
The plan had merit, using most of the Confederates in the Donelson region
to strike the Federals in the flank and rear with an army nearly the size of
Grant's. At the same time, because Cumberland City was located on the river
beside tracks of the Memphis, Clarksville, & Louisville Railroad, these same
Confederates would have the flexibility to rejoin Johnston's Bowling Green
troops by rail or boat as they retreated to Nashville. The catch was—and if
Buckner was the plan's originator, the catch may not have been accidental—
the Donelson detachment might have to be sacrificed.

When Buckner handed Pillow Floyd's orders on the night of February 11,
Pillow refused them. Despite Forrest's skirmish with the large body of Union
cavalry that very afternoon and other accumulating evidence of an imminent Federal advance, Pillow said he was leaving to have a personal talk with
Floyd. He ordered Buckner to stay where he was.[10]

                              *   *   *

"[I]f we can have ten days[,] we hope to make bomb-proofs over the guns,"
Jeremy Gilmer had informed headquarters in his letter of February 10.

On February 12, hardly minutes after Pillow boarded a steamboat for
Cumberland City to find Floyd, the Confederates began to realize that they
would not have ten days. Time was up. One by one, unit commanders discovered Federal infantry in their front in significant and multiplying numbers.

Confederate reinforcements continued gathering at the fort, pitching in to help with the massive trench-digging effort that had been underway for days. The Eighteenth Tennessee's Colonel Joseph Palmer, the majority of whose 685 men arrived on the 8th with no tents "or other protection from the weather and scarcely any cooking utensils," reported that his regiment worked night and day on rifle pits and trenches "without relief or rest" from the 9th to the 12th. Palmer's superior, Third Brigade commander Colonel John C. Brown, wrote that his men were put at the job without even the necessary entrenching gear.[11]

Some Confederate units arrived barely before the Federals did, and the result was chaotic. Near the Dover wharf, the newly-encamped Fifty-First Virginia had its pickets driven in, was hurried to a position next to Buckner's troops on the far right, then marched still later in the day back to the left near Dover, a sector under the immediate command of General Bushrod Johnson. By dusk, Johnson had thrown out pickets on the westward-leading Wynn's Ferry Road to protect the extending of abatis in that area, and the work of these laborers quickly became life-threatening. Johnson's pickets as well as the work party were sent running for cover by enemy fire. One man was killed inside the trenches, another outside, along with a third wounded.[12]

On Buckner's north end of the Confederate position, Third Brigade commander Brown reported that his works were barely half-finished when the enemy appeared before them around noon. "From then on, incessant sharpshooter fire made it necessary for the fatigue parties to improve the trenches by night," he reported; working by day was "almost impossible." Colonel Roger Hanson of the Second Kentucky Infantry, manning the Confederate right, reported that Smith's arriving Federals were "pressing in our front with the evident intention of investing our position." In a sentence that described the situation of the entire Southern infantry and artillery that day, Hanson added: "Nothing was done to oppose or prevent [the enemy's] progress."[13]

Nothing, that is, except for Forrest's cavalry. Forrest reported spending five hours harassing the Federal onrush, mostly on the opposite end of the line from Hanson. Periodically, he sent couriers back to the fort with word that the enemy was advancing in large numbers and enveloping the Confederate defense line, but after his charging cavalrymen suffered the stinging ambush by the Eighth Illinois Infantry, he fell back, "no infantry being near to support me." In messages to the fort he warned that if infantry support was not supplied the fort would be surrounded. No support came, and it was probably too late, anyway. The couriers returned with orders only for him to return his cavalrymen to their own lines.[14]

Grant had counted on Pillow to let him approach without a fight, and Pillow had done it. He had been so preoccupied with digging his own trenches that he forgot that an advancing Grant would have no trenches at all. The Federals' McClernand-generated march plan, which Grant had earlier approved—had strung out the two Union divisions along different roads only loosely connected, all but begging for ambush. Grant had approved this plan probably out of contempt for Pillow, and his contempt turned out to be even more justified than he could have hoped. On the morning of the march, of course, Pillow was not at Donelson at all.

Pillow appeared to doubt that Grant would dare to face his fort, Buckner later reported—at least in any immediate way. Buckner may have been correct: on the 10th Pillow had written Floyd that his fear was not that Grant would attack but that, rather, the Federal general would "attempt to cross the country south of my position and cut my communication by river, thus depriving me of supplies" from Clarksville and Nashville. He added, though, that this potential enemy route was so "exceedingly broken and rugged . . . as to be nearly impracticable for a march . . . [or for] procuring supplies for his forces . . . I think that is my safety." If Grant did find the country to the south too rugged, then he ultimately would have to take on the fort if he attacked the Confederates at all, so Pillow continued strengthening Donelson. He mentioned the progressing work on the riverside gun emplacements and the landside rifle pits and said he needed two more heavy guns trained on the Cumberland. He added that "if I am not engaged by the enemy in three or four days" he would ask for two forty-two-pounders at Clarksville, which he described as insufficient to protect Clarksville but capable of making the Donelson armament more impregnable.[15]

So early on the morning of the 12th the Confederate post commander took a steamboat to Cumberland City to see Floyd. He wanted to persuade him to leave Buckner's and his own troops at Donelson. In leaving, Pillow placed Buckner in temporary command of the fort but hamstrung him, assigning Forrest's cavalry to probe the front but directing that nothing be done to bring on a battle. In marked contrast to Gantt and the wild-eyed stampeders from Fort Henry, Forrest and his troopers had to be ordered "back inside our intrenchments" around 2 p.m. after nearly five hours of skirmishing. Buckner gave the order.[16]

*   *   *

Buckner can perhaps be faulted for not disobeying Pillow's order and trying to attack Grant's spread-out, vulnerable columns on the trek from Henry. Donelson's Confederates possessed approximately Grant's numerical strength on the 12th and—unlike Grant—could launch their sallies from behind earthworks. But Buckner was now in the process of becoming a balky hostage of fate. Instead of the East Tennessee department the Davis government had chosen him to head, he was being all but kidnapped and forced to subordinate his West Point knowledge to the whims of two political generals, the most ebullient of whom he abhorred.

In fact, Buckner liked the commander of the advancing enemy considerably more than he liked Pillow and Floyd. He had known Grant at West Point and in Mexico, where both were in a party of some two dozen that hiked the slopes of Mount Popocatepetl. Their friendship had become close. After Grant's army resignation, he had journeyed to New York to collect a debt and, put off by his debtor, got into such financial straits that his hotelkeeper threatened to evict him and confiscate his luggage as partial payment for the bill. With no way to go home, he chanced on Buckner, who was still in the army and stationed in New York Harbor, and Buckner had promised the hotelkeeper that he was good for Grant's debts until money could arrive from Grant's father.[17]

The reason Buckner was in New York at the time seems predictive of future behavior: he had been all but exiled there by the army for the same sort of principled windmill-tilting he would display in writing the Pillow articles in Nashville in 1857. Six feet tall and so muscular that among West Point's cadets he could chin himself the most times on the bar with both hands or just one, Buckner combined brawn with brains and was also boat-rockingly stubborn. His best subjects were math, history, and draftsmanship, and his pen (as he revealed so dramatically in Nashville in 1857) could be powerful and heavily ironic. He was also an inveterate reader and a solitary taker of long walks. Some of his ambles had been so distant as to occasionally extend from West Point to New York City, a two-day trek of fifty miles.

Soon after graduating in 1844, Buckner returned to West Point as an assistant professor of geography, history, ethics, and gymnastics, which he taught until interrupted by the Mexican War, in which he served illustriously. He again returned to the Point when the war ended, but was relieved of duty in 1850 over a matter that most officers would have overlooked. A rule compelling Sunday attendance at chapel services prompted him to protest, despite the fact that he himself devotedly attended these services as an example to the undergraduates. The problem, he said, was that a rule *requiring* his attendance was "contrary to law and the Constitution of the United States," and he insisted on his right to attend "not from compulsion." His challenge was pushed all the way to the secretary of war, after which Buckner was relieved of his position on the Point faculty and reassigned to New York Harbor. Buckner had proved he was unafraid to disagree with superiors when he felt himself right, but he had done it over in a matter which few officers would have considered important enough to risk reassignment over.[18]

Like Grant, Buckner resigned from the prewar army and turned to civilian work; most unlike Grant, however, he had been successful. His good fortune was at least partly due to the fact that while in New York he met and married beautiful Mary Kingsbury, a Connecticut Puritan whose wealthy father owned choice Illinois real estate, including part of Chicago's developing Loop. The young husband became agent for these holdings as well as other family properties in Louisville. So geography rather than philosophy probably accounted for the fact that although he was reared on a plantation in Hart County, Kentucky, he nonetheless never owned slaves himself. He exhibited a strong devotion to Dixie. As a West Point underclassman he had to be chided by his father for writing letters home making "contemptuous" references to "Yankees."

If anything, his Southern sentiments were only multiplied by living in New York and Chicago, two cities attracting large numbers of European immigrants. In 1855, he founded a short-lived Chicago newspaper associated with the immigration-hating American Party, and two years later he was shopping for a home in the South.[19]

After secession began breaking up the Union, Lincoln offered Buckner a Federal commission. The new president was doing all he could to keep Kentucky in the Union, and Buckner as head of the Kentucky State Guard had molded it into an imposing force of more than ten thousand men. But Buckner's Guardsmen and Buckner himself sympathized emphatically with the Jefferson Davis government. When their state refused to secede, virtually all of them enlisted with the Confederacy, their commander included.

So Grant and his old friend and onetime benefactor found themselves on opposite sides of the Fort Donelson trenches on February 12, 1862. And despite his West Point training, Buckner disregarded the tactics manual and simply followed Pillow's orders to bring on no attack. His stubbornness and resentment of Pillow may also have contributed to his obedience. Even if only subconsciously, he may have felt gratified to see Pillow showing himself yet again to be a deficient soldier.

The window of opportunity for a Buckner attack on Grant was open only a few hours. Around noon Pillow returned from Cumberland City and resumed the Donelson command. He had not found Floyd, who was absent at Clarksville, and, when informed of Grant's advance, he had hurried back to the fort. Pillow characteristically sent telegrams not only to Floyd but also outside the chain of command to Floyd's superior, Johnston. He informed both superiors that the Federals were advancing and that Buckner's men were needed at Donelson to fill the long trench line that Pillow himself had laid out and ordered to be dug. He informed both Floyd and Johnston that

he, Pillow, was going to keep Buckner's men at Donelson until ordered otherwise—although he already *had* been ordered otherwise.

That day, Johnston and Floyd exchanged telegrams. Johnston inquired
about Floyd's campaign strategy, and Floyd responded with the Floyd–Buckner plan to operate from Cumberland City and try to hit Grant's flank from
the south. When Johnston received word from Pillow that Grant already was
on the march, the Confederate western commander decided in favor of Pillow. It appeared too late to activate the Floyd–Buckner plan. Johnston ordered Floyd to Donelson.[20]

*   *   *

By February 12, mounting optimism had replaced the "deep gloom" Pillow
had found on first entering Fort Donelson. The presence of Buckner's crack
Kentuckians and the arriving regiments of Floyd, already battle-bloodied in
western Virginia, surely helped morale, along with the arrival and almost immediate engagement of Forrest's bellicose horsemen.

Pillow lent his own hand to the raising of Donelson spirits, although how
much he did so is open to question. He continually harangued the sweating
trench-diggers with pep-talks that were arrogant and soaringly condescending. In his February 9 special order assuming command, he had called on
them not only to hold Donelson but also to "drive back the ruthless invader" from Tennessee soil "and again raise the Confederate flag over Fort
Henry." He claimed for them a battle cry proclaiming "liberty or death" as
the sole alternatives. In a speech to the Irish-Americans of Randal McGavock's Tenth Tennessee, Pillow recalled that some of their fellow Irish-rooted
countrymen had been with him in Mexico as well as recently at Belmont,
and he said he trusted that these sons of Erin would "prove true to your
adopted South.

"I come here to drive the Hessians from this neck of land between the
rivers," he declaimed, "and to replant the stars and bars upon the battle-
ments of Fort Henry. I will never surrender! The word is not in my vocabu-
lary . . . Many of you know me personally, certainly all of you by reputation,
and I want you to go now where I command you."

McGavock, Harvard-educated and a former Nashville mayor, was present
for Pillow's self-glorification that day. He noted in his journal his exceeding
personal "regret" that Pillow had been put in command of Donelson, and
not just because of his overbearing pride. Noting Buckner's arrival there in a
subordinate capacity, McGavock scribbled his concern about how the two
would get along in view of the scorching 1857 newspaper articles. Pillow, Mc-
Gavock wrote, "is a vindictive man and not likely to forget."[21]

Thursday, February 13

Bloody False Starts and a Cold North Wind

B\Y MORNING OF THURSDAY, February 13, as Grant breakfasted with key
subordinates in a farmhouse headquarters opposite the Confederate right,
a lesser man would have been perceptibly uneasy.

Confederate commander Albert Sidney Johnston was reported to be already moving as many as forty thousand troops in the Donelson direction
from Bowling Green. Grant did not know how many of these had reached
the fort, but by the morning of February 13 he did know that it already contained enough to merit the presence of four generals. A few prisoners taken
in the previous day's skirmishes told their captors the fort held between
twenty and twenty-five thousand Confederates commanded by Floyd, Pillow,
Buckner, and Bushrod Johnson.

And Grant's potential for trouble with Halleck was growing more ominous. Grant was already in front of Donelson when he received the dispatch
Halleck wrote on the 10th instructing him to entrench at Fort Henry and
hold it. This, surely, was a jarring moment. Halleck's unresponsiveness to
Grant's wires informing headquarters of his plans to attack Donelson had
been followed by the picks and shovels with which to entrench at Fort Henry. Grant faced the possibility that at any moment Halleck could brand the
Donelson assault as disobedience to the order to dig in. Halleck's enigmatic
behavior made it all the more obvious that this Donelson business needed
to be finished in a hurry.[1]

Located on higher ground, the Donelson works were bounded on both
sides and even intersected by the swollen creeks, but they were nowhere
near being flooded out as Henry's had been. They also now bristled with riflemen, cannoneers, and long outer fortifications. All through the previous
night, Grant's soldiers had listened to the sound of Confederates working to
strengthen the fort's defenses. Some of Grant's men were soon to learn that
overnight these entrenchments had become ditches five feet wide and two

feet deep. The Confederates had cut down young trees and piled them lengthwise along the outer margins of the trenches and covered them with dirt from the ditches. The defenders now stood behind a wall that at the more critical points was five feet thick and five feet high. From there, they could fire downward across an entangled mass of other trees that had been felled outward to make an abatis. Except for the spot where the ridges were broken by backwater in the Indian Creek valley, there were some two curving miles of these ditches ringing the fort on its land side, requiring a Federal investment line considerably longer. It was too strong to storm without the gunboats, and too large and dangerous an expanse to even surround with just fifteen thousand troops.[2]

For the attackers, though, there were a few bright spots. Some of the adjacent hills were taller than the ridges along which the enemy's outer works ran, and the entrenchments had been arranged in such a manner that Confederate troops could not reach some of them without exposing themselves to the fire of Union sharpshooters.

But there were few reliable maps of these hills. With both Smith's and McClernand's divisions on the scene and spread out, Grant's force still proved to cover barely more than half the Confederate front this morning. The two days' rations that Grant had ordered carried on the back of each soldier would be depleted by this day's end. Grant had also specified that three days' additional food supplies *could* be brought later in wagons, but, probably because the Henry expedition was water-borne and wagons were scarce, he issued no mandatory directive about that, seemingly leaving it up to the commanders of the individual brigades and regiments. This meant that a lot of his men were going to have to fight on low rations, or none.[3]

Grant was all too aware of his position's growing tenuousness. He was not the sort of person to be cowed by it, or even to admit it to close associates, but correspondence from his headquarters, though written with his customary succinctness, gives him away.

NEAR FORT DONELSON, February 13, 1862

General HALLECK:

Send all [arriving reinforcements] to Fort Henry. They can be transferred here, if required, and there is now appearance that that point is in danger. One gunboat should be there.

U. S. GRANT,
Brigadier-General

Henry was "in danger" because it was suddenly vulnerable to almost any kind of force Polk might decide to send down from Columbus; Grant had decided to denude Henry of even the rearguard he had left there. Finding that neither the gunboats nor the new troops sent by water around to the Cumberland had yet arrived, early on the 13th he had ordered most of Lew Wallace's twenty-five hundred men to march out of Henry and join the lengthening lines at Donelson.

To be safe, chief engineer James B. McPherson later reported, it was also on this day "decided best to send a detachment from Fort Henry up to the railroad bridge at Danville." The object was to totally "destroy one span . . . for we were apprehensive, as all the gunboats were required in the Cumberland River, that the enemy might repair the trestle work which had been destroyed and send over re-enforcements to Donelson or make a diversion by trying to capture Fort Henry."

Had the Danville bridge been left intact, Polk at Columbus could send troops down by rail and take Grant's Donelson attackers in the rear, cut them off from the base Halleck had ordered established at Henry, and force Grant to fight on two fronts against prohibitive numbers. Grant knew he had plenty to contend with on *one* front. Around this time he sent the following wire to a postal official charged with expediting military mail.

[A. H.] MARKLAND, Special Mail Agent:

Send the mail steamers as soon as possible after receiving this. All is well here, but we have a powerful force (in front of us). Johnson, Buckner, Floyd, and Pillow are all said to be here.

U. S. GRANT

Grant wanted to insure that his access to messages to and from Halleck and other prospective sources of aid, as well as their access to any messages he needed to send from Donelson, was as expeditious as possible.[4]

He had a second, although distinctly secondary, reason for summoning the Henry garrison. He was uneasy about Lew Wallace. Like McClernand, Wallace was possessed of imposing Midwestern clout, and Grant, whose sensitivity was no less deep because he usually kept it out of sight, had either noticed or been made aware that Wallace was infuriated about being left behind. Grant took care not to wound the feelings of others, at least not until he had determined to rid himself of them. Surrounded by more vaunted and better-connected subordinates, the Henry–Donelson field commander was learning to be as prudent and careful in army politics as he was fearless and even reckless in battle.

On February 11, Grant had had one of his staff members, William S. Hillyer, discreetly write to Wallace to mollify him:

I was surprized to hear that you were to be left behind—and so was Gen Grant . . . He left to Gen McClernand and Gen Smith the [question of which] forces [were] to be left behind—he told me to day that he would give you a Division as soon as the new troops arrive and that he would see that you should have a good position in the next fight. Let me beg of you as your friend that you keep quiet for a day or two—and you will have a position that will suit you in every particular—having no intermediate commander. Be assured that . . . had I thought it possible that a General would be left behind and 7 colonels ordered forward I should have made a more active effort to change it. P.S . . . This thing will work to your advantage—Gen Grant has given positive assurance to me that you shall have a Division in a few days . . .5

Shrewdly, Grant had arranged to gratify Wallace without embarrassing his own admired friend and mentor, Smith.

When the Henry troops arrived, Grant turned them over to Smith, from whose division they had originally come. But he returned them minus Wallace, who now would command the Nebraska and Ohio regiments coming from Cairo with Foote's fleet of ironclads. As a division commander, Wallace now would be no longer under Smith and answerable only to Grant himself.

Like the Confederates, Grant assumed that the gunboats would play almost as critical a role as at Henry. If they could get past Donelson's water batteries and block the Confederates' river route to the supply depots of Clarksville and Nashville, Grant could close the noose with the reinforcements from Henry and Cairo. But Grant did not know exactly where the gunboats were or when they and Thayer's infantrymen might arrive. Sensing that simply to sit and wait invited trouble, he decided the best way to keep the Donelson garrison inside its walls until his help came was to indicate that the Federal force was confident—while doing nothing to incite a battle that could expose the charade. He issued appropriate instructions to subordinates.6

Grant gave yet another indication of disquiet on Thursday morning: He asked for help from the lone gunboat that so far had reached Fort Donelson. Very early in the morning he dispatched a message to Commander Walke on the *Carondelet*. He informed the naval officer that the infantry had arrived on Donelson's land side the previous day and that its investment was progressing. He added, a little prematurely, that most of his artillery had found shooting sites. If Walke would just "advance with your gunboat at

10 o'clock in the morning," he continued, "we will be ready to take advantage of any diversion in our favor."

The gunboat captain, after firing the introductory shots Wednesday afternoon to let Grant know he had arrived, had anchored three or four miles downriver and tried to protect his crew "from the enemy's lurking sharpshooters." Now he complied with Grant's request for a diversion. He steamed the *Carondelet* to a covered position behind a timbered jut of land and, at 9:05 a.m., began firing seventy- and sixty-four-pound shot at the hilltop fortress. This barrage was so much stronger than Wednesday's that Confederate Reuben Ross, captain in charge of some of the Donelson riverside guns, failed to realize that the *Carondelet* was the same gunboat that had fired the day before. Ross reported that this new vessel's long-range salvos were "terrific." He thought they constituted an all-out attempt to knock out the two heaviest Confederate cannons.[7]

But that did not happen, and the Confederates soon showed that their own guns were hardly to be sneered at. While Walke fired 139 shells at Donelson, he had to endure a prolonged response from all the Confederate guns. Most of the enemy cannonade overshot the boat, Walke reported, "but two [struck] us, one of which was 128 pounds solid (shot). It passed through our port casemate forward, glancing over our barricade at the boilers, and again over the steam drum, it struck and, bursting our steam heater, fell into the engine room." It "seemed to bound after the men . . . like a wild beast," wounding a dozen sailors, seven badly. It also sent a hail of splinters shooting through the vessel like needles and arrows. Some of the Union wounded were so distracted by the suddenness of the missile's crash through the wall and the plight of fellow sailors that they failed to comprehend their own wounds, Walke later remembered, "until they felt the blood running into their shoes."[8] That, when he heard about it, could hardly have reassured Grant, either.

* * *

As Walke opened fire at 9:05, Federals in Smith's Second Division were marching past the yard of Grant's headquarters. The Third and Fourth brigades under colonels John Cook and Jacob Lauman had been ordered to probe the Confederate right in concert with the expected attack by the *Carondelet*. Lauman was on the extreme Union left around 10 a.m. as, with the gunboat's demonstration well underway, he moved his men to the summit of a ridge opposite the Confederate works. There he exceeded the intent of Grant and maybe also Smith, although Smith's orders carried ambiguous implications. Instructed to "press forward as steadily and rapidly as the ground would admit and—if the opportunity offered—to assault with the bayonet," Lauman ordered the Twenty-fifth Indiana to fix bayonets, charge, and, "if possible, drive them from their works."

Colonel James Veatch would later report that his Hoosiers could barely see the fortifications "here and there" through the thick timber and had no idea how far away or how extensive they were. But he had his orders, and he deployed his flank companies as skirmishers and set out. The advancing vanguard found that the Confederate lines extended farther left than they had expected, so they moved in that direction and onto a hill. From there they covered the advance of their onrushing comrades by firing on the rifle pits and preventing the use of a six-pounder that Confederate cannoneers were trying to turn onto the left flank of Lauman's main body.

Lauman's troops already were trying to duck minie balls, and worse, from their front and right. His men had charged down into a valley from which they faced a climb to the Confederate-held heights, and there "the enemy poured on us a terrible fire of musketry, grape, and canister, with a few shells.

> The rebel breastworks were now in plain view on top of the hill. The heavy timber on the hillside had been felled, forming a dense mass of brush and logs. Through and over these obstacles our men advanced against the enemy's fire with perfect coolness and steadiness, never halting for a moment until they received [Lauman's own] order [to do so]. After a halt of a few minutes they again advanced within a short distance of the enemy's breastworks, when their fire from a six-pounder field piece and twelve-pounder howitzer on our right was so destructive that it became necessary to halt and direct the men to lie down to save us from very heavy loss.[9]

To their right, the Fourteenth Iowa of Colonel William Shaw, ordered to "advance with the Twenty-fifth Indiana upon the works in front and take a battery of two guns," went forward under heavy small-arms fire until Shaw's men passed the cover of a ridge on their right. Sergeant Kiner would come to note that several of his comrades had climbed trees that morning to "get a peep at the rebel Fort" but now saw all of it they wanted. They found themselves the targets of heavy grape-shot from the right, but they were lucky: "the range was too high." Ahead, though, the ground was uneven amid all the fallen logs and tree branches, and Shaw halted to shield his men from the cross-fire from the right while trying to decide on the best formation to order his men into, "it being impossible to advance in line of battle." Looking to his left, he saw that Lauman and the Hoosiers, too, had stopped in the face of their intimidating task. Shaw waited to see which way Lauman's men were going to go, toward the guns to the right or the rifle pits in front. Beforehand, Lauman had ordered Shaw toward the guns, but now Lauman's men advanced in neither direction, staying where they were, and Shaw continued to wait.[10]

Off to the right of Lauman, Cook's brigade had advanced down into the valley, too, until without warning his Seventh Illinois ran into a sudden, short-range cannonade on its colors. The fire, from a battery Cook had had no prior awareness of, instantly killed Captain N. E. Mendenhall of Company I and bloodied several infantrymen. Private Edward Buckner of the Twelfth Iowa's Company A was shot dead through an eye. With the heavy timber having kept their own battery from getting into a covering position, Cook's men moved back out of range.[11]

* * *

Above them on the ridge to their front, manning the far right of the Confederate defense, was Colonel Roger Hanson's Second Kentucky Infantry, part of the so-called "Orphan Brigade" of Kentucky secessionists representing their unseceded state. They had arrived the day before, and four companies of them had had to try to sleep in the rifle-pits that evening. It was a difficult doze, despite "balmy and springlike" weather in which, one of their attached artillerymen would recall, the "stars twinkled with unusual brightness, the moon beamed with tranquil light . . . and not a sound was heard save a shot now and then from a stray picket . . ." But they were nervous. Expecting a Union attack in the morning, Hanson had rushed the rest of his men into the trenches soon after daylight.[12]

The Kentuckians received their baptism by fire when Lauman's Seventh and Fourteenth Iowa began their charge up the hill. A bullet in the initial Federal volley took Company B's Sergeant Neil Hendricks in the chest. Many of Hendricks's fellow Orphans then began to dodge every round they heard. Colonel Hanson—who walked with a pronounced limp from an old wound received in an antebellum duel over a woman—lurched along in their midst and told them to take no notice of the bullets. By the time the little missiles were audible they were already past, he coolly asserted. Then one came so near Hanson that he himself ducked, prompting his troops to grin. "Boys," he amended with a red-faced laugh, "you may dodge a little if they come too close."[13]

Later, in writing his battle report, Hanson would praise Lieutenant Thomas K. Porter's battery at the Confederate right center, saying it "always fired at the right time and to the right place." Positioned to the left of the Second Kentucky and Colonel Joseph Palmer's intervening Eighteenth Tennessee, Porter's were the guns that had enfiladed Cook's Iowans as they

ROGER W. HANSON

rounded the hill, quickly driving the Midwesterners back to its shelter. The Porter battery became a magnet for the bullets of Union sharpshooters and infantry as well as Federal artillery shells. One of its officers, twenty-year-old Lieutenant John W. Morton, later recalled that the unit lost thirty-seven of forty-eight cannoneers who fought at Fort Donelson.[14]

*   *   *

Beneath the brow of the hill on the extreme Confederate right, Colonel Veatch and his Twenty-fifth Indiana were pinned down under "very heavy fire for two hours and fifteen minutes with no opportunity to return the fire to advantage, the enemy being almost entirely hid." Unable to detect further forward movement by any portion of the Federal line, Veatch asked Lauman's permission to withdraw his men to prevent "heavy loss where we could do no good."

In an exposed position and having difficulty moving among the felled trees and brush, the Hoosiers lost their poise as they began their withdrawal but rallied at the foot of the hill. Then, minus the services of seventy-five comrades, including fourteen killed, they waited for nightfall and then returned to the ridge they had occupied that morning. The Fourteenth Iowa, Kiner would write, lost fourteen total killed and wounded, including color-bearer William Hall, shot through the head.[15]

"Our casualties were numerous on this day," General Smith wrote. "The Reports of the different commanders partially confirmed by my personal observations satisfied me that an assault on almost any part of the entire front covered by us was not practicable, without enormous loss of life."[16]

*   *   *

About 11 a.m., the most serious breach of Grant's no-battle injunction got underway opposite the Confederate center. In the verbose battle report he wrote to Grant, McClernand would contend that, "in compliance with your order to avoid everything calculated to bring on a general engagement," for ninety minutes he had endured fire from two Confederate batteries—Porter's on McClernand's immediate left and Captain Frank Maney's on a commanding hill farther to the right—as well as more from Confederate sharpshooters. Finally, though, "deeming it within the spirit of your order—which required me, while acting on the defensive, to preserve my line and hold my ground—I ordered the fire to be returned."

He brought up Dresser's Battery to engage Maney while some of his cavalry units reconnoitered nearly all the way to Dover in advance of his infantry. The latter was using the partial cover of a ridge and some woods to spread rightward to, and across, the Wynn's Ferry Road. As they moved, Maney stepped up his fire on them again, and McClernand brought Schwartz's battery forward on Wynn's Ferry Road to duel with Maney and protect the Federal sidle toward Dover. By this time, Porter and another Confederate battery under Captain Rice Graves, located between Porter and Maney, were firing on them, too.

In addition to contending with the Confederate cannons, Schwartz and Dresser also "poured a destructive fire into a mass of infantry, which was seen still farther to the right, driving them in confusion to the shelter of their breastworks." The enemy position threatened his men's extension of their lines toward Dover, McClernand said, because it gave the Confederates a covered point from which to strike his troops in the flank as they moved to the right. The sight of the scattering Confederate infantrymen, McClernand added, led him to think his artillery had opened a hole in the Confederate

center and that he should follow up with an infantry assault and take the position that imperiled his men. Whether McClernand also saw something
larger—potential glory as smasher of the center of the Donelson defense
line—is unknowable. In any case, he ordered the Forty-ninth, Seventeenth,
and Forty-eighth Illinois to frontally assault the menacing position. He apparently gave command of the effort to a fellow Illinois politician, Colonel I.
N. Haynie of the Forty-eighth Illinois. "I considered him the better soldier,"
he later said, but his report simply designates Haynie as "senior."

Haynie, oddly enough, had been born in Dover before his parents moved
to the Midwest. He now sent word to Colonel William R. Morrison, a fellow
attorney and sometime state legislator who commanded the Forty-ninth and
Seventeenth Illinois, that the Forty-eighth was formed and ready to support
Morrison's advance. In the same message, Morrison reported, "he said he
believed he ranked me." Morrison was not pleased, but decided "that this
was no time to dispute about a question of rank." He told Haynie that he
would lead the Seventeenth and Forty-ninth to where the charge would begin, at which point Haynie could take command if that was what he wanted.
Haynie backed down. He suggested that the two of them lead the assault together, so Morrison ended up continuing in command of the Forty-ninth
and the Seventeenth. He took position with the Forty-ninth.

The three regiments surged forward, moving down their own hill some
two hundred yards through thick brush before starting the climb toward the
Confederate redoubt. The Forty-ninth on the right was able to go fastest, because the Confederates had not felled as many trees in their front as were
slowing the progress of the Seventeenth in the center and, on the left, the
Forty-eighth.

The Forty-ninth was within fifty yards of the Confederate works when it finally reached the crude but highly effective abatis and started trying to pick
its way through. There it finally received its first return fire, a devastating volley from the waiting Confederate infantrymen and artillerists. Morrison ordered his men to hold their fire until they reached the top of the works,
hoping that when they achieved that point they could wreak confusion with
a united volley that would carry them over before the Confederates recovered. But his troops had never before been under fire and botched it. They
discharged their weapons at will.

The Forty-ninth, along with the Seventeenth immediately to its left, continued to try to go forward under "the most terrible fire of musketry, grape,
canister, and shell." In his report, Morrison said that he had waited "with
much anxiety" for Haynie's Forty-eighth to make its assault on the left, in-
tending to use it as a diversion for his own final rush to the summit. But he
reported that the Forty-eighth's final attack never materialized, and he

complained officially that Haynie's unit "failed to support me. The works were, as I thought, almost ours, the Seventeenth and Forty-ninth still forcing their way forward, when I was struck in the right hip with a musket ball, [and] knocked out of the saddle . . ."

*   *   *

Along the heights in front of the two forward Illinois units were arrayed the Tenth, Forty-eighth, and Thirtieth Tennessee as well as the Twenty-seventh Alabama. Just to the rear of them was the staff of new Fort Donelson commander Floyd, who had arrived early that morning from Cumberland City and was witnessing the attack on his center in person.

Lieutenant Colonel McGavock of the Tenth Tennessee saw the Illinoisans' charge falter "within a few feet of our entrenchments," where they were "repulsed with a terrible loss." The batteries of Maney on the summit of McGavock's hill and Porter off to the right "did good work," the colonel would write in his diary that night, and "firing from our rifle pits was terrific" in a struggle that consumed just "fifteen or twenty minutes but was terrible while it lasted." His Irish-Americans had comported themselves so bravely, he noted, that he had all he could do "to keep them in the pits, they were so anxious to get out and charge . . ."

The Tenth Tennessee lost just one man killed and several slightly wounded, but Maney's battery, the focal point of fire from all the nearby Federal artillery and infantry, suffered badly, losing a first lieutenant and "about fifteen others." A gunner inserting a friction primer into his cannon had both hands blown off his forearms by a Federal shell.

*   *   *

The aftermath of McClernand's bloody, unauthorized assault on the center of the Confederate defense line dragged on for nearly an hour. The debacle ended only after participating officers discovered firsthand how futile it was and McClernand let them give it up.

Morrison had been shot out of his saddle and carried to the rear and his brigade was leaderless when Haynie, his co-commander, learned that the premise on which McClernand had ordered their charge was erroneous. The Confederates had *not* fled from the Confederate center under the initial Union barrage. They were behind their entrenchments "in force and well protected by six guns planted immediately in their rear," Haynie learned, to say nothing of the helpful cannons of Porter and Graves. A lull apparently occurred as he tried to verify this intelligence.

Well past 1 p.m., a half-hour or more after the initial charge, the Forty-fifth Illinois was ordered in on the right in support of Morrison. In moving up eight hundred yards, it passed the repulsed Forty-ninth. Again, advancing Union troops got within fifty yards of the Confederate rifle pits. There the Forty-ninth stopped and fired a volley. But Colonel John E. Smith, finding the Confederates "in great force" and himself unsupported because the Forty-ninth had fallen back, ordered his men into a ravine on the side of the hill to await help. None was sent. McClernand had apparently repented his rashness and perhaps already wondered how he would explain to Grant his significant violation of instructions. Smith had been under fire for an hour, he reported, before McClernand ordered him to retire. By that time Haynie had satisfied himself that the summit was indeed full of Confederate troops and cannon. Convinced that the Confederate center could not be taken "without great destruction and loss of life," he ordered the Forty-eighth to retreat some distance down his part of the hill to await further orders from McClernand, who quickly approved his decision.

The close-up combat in McClernand's costly and needless foray was over, but there was still dying to do. Withered leaves on the ground caught fire from the work of the cannoneers, and many of the wounded Federals, cut off from Union rescuers by the continuing fire of the Graves battery, were burned alive. Some, though, were rescued in daring fashion—by Confederates. Members of W. A. Quarles's Forty-second Tennessee, who had just arrived on the steamboat *General Anderson,* had come up from the Dover wharf to support Heiman's Tenth Tennessee in the center of the Confederate line after the Illinoisans charged the ridge. By the time the Forty-second arrived, the combat was over, but an opportunity for heroism remained. When some of the Fort Henry veterans of the Tenth darted out of their trenches to try to save from the burning leaves Federals whom minutes earlier they had tried to kill, men of the Forty-second rushed to assist in the act of mercy.[17]

McClernand's failed assault cost the Federals nearly one hundred fifty casualties and left bitter memories in men not yet familiar with war's rampant senselessness.

Having watched the battle unfold from near the center of McClernand's position, Adjutant Henry Hicks of the Second Illinois Cavalry later reflected that his fellow Illinoisans had retired in good order after losing "a large number of officers and men killed and wounded" and achieving nothing. He added: "Why that small portion of our army was sent forward to be slaughtered without proper support I could never clearly understand. To a subaltern unused to war it seemed needless . . . sacrifice of human life."[18]

*　　*　　*

Quarles's Confederates of the Forty-second Tennessee were equally "unused to war" but were getting a crash course in its vagaries. Having arrived from Clarksville on the *General Anderson* at 2 p.m., they were ordered to leave their baggage at the wharf in the warm afternoon—never to see it again. They were hurried first to the Confederate left, then to the center where they helped save wounded Federals from burning, but in each instance the action was over by the time they hurried into the assigned position. They finally were directed "into the ditches to protect us from shells and sharpshooters."

"It was here that we began to understand the seriousness of war," one wrote. "Around us lay our brethren, mangled, cold, stiff, dead."[19]

Floyd's brigade, made up primarily of fellow Virginians, also arrived at the Dover landing that afternoon. There, Captain John H. Guy of the Goochland Light Artillery was supervising the debarking of four guns and their horses and caissons under fire from Union cannons when he noticed that he and his men were being watched by a general. Guy did not find Bushrod Johnson as imposing as the stars on his collar ("he made no impression on me as an officer"), but the Virginian saluted and asked where he should position his battery.

Guy then got a better idea as to why Johnson had affected him so neutrally. The two men rode up and down a portion of the lines in front of Dover, "more or less exposed to the enemy's fire," and although Johnson did not appear particularly skittish, Guy detected in him "no manifestation of generalship." This officer who had not had the courage to overrule Daniel Donelson's disastrous siting of Fort Henry now seemed more interested in where Guy thought the guns should go than in giving his own opinion, Guy thought. Finally, though, Johnson made a decision and gave Guy an order. The captain rode back to the landing to get his pieces and was heading toward the Johnson-selected site when Pillow rode up. He asked where Guy was going with those guns. When Guy answered, Pillow got angry. He told Guy that Johnson had no authority to issue such an order and instructed the Virginian instead to report to Pillow headquarters in the Dover home of a Pillow staff member, Major Rice. At the Rice house, Pillow ordered Guy to take his guns to Buckner on the far end of the trenches. Pillow did not even notify Johnson that Guy's guns would not be coming to where Johnson had ordered them placed.

Johnson was left to find that out on his own, but he probably did not care much. He had not wanted the responsibility anyway.[20]

*   *   *

On the fort's opposite side, the *Carondelet* had kept up its solitary bombardment most of the day, halting only once in late morning to drop back down to its anchorage site and deliver its wounded to the transport *Alps*. There Commander Walke again heard "the sound of firing" beyond the fort. Doubtless assuming Grant was still attempting to capitalize on his earlier naval diversion, he again attacked, "throwing in some 45 shell and receiving but little damage." He continued firing until near nightfall, all but exhausting his boat's supply of ten- and fifteen-inch ammunition.

Having received no return fire from the Donelson batteries, the lonely ironclad retired again downriver into the gathering darkness to await the arrival of Foote. Earlier that day, Grant had alerted Walke in a dispatch that the flag-officer was on his way.[21]

Unknown to Walke, Donelson's riverside artillerists had become more optimistic over the course of his attacks on the 13th. The only casualty inflicted on the fort's water batteries by *Carondelet*'s multi-hour barrage was a single, freakish one. Captain Joseph Dixon of the Confederate Engineer Corps, who in several months of Donelson duty had had much to do with the laying out of its defenses, had given an order to fire and was stooping to pass from the first to the second gun in the upper of the two riverside batteries when a *Carondelet* shot entered an embrasure and struck a Confederate thirty-two-pounder, shearing off a bolt. The flying piece of metal struck Dixon in the left temple, shattered his forehead, and killed him instantly.[22]

By the time the gunboat ceased fire and moved back downriver, combatants on both sides had something besides fighting to occupy their minds. Over the course of the afternoon, the weather had shifted dramatically. Temperatures had plummeted. An icy north wind heralded the arrival of an arctic front, and nightfall brought a bone-numbingly cold rain that soon turned to sleet.

The Union troops were completely unprepared. Many had cavalierly dropped their overcoats beside the roads on the Wednesday march or simply left them at Fort Henry. Others had been ordered to divest themselves of the heavy garments by their commanders on their marches into Thursday's fruitless assaults on the Confederate right and center. Many of the Confederate defenders, on the other hand, had none to throw away in the first place, although some could claim the comfort of one or another of the four hundred huts General Tilghman had ordered built in late autumn. By no means all, though.

"We were without tents and bedclothes and had slept [almost] none . . . for three nights for watching in the trenches," remembered Jack Campbell of Fort Henry's bedraggled, exhausted Forty-eighth Tennessee. "The enemy annoyed us so day and night that we could scarcely sleep any or cook, every one being required in the [rifle] pits every time an alarm was given."[23]

Blue or gray, any man exposed to the elements began to shiver fearfully in the night's soaking, freezing gloom.[24]

Kiner of the overcoat-less Fourteenth Iowa, a God-fearing infantryman who eventually would become a chaplain, had contributed his blanket to the hospital after his unit's repulsed charge on the Federal left several hours earlier. As "it began to rain and get cold," the Fourteenth was not allowed to build fires because of the nearness of Confederate lines and the sharp-eyed snipers watching there. Kiner "was compelled to trust for favors from my comrades.

> My friends John Cramer and Thomas Barton each had a blanket; one of these we spread upon the ground beside a large log; this [blanket] we sat upon, leaning at the same time against the [tree]. The other blanket we spread over our heads . . . After our blankets were wet through . . . it began to freeze . . . Oh, how we did suffer from the cold . . . Our blankets froze stiff around us . . . Thus the night passed off[,] one of the hardest I had ever experienced.[25]

* * *

Thirty minutes before midnight, a weary Foote arrived at Walke's mooring-place in the dismal sleet four miles north of Donelson. The flag-officer had had to leave behind his ironclads *Essex* and *Cincinnati*, each damaged so badly at Henry that they could not be repaired in time. He had pushed hard up-river against the roiling, flooding Cumberland with just *St. Louis*, *Louisville*, and *Pittsburg*, along with the timber-clads *Tyler* and *Conestoga* and a flotilla of transport steamers. The latter carried Nebraska Colonel John M. Thayer's six thousand Midwestern riflemen.

In the Crisp farmhouse, Grant adjusted his plan. The succession of pelting rain, clicking sleet, and then muffling snow on the roof surely led him to regret a sentence he had included in his orders for the Donelson foray: "Neither tents nor baggage will be taken, except such as the troops can carry." Volunteers disinclined to lug overcoats on a sunny day's march were probably not a lot more likely to retain tents—even if ordered to by their regimental commanders. His men were in for a ghastly night because he had not anticipated a lengthy stay or worsening weather.

He now tweaked the plan to speed up a climax, not just to avoid a collision with Johnston or Polk but to escape this hell that was now freezing over.

When Foote and his gunboat fleet knocked out the Donelson river batteries the next day, Grant decided he would have the boats steam past the fort to Dover and bombard the Confederate trenches in front of the town. Then McClernand would launch an all-out assault on those trenches, smashing the enemy left and rolling it back onto its center and right. Then, Grant hoped, this lark-turned-nightmare would be over.[26]

Friday, February 14

Forrest: "Parson, for God's sake, pray"

Overnight, thermometers plunged to twelve degrees.

In snow that accumulated to two and three inches deep, two drenched and largely coatless armies endured agony along the caps of the gale-swept ridges. The men in the battle lines bore the ordeal not only without adequate clothing but, because of the deadly sharpshooters, generally without fires after dark.

The Federals had the worst of it. Not only did none of them have access to anything like Tilghman's cabins, they had not even a trench to get into to escape the wind nor more than scraps of food to sustain their stressed metabolisms. Their haversacks were all but empty.

Across the lines, the commander of the Confederate river batteries was edgy. Captain Reuben Ross's light artillery unit, converted by Pillow to a heavy-gun unit only one night earlier, had received only a few hours' training on the larger weapons. Now Ross feared that the ironclad he had dueled with most of the day might attempt to run past his cannons in the dark, position itself between Fort Donelson and Nashville, and sever the Confederate supply line. So Ross, burdened with more authority since the freak death of Dixon during the day, ordered the firing off of periodic salvoes to keep the Union sailors on the defensive. Late in the night, thinking he heard the sound of boat whistles, he became genuinely fearful and sent more shots downriver—and received orders to stop from a displeased Pillow, whose courier said the general was trying to sleep. The messenger did, however, temper the rebuke with courtly evidence of aristocratic manners: a bottle of peach brandy.

More than noise, though, had come from the river. At some point that evening, Floyd had heard about the Federal armada arriving three miles north of Donelson. He had also received intelligence that the transports carried reinforcements numbering fifteen to twenty thousand, as opposed to the actual six. As on an opposite hill men of the Fourteenth Iowa—who in the frigid dawn "looked like chunks of old logs lying beneath the snow"—were rousing themselves, propping their frozen blankets against trees in the continuing wind, and hastening to build fires because it was now daylight and "too cold to stand it longer without," the Confederate generals convened a hurried meeting at the Dover home of Pillow staff member John Rice. Pillow had his headquarters there, and, ominously, when Floyd arrived, he too—probably at Pillow's urging—headquartered in the Rice home rather than with Buckner at the more spartan Dover Tavern.[1]

At the gathering, Buckner reported, the generals considered the Federal reinforcements and decided unanimously to attack the Federal right in front of Dover "to open our communications with Charlotte in the direction of Nashville." Floyd and Buckner wanted no more of the closing trap Pillow and Johnston had got them into. Floyd, accounted a traitor across the North for his pro-South actions as U.S. secretary of war, was highly conscious of his controversiality and greatly feared becoming a Federal prisoner. Back in Virginia he had told his troops that if captured he would be hauled around in a cage as an example, and his fears of what would happen to him had only multiplied since then. According to Buckner, during the morning meeting at the Rice house "it was urged"—by Floyd and himself, apparently—that their breakout attack should be made immediately, before the arriving Federal replacements could be deployed. Buckner volunteered his division to cover their retreat if the attack was successful.[2]

Back at the river batteries, the vigilant Ross had nervously awaited renewal of the previous day's gunboat attack, and around 9 a.m. he discovered why it had not come. The lone ironclad of yesterday had become a fleet, and to the north the river was full of troop transports, with "heavy re-enforcements . . . landing under cover of their gunboats." Ross recommended to a superior that the batteries try to impede the boats' progress "with our long-range guns." He refused to take that responsibility onto his own shoulders, however, because ammunition was not plentiful. The superior sent an aide to seek permission from Floyd but got no go-ahead until well after noon, apparently because of the conference of generals. Ross finally did open fire on the immense fleet of Federal steamboats on his own authority, but his cannons got off no more than two or three rounds before the transports got up steam and withdrew.[3]

Floyd, Pillow, and Buckner—and presumably Bushrod Johnson, although he goes unmentioned in Buckner's report of the breakout meeting—were not the only generals hard at work this morning. Around 1 a.m., Lew Wallace had been awakened back at Fort Henry by a courier from Grant's headquarters telling him to bring his brigade to Donelson, leaving only guard detachments at Henry and Heiman. Wallace already had anticipated that he and his troops would be required on the Cumberland. In addition to his outrage at being left behind at Henry, he had written to his wife on February 11 of "my anxiety about the expedition" eastward: "It is wonderful how little we know in advance of the condition of the enemy." But he so itched to get there and find out that when Grant's messenger arrived, Wallace was already packed, his unit commanders had been alerted, equipment loaded, horses harnessed, and three days' rations issued. He later wrote that he was so positive he would be urgently needed (thanks in part, no doubt, to the note he had received from Hillyer) that he went to sleep the night of the 13th with his boots on and his lamp un-extinguished. When Grant's order arrived an hour past midnight, Wallace immediately ordered steamboats to cross the Tennessee to Fort Heiman and ferry Colonel Morgan Smith's Eighth Missouri Infantry to Henry. By 3 a.m. the ferrying had been completed. Wallace's entire command was on the march in the first glimmers of dawn.4

Before 9 a.m. Grant himself was also long since up and about. He rode several miles out the northernmost Fort Henry road from the Crisp house, turned right to make a wide northward arc on another road, and arrived at the downriver landing of the gunboats and transports. He ordered Thayer's men off the vessels and out into the elements to take the same winding route back past the Crisp house and then on to the center of the Federal line, taking position between McClernand and Smith. The Union commander went aboard the *St. Louis*, Foote's new flagship, to persuade the naval officer that the ironclads could overpower the fort's waterside guns and get above and behind the fort at Dover, in which event Donelson would be surrounded and its surrender "but a question of time."

Grant remained distinctly aware that his own position was vulnerable. "Matters here look favorable *in one sense*," he wrote to Halleck chief of staff General G. W. Cullum at Cairo on this day. "We have the works of the enemy well invested and they do not seem inclined to come out." The Confederates' odd lassitude was fortunate. Grant added that the Donelson force was "very strong," "well fortified," and apparently consisted of "not less than 30,000 troops," with most estimates going even higher.5

By mid-morning Lew Wallace arrived at the Crisp house from Fort Henry with his twenty-five hundred soldiers. Having just returned from Foote's Cumberland mooring-place, Grant sent the Wallace troops to the Union left to Smith, then put Wallace in charge of Thayer's Fifty-eighth, Sixty-eighth, and Seventy-sixth Ohio and First Nebraska regiments, which would be arriving from the river by early afternoon. With others, they would be designated the Third Division—all under Wallace, as Hillyer had promised the Hoosier in his note. "Your part," Wallace purports to quote Grant in a book written decades later, "will be to hold the centre and resist all attempts of the enemy to break through. You must not assume the aggressive."[6]

* * *

At this hour, the Confederates still had not begun their own "aggressive," their attempt to burst free. Pillow's division, on the Confederate left nearest the proposed escape route, was to lead the attack, but the sudden onset of icy winter apparently had benumbed some of the units and their commanders so much that they were sluggish about getting moving. When they did, the commanders of affected regiments, even those of brigades, seemed unsure of exactly what they were ordered to do.

Colonel William E. Baldwin of the Fourteenth Mississippi reported that around noon Pillow "directed the left wing to be formed in the open ground to the left and rear of our position in the lines, for the purpose apparently of attacking the enemy's right." Baldwin's brigade—the Twenty-sixth Mississippi and Twenty-sixth Tennessee, augmented by temporary attachment of the Twentieth Mississippi—led the way, moving forward "in a road leading from a point about 200 yards from the left of our trenches . . . approaching nearly perpendicularly the enemy's right." But they had gone no more than a quarter-mile when General Pillow called off the entire attack. He said it was "too late in the day to accomplish anything; and we returned to our former position in the lines."[7]

Pillow likely had more motivating his decision than his watch. For one thing, the move had barely exited the Confederate trenches when it came under fire. The Twentieth Mississippi's Major William N. Brown reported that around 1 p.m. Pillow ordered him to place his regiment with Baldwin's brigade and form in a field on the far left "for the purpose of making a sortie upon the enemy." But the order to go forward had yet to be received when "a few guns of the enemy were heard, and by the time we had advanced 100 yards a private of Company D was shot down, showing the that enemy was close at hand. We continued the march for 100 yards more, when the order to halt was given . . . with the explanation that we did not have time to accomplish what [was] wanted." The shooting ahead of Brown's men involved Forrest's cavalry, which was to lead and protect the flank of the breakout. Forrest reported that he passed the Confederate trenches, "but after maneuvering a short time" amid "some sharp shooting," he was ordered back to the trenches to supply sharpshooters to potshot Federal snipers, who from hills and trees were bedeviling the infantry.

One witness said Pillow canceled the attack out of fright. A Floyd aide riding with Pillow at the time of the aborted breakout later remembered that the striking of a soldier in a forward unit by a sharpshooter's bullet—maybe the private in the Twentieth Mississippi's Company D—unnerved the vainglorious commander. According to the aide, Pillow exclaimed that their movement had been discovered and therefore could not be continued. He then turned the column around and eventually got around to sending the aide to Floyd telling him what he had done. The messenger, Peter Otey, recalled many years later that Pillow's communication outraged Floyd, who hotly burst out that the movement would have to be cancelled, all right, not because it had been discovered but because Pillow had dawdled so long in sending the message.

The idea that Pillow was afraid does not ring quite true; on battlefields, he generally appeared brave. More likely, Pillow saw an excuse not to follow an order he disagreed with—and Floyd was so visibly angered because he understood Pillow's motive and because he himself deeply feared getting trapped. Had Floyd been brave enough to venture closer to the scene of prospective action, he might have been able to counteract Pillow's cavalier decision. In any case, by this time it was early afternoon, which does seem late for beginning such an ambitious move. Grant, though, would eventually contend that Union strength in front of the Confederate left at that time was still slim or nonexistent. The Confederates might well have marched out with little opposition.[8]

*   *   *

Three or four miles downriver, Foote prepared for the gunboat assault that Grant had urged. That morning his crews piled chains, lumber, coal bags, and similar hard objects around their vessels' upper decks and boilers to try to protect these vulnerable areas from the downward fire of Donelson's water batteries. By early afternoon they were as ready as they could be, and just before 3 p.m. they appeared in the same configuration they had used at Fort Henry. The ironclads—*St. Louis, Carondelet, Louisville,* and *Pittsburg*—took the lead while the timber-clads *Tyler* and *Conestoga* remained more than a half-mile to the rear, out of reach of most of the Donelson cannons. The first of the six vessels to appear, the Foote flagship *St. Louis,* had only half rounded the bend when the Confederates' longest-range weapon, the rifled thirty-two-pounder, opened fire.[9]

A mile in front of them and seventy feet above, Captain Ross in the Confederate river batteries found the developing advance an imposing spectacle. He also noticed a change from his earlier sparring with Walke. Previously, he thought he had discerned "extreme timidity" on the part of the Federal naval arm, "but now they advanced with much show of resolution.

As was our custom, we opened on the first one before she had half come into view and from that time cannonaded them with all the vigor and as rapidly as the perfect safety of our rifle would admit. Four large boats swung around the bend, forming the front line, two more formed the second line, and a single one brought up the rear, in company with an undistinguishable number of tugs, hospital boats, &c . . . [I]t must be confessed we felt unequally matched with this fleet, armed with ten times or more our number of their best artillery.[10]

Foote had learned at Fort Henry about the risk of employing in this new ironclad age the naval custom of fighting at close quarters, but Grant's plan—to knock out the Donelson guns and then steam to Dover, seal off the Cumberland to the south, and shell the trenches in front of the town—left him little choice. He decided again not to lie back and duel with the fort's longer-reaching rifle guns while trying to dismount or destroy its unrifled thirty-two-pounders from beyond their range. Instead he came on, steaming straight toward the water batteries, inside which Captain Ross and his erstwhile artillerists reflected on their weaponry: only two of their nine guns were effective beyond twelve hundred yards.

As Donelson came into sight at a distance of about a mile and a half, Federal sailors saw two Confederate shells splash in front of them. They continued to push hard against the Cumberland current, guns silent. They traveled a half-mile farther before Foote ordered his flagship, the *St. Louis*, to fire. The other ironclads then opened up with a fearsome flame.[11]

In an onshore ravine near the batteries, Forrest—who had never witnessed a duel of heavy guns before—sat his horse and watched in awed alarm. When his second in command, Methodist-minister-turned-major David C. Kelley, rode up, Forrest turned to him and shouted over the din: "Parson, for God's sake pray. Nothing but God Almighty can save that fort!"[12]

Foote hailed the *Carondelet* to order its commander, Walke, to have his men slow down their firing, probably in the interest of better aim. Another disadvantage that Donelson gave them, in contrast to Fort Henry, was that its guns were high on the bank, so that as the Union vessels came closer their guns continually had to be re-elevated. Because of that, Federal shells were being so far overshot that they appeared to endanger the lines of the Union infantry on the fort's other side. They also were falling into some of the Confederate rifle pits "a mile from the river, and into Dover," Jack Campbell of the Forty-eighth Tennessee remembered.

The Confederate fire, by contrast, was hitting its targets. The fort's downward-aimed shells struck the upward-facing slant of the gunboats' metal surface; this counteracted the armor's sloping shape, which was designed to cause head-on fire to ricochet. The Confederate shells were highly destructive, producing loud clanging sounds. Spotwood Fountain (Spot) Terrell of the Forty-ninth Tennessee mentioned seeing iron and wood "flying from [the boats] up in the air." Even in Terrell's highly unsteady prose, the tension in the watchers is apparent:

". . . the Bumbs, Shells ware burstings in the air with loud and wild confusion threatning sudden death and dis trucktion and stil tha [i.e., they] came onn while our [largest-caliber guns] wear threatning them with sudden distrucktion and also while [the shorter-range] thirty Two pounders wear hailing down on them with a vengance." [13]

Aboard the boats, Foote's sailors were trying to stay alive. They "heard the deafening crack of the bursting shells, the crash of the solid shot, and the fragments of shell and wood as they sped through the vessel," Walke of the *Carondelet* later recalled.

> Soon a 128-pounder struck our anchor, smashed it into flying bolts, and bounded over the vessel, taking away a part of our smoke-stack; then another cut away the iron boat-[crane]s as if they were pipe-stems, whereupon the boat dropped into the water. Another ripped up the iron plating and glanced over; another went through the plating . . . another struck the pilot-house, knocked the plating to pieces, and sent fragments of iron and splinters into the pilots, one of whom fell mortally wounded, and was taken below . . . and still they came, harder and faster, taking flag-staffs and smoke-stacks and tearing off the side armor as one tears the bark from a tree. [14]

Under such pressure to increase their retaliating fire, gunners aboard *Carondelet* loaded their rifled gun too often, and it exploded. A member of the crew serving it remembered that the concussion "knocked us all down, killing none, but wounding over a dozen men and spreading dismay and confusion among us. For about two minutes I was stunned, and at least five minutes elapsed before I could tell what was the matter." Suffering from inhaled gunpowder, he saw the shattered gun "lying on the deck, split in three pieces." Sailors started shouting that the ship was afire, and the still-dazed gun crewman, whose assigned job was pump-man, went to the pumps. He had not been there long when "two shots entered our bow-ports and killed four men and wounded several others. They were borne past me, three with their heads off. The sight almost sickened me, and I turned my head away." [15]

The *Carondelet* deck became so slippery with blood that sand had to be sprinkled on it to allow crews to continue to work the guns. Aboard the *St. Louis*, Foote seemed determined to show his fearlessness, but for him, too, as with Grant's infantry, Fort Donelson was no Fort Henry. Donelson's big guns were not silenced as Tilghman's had been, and Foote's fleet approached so close that even the defenders' smaller guns were devastatingly effective. Foote tried to parry the fort's fire by varying his vessels' speeds, but to no avail. As he drove to within four hundred, then less than three hundred yards of the fort, the proximity made it all but impossible for his gunners to correct the elevations of their weapons and strike the Confederate hillside emplacements. Much, perhaps most, of his close-in fire overshot the targets. A lieutenant in the 49th Tennessee was wounded by one of these shots.

Foote's closeness abetted the green Confederate cannoneers. Their few hours' training on larger weapons notwithstanding, the confidence of Ross's Maury Light Artillery grew as its men kept firing. Almost incredibly, the Confederate gunners reported suffering no casualties at all. John G. Frequa, a private and converted cannoneer in Captain B. G. Bidwell's Thirtieth Tennessee Infantry, aimed his thirty-two-pounder at a gunboat's smokestack and shouted, "Now, boys, see me take a chimney"; his gun fired and the target toppled, along with a flag. Frequa threw his cap in the air and yelled, "Come on, you cowardly rascals! You are not at Fort Henry!"

Captain Jacob Culbertson, commanding some of the unrifled thirty-two-pounders, complained that Pillow had ordered these smaller guns not to be fired until the enemy was in range. Culbertson feared that not firing the smaller guns would allow the gunboats to spot, then zero in on the positions of the heaviest ones, which *were* firing. But the Federals "took no advantage of it [and] fired almost at random." The gunboats finally approached to within two hundred fifty yards, Captain Ross later recalled, and he and his subordinates, having no idea how undermanned the vessels were, began to plot "how we would resist them when they landed and stormed our batteries" on the riverbank.[16]

Confederate infantryman Spot Terrell later recalled that when the gunboats came within three hundred yards of the batteries, the vessels fired grape-shot to try to chase the Confederate gunners from their weapons, and it may have been partially successful. Foote, at least, thought so. "The enemy's fire materially slackened and he was running from his batteries," he reported.[17]

Shots from the timber-clads, which at first stayed far to the rear and out of range of most of the Confederate guns, burst over the ironclads. Taking terrible punishment, the ironclads tried to turn to allow their more numerous broadside cannon to hammer the Confederate positions, but the Cumberland was narrow. In turning, the *Pittsburg* crashed against the stern of *Carondelet* and broke *Carondelet*'s starboard rudder. One of the fifty-nine shells that struck the *St. Louis* deprived the vessel of its steering wheel, killed pilot F. A. Riley, and sent a metal splinter into the left foot of the fleet's commander. Foote was standing so close to Riley that their clothes were touching when the pilot died.

Its wheel gone, the *St. Louis* drifted downstream, and Foote lurched down to the gun deck to get medical aid and encourage his cannoneers, who according to Confederate accounts were cowed by heavy Confederate fire coming through the large portholes. While Foote was down there, another shell wounded all but a single member of one of the six-man gun crews and bloodied the commander again, this time in his left arm. The *Tyler* then unintentionally completed the Confederate disabling of the *St. Louis* by colliding with her steering gear.

In all, Foote and his men suffered fifty-four casualties, including eleven killed, in an hour and a half. Mortified, he claimed in a report written to Halleck the next day that if his fleet could have continued fighting another fifteen minutes, it would have captured both batteries.[18]

As the badly damaged flotilla drifted back downriver out of range, dusk descended on the bleak and frigid ridges along with a momentary, eerie quiet. Union infantrymen hiding behind whatever cover they could find heard the abrupt cessation in fire of the big guns. In its wake, "men spoke to each other quietly, almost in whispers, wondering what the ominous silence meant," recalled Adjutant Henry Hicks of the Second Illinois Cavalry.

In another few moments it became appallingly clear to the Federals. The Confederate gunners watching Foote's broken ironclads drift downriver had waited anxiously, wondering if the boats were falling back to re-form and attack again. But when the vessels reached the bend a mile and half downstream and began one by one to vanish around it, the meaning was unmistakable. From the gunners on the hill to the infantry inside the fort to, finally, the thousands of Confederates lying in the freezing mud of more than two miles of trenches on the surrounding ridges, a delirious, wild yell went up and spread from Hickman Creek to Dover, rolling back and forth across the snowy slopes in the gathering evening.

Suffering from prolonged exposure to the weather as well as lack of sleep and well-prepared rations, the novices in the Confederate batteries had used inferior and outnumbered weapons to smash the dreaded gunboats that had decimated Fort Henry. Lieutenant Colonel Robb of the Forty-ninth Tennessee sent around to the gunners "a grateful stimulant," and morale among the defenders began to soar.[19]

Especially Pillow. Likely as soon as the last gunboat went around the bend downriver, Fort Donelson's second-in-command fired off to Johnston at Bowling Green a telegram that, of course, should have come from Floyd: "We have just had the fiercest fight on record between our guns and six

gunboats, which lasted two hours. They came within 200 yards of our batteries. We drove them back, damaged two of them badly, and crippled a third
very badly. No damage done to our battery and not a man killed."[20]

Johnston must have been relieved. During the fight Floyd had sent him
two fretting wires of a leader operating above his level. The first hinted at
fear: "The enemy are assaulting us with a tremendous cannonade from gunboats abreast the batteries . . . I will make the best defense in my power." The
second was utterly enigmatic. "The fort cannot hold out twenty minutes,"
it said, before incomprehensibly adding, "Our river batteries are working
admirably."[21]

*   *   *

Despite the smashing victory, Floyd seems to have decided almost immediately that the enlisted men's euphoria was foolish, the triumph all too temporary. The Federals "would not again renew the unavailing attempt at our
dislodgment when certain means to effect the same end without loss were
perfectly at their command," he wrote.

> We were aware of the fact that extremely heavy re-enforcements had been con-
> tinually arriving day and night for three days and nights, and I had no doubt
> whatever that their whole available force on the Western waters could and
> would be concentrated here if it was deemed necessary to reduce our position.
> I had already seen the impossibility of holding out for any length of time with
> our inadequate numbers and indefensible position. There was no place within
> our entrenchments but could be reached by the enemy's artillery from their
> boats or their batteries.[22]

In other words, Floyd—the man who had been haunted from the war's
outset by a vision of himself captured and hauled around in a cage—wanted
out of Donelson. He called a meeting of division and regimental commanders for after dark. Despite their victories of the past two days and fortifications that, Floyd's opinion notwithstanding, appeared to an objective eye
comparatively secure, many of the Confederate officers felt their men were
worn down and out by bitter weather, sleeplessness, and continual fortifying
and fighting. In the blue coats of Grant's newly arriving reinforcements,
whose numbers they wildly overestimated, they saw disaster approaching.
Floyd had feared coming to Donelson in the first place, and he now guessed
the augmented Grant army at "more than fifty thousand men." Illogically, he
advanced the opinion that Donelson was indefensible with any less than that
number behind the ramparts. He and Buckner both said they acutely felt

the danger of having their Cumberland River supply line to Nashville cut. Although Foote's vaunted gunboats had been roundly defeated, the two generals said the river route still would be closed by Federal artillery as soon as cannons could be hauled around to the riverbank south of Dover. Again, they counseled a breakout.[23]

Their problem remained Pillow. In the conference, the Tennessee brigadier seemed to reserve the right to return to his original intention of chasing Grant back to the banks of the Tennessee River, or at least north to the bank of Hickman Creek, should the morning attack meet with success.

The generals, addled by sleeplessness and claustrophobic fear of encirclement, settled—more or less—on an inexact, ambiguous escape plan. The new scenario again called for Pillow, with Bushrod Johnson as second in command, to attack with his augmented division on the extreme Confederate left and roll the Union right back onto the center. Then Buckner was to rise out of the trenches and strike the center with his own division, aiding Pillow's force in opening and walling off Forge Road from the Federals.

Before the breakout attempt aborted by Pillow the previous day, Buckner had volunteered his troops to guard the rear as Floyd's army withdrew to Nashville, and to Buckner, at least, the new plan was a return to the one Pillow had cancelled several hours earlier. But Floyd left to Pillow's discretion the field decision as to the timetable of the escape—as well as whether it could be transformed into a grab for all-out victory.

The possibility of fulfilling his promise to drive the "Hessians from this neck of land between the rivers" must have danced in Pillow's mind. If he could make that happen, he would surely attain the major general's rank that he felt was his minimal due. It was the rank President Polk had given him back in the Mexican War, the one Governor Harris gave him to assemble Tennessee's provisional army, and the one Jefferson Davis so unchivalrously denied him when the Pillow-mustered Tennessee legions were transferred to the Confederacy. Now he would cover himself in the glory for which he hungered.[24]

This loophole that it gave Pillow was not the plan's only problem. Colonel McGavock of the Tenth Tennessee confided to his diary that as soon as he heard about it he condemned it. In the withdrawal from Donelson once the Forge Road to Charlotte and Nashville was battered open by Pillow's attackers on the Confederate left, Heiman's men holding the water batteries, the fort proper, and the right wing of the trenches would be the last out if they escaped at all. It amounted, McGavock wrote, to a prospective sacrifice of his regiment and everybody else under Heiman.

Heiman himself, who likely told McGavock the plan, worried that too few troops were being left on the right to hold it if the Federals launched a counterattack there while Pillow assaulted on the left. Colonel J. E. Bailey was being ordered to remain in the fort proper, Heiman noted, while Head's regiment was to move up and occupy the long stretch of right-wing trenches vacated by Buckner's division in the breakout assault. Heiman said he "doubted very much that these positions, isolated as they were from each other, could be held if attacked, and I stated my fears to General Floyd . . ."[25]

Saturday, February 15, Morning
Commanders Misjudged

DURING THE NIGHT, more icy winds driving another snowstorm combined with artillery and rifle fire to muffle the clank and tramp of Confederate preparations.

Confederates fired on pickets of the Eleventh Illinois, in the center of McClernand's line, with such force and frequency that around midnight Lieutenant Colonel T. E. G. Ransom ordered his men to form for battle. He kept them that way for two hours. The Seventeenth Illinois, at McClernand's left-center, remained "in line of battle most of the night, and the cold rain and snow made great suffering among our men," reported Major Francis Smith.

At 5 p.m. on February 14, McClernand ordered Colonel John McArthur's brigade—the Ninth, Twelfth, and Forty-first Illinois—to move from McClernand's left to his extreme right. This closed the escape gap that had been virtually unmanned when Pillow aborted the planned Confederate breakout the day before. On his way to McClernand's right, McArthur reported, he was "hotly shelled by the enemy's batteries," and by the time he arrived he was in the dark in more ways than one. Night had fallen. Never having been at this location before in daylight, let alone pitch darkness, he had no idea "of the nature of the ground in front and on our right." Under these disorienting conditions, his men had to find places to lie down in the snow.[1]

To McClernand's left, some of Lew Wallace's new troops had filed into positions atop a high ridge with thick woods in front and behind. Atop the ridge snaked Wynn's Ferry Road, linking McClernand south of Dover with Smith in front of the fort. Wallace's right was "within good supporting distance from . . . McClernand and not more than 500 yards from the enemy's outworks; indeed, my whole line was within easy cannon-shot from them," Wallace reported. The Confederates noticed. Their artillery fired periodically throughout the night. Wallace's front, though, was just back of the crest of the ridge to allow his troops the luxury of building fires for their bivouacs. Even these blazes provided scant comfort. Wallace reported that his men "laid down as best they could on beds of ice and snow, a strong, cold wind making the condition still more disagreeable."[2]

Unknown to them, Grant's plans for these troops had undergone a radical change following the Cumberland River debacle that afternoon. He later recalled watching "the falling back of our gunboats and [feeling] sad . . . over the repulse." More than just "sad," apparently; in his report to Halleck that evening, he neglected to mention the repulse of the gunboats at all. Obviously fearful of further unsettling his commander, he left that doleful chore to Foote, who would not send his own report until late the next day. Grant thought during the battle that the Confederates had "been much demoralized by the assault" while it was underway, but then he heard their jubilation "when they saw the disabled vessels dropping down the river entirely out of the control of the men on board . . .

> . . . The sun went down on the 14th of February, 1862, leaving the army confronting Fort Donelson anything but comforted over the prospects. The weather [was] intensely cold; the men were without tents and could not keep up fires where most of them had to stay, and . . . many had thrown away their overcoats and blankets. Two of the strongest of our gunboats had been disabled, presumably beyond the possibility of rendering any present assistance. I retired this night not knowing but that I would have to intrench my position and bring up tents for the men or build huts under the cover of the hills.[3]

He in fact began preparations for entrenchment. McClernand reported being informed in the late afternoon by Grant, "as well as by the shouts of the enemy," that "the gunboats had fallen back and . . . that all aggressive operations on our part must be avoided." Colonel James McPherson, the engineer Halleck had sent along to monitor Grant, wrote that orders were readied to offload all the intrenching tools from the boats the next morning.[4]

Grant's crucial drive to beat Confederate reinforcements to the draw, quickly capture Fort Donelson, and finally impress Henry Halleck was being suspended. If four ironclads could not pass the Donelson guns, get to the Dover wharf, cut off Donelson's resupply line to Clarksville and Nashville, and blast a hole in the Confederate lines for McClernand to charge through, then certainly the two ironclads that were still serviceable could not. Grant thus faced an incomplete and long siege in which he, not the Confederates inside the fort, would become the sitting duck. About all he would be able to do was wait and see whether his career was to be ended by Albert Sidney Johnston in Bowling Green or Henry Halleck in St. Louis.

* * *

Having beaten the mighty ironclads, Donelson's Confederates felt they could beat anything. Forrest's horsemen had endured "another bitterly cold night by which the men were greatly harassed," Forrest would recall, but they were in their saddles before the gray of predawn, ready to lead Pillow's attack. This second night of icy weather notwithstanding, the pugnacious Tennessean thought the afterglow of the triumph over Foote's gunboats had put his men and the rest of the Donelson garrison "in the best possible spirits." They felt, he soon reported, "that relieved of their greatest terror they could whip any land force that could be brought against them."[5]

So did their lieutenant colonel. On the brink of his first full military battle, the Memphian was unquestionably eager to get on with it. The lesson he had learned in boyhood when the half-wild colt had thrown him into a dog pack had shaped his strategy in dangerous encounters ever since. In the face of danger, he would never dodge but, rather, advance menacingly. By presenting the most threatening aspect possible, he believed, he could force his opponent to hesitate and second-guess his own powers. In that moment of doubt, Forrest could seize the initiative and drive it home.

Forrest's experiences had molded him into an almost perfect human instrument for war. He was an ambidextrous natural lefthander who used pistol or saber with that hand. So determined was he to miss no chance to make himself even deadlier that he filed to razor sharpness not only the business edge of his saber but also its backside.

In the bloody little stampede at Sacramento, Kentucky—where he had killed some of the enemy's officers with his own hands—Forrest had begun to form a corollary to his long-held philosophy of attacking danger. By putting himself at any battle's hottest point, he discerned, he could best read the conflict's current, control its direction with his own zeal and strength, and ride it to victory. In the predawn of February 15, 1862, he wanted to get going, to begin finding that point.

Just back of the cavalry and to its right, Colonel William Baldwin's Confederate brigade of Mississippians and Tennesseans led the infantry, with Wharton's and Drake's brigades behind Baldwin to the left, followed by those of McCausland and Simonton more to the right. Baldwin's men had been formed and ready to march prior to 4:10 a.m., when Pillow arrived on the far left. Then, though, came delays "caused by regiments not arriving promptly," Baldwin would report. The regimental problems were caused by the intense cold as well as accumulating days of hard labor, exposure to unforgiving elements, lack of food and rest, and the proliferating stress of dealing with continual sniper fire and pitched battle. While Baldwin's riflemen waited to be ordered forward, one participant later remembered, "I saw many sleeping while standing in place at ordered arms."

To launch the assault with the kind of force that could give it a chance of success, virtually the whole Confederate line had to shift toward its Dover end. Buckner's men would leave their trenches on the right to occupy Pillow's erstwhile location. They would be replaced on the far right by Heiman's troops from inside the fort. With all this to be done on hilly ice-slick ground, the attack did not get moving until daybreak, about 6 a.m. Following Forrest's cavalry, the infantry had to fit itself into a "by road"—barely more than a lane—two hundred yards to the left of the lower end of the Confederate line, between the trenches' termination and the flooded so-called River Road headed south toward Nashville. The attackers swept around the trenches, turned right, and lunged forward more than half a mile before a Union picket's rifle killed a horse in Forrest's regiment, the first of much blood to stain the snow this day.

Then, approaching a little ridge called Dudley's Hill, the Twenty-sixth Mississippi in Baldwin's brigade suddenly came under a hot rattle of small-arms fire. On the slope of the ridge, Baldwin's regiments deployed while others from Virginia, Texas, and Kentucky filled in to the right in a patch of timber on ground sloping away from the road. To their left lay an open field of more than four hundred acres from which, three different times, bursts of Federal fire threw the Twenty-sixth Mississippi's maneuvering companies into disarray. Just as at Belmont, Pillow had displayed neither tactical sense nor regard for his men's safety in ordering the Twentieth Mississippi forward into the cover-less expanse. There they "were openly exposed to a destructive fire, which they were not able to return with effect," Baldwin reported. "The regiment was soon recalled, but not before its left wing had suffered heavy loss."[6]

Along the Federal line this morning, the men had looked forward to the arrival of dawn and permission from their officers to light fires to "thaw their frozen clothes," as one commander noted. They also wanted to cook breakfast or at least boil coffee, the only thing many of them had left to consume. Colonel Richard Oglesby's brigade had not had food since the 13th because the supply wagons carrying three more days' rations had yet to arrive. But at least they expected no attack, having thought they heard the Confederates digging trenches all night long.[7]

When Pillow's men struck, they ran headlong into the three regiments of Illinoisans commanded by John McArthur, a thirty-four-year-old native Scot. Commanding the detached brigade of Smith's Second Division that had been moved in darkness from McClernand's left to its far right the night before, McArthur was part of the effort to stretch the Union line from in front of the fort all the way to Dover. For that purpose, McArthur's troops had been temporarily lent to McClernand, who decided that instead of extending his already-thin line all the way to the banks of the Cumberland he could just as effectively stop it at flooded Lick Creek. But the McArthur units, arriving after dark, had not gotten as far as McClernand wished when, operating without benefit of instructions, they took positions that turned out to be more to the front than to the right of McClernand's right wing. The Ninth and Forty-first Illinois had camped on Dudley's Hill with the Twelfth just to their rear, and the conditions under which they arrived may in one way have been fortunate for them. Not having had the opportunity to settle into regular bivouac, they were more ready for battle than they might otherwise have been.

Dawn had brought McArthur a first look at his new surroundings, and he was immediately alarmed. A picket of the Forty-first Illinois came running back with word that massed Confederates were advancing on them, and McArthur shortly found that his units—camped on or behind this hill facing woods across an open field—were "surrounded by the enemy, who opened on us a heavy fire of musketry, at the same time outflanking us by one [whole] regiment on our right." McArthur tried to sidle his men in that direction to form a new line, moving the Twelfth up behind the Forty-first.

The Forty-first meanwhile charged, later reporting it chased the Confederates a half-mile. But then it had to return when the rest of the Federal line did not follow, and in that interval the Confederate tide swept back in with renewed vigor, the Forty-first's Colonel Isaac Pugh would recall. After more than an hour of furious fusillades, the Confederate Baldwin reported, the Southerners began to gain ground. Pushed "by an overwhelming force and exposed to a most terrible fire," the right of the Forty-First Illinois pulled back through the ranks of the Twelfth, and two companies of the Twelfth were "literally cut to pieces" in less than thirty minutes. The Twelfth finally followed the Forty-first, retreating six hundred yards.[8]

Forrest's cavalry, after leading the infantry out of the trenches, began the morning on the attack's left flank in the Lick Creek bottom, operating mostly in scrub trees and bushes so thick the men could barely spur their horses through it. The first hour was frustrating, but he kept pushing toward the Federal right and rear. He could see the end of the Federal line in the distance. It was moving backward across an open field in front of Baldwin, and he tried to charge it across the field. But this was in the Lick Creek bottom. He found the open ground in his front so marshy that it would not support horses, separating him from the fight.

Picking his way along, Forrest soon found himself across a second field opposite the Federal right, which appeared ready to take the Confederate

JOHN MCARTHUR

attackers in the flank as they continued pouring to their own right across the front of the Union line. Again thwarted by miry ground that would not support a charge, he feinted toward their front and right so that, with his cavalry on their right wing and Confederate infantry advancing to their left, the Federal riflemen began to pull back. The Union infantrymen were accompanied in their withdrawal by their cavalry, which Forrest's troopers could see in the distance taking no part in the fighting. Forrest's efforts, although bloodless so far, were noticed. General Bushrod Johnson, who had charge of Pillow's left, later cited the "great assistance" he got from Forrest in protecting the flank of the assaulting force.[9]

McArthur's outnumbered Illinoisans had never before been under fire, but they fought furiously, yielding ground with the greatest stubbornness,

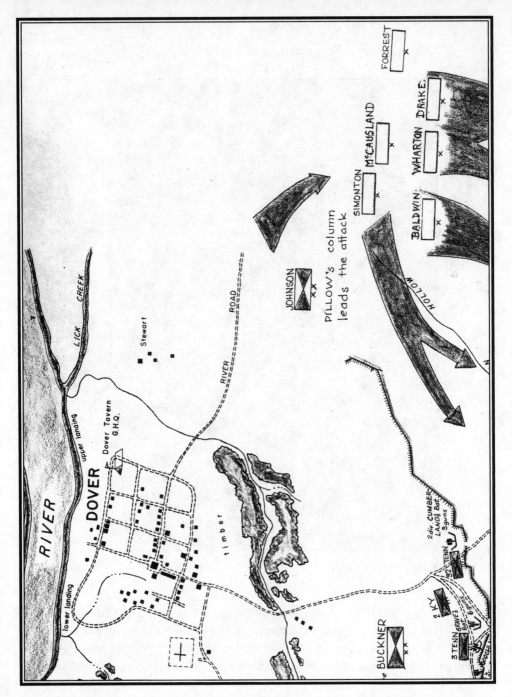

7 A.M. This first of several partial views of a series of detailed, hour-by-hour maps of the Battle of Fort Donelson's climactic day—researched by noted historians Edwin Bearss and B. F. Cooling as National Park Services staff members—shows Forrest out front on the right flank fighting mud in the

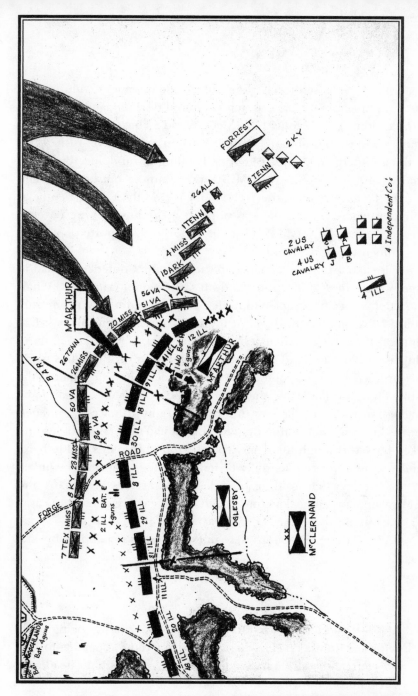

Lick Creek bottom as Pillow's troops exit Dover on River Road, enter a lane up Dudley's Hill, and begin hammering McArthur's stiff resistance and spreading across McClernand's front. *Used by permission of Tennessee State Library & Archives.*

when at all. Partly because of that, the Confederate onslaught continued to move to the right across the face, as well as around the flank and toward the rear, of the Union right. Colonel John McCausland's Thirty-sixth and Thirtieth Virginia regiments, positioned behind Baldwin as a reserve, rushed forward in thick undergrowth over rough and rolling ground and formed to the right of Baldwin's Twenty-sixth Mississippi. Fanning out beyond them had gone the First Mississippi, the Seventh Texas, and the Eighth Kentucky. But getting anywhere on this day was not easy. "The bushes were covered with snow . . . and it was very difficult to move forward," reported one Confederate regimental commander.[10]

For their breakout to have a chance to succeed, the Confederates had to find some way to smash McArthur. Baldwin saw Colonel Gabriel C. Wharton's unoccupied Virginia brigade to his left and ordered it up a ravine running toward McArthur's right flank. At the same time, he sent his own leftmost units on the attack to their left. McArthur's men pushed back hard, advancing again. McCausland's Virginians, coming in on Baldwin's right, had been ordered to fire as soon as they saw Federals, and they halted the Union thrust with a volley. Then they charged. McArthur's men began to be overwhelmed, struck in the flank by fire from the right from fresh Confederate troops as his own ammunition ran low. Forrest had taken most of his unit and picked his way through thick underbrush around Dudley's Hill to harder ground, continuing to circle to the Federal right and rear until he linked up with the infantry. The yelling brigades of Wharton's Virginians and Drake's Mississippians and Arkansans, joined by some charging Forrest cavalrymen, helped finally throw the Federals backward.

By 9 a.m., McArthur's Illinoisans were out of ammunition and all but out of the fight.[11]

*   *   *

At 8 a.m., McClernand had realized the assault on his right was being made by greatly superior numbers. He sent a request for reinforcements to Lew Wallace on his left, and Wallace passed the message on to Grant's headquarters at the Crisp house. But Grant was not there.

In the morning's early hours the Federal commander had received a message from Foote asking to see him. Foote explained that his wounds from the previous day's battle were too severe to allow him to come to Grant. Assuming that Pillow was running things in the fort—and knowing that the garrison had made no attempt to break out earlier, when fewer Union men hemmed them in—Grant later professed to have "no idea that there would be any engagement on land unless I brought it on myself." So he left, after reiterating to division commanders McClernand, Wallace, and Smith that they were to hold their positions and, to prevent a repetition of Smith's and McClernand's senseless assaults of Thursday, they were ordered to do nothing to bring on an engagement until they received further orders. In an appalling lapse by a commander in his second battle, Grant left no one in command in his stead.

He set out for Foote's landing that morning on his favorite mount—Jack, a medium-sized and sure-footed stallion. His mood was glum. A few hours earlier, referring to the defeat of the gunboats, he had written to Julia that "(t)he taking of Fort Donelson bids fair to be a long job." Grant and Jack had to traverse at least four miles of roads so solidly frozen by the night's intense cold that the icy glaze "made travel on horseback even slower than through the mud." On the way, Grant could hear sounds of battle across the miles of tree-covered hills behind him on the Federal right, but a soldier with the Twentieth Ohio, which the general met traveling southward as he himself headed north, later recalled that the noise was no worse than the assaults McClernand had launched earlier in the week.

Grant finally reached the banks of the Cumberland. He then was taken by a small boat to the *St. Louis,* where Foote handed him a cigar. Grant's already-low spirits surely sank further as he listened to Foote tell him how long the "long job" was going to be. Foote proposed taking his battered ironclads back to southern Illinois for ten days of refitting while the infantry dug in around Donelson.

Ten days. Grant did not know if his career as commander had that many left.[12]

*   *   *

Unknown to him then, the Confederates were breaking his siege. By the time Grant and Foote began their parley in ignorance of the extent of the tumult several miles away, McClernand was seeing his brigades bled away piecemeal. Soon after he dispatched the first courier to Wallace requesting reinforcements, he sent another "to urge the absolute necessity of prompt and efficient succor." The second was carried by McClernand's elderly assistant adjutant, Mason Brayman, who was so shaken by McClernand's plight that he was weeping. Brayman's tears had been prompted by a report from Colonel Oglesby that McArthur's entire gallant, much-bloodied brigade was now falling back, opening Oglesby's right to Confederate fire from his right flank as well as his front.[13]

Without Grant, there was little chance McClernand would receive the desperately needed reinforcements from his fellow division commanders—or from headquarters. In the absence of its chief, the Union command was as

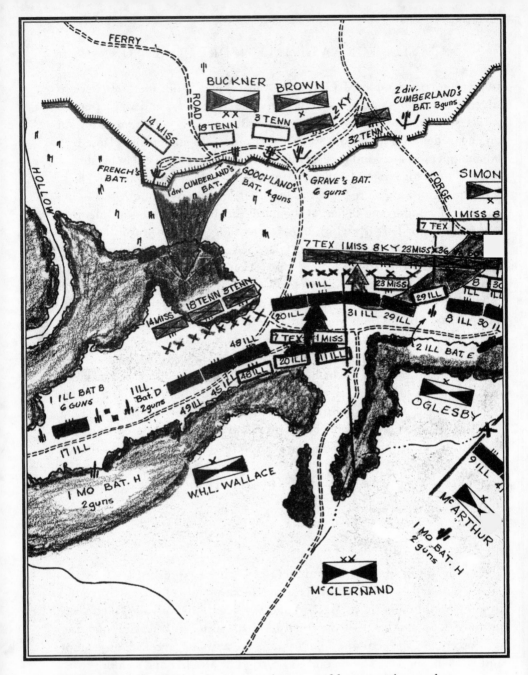

8 TO 9:15 A.M. Forrest keeps pressing toward hotter action as the Confederates threaten Oglesby's brigade after driving McArthur off Dudley's Hill and across Forge Road, the vital flood-free escape route to Nashville. *Used by permission of Tennessee State Library & Archives.*

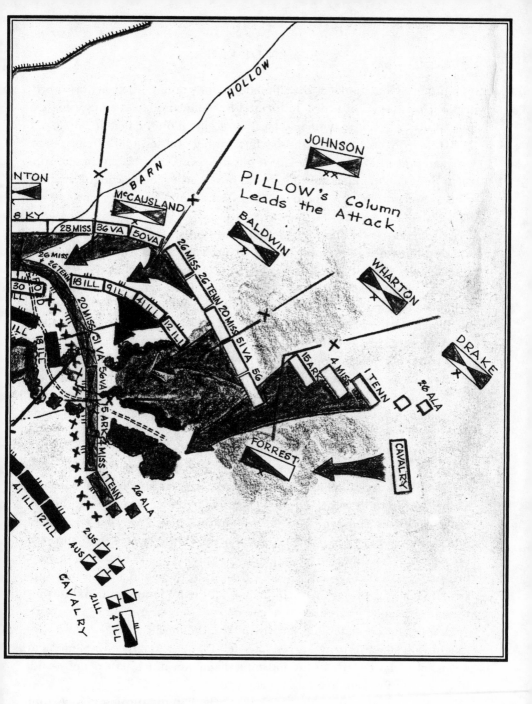

potentially dysfunctional as the Confederate one. Smith, the celebrated professional soldier, had little use for McClernand, the late-coming political one. Wallace, junior to both, had hardly got settled on the field in command of his new division. And Grant's staff, knowing McClernand's bent toward exaggeration and aware of the gist if not the specifics of his plotting to supplant their commander, was uneager to hurry aid to the ex-congressman. If all that was not enough, there was also Grant's emphatic pre-departure orders against movement.

Arriving at the Crisp house, McClernand's breathless couriers were given nothing but word that Grant would get their messages when he returned from his meeting with Foote. Likewise, McClernand's first messenger to Lew Wallace and another to C. F. Smith returned with the same reply: Grant's orders were to remain where they were. So for at least another hour, nothing happened on the Federal left, Wallace agonized in the center, and McClernand was swept away on the right.[14]

Captain S. B. Marks, commanding the Eighteenth Illinois after its colonel suffered a severe wound to an arm, was manning Oglesby's right. Marks soon would report that the Confederates approached him through the underbrush diagonally, at an angle of about 20 degrees with his lines, in columns six or eight files deep.

Marks described the Confederate battle style on this day in the thick undergrowth that covered much of the battlefield as like street fighting, with the enemy firing and falling back. The Eighteenth eventually tried to extend its line to the right to prevent being outflanked after McArthur withdrew, but some of the companies on the left did not hear the order and stayed where they were. As Marks later recounted, Confederates then stormed through the resulting gap "in overwhelming numbers and with such rapidity that both Federal wings were speedily flanked by them and almost surrounded. The majority of our men had exhausted their ammunition, and further resistance seemed useless. It was deemed prudent to retire."[15]

Despite the Confederates' surprise attack, the mostly green Union troops fought with steely ferocity. Forrest later felt that the attack's critical moment was reached fairly early in the morning, likely not much past 9 a.m.—and, from the Confederate perspective, bungled.

Forrest had guarded Bushrod Johnson's flank in the turning of McArthur and the Union right, then kept moving toward the center of the field and the hotter fighting. He left to the erstwhile Fort Henry cavalry commander, Gantt, the less-demanding duty of screening the Confederate flank.

Forrest came driving across the face of the front just behind the Confederate infantry. He had been in so many civilian battles, including face-offs with mobs, that he could sense accumulating desperation in an opponent at the point of dawning defeat. He felt that kind of slippage toward panic now in many of the Illinoisans on Oglesby's right, who were running out of ammunition. Forrest probably did not know about their failing cartridge-boxes, but he had seen that they were beginning to move backward in groups that were not stopping to fight anymore. In some cases, he later said, they were raising white flags. Forrest viscerally understood the psychology of battle; he sensed that the moment was ripe to turn these small signs of hopelessness into a wholesale rout.

He approached Bushrod Johnson and beseeched him for permission to lead an all-out charge on the islands of fierce resistance amid these rivulets of rearward-streaming Federals. Johnson was the wrong man to ask. After having had Pillow so sharply countermand his order concerning a mere gun emplacement two days earlier, Johnson was hardly eager to take more responsibility on himself amid a battle. No, Johnson told Forrest; the Federals might be trying to draw them into an ambush.[16]

The Federal right continued to melt away, though much more slowly than Forrest thought necessary. When Grant came ashore from the *St. Louis* in late morning, he found Captain Hillyer of his staff "white with fear . . . for the safety of the National troops," Grant later remembered. "He said the enemy had come out of his lines in full force and attacked and scattered McClernand's division, which was in full retreat." Grant remounted his stallion determined to get to the scene of the fighting as swiftly as possible, but the attack had come on the right of his three-mile line, the road remained slick with ice and mud, and, as he later recalled, he was "four or five miles to the north of our left."[17]

As he spurred Jack onto the icy road, his mind had to have been aswirl with recrimination against both Foote and himself. If the old salt had not prevailed on him to come up here to the boats this morning just to disclose that the gunboats would be useless for ten days, this Confederate attack, however strong, could have been swiftly met and countered. But then, too, if he had thought to leave someone else—old Smith, for example—in command, it never would have been allowed to happen, either. Going off to see Foote . . . leaving no one in charge . . . big mistakes! Halleck would have a stroke. Something had to be done to stop all this and fix it. Now.

* * *

At the front, the remainder of McClernand's division now looked doom in the face. The Forge Road to Charlotte and Nashville had now—around 10:30 a.m.—been battered open by the drive of Pillow's augmented force.

But the ferocity of the Federal defenders was beginning to tell. As the Confederate host fell on McClernand's individual brigades in turn, it was larger and more powerful than each. But the Southerners no sooner managed, with great effort, to overwhelm one of these brigades before they found the next battling them just as stoutly, usually with the aid of remnants of those previously pushed back. Because it was coming down the Federal line from its right toward its center, the Confederate drive kept encountering new resistance from each Federal brigade in turn. That made it seem to the Confederates, as they pushed to their right across hill after hill, that the enemy was being continually reinforced. It was just the sort of yard-by-yard, costly fight Forrest had sought to avoid with his request for an all-out charge. Such an onrush could have swept away the clots of opposition and turned the battle's slow, labored Confederate flow into a hemorrhage.

Instead, the progress of Pillow's five infantry brigades against the impassioned Federal defenders and their seemingly continual reinforcements was fitful and slow. About 9 a.m. Pillow sent a message to Buckner to ask what he was doing. With Floyd perhaps realizing he was out of his depth on a battlefield of this magnitude—or perhaps just not wishing to get too close to prospective captors—the gregarious Pillow seized command of the field by default. He was wondering why his assault was getting no significant aid from Buckner, who had proposed in the previous night's council of war to attack from the left-center of the Confederate trenches and take the retreating Federals in their front as Pillow was smashing their flank.

It turned out that Buckner had been delayed leaving his rifle pits on the Confederate right because of the slipperiness of the icy, snowy hills his men had had to descend and climb to get in front of Dover—and apparently also because Colonel John W. Head's Thirtieth Tennessee was late arriving to occupy the trenches Buckner was abandoning in his shift to the left. When Buckner did get his men to the Confederate left center to take over an area previously occupied by Pillow, he found the line so deserted that a cannon had been left unattended.[18]

There were plenty of Federals for that cannon to fire at, however. Private William L. McKay of the Eighteenth Tennessee recalled that after marching to the left, his regiment was first positioned just under the brow of a hill that sheltered it from "shells, grape shot + musket balls that seemed to me so thick that I could hold up my hand and catch it full." Buckner, however, seemed to take no notice. McKay later recalled that Buckner awed his men with his calm indifference to the danger. "He walked to the crest of the hill 15 or 20 steps in front of our line and walked back and forth with his hands behind him while the shells—solid shot and musket balls[—]was cutting the dirt both before and behind him. I don't know how long he remained there, but it seemed a long time as we were looking to see him fall every moment."

Buckner listened to the sound of Pillow's attack and tried to soften up the resistance in his front with artillery fire. But he decided not to attack. He later explained that because "of the heavy duty which I expected my division to undergo in covering the retreat of the army, I thought it unadvisable to attempt an assault at this time in my front until the enemy's batteries were to some extent crippled and their supports shaken by the fire of my artillery."[19]

The thick trees and undergrowth hid most of Pillow's effort farther to Buckner's left. But Buckner may have been able to glimpse some of the units of Pillow's right—the Seventh Texas, Twenty-third Mississippi, Eighth Kentucky—starting to battle to his left front against Oglesby's Illinoisans. Buckner's problem was two Federal batteries, an oversized one on Wynn's Ferry Road facing his center and another, smaller one in front of his left, each supported by infantry. The one to his left—the four guns of Adolph Schwartz's Second Illinois Battery E—lay between the Eighth and the Twenty-ninth Illinois, while the larger cluster, eleven bristling cannons facing the Confederate trenches from along Wynn's Ferry Road, was anchored by a half-dozen commanded by Captain Edward McAllister of Battery B, First Illinois Light Artillery. Dug into earthworks ordered thrown up by McClernand the night before and supported by several Illinois infantry regiments, these gunners had been throwing shells at the Confederates since before daylight while enduring hot replies from enemy batteries on their left, right, and center.

Around 9 a.m., Buckner received Pillow's first message urging him to stop waiting and "advance to relieve his forces." Buckner—possibly because of his wish to preserve as many of his men as possible to cover the Confederate retreat toward Nashville—responded minimally. He sent Tennessee Colonel John C. Brown's brigade out against the McAllister position: the Fourteenth Mississippi as skirmishers followed by the Third and Eighteenth Tennessee. These units had to march in front of the six guns of Graves's Confederate battery on Buckner's left, requiring Graves to find targets other than McAllister. Nonetheless, some of their own shells hit so close to the advancing Confederates that forward progress was hindered, halted, and in some cases stampeded. But the Mississippians and Tennesseans moved some four hundred yards into a field of ten or more acres, picked their way through an abatis, and charged into the "murderous fire" of the McAllister guns. Chaplain Thomas H. Deavenport of the Third Tennessee later remembered being "ordered out of our rifle pits to charge a battery near a half mile from us. We went and fought a long time but did not take the battery."[20]

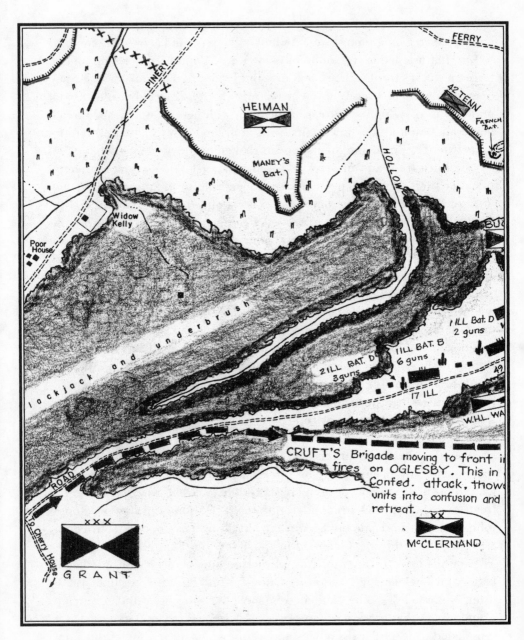

10:30 A.M. Oglesby's Illinois units, running out of ammunition, finally fall back as the Confederates bend McClernand's line backward and Forrest continues moving toward the center of the fighting, likely up Forge Road. *Used by permission of Tennessee State Library & Archives.*

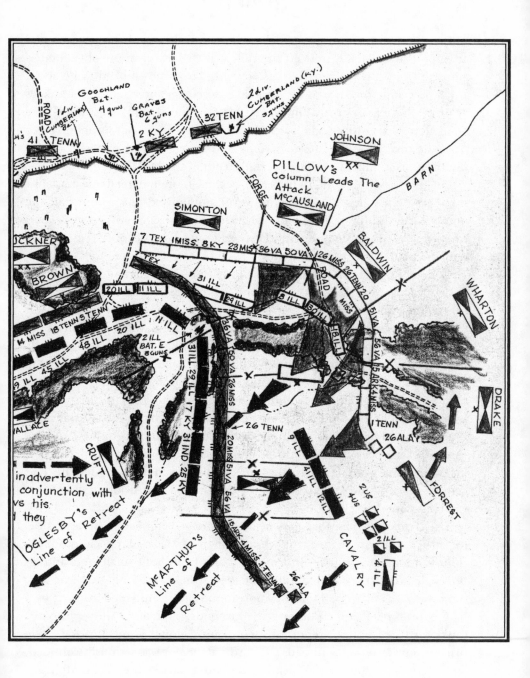

Despite being outnumbered and outgunned, they made an impassioned attempt. Private McKay noticed a particularly striking example of Confederate zeal: "a member of the 14 Miss, a young boy [who] looked to be about 15[,] . . . calling on his regt for gods sake to reform and charge the Yankees again[.] the tears were rolling down his face and I think he would have gone alone if an officer had not taken him to the rear." But by about 10:30 a.m., the three Confederate regiments were bogged down opposite several Illinois units in some woods to the right front of the McAllister guns.[21]

Buckner *was* hitting the right center of the Union line head-on with fewer numbers than Pillow's. He also, however, committed only about half the numbers he did have. Four more of his division's regiments—the Second Kentucky and the Thirty-second, Forty-first, and Forty-second Tennessee—remained in reserve in the trenches.

Colonel Roger Hanson and his Second Kentucky waited all morning and busied themselves. Assigned to support Graves's battery in the Confederate center, they were asked at about noon to supply ammunition for the Fourteenth Mississippi, which was running out of it while fighting in front of the trenches. Hanson obliged that request and also had his men deliver a destructive fire into the flank of the Federals opposing the Mississippians. Although his post-battle report does not say so, Hanson also had to have later seen Buckner beginning to withdraw Brown's brigade back to the trenches from its stymied position in the woods to Hanson's right. About that time, Colonel John McCausland, fighting farther to the left, approached and appealed for support as the Pillow push slowed. McCausland said that unless his Virginians were reinforced, "the enemy would retake what he had gained; that . . . the enemy were bringing forward new troops and in overwhelming numbers."[22]

The fighting to Hanson's left front was savage. The Federal line was being struck not only by fire from the riflemen of McCausland's and Simonton's Confederate brigades in front, but also from both small-arms and artillery fire from the Confederate trenches, which were only three or four hundred yards off. The Eighth Illinois found itself "enfiladed at turns by a battery on the left, which never ceased to pour grape and canister into our ranks for three hours," reported Lieutenant Colonel Frank Rhoads. "The fire was murderous . . ." Rhoads's subordinate major was seriously wounded, and his acting adjutant "fell dead in the latter part of the battle, after . . . bearing an order from Colonel Oglesby. Captain Robert Wilson was dangerously wounded . . . Captain Joseph M. Hanna (color company) next fell, dangerously if not mortally wounded, cheering his men to die by their colors. Lieutenant Marsh, Company B, and Lieut. H. A. Sheetz (color company), both fell dead at their posts . . ." Rhoads's orders had been to hold the

JOHN MCCAUSLAND

crest of the snowy ridge along which he had been positioned, and he later reflected that the Eighth followed its orders, "but at the cost of 54 killed and 186 wounded (many mortally)."[23]

Perhaps a thousand yards to Rhoads's left, where the Wynn's Ferry Road turned west from its southward path out of the Confederate trenches, members of the Twentieth Illinois had heard fighting to their right for two hours before being warned that Confederates were advancing on them. Then their skirmishers were driven back, and they saw Confederates coming over the crest of the hill along which the Twentieth was positioned. "Not waiting to receive their charge, I ordered my command to advance," reported Colonel C. C. Marsh, and his men drove the Southerners "steadily before them till they broke and ran."

This may have prompted McCausland's call for help from Hanson. Perhaps around 11 a.m., with Buckner gone to the right supervising the Brown attack and withdrawal, Hanson was mulling how to answer McCausland when Confederate cavalry galloped into view. The horsemen followed Wynn's Ferry Road down into a ravine, where they proceeded to charge the large emplacement of McAllister's cannons.[24]

*   *   *

Forrest had continued all morning to press his flanking work in the direction of the hottest fighting.

His troopers already had galloped up the now-open Forge Road and then down one of its byways into a ravine. There, in brief but hard fighting, they captured three guns of the Second Illinois Battery E. The Eighth and Twenty-ninth Illinois Infantry had just fallen back, leaving behind the battery. The artillerists—minus their wounded commander, Lieutenant Conrad Gumbart, and a total of twenty-three dead horses—were trying to haul their cannons backward when the Confederate cavalrymen struck. Forrest's horse was shot under him but kept moving, but the mount of his youngest brother, Lieutenant Jeffrey Forrest, went down so swiftly and violently that it rolled onto and painfully mashed its rider. With the Gumbart guns taken and left behind, the cavalrymen kept going down the ravine byway toward its intersection with the Wynn's Ferry Road and ever louder small-arms and cannon fire.[25]

Up there the Eleventh Illinois, personal regiment of Colonel W. H. L. Wallace before he was elevated to brigade command, and the Thirty-first Illinois of Colonel John "Black Jack" Logan had had the ill luck to be caught in a crossfire. They were at the vortex of collision between the rifles of Simonton's Seventh Texas and the First Mississippi infantry at their right front and, farther ahead, the blistering fire of three different artillery units in the Confederate trenches. Already, Colonel T. E. G. Ransom's Eleventh had withstood an initial forty-five minute onslaught that had killed or wounded thirty-five of his men, only to see Confederate colors appear among another large attacking force within a hundred yards of their front. The resulting second fight was also "exceedingly . . . bloody," Ransom reported, but "after great loss on my part the enemy again fell back." Then he "was again attacked by a heavier force on my right flank." By this time, brigade commander Wallace had given orders for a retreat by his whole brigade along Wynn's Ferry Road toward the Federal center, but the Eleventh was so embattled that the Wallace order never reached it. Ransom moved his men to the right to meet the new threat and to support Colonel Logan of Oglesby's teetering Thirty-first Illinois.[26]

"Black Jack" Logan, like McClernand, had been a southern Illinois Democratic congressman, and when Grant first encountered him while helping muster Union troops for Illinois, he was leery of Logan's prewar reputation. The Illinois politician had been vociferous in his support of the Fugitive Slave Act and of laws to ban free blacks from Illinois, and he had won reelection over his 1860 Republican opponent by a landslide in a district originally

JOHN A. LOGAN

settled by Southerners and initially sympathetic to the South. When local leaders asked if Logan could address his new regiment of state volunteers, Grant hesitated before consenting; he only did so because Logan would appear alongside the outspoken unionist McClernand. But Logan followed McClernand's speech with one "hardly equaled since for force and eloquence," Grant wrote. "It breathed a loyalty and devotion which inspired my men to such a point that they would have volunteered to remain in the army as long as an enemy of the country continued to bear arms against it." Logan went off to Bull Run to fight as a private with a Michigan regiment before returning home to recruit the Thirty-first Illinois, and his personal example had recast the loyalties of his whole district. It exceeded its quota of Union Army volunteers.[27]

At Fort Donelson, Logan reaffirmed his patriotism in emphatic fashion. His regiment suffered 176 casualties including Logan himself, who sustained wounds to his left arm, shoulder, and thigh.

By now, late morning, the whole Union right had been turned back past perpendicular. The Dover end of the Federal line had become a salient whose bend to the right had been held tenaciously by Logan's Thirty-first

Illinois. Next in line to the left, occupying the center of the bend, fought the embattled Eleventh. To its front, it already had seen the Eighth, bloody and all but ammunition-less, further slaughtered by a dismaying volley from its reinforcements, after which the Eighth retired in confusion to the rear. Then Logan sent word that the Thirty-first, too, was out of ammunition, and the Eleventh had sidled to the right to cover the Thirty-first's withdrawal from the line.[28]

Then Forrest arrived, and the Eleventh fell out of purgatory into hell on earth. The Illinoisans now suffered the last of their three hundred thirty-nine casualties, the most of any Union regiment in the battle. Lieutenant Colonel Ransom had just retaken command of the unit after being treated for a wound, and as soon as he saw a battalion of Confederate cavalry striking both his left flank and his rear, cutting him off from the leftward units that were all that remained of the Federal right, he ordered a retreat. It was too late, Ransom himself would recall. Most of his men, surrounded, were forced to cut their own individual ways back into the Union lines "with terrible loss. I found what was left of the Eleventh a few hundred yards in the rear of our first position," Ransom later reported.

But not every member of the Eleventh who was still alive got out. Lieutenant James Churchill, attempting to fight his way to safety when Forrest's troopers struck from behind, chose a spot in the line of horsemen to try to break through. He saw a Confederate cavalryman to his right with a rifle pointed at his head, and he was trying to bring around the revolver in his left hand when the trooper's bullet struck him. He "fell on, and among, a pile of dead and wounded," he later remembered. As he dropped, another bullet "struck me in the center of the right hip-socket from above, splitting off the outer half"; it traveled down his thigh and "lodged above the knee . . . I attempted to get up, but could only raise my head—my hips and lower limbs were as of lead."

McClernand's whole line was now gone, punched into bits and pieces of its various units, retreating in disorganized clots, many of the men holding up empty cartridge-boxes to show that they had not quit until left no choice. The Confederates, with Forrest now in their vanguard, were driving slowly but steadily toward the center of Grant's stunned army.

The battle passed over Lieutenant Churchill and moved on across the bloody, melting snow. Confederate stragglers appeared, and they began "robbing and tearing the clothing from the dead and wounded," Churchill soon remembered. "I remonstrated, and told them that it was not in accordance with civilized warfare; that there was no objection to their stripping the dead, but the wounded required all they had to keep them from freezing."[29]

*   *   *

By late morning, there were multitudes of freezing wounded on both sides. The fighting was so intense and prolonged over such expanses of wooded and broken terrain that, Forrest would later recall, units "were scattered and mixed in fragments." Some Confederates—seeking a new supply of ammunition, or helping the wounded, or just trying to get out of the cold—went into Dover, where Forrest saw many huddled "around the fires and up and down the river bank." Before noon, Confederate hospital boats were arriving for casualties being gathered into the town's hotels. Federal cannons zeroed in on these buildings, and it was about 1 p.m. before Union fire was finally diverted by the raising of hospital flags high enough to be seen across the lines.[30]

Similar dangers threatened Union medical facilities. Lieutenant Colonel William Erwin of the Twentieth Illinois, a veteran of the Mexican War, died of a wound to the chest "without a murmur and without a struggle" in a farmhouse field hospital just to the rear of some of the most desperate fighting. The Eleventh and Thirty-first Illinois were making the last stand of Mc-Clernand's division as the surgeons worked with increasing urgency in this makeshift facility on a lane running up so-called Bufford Hollow from Wynn's Ferry. As the Confederates moved forward, many of McClernand's wounded rapidly crowded into the place. "The slightly wounded, the mangled, the dying, and the dead" were brought in indiscriminately in "a scene which baffles description," reported Third Brigade surgeon Thomas Fry.

The scene got worse in late morning when the surgeons found the farmhouse suddenly hosting a horde of the able-bodied. "Hundreds of armed soldiers rushed in and remained," Fry reported, "until a volley of musketry from the enemy caused them to seek other and safer quarters." This Confederate firing at the hospital, like the Federal cannonading on the Dover hotels, was unintentional and halted when the hospital flag was spotted, but it led Fry and a subordinate surgeon to leave for safer quarters themselves. They took with them "all the wounded" who were in sufficient condition to be moved.[31]

Even to those familiar with the ravages of war, the field hospitals were chambers of horrors. John Brinton, Grant's medical director, was shocked by what he saw in one clinic. Brinton was reunited at Fort Donelson with a surgeon from an Illinois regiment who at Cairo a few months earlier had begged Brinton to perform an amputation for him. Brinton refused, saying that to comply would damage the man's standing in his unit; instead, Brinton assisted and instructed during the surgery. Now, riding around inspecting facilities during the Donelson fighting, he was told of a "great surgeon" operating in a nearby field facility. Curious to see this eminent physician, Brinton was directed to "the second story of a little country house." There he followed "bloodstained footmarks on the crooked stairs, and in the second-story room stood my friend of Cairo memory. Amputated arms and legs seemed almost to litter the floor. Beneath the operating table was a pool of blood, the operator was smeared with it and the surroundings were ghastly beyond all limits of surgical propriety." Hailing Brinton, the regimental surgeon extended his arm toward the limbs on the floor and said: "I'm getting along. Just look at these." This particular doctor, Brinton added, "seemed to have done good work," but that was hardly the case with every field physician. Fry complained of one "efficient and skillful surgeon when sober" who that day was so drunk as to be useless.[32]

Many soldiers never made it even to these butcher shops. Lieutenant Churchill of the Eleventh Illinois lay where he had fallen as the battle rolled past amid a cacophony of cries from his fellow wounded. Some youthful voices called for "Mother" while others shrieked "in great agony," groaned, or vehemently cursed. Presently, a trio of Confederate medical personnel came along looking for Federals with enough prospects of recovery to become prisoners of war. When they looked at Churchill and he asked what they planned to do with him, they said they did not plan to do anything. "They told me my right hip and thigh were both broken, that the blood was fast dripping from the left leg, (and) that it was no use to haul me off, as I would peg off before morning." They pulled another wounded man from beneath him, and Churchill's head, previously lying on the other wounded man's stomach, now fell onto the snow-covered ground. The head of a corpse pressed at Churchill's right side, the head of a second dead man was jammed against Churchill's own head, and yet another head, of a wounded man, lay over his heart. He asked the wounded man where he was wounded, but the man made no reply, and Churchill felt around until one of his fingers went inside a "large bullet hole" in the man's chest.

Looking around, he realized that he had fallen over a tree limb two inches in diameter and that the limb was causing part of his physical agony. He asked some Confederates nearby to lift him off the limb and away from the head of the dead man with whom he was engaged in such an uncomfortable tête-à-tête. One of the Confederates grabbed his ankles and abruptly lifted them three feet off the ground, causing Churchill's thigh bone to cut into the muscle around it. He screamed. After they tried one more lift with a similar result, "I told them to never mind, and they departed."[33]

*   *   *

By mid-day, the Confederate onslaught had rolled up the brigades of McArthur and Oglesby and slammed into the front and flank of McClernand's third and final brigade, W. H. L. Wallace's. Its principal anchor was a cluster of guns—two twenty-four-pounder howitzers, two twenty-pounders, along with another, unspecified cannon from Ezra Taylor's Battery B—commanded by Wallace's captain of artillery, Edward McAllister. McClernand had ordered them dug-in the night before on Wynn's Ferry Road, at the head of another ravine.

By noon, Forrest had cut the last legs from beneath the Eleventh Illinois. He had helped Mississippi and Virginia infantrymen smash the McClernand salient and fold the end of the Federal line back on itself. Then he encountered Pillow, who asked if the cavalryman knew anything about Buckner, whose advance had been so inconsequential that Pillow could discern neither it nor any effects of it. In his direct way, Forrest said he had been too busy to know anything about troops other than those he was supporting.

"Well, then, Colonel, what have you been doing since I saw you last?" Pillow inquired, just as directly.

"Obeying orders, General, by protecting your left flank," Forrest said. He then pointed to the Gumbart guns as well as captive men of the Eleventh Illinois.[34]

Pillow congratulated him, then said he was going to find Buckner and galloped off further to the right toward the trenches. There he found that Buckner had made his feeble attack on the McAllister positions but had finally fallen back and was again within the trenches. Pillow ordered Buckner's erstwhile attackers—John C. Brown's brigade—out again, this time toward the right of McAllister's clustered guns to try to flank them from that side.[35]

"We had scarcely gained the pits," the Third Tennessee's chaplain Deavenport later remembered, "when a battery began to shell us at a furious rate. I heard someone behind us and on turning around saw Colonel J. C. Brown . . . jump from his horse, wave his sword over his head, and cry, 'Men of the 3rd Tenn., come out of the pits.' The men . . . at once obeyed. A line was formed and . . . Soon the order came to move forward."[36]

Pillow obviously was impressed with what he had seen of Forrest's fearlessness in the face of artillery. While Brown began to get his men out of the trenches, Pillow sent the cavalryman an order: leave Gantt on the left flank and bring the rest of his men to the right. Brown's men had just moved out, Buckner with them, when Forrest arrived, and Pillow pointed toward the McAllister guns. Could Forrest take them? he asked. Appealing to Forrest's pugnacious pride and competitive instinct, he added that previous attempts had been made in vain. "I can try," Forrest answered.

Roger Hanson of the Second Kentucky, at the opposite end of Buckner's position from Brown's, then watched Forrest make two "gallant but unsuccessful charges" on the guns in the ravine. Forrest was arranging his squadrons for a third assault when he noticed the Second Kentucky nearby to his right and sent to ask Hanson for infantry aid. Already agonizing over McCausland's message that help was needed on this part of the field to head off a possible Union counterattack, Hanson concluded in Buckner's absence to take the responsibility on himself.[37]

Hanson joined Forrest in the shallow vale where his troopers were forming up. Out in front of them, Hanson saw an open area that had been occupied as a camp, likely by the Twentieth or the Forty-fifth Illinois the night before. Beyond it, Union infantry had taken position in timber and thick undergrowth. Hanson issued his instruction to his riflemen: double-quick across the open ground without firing their weapons until they reached the woods. He later reported he lost fifty men crossing the open area, but his order was "admirably executed" and the Federals "stood their ground until we were within 40 yards of them." At that point, though, the Confederates had reached the woods, where they loosed a hail of rifle fire, under which the Federal infantry hastily withdrew in confusion. With perhaps a bit of his wry humor, Hanson added: "This was not, strictly speaking, a [bayonet charge]—but it would have been if the enemy had not fled."[38]

Forrest's troops, mounted, reached the guns first. As was becoming his habit, he struck from the flank, going for the cannoneers, while Hanson came head-on. Both infantry and cavalry arrived at a lucky time: McAllister had just minutes earlier run out of ammunition and received an order to retreat, and Federal resistance around the cannons was limited to small-arms fire from the gunners and their companion infantry, the Forty-fifth Illinois. In the face of Hanson's bayonets, the infantry quickly dissolved, probably because the big twenty-four-pounder cannons no longer had anything to fire and could no longer offer protection to themselves or their supporting riflemen. Even more luck may have been involved. Brown's brigade of Buckner's division could be seen advancing in the distance, moving across a hill in the direction of the Federal center with obvious intent to flank McAllister from the far side; the Federals probably saw Brown coming.

McAllister reported getting an order—probably from his brigade commander, W. H. L. Wallace—to retreat down Wynn's Ferry Road toward the Federal center. This was soon after the Thirty-first Illinois ran out of ammunition and the Eleventh was cut off and swept away by Forrest, collapsing the salient that was Oglesby's last stand. Wallace, now flanked, ordered a general retreat of his brigade a half-mile backward on Wynn's Ferry—and everybody around McAllister rushed to comply. "[B]efore I could throw my saddle on my horse," McAllister reported, "I was left by the Forty-Fifth [Illinois] Regiment . . .39

"I got all the teams I could and hitched onto the left gun, but it was so heavy we could not haul it through the brush, and abandoned it . . . I started with two teams to hitch up the right piece, but before reaching it received a heavy volley from the enemy, then in full sight and charging on the gun. All attempt to save it then was hopeless, and I reluctantly ordered my drivers to retreat and followed them."40

There was so much gore around the guns from men and animals that at one point it pooled and splashed the cavalry's hooves before freezing in the snow. In Forrest's charges along this part of Wynn's Ferry Road, his horse, hit by seven bullets, fell from loss of blood. Supplied a second mount by a young Baptist minister riding with him, Forrest swung up and moved on, but his replacement horse was as ill-fated as the first. His and Hanson's men pushed on down Wynn's Ferry Road through the ravine toward more Federal guns, and the second horse took a bullet when Forrest headed forward to reconnoiter. Leaving Major Kelley to finish the reconnaissance, Forrest had started easing the wounded mount slowly back toward Confederate lines when a cannon ball passed completely through the animal just back of the saddle-blanket, drenching its rider's boots with blood and momentarily numbing his legs. Forrest staggered back to join his men around the final guns they had captured.41

Forrest had taken a heavy hand in breaking McClernand's final line. In doing so, he had broken with the traditional role of the cavalry in his era, which was limited to reconnaissance and an occasional charge, leaving grittier combat to infantry. Until Hanson's Kentuckians came to his aid, he had taken on the pivotal McAllister cannons on his own. In finishing off the Eleventh Illinois at the bend of McClernand's salient and then the McAllister guns almost immediately afterward, his fist had struck the blows that sent the last of McClernand's men reeling from the field.

*   *   *

"The roar never slackened," wrote Lew Wallace. "Men fell by the score, reddening the snow with their blood. The smoke, in pallid white clouds, clung to the underbrush and tree-tops . . . Close to the ground the flame of musketry and cannon tinted everything a lurid red."42

Much earlier that morning, General Wallace had struggled over whether to obey Grant's order simply to hold his position while, as Wallace at that moment understood it, Grant was arranging for another attack by the gunboats. When the second McClernand message arrived, though, "stating substantially that the enemy had turned [McClernand's] flanks and were endangering his whole command," Wallace decided circumstances demanded that he ignore the Grant directive. He sent Colonel Charles Cruft of his own First Brigade—the Thirty-first and Forty-fourth Indiana and the Seventeenth and Twenty-fifth Kentucky—hurrying to the right, the Twenty-fifth Kentucky in the lead.

Its men could not even stop to form into line because of "the pressing request of a messenger from one of the Illinois regiments, then to the right, to hurry forward and engage the enemy." As they passed McClernand's headquarters, McClernand ordered the Kentuckians' commander to "go at double-quick" and provided a guide to show them the way. But when they got under fire from Confederate artillery, the guide told the Twenty-fifth's commander, Colonel J. M. Shackelford, to go around a hill to his front. After that, Shackelford claimed, the guide vanished.

"I then proceeded in utter ignorance of the point at which I was needed and the position of the enemy," the colonel reported, "until I came up in the rear of one of General McClernand's regiments . . . the colonel came running down . . . and appealed to me to come to his rescue, stating that his men were about out of ammunition. I halted my regiment, formed them, and led them up in the face of a most galling and terrific fire."[43]

Cruft's men had been sent to try to keep Oglesby's Illinoisans from being swept away, and they went in just to the right of Logan's embattled Thirty-first Illinois. But they arrived too late. Cruft reported that the Confederate fire from their right continued to be "very severe," and the push of the Southerners—Virginians under McCausland and Wharton as well as Baldwin's Mississippians—came as close as twenty feet to the Union line, continuing furiously for several minutes. A rightward portion of the Twenty-fifth Kentucky was asked to stop firing because it was hitting Federals in front, but as soon as it did, Oglesby's bloody Eighth Illinois, the troops who had been fired into "retreated in confusion" in such mass that the Twenty-fifth's right companies became separated from those on the left. At that point Cruft's units suddenly found they had become the Federals' extreme right and were out in front of the rest of the line by half a mile.

They had to withdraw to the next hill to bring themselves back into line. Then, like the rest of Cruft's men, they began to give ground slowly and hold on as the Confederate sweep around the Union right finally spent itself.[44]

*   *   *

The Confederates had now opened the Forge Road, the desired escape route to Nashville, by a half-mile or more. But for days Pillow had promised his troops that he would chase the invader back to the Tennessee River, and, in the opinion of Lew Wallace, he decided to do it.

"General Pillow's vanity whistled itself into ludicrous exaltation," Wallace later wrote. "Imagining General Grant's whole army defeated and fleeing in rout for Fort Henry and the transports on the river, he . . . ignored Floyd [and] . . . rode to Buckner and accused him of shameful conduct[, then] . . . ordered Buckner to move out and attack the Federals . . . up [Wynn's Ferry] road . . . toward our cent[e]r."[45]

Whatever Pillow may have imagined, by ordering Buckner to proceed on down Wynn's Ferry—instead of halting to hold Forge Road open while the rest of the Donelson garrison marched out to Nashville—Pillow made a monumental mistake that would not be his last on this fateful day.

Pillow thought he had won the great battle of the western theatre. He proceeded to dash off to Albert Sidney Johnston a Napoleonic wire he no doubt knew Jefferson Davis would read. "On the honor of a soldier," it exulted, "the day is ours!"[46]

29

Early Afternoon

Grant, Pillow, and Disaster in the Balance

IT WAS SNOWING AGAIN but warmer. Some of the snow on the ground was melting as, a little after noon, Grant rode hard southward through ice-laced mud as Buckner and John C. Brown pushed up Wynn's Ferry Road.

When Grant came ashore from Foote's flagship to find the blanched Captain Hillyer, the Union commander was doubtless as astounded as a man of his restrained temperament could be. Two days earlier, when Brinton had come to him voicing fear that the enemy might "sweep down" from the heights around Dover and capture an exposed hospital with its supplies, Grant had told the doctor that the danger was all but nonexistent because "the enemy are thinking more of staying in than getting out— I know him."

By "him" Grant of course meant Pillow. He rarely disparaged other officers, but in correspondence he sometimes referred sarcastically to the Tennessean as "the great Gen. Pillow." Once Grant had suggested that Pillow's pretenses at heroism were both hollow and calculated. "I do not say he would shoot himself, ah no!" he had written his sister regarding Pillow some months before. "I am not so uncharitable as many who served under him in Mexico. I think, however, he might report himself wounded on the receipt of a very slight scratch, received hastily in any way, and might irritate the sore until he convinced himself that he had been wounded by the enemy."[1]

At Donelson up to this point, Grant had correctly assumed that the overbearing Pillow would dominate Floyd and be Donelson's *de facto* commander. He erred, though, in believing that Pillow on this day, February 15, would be more cowed by the Federal legions than he had been on February 12, 13, and 14. Grant employed too much logic to assess a man who was erratic and always passionately ambitious. Grant assumed Pillow would continue cowering behind Donelson's walls, he later wrote, because "conditions for battle were much more favorable to us [now] than they had been for the first two days of the investment. From the 12th to the 14th we had but

262

15,000 men of all arms and no gunboats. Now we had been reinforced by a fleet of six naval vessels, a large division of troops under General L. Wallace and 2,500 men brought over from Fort Henry belonging to the division of C. F. Smith." Why, then, would the Confederates suddenly want to fight? This excuse-seeking reasoning ignores a crucial truth, though. Pillow had seen and understood the importance of the smashing of the "fleet of six naval vessels" the evening before. Grant had heard the whole Confederate army's exultant yell at the sight of the crippled monsters limping off down-river. By leaving the field to see Foote he underscored the profound depth of his *own* belief in how all-important the gunboats were—and how their defeat had shaken him to his boot heels.[2]

Although he would recall that "the roads were unfit for making fast time," the expert horseman set off on Jack at a gallop. Grant had long held a superstition against returning anywhere by the same route he had taken to get there, and he may have worried that in the midst of this calamity he was returning to his headquarters by the same road he had taken to get to Foote's flagship. He could do nothing but press on, though. He first reached Smith's troops on the left, where his old commandant had followed the early-morning instructions to stay put and content himself with keeping up skirmish and artillery fire. Smith now told him that there had been no fighting here, that it had all been on the right wing. Grant replied with the quick coolness that was his essence under stress and with words that showed his mind had not been idle on the ride.

"If the enemy has massed so heavily on our right, he must have weakened his front here on our left," he said. "Hold yourself in readiness to attack with your whole command. Look out for a place to make the assault while I go over and see McClernand and Wallace."

"I'll be ready to advance whenever you give the order," Smith said.

The aplomb of Smith, together with the lack of action on that wing, was reassuring.

"In reaching the point where the disaster had occurred," he later remembered, "I had to pass the divisions of Smith and Wallace [and] . . . I saw everything favorable to us along the line of our left and centre." Then he memorably employed his gift for understatement. "When I came to the right[,] appearances were different."[3]

* * *

Lew Wallace, having sent Cruft's men off cross-country to aid McClernand in the early morning, later moved his remaining brigade—Colonel John Thayer's Ohio and Nebraska units—to the right perhaps a mile onto Wynn's

Ferry Road in the direction of the increasing tumult. The clock had passed noon when Wallace sat a horse among Thayer's volunteers atop a hill on Wynn's Ferry Road facing northeastward toward the Confederate trenches. He was discussing matters with Captain John Rawlins of Grant's staff, he later recalled, when he heard "a great shouting" coming from his right. An orderly sent to investigate dashed back to report that the road and adjacent woods in that direction were crawling with routed Union troops headed that way. He described it as a "stampede" that choked the road with men, horses, and wagons. Then the "fugitives . . . came crowding up the hill in rear of my own line, bringing unmistakable signs of disaster," Wallace officially reported at the time.

The scene became crazed. A mounted officer came galloping down the road shouting "We are cut to pieces!" in obvious terror. Rawlins pulled his pistol to fire at the horseman to prevent him from spreading wholesale panic, and Wallace had to grab Rawlins's arm to keep him from extending to an officer the standard policy toward fleeing enlisted men. Moments later, according to Wallace's memory decades afterward, the hatless and wild-eyed rider was followed by a much more placid one, McClernand Third Brigade commander Colonel W. H. L. Wallace. This second Wallace's "coolness under the circumstances was astonishing," the first Wallace recalled. By the time Lew Wallace wrote his memoirs, that impression would be so strong in the mind of the lifelong writer that he would picture the brigade commander riding at a walk, one leg crossed over his saddlehorn like a home-bound "farmer from a hard day's plowing."

The general described the colonel as followed by four to five hundred men falling back, not out of fright, but because they were out of ammunition. The general told the colonel that the ammunition wagons were a little farther down the road. The colonel informed the general that the enemy was close behind and that he barely had time to put his men in line of battle.4

This "stampede" may not have been quite as much of a surprise as it appears in the dramatic memoirs of the *Ben-Hur* author. Colonel Wallace already had sent word to General Wallace that he was coming. His assistant adjutant would later recall that after Oglesby's line began breaking behind McArthur's, Colonel Wallace sent him to McClernand to ask for permission to withdraw and form a new line. The assistant adjutant, Captain Israel P. Rumsey, said McClernand reluctantly assented, and when Rumsey returned, Colonel Wallace "then gave me the order . . . to form the new line changing front to the right. I did so, and he immediately started for the right, where Colonel Ransom with the Eleventh Illinois was fighting hand to hand with the rebels. [Wallace] then sent Davis of his staff with word to Lew Wallace." Receiving the reply that the general "would be glad

JOHN A. RAWLINS

to" help, W. H. L. Wallace then "rode rapidly" to the general, Rumsey remembered, and "suggested what seemed to him necessary to save McClernand's Division and perhaps the day; which was that he, Lew Wallace, should bring his fresh troops to our front and hold the rebels while we replenished ammunition and Colonel Oglesby and McArthur rallied."[5]

General Wallace's report does say that behind the first terror-stricken wave of battle fugitives came parts of McClernand's units moving toward him in perfect order with their brigade commanders all calling only for more ammunition with which to fight.

"The crisis was come," Wallace's official report continued. "There was no time to await orders. My Third Brigade had to be thrust between our retiring forces and the advancing foe."

So, once again, the young general disobeyed the instructions Grant had left in his absence. He hurried Thayer's men a bit farther down the road to where the little hill they were on began to break slightly downward. Placing them in line of battle astride the thoroughfare at right angles to his former position facing the Confederate trenches, he sent to his rear for all the cannon that could be quickly gathered. The closest were two from Taylor's Battery B, First Illinois Light Artillery, that had been with W. H. L. Wallace, and all of Battery A. He placed them in the road with the First Nebraska and the

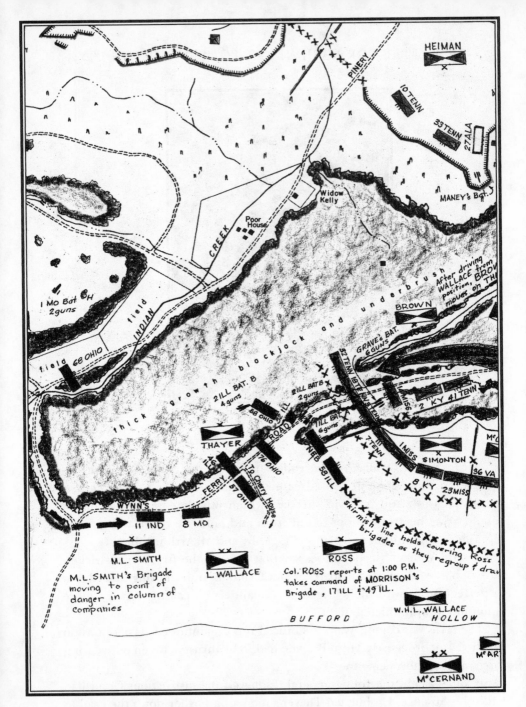

12:15 TO 1 P.M. After Forge Road clears, Forrest leaves some of his cavalry to guard Pillow's flank, then teams with Hanson's Kentucky infantry to smash the McAllister cannons in the center. Led by Buckner, the Confederates push Oglesby's and W. H. L. Wallace's brigades westward along Wynn's Ferry Road. *Used by permission of Tennessee State Library & Archives.*

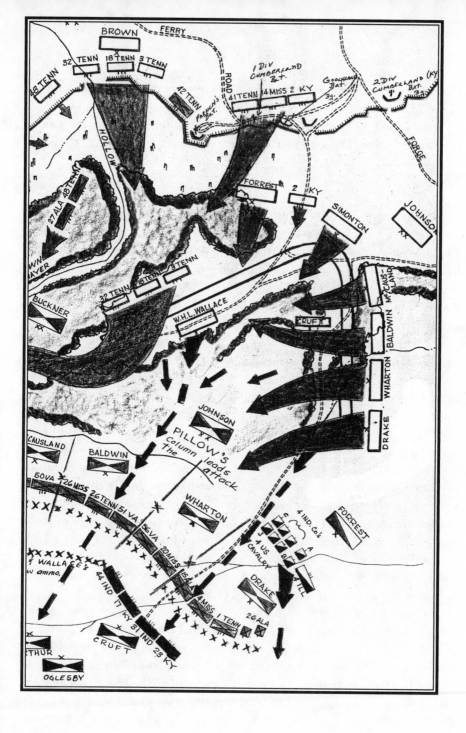

Fifty-eighth Illinois on their right and the Fifty-eighth Ohio plus a company of the Thirty-second Illinois on their left. Behind these he positioned another Ohio infantry regiment and two more from Illinois. Just to the rear of these, many of McClernand's remnants busily filled their cartridge boxes.[6]

*   *   *

The slight lull that gave Lew Wallace time to rearrange infantry and artillery units and dam the ebbing Union tide probably occurred because John C. Brown's men—the Third, Eighteenth, and Thirty-second Tennessee followed by other Buckner units—assumed their job was all but finished. Brown's troops had marched out of the trenches that morning with three days' rations. Their commanders all had understood their primary task was to block off the further reaches of Wynn's Ferry Road and enable the Donelson army to take the Forge Road south to Charlotte and Nashville. Wynn's Ferry was now effectively blocked. Forge Road had been opened. All that seemed left to do, under this new order from Pillow to attack down Wynn's Ferry Road, was to perhaps buy more time for the general retreat by pushing the Federals backward up Wynn's Ferry as far as they were inclined to go.

Brown's men required some little time themselves. They needed to refill their cartridge boxes and dry their flint-lock muskets. The weapons had gotten drenched in the morning's fighting through dense undergrowth which the heavy, wet, continuing snow of the morning kept thickly covering while simultaneously melting. The Federals that Brown's men were chasing, the broken elements of W. H. L. Wallace's brigade, were now nearly out of range of the Confederate artillery, so that, as Colonel Joseph Palmer of the Eighteenth Tennessee later reported, "it was not deemed consistent with the [previous night's] orders for the movements of the whole army that day . . . to pursue the enemy any farther in that direction."[7]

Now the Wynn's Ferry Road and the hollow to its right brought Brown's brigade to the rise whose brow Lew Wallace had crowned with his hastily assembled Federals. The Union position was so masked by undergrowth and trees that Brown's skirmishers could not see how it lay or how many men defended it. Thinking that the Union artillery could not be supported by more than a thousand troops, the Confederates charged upward. At about a hundred yards, Brown would report, "we were met by a fire of grape and musketry that was terrific" but which passed "above our heads." Lieutenant Colonel Thomas M. Gordon of the Third Tennessee, wounded, ordered the regiment to fall back under cover of the hill, but they had retreated only a hundred yards or so before a dismayed Colonel Brown stopped them, along with the Eighteenth.[8]

Brown sent forward two companies double-quicking off to the left and right as skirmishers, and their rifles were quickly heard, the Third Tennessee's chaplain Deavenport later remembered.

"The other four [companies] were left standing under this dreadful fire. This is the time to try men. While they are firing themselves, they have something to occupy the mind, but compell them to stand under a heavy fire with nothing to do, they will grow weak in the knees."9

Buckner called for artillery from Graves's, Porter's, and Jackson's batteries— along with Colonel Robert Farquharson's Forty-first Tennessee Infantry in Brown's immediate rear—to break the Union line and pursue the Federals further or to hold the position Brown now held astride Wynn's Ferry. To Buckner's wondering consternation, the artillery and infantry reinforcements he had called for were suddenly denied by Pillow. Brown's men made three separate lunges at the Federal position, but were repelled each time by the First Nebraska and the Chicago cannons. Wallace's report would say the foe then "retire[d] to their works pell-mell and in confusion."10

Wallace's report, though, attempted to take all credit for an extraordinary turnabout in which Wallace was not the major player. The Confederates did return to their trenches, but they hardly fled. Brown would claim that, with the help of the Fourteenth Mississippi, he was about to renew his attack on Wallace when a singular circumstance prevented him. Without consulting or even apprising Floyd, Pillow, repenting of his ambitious aggression down Wynn's Ferry Road, suddenly reversed himself and did what to Buckner and many other officers was the unthinkable. He ordered Confederates along the entire front to return to their rifle pits and abandon the two miles of ground they had bought with such blood in the previous seven-hour onslaught.

*　　*　　*

Buckner, furious, resisted. "[A]fter the battle . . . had been won and my division . . . was being established in position to cover the retreat of the army, the plan of battle seemed to have been changed," he wrote three days later.

He obeyed the dismaying order only after receiving a reiteration of it from Pillow. Then, unchased by Federals, he reluctantly pulled his men nearly back to their trenches. In the process, he happened onto a mystified Floyd, who just a little earlier had ordered him to solidify their position on the road. Floyd later wrote that his intention was to have Buckner's men hold that position overnight to prevent the Federals from re-closing the Forge Road.

The problem was that in the breakout planning meeting neither Floyd nor anyone else had set the approximate time of retreat, leaving it to be determined by the progress of the fighting. And now nobody could fathom

GIDEON JOHNSON PILLOW.
Courtesy of the National Archives.

Pillow's thinking. When Buckner encountered Floyd and told him what Pillow had ordered him to do, Floyd became as angry as Buckner. He ordered a halt to Buckner's withdrawal until he could find and confront Pillow. In an ensuing conference, Floyd hotly asked Pillow what they had been fighting for all day. Then he answered his own question: "not to show our powers, but . . . to secure the Wynn's Ferry Road—and now after securing it, you order it to be given up."

Pillow, cowed, explained his order. He said the exhausted Confederates needed rest, food, and a re-supply of ammunition; the wounded had to be gathered from the field; the skeleton garrison that had been holding the Confederate trenches while he and Buckner had attacked out of them should not be left there to be sacrificed. The completeness of their triumph afforded them the time to do all these things, Pillow contended.

Floyd finally bowed to the directive of his second-in-command, later reporting that it seemed the only choice left to him. This was because he had seen movement by the Federals opposite Buckner's denuded former position in the trenches in front of Fort Donelson. He ordered Buckner to comply with Pillow's order, after all, and return as quickly as possible to his former position on the extreme right—"which," Buckner later quoted Floyd, "was in danger of attack." The day was far gone and time was running out, Floyd also reasoned; the crucial element of momentum was passing to—or being seized by—the Federals. Some twenty thousand Union reinforcements were arriving, the Confederates believed, and Buckner's lightly protected former position on the right of the Donelson defenses was in extreme jeopardy.[11]

Pillow later tried to explain his inexplicable order, which left virtually no one guarding the vital Forge Road, by incomprehensibly repeating the goal espoused in the post-midnight council by Floyd and Buckner: to open an escape route. But Pillow wrote that opening it "had occupied the day" and the weary Confederate units needed to go back inside their previous lines to re-form ranks and pick up rations and other supplies. He did not say why Buckner's men, who by Buckner's order already had these supplies with them, were not allowed to hold their positions on Wynn's Ferry Road while the others returned to collect their knapsacks. Maybe he did not know Buckner's men already had them. Possibly he was thinking only about himself and his own men, who not only did not have this equipment but also had been fighting since shortly past daybreak after suffering from cold and sleep-deprivation for at least forty-eight previous hours. Maybe he did not think the skeleton force occupying the extreme right could hold it alone long enough for the others to get their gear and withdraw. Whatever he thought, Pillow certainly had no idea the Federals could recover from their bloody drubbing.[12]

*   *   *

He also had no way of knowing that his great victory of the morning had been won over a leaderless foe—and that by 1 p.m. the foe was leaderless no longer. About 1:30, in fact, Grant finally arrived where Thayer's Midwesterners and their Illinois cannons had just dealt the final repulse to Brown.

Grant had gotten more worried the nearer he came to the scene of the fighting. Somewhere on his gallop across the front, he suffered a crisis of confidence—or as close to one as his desperate resolve would permit. On the ride, he sent a shaken-sounding message addressed to Foote or whatever subordinate the naval chief left in command on the river after departing for Cairo.

> *Head Quarters, Army In The Field,*
> *Camp near Ft. Donelson, Febry 15th 1862*
>
> *COMMDG OFFICER G.B.* [Gunboat] *FLOTILLA*
>
> *If all the Gun Boats that can, will immediately make their appearance to the enemy, it may secure us a Victory. Otherwise all may be defeated. A terrible conflict ensued in my absence, which has demoralized a portion of my command. I think the enemy is much more so. If the Gun Boats do not show themselves it will reassure the enemy and still further demoralize our troops. I must order a charge to save appearances. I do not expect the Gun Boats to go into action, but to make their appearance, and throw* ["a few" is crossed out here] *shells at long range.*
>
> *Respectfully,*
>
> *U. S. Grant*
> *Brig Gen. Commdg.*[13]

Probably for the benefit of his own mind as well as that of the naval officer who received this message, Grant put the best face possible on the facts
as he knew them, while nevertheless making it clear that the circumstances
were dire. Indicating that if the gunboats did not "immediately make their
appearance to the enemy" a defeat was highly possible, he emphasized that
he was requesting only an "appearance," not an attack, by the navy. He may
also have been hinting at Foote's culpability in the calamity by adding that it
all "ensued in my absence," which had occurred at Foote's request. He went
on to write that some of his army had been "demoralized," but, with the
dogged optimism that had sustained him during his life's previous reverses,
he rushed on to say (while providing no evidence) that he thought "the enemy is much more" demoralized. Then, lest he sound so confident as to lead
the navy to think its aid could be done without, he wrote that non-appear-
ance by the gunboats would "reassure" the Confederates and dishearten the
Federals "still further," making a defeat that much more probable. The situation was so serious, he added, that he would have to "order a charge" just "to
save appearances."

Grant's message is one of the more extraordinary documents ever written
by a man whose contributions to military literature would become conspicuous for their succinctness, candor, and unassuming heroism. The note's ultimate message is that even at this moment when victory appeared so distant
that it seemed almost fantasy, the little man in the rumpled blue coat refused to settle for less than at least a tie. No matter how demoralized his men
were, he was going to fight, and if the navy did not want to be embarrassed,
it had better at least look aggressive. The only acceptable response when
your forces were attacked was to counterattack—and to appear to be doing it
with every means you had.

By the time he reached the Federal right, Grant looked cool and uncon-
cerned, Lew Wallace would remember. Accompanied by chief of staff J. D.
Webster, Grant rode up to McClernand and Wallace at the right center of
the buckled Union line and, with an unsmoked portion of Foote's cigar still
in his mouth, returned their salutes. In one hand he held a few pieces of paper that looked like telegrams.

McClernand, as shattered as his division by the lack of timely aid that
headquarters could have provided, made a bitter observation that likely put
the nail in the coffin of his relations with his commander. In this dark hour
of trial for both, the politician pointedly referred to Grant's disastrous absence with an angry growl:

"This army wants a head."

Grant had no trouble imagining what use McClernand would make of
that criticism. The ex-congressman would begin, no doubt, by sending it to

every newspaper editor he knew, as well as his longtime acquaintance in the White House. Grant may well have given McClernand the sharp look by which he had been known to cow rowdy enlisted men. His reply to McClernand was milder, but perhaps just as pointed. "It seems so," he said.

As the full measure of the disaster that had befallen McClernand sank in, Grant "flushed slightly," Wallace recalled. Still in the defensive mindset in which he had left Foote that morning, he told the two division commanders to pull their troops back onto the hills beyond cannon range and start digging while they awaited reinforcements that were on the way. After encountering Wallace's damming of the human flood down Wynn's Ferry Road, he was told, the Confederates seemed to have halted their offensive. That would give the Federals a chance to entrench; dug in, they could hold while Smith assailed the Confederate right and perhaps recaptured a little Union momentum.

Then, in the space of a few moments, Grant showed he was a general in essence, not just in uniform. Somebody said the road to Charlotte and Nashville was now open. Noticing common soldiers "standing in knots talking in the most excited manner" while getting no orders from their officers, he paid attention to what they were saying. Some remarked that the Confederates had emerged from their fortifications with, as Grant later remembered, "knapsacks, and haversacks filled with rations." This indicated to the men in ranks that their attackers planned to stay outside the trenches and "fight as long as the provisions held out."

Their commander swiftly combined the fact of the open Charlotte road with that of the full Confederate knapsacks and divined their true significance. The Confederates were not, as Grant had so confidently assured Brinton two days earlier, "thinking more of staying in[side Fort Donelson] than [they were in] getting out." Pillow had been trying to flee but now was retiring from the field. The situation in the trenches all along the Confederate line had to be highly disordered.

Grant now saw a way out of the abyss, with or without the gunboats. With what surely was ecstatic—if almost totally private—joy, he made one of the most important decisions in American history and tossed aside the abhorred siege plan. In "his ordinary, quiet voice," Wallace later wrote, Grant said, "Gentlemen, the position on the right must be retaken."14

He then turned and galloped away, back toward Smith's left. En route, he explained to Webster his change of purpose. He realized that in his hopeful note to Foote he had captured the reality of the situation better than he could have known at the time.

"Some of our men are pretty badly demoralized," he said with as much excitement as he was capable of, "but the enemy must be more so . . . he has attempted to force his way out, but has fallen back. The one who attacks first now will whip, and the enemy will have to be in a hurry if he gets ahead of me."15

* * *

It is impossible to know what thoughts swirl in any man's mind at a given moment unless he purports to recall them, and often not then.

More than two decades later, Grant would write that he thought about entrenching as Foote had advised, then about Pillow's withdrawal from the field and his soldiers' descriptions of the loaded Confederate knapsacks. But it seems likely that other ideas, too, goaded him toward his decision to forego digging in and, instead, to launch an all-out counterattack.

There were, of course, Johnston and Polk and the possibility that, seeing the Federal infantry stalled in front of Donelson and the gunboats returning to Cairo, the Confederate theatre commanders might reinforce Donelson and attack with heavier numbers than Grant's. There was also the possibility that Halleck would lose his last vestige of patience with this subordinate whom he so plainly disliked and send a better-credentialed officer to rescue, and relieve, him—especially after the subordinate had been trounced, if only for one day, by the lightly regarded Pillow. A crushing defeat by the Tennessee politico was surely the most mortifying prospect Grant had ever faced as a soldier. Finally, there was the contemptuous observation made by McClernand. His comment—"This army wants a head"—unmistakably displayed the ex-congressman's conviction that the Henry–Donelson campaign lacked a fit field commander. Whom McClernand thought Grant should be replaced by went without saying.

It was one of the handful of most pivotal moments of the war. What would have happened had Grant done what most peers would have, which was follow Foote's guidance and entrench? How much longer would Halleck have waited to sack him? And how long after that would it have taken Lincoln and the Union to find another Grant, a general inclined to attack and face the fact that this was a war, not merely a disagreement among countrymen that could be healed with skirmishes? Would they, in fact, have been able to do it at all—and in time to keep a "Peace Democrat" from replacing Lincoln in the White House in 1864?

Grant's decision was probably reached over the course of an hour. On his ride from the river, he had realized that the Confederate right had been robbed of strength to enable the fueling of such an onslaught on its left; he mentioned it to Smith on first arriving at the Union lines. At the time, though, he thought of Smith's sector as simply the place to launch the "attack to save appearances." When Grant reached the right center, the soldiers' talk of Confederate knapsacks filled with three days' rations and the reminder that the Forge Road had been opened, coupled with the Confederates' puzzling retirement from the field, had to have been received by his mind like sudden, unaccountable gifts from the gods. They expanded his sense of the possibilities from the mere attempt to "save appearances" to a bid to reclaim the day Pillow assumed was won.

These charities of fate gave Grant all he needed to change his mind. The McClernand aspersion just added bile.

*   *   *

Gambling that his reasoning was correct—that to sweep the Union right all the way back onto its center the Confederates had robbed much strength from in front of the Federal left—Grant made his decision to launch a powerful counterstroke. He would deliver it across the entire line, beginning on the end where he thought Pillow and the Confederates would be weakest. With Webster, he headed for the headquarters of his West Point mentor Smith, telling Webster that as they passed he was to employ a powerful weapon of psychology: "Call out to the men . . . : 'Fill your cartridge-boxes, quick, and get into line; the enemy is trying to escape, and he must not be permitted to do so.'"

At Second Division headquarters, Grant found the fifty-four-year-old Smith waiting for him, sitting against the trunk of a tree. As usual, Grant did not waste words or time. Riding up, he immediately said: "General Smith, all has failed on the right. You must take Fort Donelson." Smith, he added, was to quickly throw at the enemy trenches in his front his entire division— which was fresh, having participated in no fighting all day. In the Confederate trenches, Grant said, Smith "would find nothing but a very thin line to contend with."

The older man's reply was immediate and even more laconic than Grant's order. "I will do it," he said.[16]

Smith's charge that afternoon did not reach Fort Donelson, but it did the next best thing. First Smith directed John Cook's smaller brigade, made up of the Twelfth Iowa and the Fiftieth Illinois, to throw a forceful feint at the troops in their front. Then the old man himself led Lauman's large brigade—the Second, Seventh, and Fourteenth Iowa plus the Twenty-fifth Indiana—to the left of Cook's, toward the very end of the Confederate line. To the Second Iowa he shouted Grant's instructions that they had to take the fort. They must fix bayonets, he added. He would lead them. He then got out front of his men. Fearing that his young volunteers would become edgy and prematurely open fire, he positioned his horse and his own body

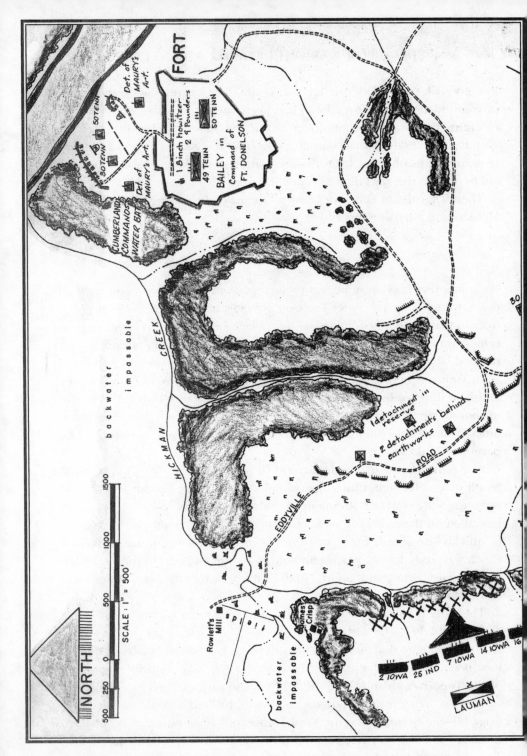

2:15 TO 3:15 P.M, UNION LEFT. Grant, saying that "all has failed on the right," launches his counterattack, sending Smith at the head of Lauman's and Cook's Midwesterners in an assault on the depleted Confederate trenches in front of the Union left. *Used by permission of Tennessee State Library & Archives.*

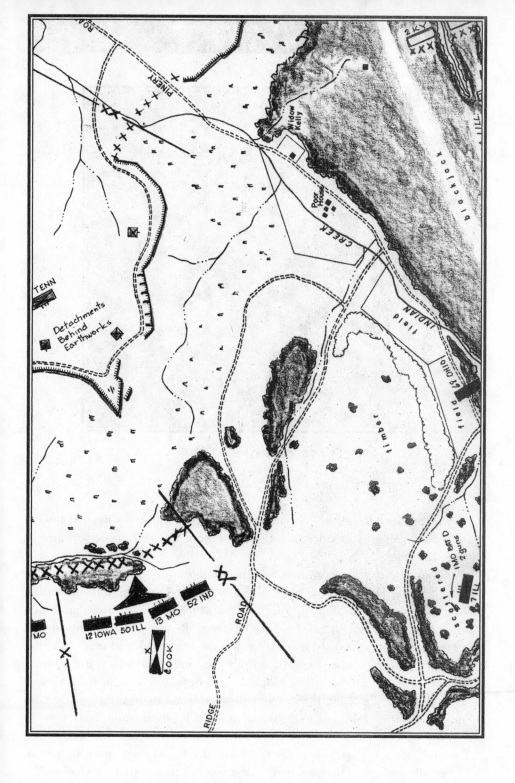

CHARLES FERGUSON SMITH.
Courtesy of the National Archives.

to prevent it. Behind the old career soldier, the volunteers headed toward the outer ring of Confederate trenches, directly in front of the fort and its river batteries.

Slipping and sliding off their hill, the Iowans and Hoosiers came without a shot across a creek at the bottom of a ravine and then upward into firing that started coming from the rifle pits that Buckner's men had abandoned early that morning. Spread along the Eddyville Road leading northwestward out of Donelson, these trenches lay atop that next snow- and mud-slick rise, one denuded of timber except for the thick abatis into which the downed trees had been fashioned. The tangled mass, designed to delay the attackers and allow the Confederate rifles and shotguns time to do their work, was so nearly impenetrable that one soldier thought a rabbit would have trouble getting through. There the already warm Confederate fire got hotter. The Federal formation became ragged, causing the hard-bitten Smith to turn in his saddle and shout threateningly: "Damn you, gentlemen, I see skulkers!"[17]

This end of the Confederate trenches was manned by a mere skeleton force, just three companies of the Thirtieth Tennessee, their fire supported by the guns in the fort as well as by Porter's Confederate battery to the attackers' right. When the Federals reached the abatis, they necessarily slowed. Smith put his cap on the point of his sword, raised it high, and picked his way upward as he called out to the men behind him, "No flinching now, my lads, here, this is the way, come on." The brigade followed. At other times he was less paternal, shouting at them with typical old-army profanity that while war was his "business" and had given him this unwelcome job of being here on this bullet-blasted, snow-slick slope this afternoon, they by contrast had volunteered for the task, had come willingly out of civilian safety to shed blood for their country, and now, by God, they were going to get to.

"Come on, you volunteers, come on," he harangued them. "This is your chance. You volunteered to be killed, and now you can be." As Smith's troops neared the crest with bayonets brandished, the Fourteenth Iowa was finally allowed to fire. Having restrained their trigger fingers through all they had had to endure scrambling up the obstructed slope, they loosed a volley that was delivered as if from "the maddened regions of despair," Sergeant Kiner would remember. They "seemed to shake the very earth" as they mounted the Confederate parapets with clashing bayonets.

For a few moments the fighting was from up close. Smith's adjutant general would later write that the old soldier, "calm but terrible" astride his horse, could have "placed his hand on the heads of the rebels who were firing on our advancing men." But not for long. As Kiner wrote, "The shock was more than rebel courage could stand."

Most of the few Confederate defenders scrambled out of the rifle pits and fell back across a deep ravine and through one of their camps to the next ridge, while the remainder fell to Union steel. The onrushing Federals chased them through the camp toward the inner hill topped by the fort. They then were slowed when the Fifty-second Indiana, instead of following orders to support the Second Iowa, came up in confusion and, stopping in the already-taken Confederate trenches, fired wildly into the rear of their advancing comrades. The troops into whom they fired were fighting hand-to-hand again. The Second Iowa ran out of ammunition and fell back behind the captured rifle pits, replaced by the Twenty-fifth Indiana.[18]

Both Smith and his mount were hit by fire, he would later confide to his journal, but he added that by his behavior he managed "to encourage and keep in position the Vols." Only luck and the paucity of Confederate defenders can explain how Smith managed to escape death atop a horse with his hat and sword raised to focus the attention of his men.

The Second Iowa's similarly conspicuous color-guard was not as fortunate. According to the regimental report written three days later:

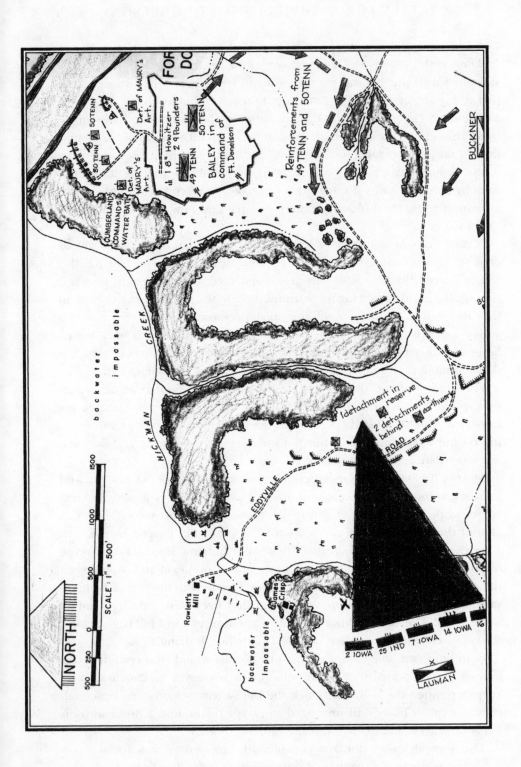

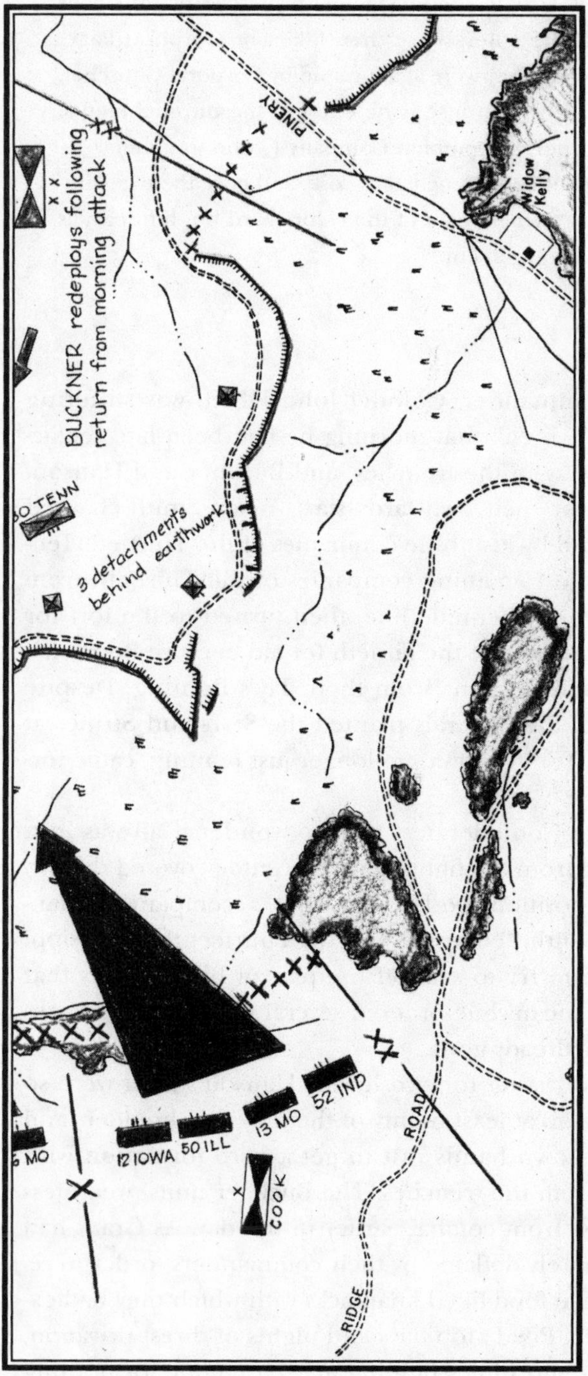
PINERY
Widow Kelly
BUCKNER redeploys following return from morning attack
30 TENN
3 detachments behind earthwork
MO
12 IOWA
50 ILL
13 MO
52 IND
COOK
ROAD
RIDGE

2 TO 5 P.M, UNION LEFT. In fighting that rages until nightfall, Smith takes the trenches on the Confederates' extreme right before Buckner's men can get back into them, but the Federals cannot carry the Confederate fallback position on the next ridge. Smith brings up cannon, points to the Confederate bastion overlooking the Cumberland River, and gives Cook his order for the next morning: "Take it, sir!" *Used by permission of Tennessee State Library & Archives.*

Color Sergeant Doolittle fell early in the engagement, pierced by four balls and dangerously wounded. The colors were then taken by Corporal Page, Company B, who soon fell dead. They were again raised by Corporal Churcher, Company I, who had his arm broken just as he entered the intrenchments, when they were taken by Corporal Twombley, Company F, who was almost instantly knocked down by a spent ball, immediately rose, and bore them gallantly to the end of the fight. Not a single man of the color-guard but himself was on his feet at the close of the engagement.[19]

*   *   *

The defenders' brigade commander, Colonel John Head, was suffering from near pneumonia. At daybreak that morning he had been late replacing Hanson's Second Kentucky in the trenches, and Buckner and Hanson, in turn, had blamed Head for their own tardy start. When Smith charged the Buckner trenches manned by just three companies of the Thirtieth Tennessee, Head ordered the two remaining companies of the Thirtieth from the extreme left of his three-quarter-mile line, then turned to the fort for the Forty-ninth Tennessee and part of the Fiftieth for aid because Buckner's just-returning infantrymen were spent from their day's fighting. Despite Head's efforts, about 3 p.m. the Federals planted the Stars and Stripes at the trenches' far end as the Twelfth Iowa, no longer just feinting, came forward, too.[20]

Now, suddenly, it was the Confederates' turn to wonder if all was lost. Hanson's men, just returned from the fighting in the center, covered the two miles back to their former position too late. Buckner, accompanying Hanson, brought up the Eighteenth Tennessee and the Fourteenth Mississippi from farther down the line to try to seal off the part of his trenches that Smith had yet to reach. He meanwhile ordered several unsuccessful attacks to try to retrieve the portion already gone.

The fighting was furious, lasting for two hours. Hanson's men were so weary that Buckner had to grab at least twenty of them by the shoulders and place them in line with his own hands just to get a core formation with which to try to oust Smith from the trenches. The Buckner units' weariness stemmed apparently not just from combat earlier in the day. As Grant had assumed, their spirits were surely deflated by their commanders' order to return to their trenches with the food-filled knapsacks with which they had expected to march to Nashville. Piled atop days and nights of direst privation, the realization that all of the morning's fighting may have gone for nothing must have been crushing.

But by sunset Buckner had at least held off the Federals and established a new line on the hill to which Head's defenders had initially retreated. Hanson thought the new position stronger in natural features than the old one, but his men were so fatigued from working so hard with so little clothing to protect them from the elements that digging new rifle pits proved "utterly impossible."

Soon after nightfall the Third Tennessee, which also had helped stem Smith's Union tide, "lay down, the weary to rest and the wounded to die," recalled chaplain Deavenport. "We had worked and fought all week, had eaten or slept but little, and were all nigh worn out." Faced with a Union force that Buckner believed to be three to five times the size of his own, the division commander was becoming certain that, with his right already pushed back and part of his trenches now in enemy hands, he would be unable to stop the horde that he was sure Grant would throw at him at dawn.[21]

*   *   *

While Buckner was trying to retrieve his old position from Smith on the Confederate right, Lew Wallace was having more success complying with Grant's order to retake the lost Federal ground on the line's other end—thanks in great part to Pillow's order pulling the Confederates back to their own trenches. About 1 p.m. Brigadier General Bushrod Johnson, personally overseeing Pillow's wing of the morning attack and watching his troops push McClernand backward hill by hill, was with Drake's brigade on the left side of the attacking force when he noticed that he no longer had support on his right. Johnson asked for reinforcements and was ordered to report to Floyd inside the original Confederate perimeter. When he arrived, Floyd refused him his reinforcements. Johnson suggested that his men should attack the Federal position in his front, but Floyd demurred, telling him just to "display" Drake's brigade while the rest of the attackers retired within the trenches. Johnson did as ordered, then himself returned eight hundred yards to the works. There he watched as Drake's men—the Fourth Mississippi, Fifteenth Arkansas, Twenty-sixth Alabama, and a Tennessee battalion—came under attack by Lew Wallace.[22]

The all-out effort on the Union right got going after Smith's on the left. That was partly, probably, because McClernand had been designated to lead it, but McClernand's command was in such tatters that he uncharacteristically deferred to Wallace. When Wallace's counterattack did begin, the Eighth Missouri and Eleventh Indiana, helped on the right by Cruft's brigade of Hoosiers and Kentuckians, stormed the hill Drake occupied.

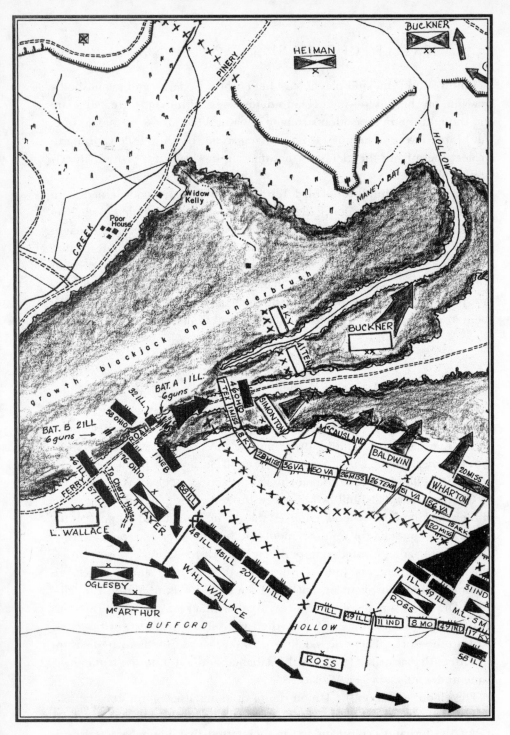

2:15 TO 3:15 P.M, UNION RIGHT. On Grant's right, after Buckner's drive has been checked by Lew Wallace, Confederate units start withdrawing in compliance with Pillow's stunning order to go back to the trenches. Forrest is sent to the Confederate left again, this time to aid Drake, who is on "display" to cover Pillow's withdrawal. *Used by permission of Tennessee State Library & Archives.*

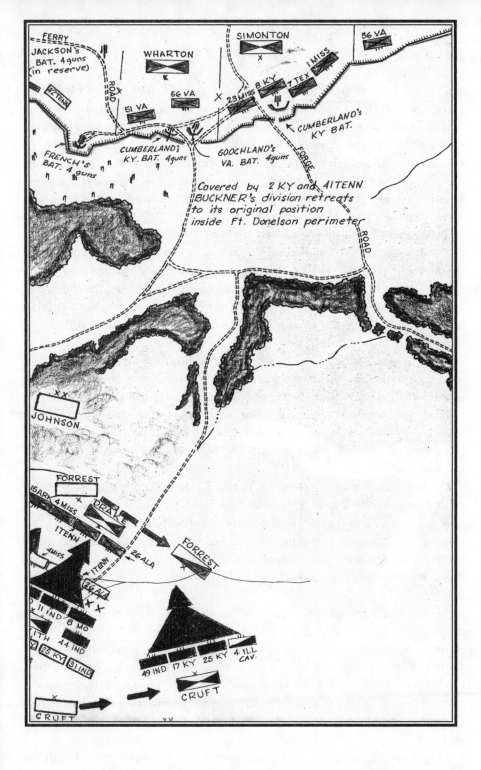

Refused help from other quarters, Johnson prevailed on Forrest to take his troopers to Drake's aid. The Federal assault was so powerful, though, that Forrest uncharacteristically advised Drake to withdraw, then helped him conduct a fighting retreat. Brigade commander Colonel Morgan Smith of the Eighth Missouri, who had most of a cigar shot away from his mouth during this part of the fight, reported that, in the forest and dense underbrush dotting the hill, in "two instances their (Confederate) skirmishers and ours were occupying each side of the same tree for cover."

Wallace's push ultimately carried them to within one hundred fifty yards of the trenches at the Confederate right center, driving Drake into them as the Federals cheered. But the Confederate withdrawal on this part of the field had less to do with Wallace than with other problems. Buckner had called for reinforcements on the right to regain his lost trenches, and that made it unwise to send out more troops to Drake's aid on the Confederate left, Johnson later reported. [23]

After dark, Grant and Smith continued to improve Smith's position. As soon as his men had captured the rightmost part of the Confederate rifle pits, Smith had ordered up five cannons—batteries H and K of the First Missouri Light Artillery—to help hang onto them. His adjutant general, Thomas J. Newsham, later remembered bringing up two ten-pounder Parrott guns and, after they had opened fire, Smith sent him back for two twenty-pounders.

On his second mission Newsham passed Grant, who asked if Smith needed anything. Without having consulted his chief, Newsham requested the return of some of Smith's former regiments that had been sent to the right on loan to McClernand's command the day before. Newsham specifically asked for the Ninth Illinois, which had been in some of the heaviest fighting on the right that morning and was, in Newsham's words, "a regiment that Gen. Smith loved."

Smith and Newsham positioned the twenty-pounders and ten regiments, with more arriving from McArthur's brigade, of which the Ninth Illinois was a part. McArthur's whole brigade was now returning from McClernand. Newsham and his commander were about to go back to their camp for the night when, Newsham would later recall, Smith took particular notice of one of the regiments "drawn up in line of battle." It included, in Newsham's estimation, about fifty men with bandages on their arms and legs.

"The General asked me what regiment it was; I answered the Ninth; he asked what those white bandages were on the men for? I told him they were on men who, when they heard that *he* wanted them, had left the field hospital and joined the regiment to do and die for him."

At that, Smith "at once took off his cap and rode down the front of the regiment bareheaded." The regiment stood in silence, perhaps in wonder, until this tough old man they so admired had passed completely by them. Then, Newsham recalled, "a cheer from their full hearts broke forth that told him how they appreciated the mark of respect he had paid them."

Smith and the aide then returned for the night to their dreary bivouac beneath a white oak tree—"wet, cold and hungry" with nothing to eat and only "a great fire to warm us." They had given up their tents to the wounded.[24]

*   *   *

Grant was grimly elated. In the space of not much more than three hours he had pulled back from the brink of a defeat that would have been disaster for the life of the Union and his own career—and had pushed to the threshold of the greatest Federal triumph so far in this war. And he knew it. As he had said in early afternoon, the side that followed Pillow's implausible withdrawal with an attack would win, and he had made sure his Federals were the ones who attacked. Now, after sunset, with a strong force already occupying one end of the erstwhile Confederate rifle pits and with artillery hauled in to enfilade adjoining Confederate positions, Grant ordered a dawn assault all along his line to finish the business. He was so anxious to get it done that there is even indication that he considered a night attack. He assured subordinates that, in Brinton's words, "in the morning . . . we would be in."[25]

The mood on the Confederate side of the trenches depends on the recollection. Floyd, Pillow, and Buckner, to varying degrees, each characterized their troops as weary or exhausted. The more bellicose Forrest, by contrast, saw the Confederates as "flushed with victory" and confident about the outlook for the next day. John Morton, the lieutenant with Porter's decimated battery on the defenders' imperiled right, later recalled that even he and his remaining men felt that "affairs were progressing agreeably for the Confederates." Although they did not say so, though, both men had to have been troubled by Pillow's decision to pull them back from all the ground they had won.

As the evening wore on, the Confederates put their wounded aboard steamboats bound for Nashville, along with more than two hundred Union prisoners. Most of the enlisted men expected to resume the fight the next day.[26]

*   *   *

After nightfall, the Confederate generals and their senior subordinates gathered in Dover at the John Rice house, just up the street from the Dover Hotel. Floyd proposed that the next morning they recover from Pillow's

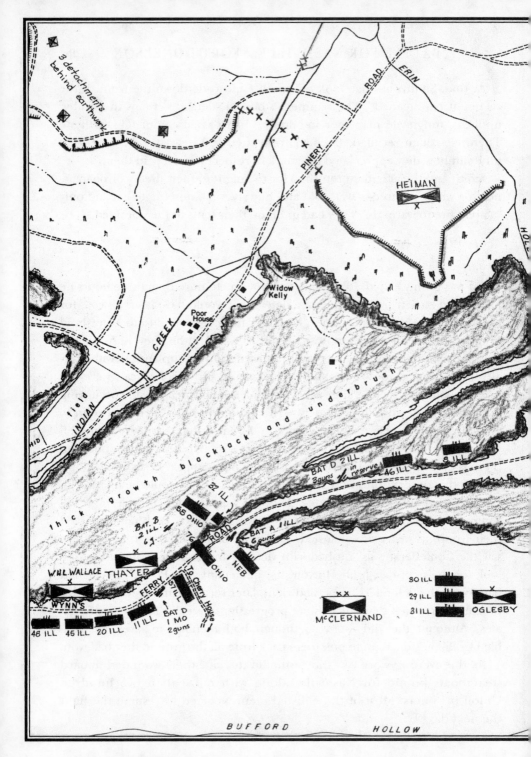

2 TO 5 P.M, UNION RIGHT. On the Union right, Lew Wallace responds to Grant's order to retake two miles of ground lost in the morning but by now largely vacated by the Pillow order to withdraw from the field. As Union

cavalry reaches the Forge Road escape route, Wallace camps facing the
Confederate trenches in front of Dover and, on Grant's order, readies an
assault for dawn. *Used by permission of Tennessee State Library & Archives.*

critical mistake by trying for the third time in three days to march, or cut their way, out.

Just before the meeting convened, Colonel McGavock of the Tenth Tennessee rode to headquarters. Buckner had yet to arrive, and McGavock reported finding Pillow sitting quietly while Floyd wrote a battle report to General Johnston in Nashville. When Floyd finished, he read it aloud. Dated "Fort Donelson, Tenn., February 15, 1862—11 p.m.," its message was incomprehensible. "The enemy having invested our lines, it was determined to attack them, which we did this morning at 5.30 o'clock," it said. Equivocally praising the work of Pillow, Buckner, and Johnson, it mentioned the "steady and determined courage of *many* of our troops," but also noted the *enemy's* maintenance of "a *successful* struggle, which continued for nine hours, *and resulted in driving him from the field* . . . They have a force of 42 regiments [all italics added]." The recipient would have to wonder not only what happened but who won.

While they waited for Buckner to arrive, the officers talked about the day's fighting. McGavock asserted that if the guns Wallace had amassed on Wynn's Ferry Road had been charged and captured earlier in the battle—which he thought could have been done by Heiman's brigade in the Confederate center, of which his Tenth Tennessee was a part—the Federals could have been "driven entirely away." Pillow responded that if Buckner had just kept his promise to attack on time, "the enemy would have been routed."27

Floyd announced that Confederate scouts had spotted more Union transports four miles north of Donelson, and troops were being marched off them. Donelson's defenders could not successfully contend with these new reinforcements, he added. "A considerable proportion" of the army, however, could be extricated from Grant's tightening noose with a renewed smashing of the Union right the next morning, he said. To that end, he ordered the brigade and regimental commanders to have their men ready to move out of Donelson by 4 a.m. on the River Road, along which they had exited the Confederate trenches to fight the previous morning. Accordingly, Brown's brigade of Buckner's division and Bushrod Johnson's leftward portion of Pillow's troops were ordered to begin forming up on the Confederate left again, this time with Brown's artillery spiked and abandoned and Johnson's troops advancing again around the left of the Confederate trenches. All along the perimeter during the shank of the frigid night, preparations proceeded toward another breakout.28

Chaplain Deavenport of the Third Tennessee recalled that around midnight his unit's commander, Major Nat Cheairs, ordered men of the Third to quickly prepare themselves something to eat and get "ready for action . . . We fell in and started in the same direction we had started the previous morning. All of us supposed we were going back there to fight . . . It seemed a strange move, as the enemy were pressing us on our right at dark . . . We marched about a mile and a half."²⁹

Across the way, the Federals were preparing, too. The river transport vessels that Floyd had heard about had disgorged five fresh infantry regiments: the Fourteenth and Fifteenth Illinois, the Twenty-third Indiana, and the Fifty-sixth and Seventy-eighth Ohio. In what had been Buckner's camp behind the trenches along Eddyville Road, pickets of the Second Iowa were fired on several times as they waited for dawn. A bit farther to the right in the same trenches, men of the Fourteenth Iowa camped around cannons of the First Missouri Light Artillery. One of these campers, Sergeant Kiner, later recalled that it was a miserable experience:

> As we sat upon the side of the embankment that night, which was cold and freezing, our hearts were often pained by the groans of the poor wounded who lay bleeding upon the field . . . we felt sad and weary . . . and had but little to eat . . . [D]uring the day the snow had melted away and left the ground wet and disagreeable, and during the night when we sat down our clothes would freeze to the ground. My two great toes froze so badly that they were sore for several months. During the night we met with no difficulty from the enemy, though we were so close that we could distinctly hear them moving about behind the inner works of the fort.³⁰

Colonel John Cook, commanding Smith's Third Brigade, had his men resting on their rifles nearby. He and they no doubt awaited the coming day with profound consciousness of another bloody job ahead. The laconic Smith, before leaving to go back to his oak tree for the night, had nodded at the inner fortress beyond the new Confederate line in their front and had given Cook a starkly simple command for the next morning: "Take it, sir!" At least, though, the cover of Buckner's old trenches now afforded many of the Federals the chance to build their first fires in three nights.

A mile or so across the battlefield, beside Wynn's Ferry Road at the place where it entered the center of the trenches that were still Confederate, the Eleventh Indiana was within eight hundred yards of Confederate cannons and enduring another fireless evening—on a night that its colonel, George McGinnis, called "one of the coldest" yet. Waiting to form a new line of battle and charge the breastworks, many of his men attended to their own wounded as well as those of McClernand's First Division, who now lay all around and among them.³¹

One lying out there in the dark was Lieutenant Churchill of the Eleventh Illinois, shot in the hip by one of Forrest's cavalrymen during the day's climactic Confederate assault on the left. After the fighting ended on that part of the field and afternoon had dragged shiveringly into evening, Churchill listened to the ever more hopeless cries of his fellow wounded.

> Some of these nearby I could individually recognize as they grew fainter and fainter and finally ceased altogether. The soldier on my left . . . had stopped groaning before the last battle. I put my hand on his forehead and found he was cold. The heads of the other two dead men felt like ice. I was bareheaded, having lost my cap when I fell the first time. I could tell it was growing very cold and judged it must be 15 or 20 degrees below freezing. The trees snapped, and branches and twigs moved with a sharp, crispy sound. Night had fallen, and I was evidently between the opposing picket lines. All hopes of being taken from the field vanished . . . My head was resting against that of the dead man on my right and was getting very cold. In attempting to raise it, I found it stuck fast; my hair had frozen to the ground.[32]

Sunday, February 16

A White Rag Rebuffed

Even before Floyd dismissed the Saturday night gathering of Confederate generals at the Rice house, couriers began arriving with ominous intelligence. One reported the sighting of massing Union troops and artillery in front of Buckner's position. A second soon afterward informed Floyd that more heavy columns of Federals were moving across the front of the Confederate works toward the left, where the escape attempt was to be renewed.

Just after the officers' meeting had broken up, some of them—including Floyd, Pillow, and Buckner—were still discussing matters in Pillow's room shortly before 2 a.m. when a messenger rode in from the center and said dogs were barking in the Forge Road area. This, combined with the earlier report of enemy troops moving to the left, indicated that the Federals were reoccupying their leftmost positions of the previous morning, endangering the planned exit route. Floyd told Pillow to have this investigated, and Pillow sent out two scouts. They were soon back with the alarming word that campfires were blazing along what had been the Union right the previous morning. Pillow, hardly eager to believe the Federals had simply marched back onto all the Confederate-won ground that he had ordered abandoned in the afternoon pullback, sent for Forrest.[1]

Forrest had been catching a brief rest after a day in which the latest of fifteen Donelson bullet marks had tattered his overcoat. After his second horse of the day had been blown from between his legs by that Federal cannonball, he and his men had spent most of the rest of the afternoon and evening, at Pillow's order, scouring the battlefield for captured weapons and Confederate wounded. According to Forrest's authorized biography, they picked up "as many as five thousand stands of small-arms and a large quantity of blankets and knapsacks."[2]

When Forrest entered Pillow's quarters at the Rice house and Pillow told him the Federals were said to have reoccupied their morning positions on the left, Forrest archly disagreed. He explained that he had been two miles out the Forge Road at nightfall and all over the battlefield as late as 9 p.m. and had seen no enemy except stragglers looking for wounded. Pillow asked him to send out men to confirm this, as well as to check the status of the ford crossing swollen Lick Creek on the River Road. Forrest left. While he was gone, Pillow ordered commissary and quartermaster officers to burn all their supplies at 5:30 a.m. in preparation for the breakout.[3]

The scouts Forrest sent to Forge Road returned to say they had found only stragglers and wounded. They also reported having seen fires, but Forrest said he believed these were only old Federal camp blazes of the previous evening, fanned to renewed life by the wind or re-ignited by residents of the area out of kindness to the un-evacuated wounded. Then another scout, not one of Forrest's, arrived from the same part of the field and reported that the woods in that area now were "perfectly alive" with Union troops. Pillow sent still another scouting party to the area.

Then the men Forrest sent out along River Road returned and reported that the Lick Creek ford was so flooded that it was "not practicable for infantry," the mud being "half-leg deep" and the water reaching the saddle-skirts of horses. Confederate medical personnel had found a significant portion of the troops already suffering from frostbite, and the prospect of ordering frostbitten and under-clothed foot soldiers to attempt to cross a hundred yards of ice-flecked water was daunting. The generals agreed that they should not do it.[4]

"Well, gentlemen, what is best now to be done?" Floyd asked.

Nobody answered.

Floyd asked the question again, this time putting it pointedly to Pillow. The Tennessee aristocrat hesitated. Then he said he favored fighting their way out immediately, under cover of darkness.[5]

Turning to Buckner, Floyd posed the same question. Buckner replied swiftly, arguing strenuously against the idea of a nighttime battle. To make such an attempt in the dark against a vastly superior enemy—with Confederate troops worn to exhaustion by fighting, hard labor, and prolonged overexposure to bitter weather with inadequate food and clothing—would cost three-fourths of the Donelson army. He ran through a litany of additional problems. Their ammunition was nearly gone. They were facing an enemy they believed was four times as numerous. Fresh Union reinforcements would oppose their breakout. On their line's pierced northern end, the fort would fall, and with it the water batteries. The feared Federal gunboats would reappear and rake the Confederate troops with fire from the rear while the same troops were being opposed by infantry in their front and on their right flank. The combination would result in all but annihilation. In the unlikely event that they escaped their entrenchments before the movement was discovered, they would be caught on the road and massacred.

What Buckner did not have to say but doubtless meant was that these disasters were all the more likely to befall any army, however valiant, acting under the instructions of Gideon Pillow. Buckner professed to take extraordinary pride in being responsible to the soldiers, and he had seen too many Confederates killed and maimed for nothing on this bloody Saturday. The fault lay in great measure in Pillow's overbearing usurpation of authority and Floyd's irresolution. (Although Buckner certainly did not say so, his own battlefield departures from the previous night's plan and his laggard responses to Pillow's orders also shared some of the blame.) Buckner now shrank from shedding more Confederate blood, trying to do over again what already had been done and wasted. His recital of their woeful prospects was an impassioned denunciation of Pillow, underscoring the depths into which the Tennessean's vainglorious blunders had sunk them all. Buckner bitterly added that he "did not think any general had a right to make such a sacrifice of human life" as Pillow had recommended.[6]

Forrest, although only a lieutenant colonel, demanded a say. He told Buckner that his cavalrymen could not only cut a hole in the Federal line anywhere they were asked to but also could fend off any attackers to the rear. But Forrest was as much of a battlefield neophyte as Floyd, and the senior commander sided with the far more experienced Buckner. When talk turned to how a retreating Confederate column would have shells rained on it by Union artillery, Forrest turned his back and left.[7]

Pillow then proposed holding out at least one more day. During that time, enough steamboats might be brought from Nashville to get most of the troops across the Cumberland, from which they could be taken to Clarksville or Nashville. Buckner vetoed that, too. Smith's possession of the Confederate trenches on the right, he said, assured that Buckner's men could not hold their new line a half-hour past daybreak.

"I think you can, sir!" Pillow challenged.

Buckner had had more than enough of what Pillow thought. He angrily responded that he knew his position and how many men were on hand to defend it—four thousand—while Grant could throw against them almost any number he cared to. Although Buckner did not say it here, they all knew that the right of his line was the end nearest the newly arriving Union reinforcements downriver.

But, more important, Buckner knew Grant, the Mexican War quartermaster who could not be kept out of battles. This was the same Grant who two months ago had attacked the Confederate camp at Belmont under the very brow of the cannon-bristling bluffs at Columbus. With Smith's lodgment in the Confederate trenches already made, Ulysses Grant would not hesitate to throw into that breach every rifleman he could muster. And opposing them? Buckner mentioned how to resist Smith that afternoon he had had to use his own hands to line up Hanson's Second Kentucky, "as good a regiment as there is in the service."

Pillow, apparently shaken, characteristically abandoned most of the humanitarian reasons he had earlier cited for ordering the wholesale pullback into the Confederate trenches. A subordinate officer in the meeting recalled Pillow saying that Smith's possession of the Buckner rifle pits on the right provided the Federals with "an open gateway" to the Confederate river cannons that held back the gunboats, and that the garrison "ought to cut our way out, carrying with us as many as possible, leaving the dead and wounded on the field."

Scarcely masking his contempt, Buckner emphatically refused. Generals, he said, "owed it" to their soldiers, "when further resistance was unavailing, to obtain the best terms of capitulation" that could be had.[8]

Buckner did add that he understood the role of the Donelson garrison to be to hold off Grant's Federals until Albert Sidney Johnston's Bowling Green army could retreat to Nashville. If Johnston's retreat had not yet been accomplished, Buckner said, he believed "we should attempt a further defense, even at the risk of the destruction of our entire force, as the delay even of a few hours might gain the safety of General Johnston's force." Floyd said Johnston's army had already reached Nashville. Buckner "then expressed the opinion that it would be wrong to subject the army to a virtual massacre . . ."[9]

Around then, Forrest re-entered the room. What he had been doing outside can only be surmised, but from what he soon said it seems likely he had reminded himself that committing physical violence against superiors would be viewed as bad form and that he should calm down and lend his support to Pillow, the only one of the three generals who wanted to fight. But as Forrest entered, he heard Floyd saying he "could not and would not surrender himself." Doubtless aghast, Forrest turned to Pillow, the only one of the generals with whom he had had a prior relationship. He asked if they were going to surrender the army. Pillow said they were. Forrest became more agitated. Dismissing Buckner's talk of the inhumanity of demanding still more sacrifice from their troops, he made an impassioned little speech. He said he had promised the parents of many of his young troopers to protect them to whatever degree that was in his power, and he was going to take his cavalry out if it saved just one man. Getting more heated, likely stabbing the air with the index finger of his powerful left hand as he lectured the generals, he said he would rather have his troopers' bones bleach the Stewart County

SIMON BOLIVAR BUCKNER. *Courtesy of Medford Historical Society Collection/CORBIS.*

hills than consign them in mid-winter to Northern prison-pens. He, by God, had not come to Fort Donelson to surrender.[10]

Forrest's passion went for naught. Floyd continued to side with Buckner, agreeing that surrender was the only course left. He now added, though, a craven corollary. The scenario he had first voiced back in western Virginia—of being captured and hauled around in a humiliating cage—reappeared all too near the forefront of his mind. Personal considerations, he said, prevented him from doing the surrendering that needed to be done at Donelson. He had a right to decide that he "could not survive" capture, Floyd soon would write. A witness recalled that Floyd based his refusal on his "position with the Federals"—referring to his controversial pro-Southern actions as U. S. secretary of war. In other words, he assumed that if captured, after being hauled around in the fearsome cage, he would hang.[11]

Pillow then declared himself equally important. "There were no two persons in the Confederacy," he was quoted by witnesses as saying, "whom the Yankees would prefer to capture than himself and General Floyd." So Pillow, too, refused to surrender. He asked Floyd whether "it would be proper for him to make an escape" along with Floyd, but the fort's nominal commander seemed not to be looking for company. He refused to make a definite reply. That was a matter each man had to decide for himself, Floyd said. When Pillow asked Buckner the same question, Buckner affirmed Floyd's answer. Buckner stiffly added, however, that it would be as bitter to him as to anyone else to surrender, but personal considerations should not govern actions of commanders. He said he regarded it as his duty to "remain with my men and share their fate."

Pillow ignored Buckner's pointed remark. He reiterated that he was leaving. According to Pillow staff member Major W. H. Haynes, Buckner then stated the obvious: "Then I suppose the duty of surrendering the command will devolve upon me." If only subconsciously, Buckner, too, was probably allowing a personal consideration, his hatred of Pillow, to influence him. Not only was surrender the only compassionate way to reward the gallantry of Donelson's beleaguered soldiers, it would underscore Pillow's blunders and assure him the infamy he deserved.[12]

Then—as later reported by Pillow, Pillow's chief of staff, and his assistant adjutant—Buckner volunteered to surrender. According to Assistant Adjutant General Gustavus A. Henry Jr., who was on hand, the discussion closed this way:

Floyd: "General Buckner, if I place you in command, will you allow me to get out as much of my brigade as I can?"

Buckner: "I will, provided you do so before the enemy receives my proposition for capitulation."

Floyd (turning to Pillow): "I turn the command over, sir."

Pillow: "I pass it."

Buckner: "I assume it. Give me pen, ink, and paper, and send for a bugler."[13]

Forrest, agonizing, again protested, arguing that "there is more fight in these men than you all suppose." Angrily ignoring Buckner and Floyd, he asked Pillow what he should do. "Cut your way out," Pillow said. Forrest replied that he would. Pillow and Floyd then said they would take their chances with Forrest, and the cavalryman left to get his men together. Pillow also left, then returned in a few moments to clarify, apparently for future political reasons, his disagreement with their view that cutting their way out would cost three-fourths of the command. He agreed, though, that if it could be proved that doing so would cost that many men, it would be wrong. Buckner and Floyd nodded.

"We understand you, general," they said, "and you understand us."[14]

*   *   *

Out in the Confederate camps, the troops had been going ahead with prepa-rations for another breakout. On the left, Bushrod Johnson had his men drawn up in columns and had marched around the trenches south of Dover onto the River Road, as he had done the previous morning. Toward the right, Heiman received an order to follow Johnson "without the least noise," and further down the line John C. Brown was instructed to spike his guns and follow Heiman. Colonel McGavock of the Tenth Tennessee, guarding the right of the Confederate center, wrote in his diary that the plan was for the Confederate retreat to begin before daylight: "every Reg[iment] must be ready to march by 4 oc[lock] with provisions in their haversacks, blankets, etc.," Heiman had told him.

"Agreeable to order I had my regiment ready and we marched beyond the town of Dover where we were halted," he wrote, adding that "The morn-ing was cold and disagreeable."15

It was definitely cold—an icy, light rain was falling—but for the Confeder-ates the morning would become far more disagreeable still.

Men in Bushrod Johnson's column suddenly saw some of their fellow units falling out of line. Johnson, so personally unassertive that he apparent-ly had not gotten an invitation to the conference in Dover, had had his men in column by regiments and ready to march by 3 a.m. Reluctant to trouble his superiors, he waited on the River Road until he saw regiments of Floyd's Virginia troops leaving the ranks and moving to the Dover wharf. When he inquired as to what was happening, Johnson was told that they were going at Floyd's order. McGavock, also waiting outside Dover, became impatient after half an hour and, as he put it, "began to smell a rat." He went to his superi-or, Heiman, to ask "why the delay. If we expected to make a successful re-treat, we should be moving . . . we were burning time." Heiman said he knew nothing, that he was just waiting for more orders. McGavock then hunted up Johnson, who likewise "seemed to be profoundly ignorant as to what was go-ing on." Finally, perhaps goaded by his subordinates, Johnson headed to headquarters in Dover.16

Forrest, like Floyd and Pillow, rushed to leave Fort Donelson; unlike them, he was angry, not afraid. He hurried to his cavalry camp and put the question of surrender to his men. He told them that he himself was leaving and would take out any man who wanted to go along. Absent was Lieutenant Colonel George Gantt, whose Ninth Tennessee Cavalry had stampeded into Donelson from Fort Henry a week before, and Forrest sent an aide to notify him. There was no time to waste. Buckner had said that all who wished to leave could go as long as they did it before he got in touch with Grant—which had to happen quickly to head off the renewed Federal attack that seemed certain to come at daylight. Forrest later reported sending for Gantt and his battalion three times, but Gantt, along with a couple of Kentucky cavalry companies, "refused to come." Gantt later would say that he had misunderstood the rendezvous point and had gone there to no avail. Most of Forrest's own men, as well as some from a Kentucky unit, "said they would go with me if the last man fell."

As soon as these troops were ready, Forrest reported at headquarters for Floyd and Pillow. There Floyd told him that Pillow already had departed. Pillow staff member Rice, the Dover resident, had found a small flatboat in which to take the general and Lieutenant Colonel Gilmer, the engineer, across the river.[17]

A Tennessee lieutenant later would remember overhearing part of a conversation between Floyd and Pillow at the Dover landing. Floyd, the infantryman said, was questioning Pillow's assertion that the whole army could have been evacuated across the river by boat with the return of the steamboats that had taken wounded to Nashville earlier in the evening. Pillow, seemingly wearying of the subject, threw up his hands and appeared to place all blame for the impending surrender on Buckner and Buckner's utter disdain for him. "This thing began with that court-martial in Mexico," he said. [18]

Floyd informed Forrest that he was leaving by boat rather than require his infantrymen to brave the Lick Creek ford. Sometime at or after the breakup of the conference of generals he had learned that a steamboat was to arrive from Nashville before dawn, and he had determined to commandeer it.

Before leaving, he flashed to the outside world abrupt news so different from his and Pillow's earlier announcements of the day's glorious victory that it was shocking. He wired Albert Sidney Johnston at Johnston's new theatre headquarters in Nashville:

FORT DONELSON, TENNESSEE, February 16, 1862

General A. Sidney Johnston:

Last evening there arrived in the river near Fort Donelson eleven transports, laden with troops. We are completely invested with an army many times our own numbers. I regret to say the unanimous opinion of the officers seems to be that we cannot maintain ourselves against these forces.

John B. Floyd
Brigadier-General[19]

JOHN B. FLOYD

Near where Forrest and his troopers were saddling up, Lieutenant Colonel McGavock of the Tenth Tennessee was awaiting the return of Bushrod Johnson. McGavock began to see much activity in the direction of the Dover wharf. At the landing sat two steamboats, "lights moving about in every direction and some movement . . . evidently going on of an important character." News sometimes travels faster among enlisted men than officers, and this was one of those times; word of the impending surrender, apparently from Floyd's departing Virginians, spread like wildfire. McGavock noticed that troops in his vicinity "were becoming demoralized and moving off by ones, twos, and threes up the river."[20]

*   *   *

Down at the landing, Floyd was hustling the Virginia troops onto the two steamboats, which had just returned from Nashville after transporting wounded from the Saturday fighting. Much earlier that morning, at about 1 a.m., while still commander of the fort, Floyd had ordered Major W. N. Brown of the Twentieth Mississippi, the only non-Virginia unit among the troops Floyd had brought to Donelson, to help the Virginians cut their way out, obviously as part of Floyd's original plan to accompany Forrest. A little later, though, Brown received another order, this time from Buckner. Brown was to move his regiment to the wharf to be taken out on one of two steamboats expected there shortly. Confused and probably assuming that Floyd was still in command, Brown went to him for clarification and was told that Floyd's command was leaving on the steamboats. The Virginia units and Brown's Mississippians "would embark according to the rank of the commanding officers," Floyd told Brown; parts of two Virginia brigades, each commanded by full colonels, would precede Brown's unit. Brown, waiting his turn, was "directed to place a strong guard around the steamboat landing, to prohibit stragglers from going aboard." A straggler was any man in any brigade but Floyd's.[21]

At the other end of the Confederate trenches, the rightmost ones now held by C. F. Smith's Federals, Sergeant Kiner and his fellow members of the Fourteenth Iowa "could plainly hear the enemy shifting themselves and their plunder around in an unusually brisk manner, and occasionally the sound of a bugle was heard." Kiner and his comrades assumed that the bugles were rallying a counterattack to try to regain the lost trenches, and they resignedly expected a Sabbath slaughter.

But Kiner and his fellow Iowans could not have been less correct about what the Confederates were doing. A party headed by Major Nat F. Cheairs of the Third Tennessee, at Buckner's orders, was being readied to go across the lines to Grant to ask for terms of surrender. They had to move quickly, before the Federals attacked. But they were hampered by their ignorance of protocol—none of the commanders at Donelson had ever before had to surrender. Frustration soon turned to rage. Shortly before dawn, Buckner aide Major George Cosby showed up at John C. Brown's headquarters with the orders to assemble the emissary party. It was to be led by Cheairs. Cheairs asked Brown what the proper bugle call would be to announce the party to the Federals. Brown turned on him angrily. Just order the bugler to blow every call he knew, the brigade commander exploded.

"And if that wouldn't do," Brown told Cheairs, the bugler could "blow his damn brains out."[22]

*   *   *

Another important and even less likely visitor, however, beat the Cheairs party to Grant's headquarters. On the early morning of February 16 a slave belonging to a Confederate officer got past the preoccupied Confederate pickets and entered Federal lines.

This war was not yet officially about slavery. The people who fired the first shots in Charleston, South Carolina, claimed to have done so in defense of state's rights, and the most financially important of those allowed the owning of slaves. But several more months would pass before Abraham Lincoln, in an attempt to cripple the Confederacy, would proclaim emancipation—and only in areas that were in rebellion. But a Confiscation Act passed by Congress in 1861 provided that property used with an owner's knowledge and consent to aid an insurrection was to be confiscated, and when that property was a slave, he or she was to be freed.

In the border states, better penetrated by Northern news than the Deep South, many in bondage had heard of the Confiscation Act, and they apparently included Grant's late-night caller.

As soon as he got inside Union lines, the slave reported to his new hosts that the Confederates had begun fleeing Fort Donelson. Some of the Union officers thought he had been sent to lure them into a trap. They advocated tying and whipping him. He replied that they could shoot him if he was lying. The officers then took him to headquarters and woke Grant.[23]

Out on the Federal battle line, infantrymen tried to get a little sleep in the mud as they endured another raw, cold night and awaited daylight. Morning was to be both longed for and dreaded. A victory promised to end their terrible privation, but winning it, if the Confederate example of the previous day held any clue, would be intensely bloody work. Sergeant Kiner of the Fourteenth Iowa had pondered such reflections when the murky gray of impending dawn began to make it possible to distinguish individual men in the diminishing darkness. Suddenly, Kiner and his fellow Iowans saw the last sort of man in the world they expected. "[T]o our great joy," Kiner wrote, the man they saw was "a rebel . . . making his way toward us holding over his head a white rag upon a small pole."[24]

To get to Grant, the Cheairs party first had to pass out of Cheairs's own regiment, the Third Tennessee. Seeing the white flag, Chaplain Deavenport and the Third's infantrymen began, in Deavenport's considerable understatement, "to think all was not well." Passing from the Confederate lines to the Federal ones was not easy. Nearly an hour of bugle calls and white flag demonstrations—made with pieces of ripped-up tent—had to be sent across the deep, wooded hollow between the position of Buckner's division and its former one, the trenches now occupied by Smith's men, before these elicited the attention of responsive Federal officers busily preparing for their morning assault. Cheairs's Third Tennessee was almost directly across the hollow from the Second Iowa, and finally it became light enough and safe enough for Cheairs and his truce party to pass down his own steep hill into the hollow and then up the next ridge to the trenches his men had occupied until a few hours before. There he asked an officer with the Second Iowa if he could speak to someone authorized to negotiate surrender.

The redoubtable Smith, notified, rode forward. He had passed the run-away slave to Grant's headquarters not long before and knew about the fugitive's story of Confederate attrition during the night. The old officer's tone now was contemptuously brusque in telling Cheairs what his own terms would be. "I'll make no terms with rebels with arms in their hands," he growled. "My terms are immediate and unconditional surrender."

But of course any surrender terms were not up to him. He took Buckner's note from Cheairs and led the Confederate the half-mile or so to Grant's headquarters.[25]

*   *   *

At the Crisp farmhouse, the Union commander had not had a lot of rest. He and his staff were anxiously awaiting what they expected to be a victorious but bloody morning assault.

The tent-less Smith had already come by once this evening to, no doubt, warm himself by the fire. In the process he regaled his former cadet with details of his successful attack on the trenches. "I preached to the men," he told Grant and the staff in the afterglow of his triumph. "I made them a speech—the first I ever made in my life. I cheered with them, I swore at them, and, by ___, I would have prayed with them if necessary."[26]

After finally getting to his bed in the kitchen, Grant was summoned out of it sometime around 3 a.m. to meet with the slave who had deserted from Dover. Grant and his staff had listened intently to his story, then warned him that many lives might depend on this information. If it turned out to be false, he was told, he could hang. The man stuck fast to his story: the Confederates had "been a-goin all night" from the Donelson lines, he reported.

Grant believed him—and doubtless felt even more urgency about the need to attack at first opportunity. He emphatically did not want and could not afford to capture another Fort Henry, emptied of all but token occupants. The newspapers that had berated him for the comparatively empty victory at Fort Henry would become more savage if the same thing happened at Donelson. A second such equivocal triumph would also reflect on his commander, Halleck, which might finally be more than Grant's career could stand.

He was hardly back in bed before a second visit from Smith roused him again. The old man handed him a note and told him that the Confederate who brought it was waiting outside.[27]

Surgeon Brinton, sleeping on the kitchen floor with his saddle for a pillow, later remembered that Smith was brought in by an orderly and "seemed very cold, indeed half frozen. He walked at once to the open fire on the hearth, for a moment warmed his feet, then turned his back to the fire, facing General Grant, who had slipped out of bed and . . . was quickly drawing on his outer clothes." Smith said, "There's something for you to read, General Grant," and handed Grant a letter. After Grant took it, Smith asked the staff for "something to drink. My flask, the only liquor on the Staff, was handed to him," Brinton later wrote, "and he helped himself in a soldier-like manner."[28]

While Smith defrosted, Grant read a stiffly formal communication over the signature of an old friend. "Sir: In consideration of all the circumstances governing the present consideration of affairs at this station, I propose to the Commanding Officer of the Federal forces the appointment of Commissioners to agree upon terms of capitulation of the forces and fort under my command, and in that view suggest an armistice until 12 o'clock today."

When he finished reading, Grant looked up and asked Smith for an opinion on how to reply. "No terms to the damned rebels," the older man grunted. Grant's face broke into an amused grin, and he sat down to swiftly write out an answer. Grant acknowledged in a sentence the receipt of Buckner's communication, then concluded: "No terms except unconditional and immediate surrender can be accepted. I propose to move immediately upon your words."

As soon as he finished writing, Grant read the message aloud to Smith. Brinton remembered that the old man, "erect, manly, every inch a soldier, standing in front of the fire twisting his long white mustache," replied with an emphatic "Hm!" and added that it was "the same thing" he himself had said except "in smoother words."

He then turned and went back out to allow Major Cheairs in to receive it.[29]

*   *   *

In the murky predawn, the rumor of imminent capitulation spread fast on both sides of the trenches. Gangs of Confederate enlisted men flocked to the Dover wharf, "panic-stricken and frantic," to try to get aboard the steamboats, recalled Major Brown of the Twentieth Mississippi. But it was no use. At Floyd's order, Brown's men had formed a semi-circle around the landing and "stood like a stone wall."

At almost daylight, McCausland's brigade of Floyd's division was loaded and taken across the Cumberland to safety, after which the two steamboats returned for another trip. The Goochland Light Artillery's Captain John Guy had seen them coming back. He and his unit had awakened in their camp near Wynn's Ferry Road, packed their knapsacks, and, looking around and seeing no other Confederate troops nearby, headed for the wharf to try to find out what was happening. There they discovered a great many "much excited" Confederate soldiers. Guy saw a steamboat disembarking southern troops on the opposite side of the river. He began to divine the import of these events as he watched supplies and ammunition being thrown into the river. Paranoia suddenly gripped him.

> . . . I determined not to be captured if there was any possible means of escape. The steamer General Anderson was just returning for another load of soldiers, and my only hope . . . was on the steamer. I anxiously awaited its return, but instead of coming near me, as I expected, it stopped about 100 yards above where I was standing. Several thousand soldiers had now congregated at the wharf . . . To force my way through this immense body of men was impossible [and] . . . delay was dangerous. I at once resolved, if possible, to get on board of that steamer.
>
> The only chance was . . . to wade the surging Cumberland River for some distance . . . I had a horrible conception of a prison pen. I proceeded to make my way in the direction of the steamer, keeping as near as possible to the bank of the river, though up to my waist in mud and water, and coming in contact with melting snow and ice most of the time. After no little perseverance I succeeded in accomplishing my object, though before reaching the steamer I was nearly over my shoulders in the water, very cold, and much exhausted. On board of the steamer there happened to be a barrel of whiskey, which had been bayoneted by the soldiers. I . . . at once procured some in a tin cup and drank it . . . The commotion among our soldiers at this time was very great, many of them were frantic with excitement, and attempted to get on board of the steamer, though failed . . .[30]

As the last couple of hundred Virginians tried to scramble aboard, Floyd waved his sword and shouted a welcome to "my brave Virginia boys."

They seemed to be all Floyd cared about, besides himself. With the Virginians nearly loaded, Colonel Brown sent word to Floyd that the Mississippians holding back the mob were ready to embark, too. He got no "satisfactory answer," he later reported. Then he suddenly learned that nobody else was being taken aboard. Floyd actually began "fighting off the men in my front, who . . . belonged to one of the Virginia regiments." Brown soon discovered why Floyd had started acting so strangely. Buckner sent for Brown and upbraided him because Floyd's steamboat had not already left. Buckner said that if it did not embark immediately he "would have a bomb-shell thrown into it." The new Donelson commander explained that "the honor and good faith of the Confederacy" required that at daylight he surrender everything to General Grant. Brown rushed back to the landing to try to get aboard the boat, but by then "it had shoved off and was making up the river with very few persons aboard."[31]

Claustrophobia began setting in on River Road. Bushrod Johnson arrived back from headquarters and told a mortified McGavock the sordid story. They all were to be surrendered. Pillow and Floyd had turned the fort over to Buckner and escaped to Nashville on boats. White flags were already floating over their breastworks. McGavock and members of his Tenth Tennessee were shocked and dismayed. McGavock asked Johnson if there was a chance for them to escape, and Johnson said no, that the Federals had tripled their numbers in front of the already-turned Confederate right, and Pillow and Floyd had commandeered the transport steamers. Their case was hopeless.

As news of the surrender spread through the ranks, the men erupted in rage. A captain in the Fifteenth Arkansas asked a gunner in a neighboring battery what the appearance of the white flags meant. The cannoneer responded with not a vestige of soldierly respect for higher rank:

"We're all surrendered, God damn you, that's what it means."[32]

In the wake of their abandonment by Floyd and Pillow, it was every man for himself. Over the course of the next two or three days, a significant but unknown number of Confederates departed Donelson in small groups or individually. Enlisted personnel S. G. Morgan, James Grady, L. C. English, and Bence Tubb of Company E, Fourteenth Mississippi, walked out of Dover about an hour after sunup, found a place on the Lick Creek overflow shallow enough to wade, and crossed. Around the same time of day James Chandler, orderly sergeant of Company C, Twenty-seventh Alabama, saw a white flag outside his tent and headed upriver through Dover with two other members of his regiment. At the edge of a small field beside the Lick Creek backwater, near a house on the opposite bank, they saw a group of men walking purposefully along. Chandler and his companions thought the group was Federal and detoured. But they soon met a fellow Donelson escapee who told them the group they had seen were "Confederates marching out of Dover." The little Chandler party soon crossed the flood on a half-submerged log and joined the exodus. It included more than low-ranking troops: Colonel John W. Head of the Thirtieth Tennessee. Head's near-pneumonia prompted the regimental surgeon to prescribe escape; in his condition, the physician said, Head might not survive imprisonment. Head then simply left his regiment's camp and headed south along the river.[33]

* * *

When Grant's reply to his surrender note finally wound its way back to him across the hollows between him and the Crisp farmhouse, an already-agitated Buckner was outraged. He had assumed all night that a dawn attack was coming and had hurried out the Cheairs party to head it off, but he had not anticipated the substance of Grant's reply. He and the Union commander, after all, had been fairly close friends once. He had helped Grant out of that very tight spot in New York in 1854, and now he almost certainly had hoped for a chance to negotiate a parole, rather than imprisonment, for himself and his men.

Instead, Grant had sent him a reply that, in light of their friendship, was not only ungentlemanly but also unfriendly. The Confederate found himself confined to the Donelson box into which he and Pillow had put him, and it was closing. His forces were dribbling away around him, and, with many of the still-organized regiments formed up on the River Road outside the trenches, they were in no position to repel an assault. Buckner had been suckered and abandoned by two superiors of low, or no, character. Floyd had spirited away his Virginians in steamboats only after disembarking four hundred luckless recruits whom the boats had just ferried in from Nashville; and Pillow was skedaddling in a skiff. Donelson's most resolute warrior, Forrest, had gathered up a gang of his cavalry in disgust and headed down River Road toward the freezing waters of Lick Creek ford. Buckner's command, such of it as remained, was now truly what he had maintained it was in the conference of generals: done for.

Trapped, he had no choice but to reply as he now irritably did.

> *HEADQUARTERS,*
> *Dover, Tenn., February 16, 1862.*
>
> *Sir: The distribution of the forces under my command incident to an unexpected change of commanders and the overwhelming force under your command compel me, notwithstanding the brilliant success of Confederate arms yesterday, to accept the ungenerous and unchivalrous terms which you propose.*
>
> *I am, sir, your very obedient servant,*
>
> *S. B. BUCKNER,*
> *Brigadier-General, C. S. Army.*[34]

He used the words "ungenerous and unchivalrous," Buckner eventually told a friend, to convey to Grant his feeling that in view of their prior association Grant owed his request for terms more consideration than a harsh, impersonal, three-sentence reply.[35]

*   *   *

Buckner had just dispatched his note when another former acquaintance, Federal Third Division commander Lew Wallace, was announced at the door of Buckner's Dover Hotel headquarters. Wallace had learned of the surrender only a few minutes earlier. He had got his men down to the foot of the hill crowned by the left center of the Confederate trenches, near where the Wynn's Ferry Road crossed them, and was readying his men to attack when he heard a bugle. He then saw one of the several signals Buckner had ordered raised all along his lines to head off a Union assault: a white flag carried by a Major W. E. Rogers of Mississippi, who was accompanied by a general, Bushrod Johnson. Wallace sent his adjutant forward to meet them, and the officer returned with news of the cease-fire. Then, out of what he described as "an irresistible impulse to get there first"—obviously to satisfy his curiosity but perhaps also to be mentioned in newspapers—Wallace rashly, and not very wisely, asked Rogers if he could have the flag of truce so that he could hurry on ahead to Buckner's headquarters. Rogers advised otherwise but added that he would be glad to accompany Wallace. "Our people are in a bad humor," he explained. So Wallace and the pair of Confederates rode back to Buckner's headquarters together.

Dismounting in front of the Dover Tavern, Wallace sent his name inside to Buckner and was quickly admitted. Four years younger, Wallace knew the Confederate from the old army—both men had served in the Mexican War—and he now found Buckner finishing breakfast with his staff. Buckner rose and shook Wallace's hand, "grave, dignified, silent." He did not introduce his staff, saying simply that Wallace already knew them all. That was generally true, because Wallace had visited an 1860 Kentucky State Guard encampment and was introduced to most of them then. Buckner invited him to share their remaining cornbread and coffee. From their conversation, it became obvious to Wallace that Buckner and his staff believed Grant had fifty thousand men, and Wallace did not correct their impression, feeling that to do so would be insensitive. "The idea helped soften the pangs of defeat," he later wrote.

"What will General Grant do with us?" Buckner asked. What he meant was, would the Confederates be regarded as prisoners of war and thus eligible for certain mercies? As traitors destined for the gallows so feared by the departed Floyd? Or might they expect to be simply paroled and turned loose, as Buckner doubtless hoped in sending Grant his request for surrender terms? It was no idle question. This was, after all, the war's first large-scale surrender.

Wallace, knowing nothing of Buckner's favor to Grant in New York in 1854, apparently assumed Buckner feared the worst.

"I can't say," Wallace replied. "But I know General Grant, and I know President Lincoln better than General Grant, and I am free to say that it is not in the nature of either of them to treat you, or these gentlemen, or the soldiers you have surrendered, other than as prisoners of war."[36]

Buckner responded, no doubt glumly, that that was what he had expected. During the conversation, a young Buckner aide could not suppress tears, and now, apparently attempting to protect his staff members as much as possible, Buckner added that his sole request was not to be separated from them in captivity. In what must have been a demeaning question for a man of Buckner's pride to have to ask about a onetime friend, he sought Wallace's opinion on whether he should make his request to Grant. Wallace said he should.[37]

As they talked, Federal naval officer Benjamin M. Dove arrived. After asking Wallace a few quick questions about the surrender process, Dove left, and Wallace would later learn that Dove had been sent by Commander Henry Walke to try to beat Grant to Buckner and snatch another surrender for the navy. When Dove saw that Wallace, an army officer, was already at Buckner's headquarters, he swiftly exited.

Buckner and Wallace chatted for nearly an hour, and only once did Buckner overtly exhibit the strain to which he had been subjected by the days and nights of fighting and the unceremonious decamping of Floyd and Pillow. Wallace mentioned that he found it strange that the Confederate Congress had come up with a new flag rather than vying with the Lincoln government to keep the old one. Buckner's temper flared. He brought his fist down hard on the table, as if Wallace had scant right to bring up such a subject to an honored American soldier.

"The old flag!" the Southerner burst out, perhaps thinking of the commanders his new one had most recently required him to serve. "I followed it," he said, "when most of your thousands out yonder were in swaddling clothes—in Mexico—on the frontier—and I love it yet."[38]

*   *   *

The sun was well up by the time Major Cheairs returned from Dover to the Crisp farmhouse with Buckner's response to Grant's unconditional surrender ultimatum. Grant's message and the Confederate situation had left Buckner scant alternative, so there could be little doubt about his answer, and Grant had busied himself with details. As soon as Cheairs arrived with the Buckner response, Grant readied orders for Smith's and McClernand's divisions to take possession of the fort and the rest of the Confederate trenches beyond the point that Smith's men already occupied. Then the

Federal commander and some of his staff members prepared to accompany the Confederate party back to Buckner's headquarters. It was a substantial ride, perhaps four miles or more by road, from Grant's headquarters to Buckner's: from well behind the Federal left to well in front of the right. On their way, Grant and his people met jubilant shouts from Federal troops and sullen glares from Confederates—the latter so pronounced that a Union cavalry detachment escorting the party kept pistols drawn throughout the ride.

As they went, everything but the earth itself seemed to be moving around them. All along the erstwhile front, Federal troops were pushing into the squalor, mud, and puddles of melting ice and snow behind the Confederate trenches. But these advances were haphazard, disorganized, and flecked with jealousies and resentment. Old Smith, whose charge into Buckner's rifle pits had spelled Donelson's doom, was intended to get the place of honor in taking possession of the fort itself, but he was beaten to it by W. H. L. Wallace of McClernand's division.

On the part of some of McClernand's men there seemed to be hard feeling against the other divisions for their laggard or nonexistent help the day before. Today Wallace's brigade had gotten up early, expecting to be ordered forward in a charge, when the officers heard the foe had surrendered. Wallace ordered the brigade formed up and moved forward while he himself rode on in front to see if the report was true. When the unit reached the trenches, Wallace met it there and led it on in, straight toward the walls of Fort Donelson itself. He was met by staff officers from Smith, who ordered him to halt, but Wallace, a lawyer and ex-district attorney whose words tended to be few and well chosen, refused. "General Smith is not my commander," he said, and rode on. He then planted inside the walls the flag of the Eleventh Illinois, the bloody and much-thinned regiment he had led until raised to brigade command days before leaving Cairo. He also placed guns from his brigade's battery inside the fort, where that unit soon saluted the gunboats as they came upriver to Dover firing celebratory salvoes.

("It was the greatest battle ever fought on this continent," Wallace wrote Ann Wallace the next day. He told her how the Eleventh had lost the most men of any Federal regiment in the battle. "The colors of the regiment are riddled with shot and the staff was struck twice with bullets, breaking off the spear at the top . . . Tell Helen Fisher that the pledge I made to her when on behalf of the Ottawa [Illinois] ladies she presented the flag to Co. I has been redeemed. The Eleventh lost nearly everything but their flag and their honor. It was the first flag planted on the inner fortification of Fort Donelson.")

Only preceded—by an hour or so—by the gunboat that Captain Dove took into Dover to try to grab Buckner's surrender, a steamboat called the

New Uncle Sam had taken the place of honor at the head of a grand flotilla of transport vessels. Chosen to be Grant's Cumberland River headquarters boat, it steamed past the fort, which teemed with Confederate soldiers standing around their stacked weapons. Just beyond the fort and its water batteries, the boat's passengers saw the little city of log huts that Tilghman had ordered built for winter, and then another hill topped with a school building flying a hospital flag. When the boat nosed in at Dover, reporter Charles Coffin of the *Boston Journal* leaped onto the wharf to see and try to interview some Confederates, "a care-worn, haggard, melancholy crowd."

Dover itself "had suffered greatly . . . Nearly every building was a hospital. Trees had been cut down, fences burned, windows broken, and old buildings demolished for fuel . . .

> We came upon a squad of soldiers hovering around a fire. Some were wrapped in old patched bedquilts which had covered them at home. Some had white blankets, made mostly of cotton. Others wore bright [coarse, woolen fabric used in rug-making] . . . One had a faded piece of threadbare carpet. Their guns were stacked, their equipments thrown aside, cartridge-boxes, belts, and ammunition trampled in the mud. There were shot-guns, single and double-barreled, old heavy rifles, flint-lock muskets of 1828, some of them altered into percussion locks, with here and there an Enfield rifle.

For grotesqueness, Coffin wrote, they were unequaled. Deficient in neither intellect nor courage, they included "noble men, brave fellows," he went on, but their uniforms were ragtag, "brown-colored predominating, as if they were in the snuff business and had been rolled in tobacco dust. There was sheep-gray, iron gray, blue gray, dirty gray . . . Judging by their garments, one would have thought that the last scrapings, the odds and ends of humanity and dry goods, had been brought together."39

* * *

Following the long ride with his staff and Major Cheairs, Grant entered Buckner's headquarters an hour or so after Lew Wallace had arrived. The brusque tension in the surrender notes was dispelled at once. Buckner, finished with breakfast, was smoking a cigar. His natty attire—a blue woolen overcoat and checked neck cloth—contrasted sharply with Grant's rumpled tunic. Buckner found his old friend as unassuming as his dress: "very kind and . . . polite." The Confederate relaxed a little. As soon as they had exchanged greetings, a surprised Grant asked two questions:

"Where is Pillow? Why didn't he stay to surrender his command?"

"He thought you were too anxious to capture him personally," Buckner said.

Grant grinned. "If I had captured him, I would have turned him loose," he said. Then he added a line that showed his sense of humor, his disinclination to waste words, and his recognition of their mutual utter disdain for Pillow: "I would rather have him in command of you fellows than as a prisoner."

The two men continued to make light of Pillow, hardly mentioning Floyd, the fort's nominal commander and Pillow's co-deserter. Buckner knew all too well, and Grant rightly assumed, that the *de facto* Confederate commander during most of the battle had been Pillow. Buckner said that if he himself had been in command of the Donelson army on February 12 when the Federals were advancing from Fort Henry (which Buckner technically and briefly *had* been), Grant never would have gotten close to the Donelson lines without a fight. Grant said that he never would have tried to get there the way he did had Buckner been in charge.

Outside the hotel as their talk continued, the victors' celebration was becoming a bit more formal. Grant's three divisions—Smith's, Lew Wallace's, and McClernand's—were all inside the former Confederate perimeter now with bands playing, flags waving, troops cheering, and gunboats firing off salutes in front of a host of troop-transport steamboats that had been hastily and "gayly decorated," Coffin reported.

Inside the hotel, the air got testier with the arrival of General Smith. Like Grant, Buckner had been a Smith student at West Point, but when the Philadelphia-born former commandant and the Kentucky ex-pupil met now on opposite sides, Smith refused to shake Buckner's hand.

"General Smith, I believe I am right," Buckner responded, referring to the side of this war to which he had decided to pledge his allegiance.

"That is for God to decide, not me," Smith snapped, "for I *know* I am right."[40]

So much for those old rumors of Smith's disloyalty.

* * *

As Federals began spreading throughout the Confederate position, the mind of Lieutenant Colonel Randal McGavock of the Tenth Tennessee Infantry became more tortured by the minute. After Bushrod Johnson told him back in the chaotic predawn that there was no possibility of escape, McGavock had wracked his brain in search of one. He first considered trying to cut his way out with just the Tenth Tennessee. Then he thought about finding a flatboat for his regiment's equipment and ordering every man to swim the Cumberland; then he reflected that many of his men could not swim. Finally—"in sorrow, humiliation, and anger"—he marched them back into their camp and rode north to the fort, where a white flag was flying. There he saw Dove's gunboat appear on its run past the fort into Dover, after which he rode back to the Tenth's camp and had breakfast with some of his troops.

There he descended into absolute misery. As he wrote in his journal, he watched "the Hessians" crossing the Confederate trenches unopposed and heard their joyous hooting.

"Oh! how these shouts sank into my heart," he continued. The invaders' hands sank into other things: "The [Federals] came into our encampments, bursted open the trunks of officers and robbed them of everything."⁴¹

*   *   *

In Buckner's room at the Dover Hotel, as Buckner and Grant renewed their old friendship, the clock wound toward mid-day. Not much before noon, the two departed Buckner's hotel headquarters for Grant's floating one on the *New Uncle Sam*.

The surrender was formalized in the boat's cabin. As they worked out the details, Grant too smoked a cigar. He sat on one side of a table and Buckner, accompanied at the time by his chief of staff and one other Confederate, occupied the other. Buckner "freely gave information relative to his positions, his forces, their disposition, and his intentions" during the battle, according to reporter Coffin:

> He [had] expected to escape and claimed that the engagements on Saturday were all in favor of the Confederates. No opprobrious words were used by anyone. No discussions entered into. He asked for subsistence for his men, and said that he had only two days' provisions on hand. He had favors to ask for some of his wounded officers [doubtless regarding their medical care and notification of their families], all of which were readily acceded to by General Grant[,] who was very much at ease . . . conducting the business with dignity, yet with dispatch.⁴²

*   *   *

When Grant asked about the number of troops in the fort, Buckner said his present force would number between twelve and fifteen thousand. Later, however, perhaps to downplay the magnitude of the Union victory, he reported the number as never more than twelve thousand. To Grant, he mentioned the departures of Floyd and Forrest, and that they each had taken troops with them. In response to a Buckner request, Grant agreed to let the captured Confederate enlisted men retain their blankets and other personal belongings, while the officers could keep their side-arms.[43]

Formalizing the surrender was a daunting task that took most of the rest of Grant's day. Handing over one half-disciplined volunteer army to another was no easy matter. As Grant said in a letter to Julia dated that day, his men had achieved "the largest capture I believe ever made on the continent," and the task of dealing with it was enormous.

The numbers, at that point in the war, were staggering. Despite all the attrition, the best estimates are that from 16,500 to 17,500 Confederates were sent out over the next two days to Cairo aboard transport steamers, bound for prisons farther north. The enlisted men who were marched onto these boats were restricted to the lower deck while officers could roam throughout the vessels. Wounded members of both armies filled "saloons and cabins, berths and state-rooms," journalist Coffin reported.

The scale of casualties was also enormous. The number of Confederate killed and wounded was variously estimated between fifteen hundred and two thousand; Pillow later said 1,134 wounded Confederates had been taken out of Dover before the surrender and that approximately four hundred more were among the captured. Union casualties were reported at five hundred killed, 2,108 wounded, and 224 missing, not counting the gunboats' nine dead and forty-nine hurt.

In a dispatch sent that afternoon to Halleck in St. Louis, Grant estimated that the Confederate weapons captured included "about 20,000 stand of arms." The ordnance booty would come to be totaled at forty-three pieces, including fourteen heavy guns.[44]

As Grant ran through these numbers, he was possibly struck by the suddenly awesome symbolism of his headquarters boat's name. He likely had chosen the vessel simply because "Uncle Sam" had been the nickname his initials had got him at West Point, and it had stuck. Now, though, by virtue of Buckner's capitulation, Sam Grant had captured a whole army. Overnight, he had become a new Uncle Sam himself—and had taken a long stride toward saving the other one.

*   *   *

Almost as soon as they got inside the Confederate perimeter, some of Grant's volunteers began acting more than ever like volunteers—and so did Buckner's. Some of Grant's started shamelessly looting, while some of Buckner's continued what members of the garrison had begun doing as soon as they heard they were to be surrendered—just walking away and fading over the horizon. The Confederates were aided in their fugitive endeavors by Grant's humanity; he consented to let the Southerners bury their dead. The Federals then became so accustomed to seeing Confederates walking around the battlefield supposedly looking for dead comrades that they paid them little attention.

Many of the Union troops were too busy rifling the captured supplies to notice much anyway. Almost immediately, Grant's volunteers began unabashedly looting. The saddle horse of Colonel McGavock of the Tenth Tennessee, hitched in front of a Dover hotel, was stolen—"I think . . . by a field officer," McGavock said in his journal that night. McGavock complained about the theft to Grant himself. Grant assured him that if McGavock could find the animal Grant "would make the man give him up, but that he would have to be turned over to [the] Quarter Master."

As the day wore on, Federal soldiers were seen "luxuriating like children in the hogsheads of sugar," reporter Coffin wrote. "Many a one filled his canteen with New Orleans molasses and his pockets with damp brown sugar." In a Dover store Coffin found a squad shamelessly shoplifting seemingly useless items: a mirror, brass candlesticks, "a package of bonnets." It was a carnival of happy thievery, which the hosts of surrendered victims could only watch in helpless fury. 45

Grant can hardly be blamed for being unready for such behavior. No army this size had ever been surrendered on the American continent, and no army of volunteers the size of Grant's had ever captured one. He had issued periodic orders against looting since he took command at Cairo, and at Donelson he did direct, though far too late, that all captured property be turned over to the quartermaster. He added that "[p]illaging and appropriating public property to private purposes is strictly prohibited." Plainly having heard what was happening and manifesting a desire to stop it, he ordered both Smith and McClernand to detail four whole companies each to gather booty. Smith, he continued, was to send twenty-five men just to prevent individual soldiers from shipping property captured at Donelson and to search the transport boats for any already shipped.

Buckner prevailed on his old friend to try to stop some of the worst abuses, protesting that Confederate officers and men were experiencing treatment that violated Grant's earlier surrender directives. Over the course of the afternoon he sent Grant notes about Union excesses that were both inhumane and villainous. "Thousands . . . have been standing nearly all day in the mud without food and without fire," the captive general said in one that also complained that such items as Confederate officers' firearms and enlisted men's blankets were being taken from them. "There seems to be no concert of action between the different departments of your army in reference to these prisoners," he wrote, suggesting that Grant either order his "interior guards" to respect passes handed out by Buckner himself or name a Federal officer to be located in Buckner's headquarters to issue passes Buckner vouched for. Grant quickly ordered that Buckner be given the authority to issue them.[46]

In marked contrast to the brusqueness of his reply to Buckner's request for surrender terms, Grant on the rest of this day could hardly have been more cordial, cooperative, and forthcoming in response to Buckner's requests. His attitude toward his old friend had been exemplified by his offer to return the great favor Buckner had done him more than seven years earlier in New York. Just after their formal surrender meeting broke up on the *New Uncle Sam*, Buckner told a friend years later, Grant took the downcast Confederate aside. He knew that in whatever general officers' prison Buckner was to be sent to, he would need money to buy newspapers, books, stationery, and other items with which to while away his time.

"Buckner, you are, I know, separated from your people, and perhaps you need funds," Grant said. "My purse is at your disposal."

Graciously, Buckner declined.[47]

* * *

What may have been the most deliciously satisfying day of Grant's life was doubtless soured a little by its necessary paperwork, and he and his staff began writing a flurry of orders, dispatches, and letters. The document that must have given him the most satisfaction was obviously one of the earliest— his telegram notifying Halleck. It could not have been more businesslike. Unlike after Fort Henry, it included no "Hoping that what has been done will meet the approval of the Major General commanding the Department." This time there could be no question.

> *Maj. Gen. H. W. Halleck:*
>
> *We have taken Fort Donelson and from 12,000 to 15,000 prisoners, including Generals Buckner and Bushrod Johnson; also about 20,000 stand of arms, 48 pieces of artillery, 17 heavy guns, from 2,000 to 4,000 horses, and large quantities of commissary stores.*
>
> *U. S. GRANT,*
> *Brigadier-General, Commanding*

But besides Halleck and the Buckner entreaties, there were myriad other matters to handle. Lew Wallace was quickly ordered back to Fort Henry to guard against any threat there from Polk's now-flanked force at Columbus.

Wallace and McClernand, the most political of the three division commanders, received only minimal and perfunctory praise in a longer dispatch
Grant wrote to Halleck, which gave most of the victory credit to Smith.

But Grant seems to have taken care to try to keep the well-connected Wallace mollified. Aide W. S. Hillyer, who had written Wallace that encouraging
note when he had first been left behind at Fort Henry, now penned the
Hoosier another one. Including a little soldierly humor, it apparently responded to another Wallace protest at being again consigned to Henry, away
from potential ensuing action, after he had stopped the climactic Confederate assault the previous afternoon. "You are not going to be left behind,"
Hillyer assured Wallace. "I know Gen Grants views. He intends to give you a
chance to be shot in every important move." Hillyer then explained that no
troop movement was imminent, and when one was, Wallace would not be
forgotten. "We cannot advance for some days . . . You will not be left at Ft
Henry unless it be to defend against a threatened attack. God bless you. You
did save the day on the right."[48]

*　　*　　*

While Grant tackled the surrender details on the *New Uncle Sam* on this first
day of the rest of his life, another passenger aboard the headquarters boat
was feeling redeemed as well. Lieutenant Churchill of the Eleventh Illinois
confronted the miraculous prospect of remaining alive.

At intervals during his torturous night between the lines, he had shouted at
the top of his lungs—not calling for help, he later remembered, but, rather,
"to see if my voice was growing fainter." He found it odd that he could discern
no change in it. Eventually "welcome streaks of light began to appear in the
east," and soon after dawn he saw an assistant surgeon from his unit searching
the battlefield for dead and wounded. Churchill called to him. When the surgeon reached him, Churchill was told Fort Donelson had just surrendered
and that he himself had been presumed dead. The doctor handed him a rub-
ber canteen full of whisky, which "I drank of . . . until he took it away."

The surgeon momentarily left and returned with several members of
Churchill's company, who lifted him onto a camp cot, covered him with a
blanket, put another beneath his head, and carried him away from the
bloody piece of icy earth on which he had lain with so many others for twenty-two hours. They bore him to the bank of the Cumberland, where he was
taken aboard Grant's headquarters boat because the hospital steamers were
already full.

"My boots, pants, and stiffly frozen clothing were cut in pieces to get them
off," he later recalled. "[T]hen my cot was carried aft and set down beside

that of Colonel John A. Logan [of the Thirty-first Illinois], who had been wounded in the arm. In a few minutes General Grant's chief surgeon examined my wounds, and told me he could do nothing for me, as all the appliances that my wounds would require were in use."[49]

*   *   *

This singular day that had dawned so differently eased toward evening as the first loads of Confederate prisoners were herded aboard transports. The boats then cast off and steamed downriver toward Cairo "from under the walls of Fort Donelson, which frowned grimly on the captured and the victorious alike," wrote Lieutenant Morton of Porter's Confederate Battery.

The Tenth Tennessee Infantry and some of its junior officers were among the departing, but Colonel Randal McGavock was not among them. Now horseless, he "passed the afternoon and evening mostly in my room at the hotel with some of the officers of our Reg."[50]

On the *New Uncle Sam* at the Dover wharf, the general who had won this unprecedented Federal victory turned out such a large volume of orders, dispatches, and correspondence as to suggest that he labored with his pen far into the evening. One of the final letters, probably, was the one he wrote to Julia that night. It was considerably longer than usual, particularly given how very busy his day had been. In it, he responded to a question from his wife about the Kountz charges. Since her letter is no longer extant, it is not clear what her question was or how much she knew about the entire Kountz affair. In memoirs written more than thirty years later, she provides details that are either twisted by time or by whoever related them to her—but it is plain, from both what she said later and from the fact that she wrote to her husband about the charges in the midst of a battle campaign, that she regarded them as very important at the time. Her memory, though faulty, indicates her idea of Kountz's influence. Her recollection was that Kountz had been appointed not by McClellan but by President Lincoln.

In his reply to her letter, her husband wrote that she should not worry, that Kountz was a man of no character whose charges were baseless. Beneath these, on this inordinately busy day he took the time to pen ten additional lines that afterward were crossed out and rendered illegible. He either did it himself that night, or he or someone else did later.[51]

PART IV

SPOILS

February 16, Forrest Leaving

"Damn Your Judgment"

NATHAN BEDFORD FORREST had never been and would never be a man who surrendered easily. Outraged and angry as he hurried to exit Donelson's collapsing lines, Forrest exemplified the tenuous discipline of the Civil War's early volunteers.

In a cemetery just outside Dover, Forrest gathered as many of his officers as possible in the short time he had and told them to give their men the option of going or staying. As for himself, he added, he was going, and not just if he could save but one man, as he had informed the generals. He was going if it cost his own life.

Every man of his command who got the chance decided to go with him—about five hundred in all. They were joined by a ragtag collection of soldiers from other units whose numbers have been estimated anywhere from two hundred to one thousand. Having ascertained that the scurrying Floyd and Pillow had made other arrangements, Forrest was about to give the order to head out River Road when he noticed a soldier of another unit sitting a horse nearby. He invited the man along. Private John S. Wilkes, a member of John C. Brown's Third Tennessee Infantry, replied that he felt he should stay with the men of his regiment. Forrest turned away waxing disgusted and profane.

"All right," he growled. "I admire your loyalty, but damn your judgment."[1]

The additions to Forrest's ranks included artillerymen from Porter's battery who had unhitched their horses from the caissons, as well as gangs of infantry walking or riding double with the cavalry. The motley procession passed out of the Donelson trenches and, a little way beyond, was met by a lieutenant and three enlisted men who had been sent ahead to scout. A heavy Federal force was moving to block the route, they reported. In disbelief, Forrest asked for volunteers to recheck, but in this harrowing hour none came forward. He then gave command of the column to Major Kelley and went himself, taking along his brother Jeffrey. Before galloping off, he

matter-of-factly instructed Kelley that if he were killed on this reconnaissance, Kelley was to keep the column advancing along the planned route.

At the site of the reported blockage, the Forrest brothers found just a rail
fence. They assumed that in the murky darkness it must have looked to the
scouts like infantry, and they decided the same sight had been what so drasti-
cally influenced the generals' surrender decision an hour or so earlier. The
brothers then rode off to the right up Dudley's Hill, from which Pillow's assault had driven McArthur the preceding morning to open the Forge Road.
On the hill, the Forrest siblings found only campfires and huddling Union
wounded, who indicated that the only able-bodied Federals they had seen all
night were a few scouts. Forrest considered sending this information to
Buckner, then assumed the surrender had already begun.

Two years after the war, Forrest would maintain that his "personal reconnaissance of the ground" confirmed that the Forge Road, which the Donelson army had spilled so much blood to open on Saturday, was still open in
the predawn of Sunday—as he had argued so hotly, and so unsuccessfully, in
Floyd's post-midnight council of generals. He contended that the whole
army that Buckner surrendered could have been withdrawn on it and saved.
But he never asserted that he and his brother had gone all the way *to* Forge
Road, which lay *beyond* Dudley's Hill. And instead of changing plans and taking his Donelson fugitives out on the comparatively dry-surfaced Forge
route, when he returned to the column on River Road he continued out that
way, knowing he had to cross a flooded ford. Perhaps he assumed there was
no longer time to switch routes.[2]

Forrest and his brother rejoined their column as it approached the Lick
Creek ford. The hundred yards of water was lined with ice along the bank
and appeared too deep for horses to cross without swimming. Again, Forrest
asked for a volunteer to check, and then again, when no one immediately responded, he took the job himself, splashing into the flood. As scouts had reported earlier to the council of generals, the water rose only saddle-blanket
deep on his horse, and the men followed. With lookouts posted on all sides,
they took up the march toward Cumberland City, Charlotte, and Nashville.

Progress was slow. They moved cautiously, keeping out advance and rear
guards as well as scouts and flank elements in case of pursuit from Fort
Donelson or collision with other Federals who might have invaded the area.
And they were exhausted from four nearly sleepless days of battle. But they
kept going all day and covered nearly twenty-five miles. The hiking stragglers
were as fortunate as the riders. It was so cold the latter had to keep dismounting and walking to keep from freezing.[3]

February 16, Nashville Under the Gun
"A Perfect Panic"

As FORREST AND HIS FOLLOWERS passed Lick Creek ford and headed down the road toward Nashville, readers of the Tennessee capital's newspapers were digesting and hurrah-ing latest bulletins of the great victory Pillow and the rest of the Fort Donelson garrison were reported to have won the day before.

Informed that the Confederates at Donelson were heavily outnumbered, people from around the region had converged on the capital to obtain the most recent reports as the fighting progressed and the various dailies published continual extra editions. A midnight dispatch reported that the Confederates had driven the Federals from the field and inflicted heavy casualties. The news was duly headlined and roundly celebrated. Nashvillians breathed sighs of exultant relief from their fear of the armored gunboats, which, had they got past Donelson, could have sailed up the Cumberland and bombarded the un-entrenched city.

Later in the morning, as many dressed and set out to Sunday church services, a horrifying new rumor began to spread. Given added momentum by the refusal of Governor Harris and General Johnston, both now in Nashville, to make any comment, the new talk had it that before sunup Donelson and its entire force had run up the white flag. Nashville's crowds trembled. They had been warned by a strident Dixie press about the consequences of Federal victory:

"We shall see plunder; insult to old and young, male and female; murder of innocents; release of slaves, and causing them to drive and insult their masters and mistresses in the most menial services; the land laid waste; houses burned; banks and private coffers robbed; cotton and every valuable taken away before our eyes, and a brutal and drunken soldiery turned loose upon us."[1]

Beauregard, visiting Nashville on the way to Bowling Green scarcely a week earlier, had only magnified such fears. The Creole publicly asserted that the lascivious and venal watchwords of every Federal soldier were "beauty and booty." Now, with Fort Donelson gone, the horde of thugs was on its way, unimpeded.

Albert Sidney Johnston and his staff had gone to bed in Edgefield Saturday night as happy as the general populace, having received around midnight the Pillow and Floyd dispatches claiming victory. Colonel Edward W. Munford, Johnston's aide-de-camp, was asleep in the same room with his chief when they were awakened shortly before dawn by a messenger with more Donelson dispatches. Munford lit a candle and at Johnston's direction read aloud "the astounding official statement that the place 'would capitulate at daylight and the army be surrendered by Buckner, Floyd and Pillow having left on steamboats for Nashville.'" Munford recalled that Johnston, lying on a camp cot in one corner of the room, "was silent a moment," then asked to hear the chilling message again. Munford complied.

"I must save *this* army," Johnston then said. He ordered the rest of his staff awakened and set to hurrying the balance of his Bowling Green troops across the Cumberland as fast as possible. A week earlier, he had warned that loss of Donelson could maroon the Bowling Green army on the north side of the river, separated from the Polk wing by not just one major river but two. Now he rushed off a succinct telegram to Beauregard, who was taking command of the Polk wing until the two demi-armies could reunite again somewhere well to the south or southwest.

"At 2 a.m. today Fort Donelson surrendered," the doleful wire said. "We lost all."[2]

Worship in most Nashville churches, already begun, was abruptly cancelled, and Governor Harris was seen moving feverishly about the city. Having received the news of the Donelson defeat around the same time as Johnston, Harris had crossed the Cumberland to Edgefield early in the morning to confer with the general, who advised him to adjourn the legislature "to some other place" and evacuate the state's records as soon as possible. Johnston said he already had ordered a train for Harris's use. "You can do no further good here now," the general added.

The governor gathered as many members of the legislature as he could for an informal emergency meeting and within hours issued a call for them and the rest of the members to reconvene in Memphis on February 20. The state records were then dumped on a train alongside Harris as, by mid-afternoon, he and the heads of his departments of government got rolling out of town. A Nashville woman jeered his unceremonious departure in her diary: "Oh! Isham, gallant, chivalrous, courageous and swift on the run Isham—we are —yours in haste.'"

Financial institutions opened on this Sabbath to allow depositors access to their accounts—and were so immediately cleaned of their deposits by patrons and bankers that a furloughed Confederate soldier visiting a Union Planters branch downtown saw a cashier emerge from the vault with a five-dollar gold coin that he said was "all that was left . . . Someone had dropped it." By late afternoon, the value of Confederate-printed currency had dropped, too. Passers of Confederate currency could only do so at a discount of its nominal worth.[3]

Doctor Samuel H. Stout, administrator of the so-called Gordon Hospital in the riverfront Gordon warehouse near the foot of Broad Street, was eating at the City Hotel, he later recalled, when "some one pretending to be a courier of Captain Lindsey, commander of the post, rushed down the street on horseback and, stopping before the door of the Gordon Hospital, cried out in a commanding voice, 'The Yankees are coming; are just below the city. Captain Lindsey has sent me to order every sick and wounded man, able to do so, to leave his bunk, and try as best he can to make his way to Murfreesboro.'" When Stout returned to the hospital after his meal, he found every one of his patients, including ones barely mobile, already on the street and full of fear. With difficulty, he got them back into their beds. He said he would like to see the unidentified and presumably unauthorized messenger hanged.[4]

Everybody who could was already following the example of Governor Harris and fleeing, while the rest vied for shares of the food and other domestically usable military goods stashed in the depots and warehouses. By afternoon the city was in full, shameless stampede, and new terrifying rumors made the rounds. One had it that Harris had decreed all women and children must get out of the city within three hours, after which the place was to be shelled. According to another, the Union army of General Don Carlos Buell, with nothing in its path since Johnston pulled out of Bowling Green four days earlier, had swooped down on Springfield, Tennessee, only twenty-five miles off. He was expected by 3 p.m. in Edgefield, the suburb on the Cumberland's opposite bank from downtown. There, it was said, Buell would link up with a fleet of gunboats that already had passed Clarksville and whose captains planned to rain destruction on Nashville. Individual firearms could be of no avail against a gunboat, but their scarcity was keenly felt by residents, who had seen most of their serviceable weapons recently collected by the government for the army.[5]

*   *   *

But before Nashville braved the advancing Federals it would have to endure the retreating Confederates. Johnston's little army, now down to barely ten thousand effectives exhausted from marching through rain, snow, and ice on the last leg of their headlong rush from Bowling Green, began arriving in the city about noon. Guarded front and rear by hardy Texas Rangers, some had walked as many as thirty miles in the past twenty-four hours. Many had seen comrades freeze to death camping on the road.

Most of the marchers hustled—or *were* hustled, not only by their officers but by the residents—straight through town without stopping. In keeping with a decision by Johnston not to try to defend this city that throughout the fall and early winter had all but ignored his calls to fortify, they headed on through toward Murfreesboro. The capital that had sent so many Confederate soldiers off to battle with cheers and martial music a few months earlier now derided them in near-hysteria. John M. Taylor, one of the soldiers who marched through Nashville, later wrote that he and his fellow members of the Twenty-seventh Tennessee would never forget "the taunt that was thrown out by by-standers on the streets" that day: "that we were leaving the people and our capital city to the mercy of the Federals." Many of the hooters, Taylor added, appeared to be dodging that job themselves; they were "young and vigorous, and ought to have been with us, with muskets on their shoulders . . . they would have swelled our ranks considerably."[6]

These troops were already familiar with municipal hysteria. On February 13, Buell units had moved quickly into the vacated Confederate lines around Bowling Green and shelled the city. Homes containing women and children quickly emptied "in such consternation, confusion and alarm" as Texas Ranger chaplain B. F. Bunting had ever seen. "Women were seeking the fields with their little ones clinging to them, or wading through the frozen snow. Some took possession of carriages, some of wagons, others mounted on horseback, and the hurrying, living stream of frightened humanity rolled . . . southward towards —Dixie."[7]

All of the Bowling Green civilians who reached Nashville found the same scene on a larger scale.

"A perfect panic reigned throughout the whole city," a unionist among the stampeders would soon tell a newspaper in Ohio. The appearance of Johnston's retreating army compounded the public fright in more ways than one. Another rumor began to circulate, apparently from the Texas Rangers: the Confederates were going to burn Nashville to the ground themselves rather than leave it and its bulging supply caches to the Federals. The Rangers, purportedly on orders from higher up, had burned buildings in Bowling Green containing abandoned military materiel and were accused—unjustly, a letter from Chaplain Bunting would soon contend—with firing other structures as well. "That was done by the citizens," Bunting wrote to his hometown newspaper. ". . . Had it not been through the efforts of the officers and soldiers there, the greater part of the place would have been destroyed."[8]

In Nashville, wild-eyed civilian refugees and retreating soldiers created a huge traffic jam. Long lines of each continually found themselves blocked by the attempted passage of each other in opposite directions, especially across the seven-hundred-foot suspension bridge to Edgefield. Bunting's contingent of Rangers had stopped ten miles short of Nashville to feed at 4 p.m. and then again "took up the line of march in extra-'double quick' in order to get over the bridges at Nashville that night. About 11 o'clock the wagon train was within two miles of the river, but the road was perfectly jammed. This caused a halt, and a movement only by jerks."[9]

Alongside Johnston's Bowling Green force on this Sunday came the first loads of bloody survivors of Fort Donelson's final day of battle. In anticipation of their arrival, Nashville had already earmarked its schoolhouses and many other buildings, estimated at between twenty-five and thirty in all, to shelter more than three thousand Confederate wounded or sick.

Some Union prisoners from Donelson also arrived that morning on the steamboat *John B. Runyon*. Most of them were taken to the large and unfinished Maxwell House Hotel, which for the war effort had been restyled Zollicoffer Barracks. One of these prisoners, A. F. Gilbert of the Seventeenth Illinois, was brought cold biscuits and hard-boiled eggs by a member of the Confederate Nurses Association who turned out to have a name he recognized. Mrs. John Bell was the wife of the Tennessean who had been the "Constitutional Union" candidate for president less than a year and a half earlier, running last in the four-way contest with Lincoln, Breckinridge, and Douglas. Gilbert later recalled that Mrs. Bell "delivered a homily on the cruelty of wars in general" and said that this one never would have occurred had her husband been elected.[10]

To prepare for the coming of the horde of Donelson wounded amid the disorder of the departing, all those previously hospitalized from Donelson's earlier fighting and still able to walk were ordered out into a field camp south of town. From there they were hauled to railroad stations to be sent painfully farther south. A Confederate quartermaster in Chattanooga, alerted that he was soon to receive "some thousand or twelve hundred sick and convalescent soldiers from this [Bowling Green] Army and from hospitals at Nashville," was appalled at the condition of the first load of three hundred.

"They had been stowed away in box and cattle cars for eighteen hours, without fire, and without any attention other than such as they were able to render each other," he later recalled. "Tears filled the eyes of many at the depot when these poor fellows were taken from the cars, so chilled and benumbed that a majority of them were helpless."[11]

The unfortunates apparently had been loaded into the "box and cattle" cars because passenger compartments already were filled ("to suffocation," one observer wrote) with a writhing mass of fearful humanity. As many as seven trains left Nashville that day crammed with women and children and with so many men riding outside that they covered the tops of the cars. Another train, a special one carrying the family as well as the "personal baggage, furniture, carriage and carriage horses" of Nashville & Chattanooga Railroad president V. K. Stevenson departed just past nightfall, perhaps to avoid unwanted extra riders. One party invited aboard was that of Abraham Lincoln's sister-in-law, Mrs. Emily Todd Helm, wife of the commander of the Confederate First Kentucky Cavalry. Three decades later, she recalled that Stevenson "kindly allowed me and my children and servant to get on board" his flight to Chattanooga "in time to secure a room in the only hotel there."

Stevenson, a Confederate major and quartermaster over Nashville's huge stocks of supplies, seemed to unceremoniously shed his public responsibilities, although he afterward claimed he had urgent military transport business in Chattanooga. Other prominent fugitives included ex-U.S. Representative Andrew Ewing as well as John Overton, reputedly the richest man in Tennessee.

The citizens who escaped by train, from Stevenson to those clinging to the tops of the railroad cars, comprised the lucky of Nashville. Every available private vehicle of any type was hired at wildly inflated prices, and "only the wealthy could enjoy the luxury of a ride . . . Large numbers, in their eagerness to escape from the city, left on foot, carrying with them such articles as they wished to preserve, either as mementoes or for their comfort." Behind, they left thousands of the poor who "had no alternative but to remain and make the best disposition of themselves that they could." A Methodist minister later recalled that throughout the rest of the day thousands of civilians followed the retreating army amid the simultaneous removal of "sick, wounded, dying, and dead soldiers.

"The scene beggars description," he added.[12]

The departures continued throughout the afternoon and evening, and the outflow of humanity began to be balanced by an influx of new arrivals. First was Johnston's Bowling Green army. Then, beginning in a trickle that would increase dramatically over the next couple of days, came small gangs of the fugitive infantrymen who had made their individual ways out of Fort Donelson. They were traveling with no military chain of command left to control them, further increasing the municipal chaos. When night descended on possibly the most terrifying day in Nashville history, the disorder only spread, with "yells, curses, (and) shots" ringing out "on all sides."

On all with the ill luck to be in Nashville or its environs, in the evening more winter rain began to fall. The soldiers tore down rail fences for fires for their camps and stole corn and hay for their animals. The Ewing estate south of Nashville was later reported "perfectly ruined" by the Confederate troops, who were furious at the turn of events and at the ex-congressman and the rest of those rich enough and lucky enough to leave and avoid the consequences. They fed their horses on sofas in the Ewing parlor and, in apparent blanket resentment of anybody with influence, were quoted as saying, "Damn him[,] he got us into the trouble and is now the first . . . to run away."[13]

Around midnight, the mounted Texas Rangers filed past the jam of wagon traffic on the suspension bridge over the Cumberland and headed out the Murfreesboro pike, but they had to travel four more miles before they could find an unoccupied spot on which to make camp. "Here, about 10 o'clock p.m.," Chaplain Bunting wrote, "we had the satisfaction of turning into a field and put up for the night, supperless and tentless in a pelting rain."[14]

*   *   *

Back at Fort Donelson, the captured Confederates were enduring misfortunes of their own.

Captain Jack Campbell of the Forty-eighth Tennessee later recalled standing "around all day in mud shoe-mouth deep guarded by the enemy." Some of the Federals shot themselves handling the captured, loaded Confederate rifles, Campbell wrote; they also shot several Confederates. They broke into the trunks of the captives and took what they wanted. At Buckner's headquarters, Campbell confided to his diary, a Federal colonel named Sweeney had proclaimed "that the Federal government was going to crush out the rebellion if it had to kill every man, woman, and child in the Southern states," and that Buckner, "an unarmed prisoner, indignantly replied that [the colonel] was a monster and a brute and that there was the door, take it."

Chaplain Deavenport of the Third Tennessee later remembered that they "were driven through the cold mud" all day. Around 11 a.m. the Third was marched from its position in Buckner's final fall-back position on the right side of the Confederate line down to Dover on the left to stack arms:

> We were ordered to leave our baggage and return for it . . . While [we were] stacking arms, our captors plundered our camp and took all the best of the clothing and blankets. Many a poor fellow was left without a blanket or a change of clothes. At length, about two hours after dark, we were marched on

the boat and stored away in the hole [sic] which was about four feet from floor to [ceiling]. Worn out, and almost indifferent to what fate might befall me, I dropped down and was soon asleep . . . [15]

Jack Campbell had been separated from the rest of the Forty-eighth Tennessee and, he informed his diary, was put aboard the *Neptune* with the Third. He was so exhausted that he went to sleep in the *Neptune's* hold with his pistols and sword still buckled on, as he had done for the previous week. He slept soundly and "was permitted to come out of the stinking hold by eight o'clock," he recalled. "We received some crackers and raw meat to make our breakfast upon."

He spent most of the next day, Monday, February 17, trying to get permission to "go down the line of [transport] boats and hunt up my regiment." [16]

Like so many others, soldier or civilian, in Tennessee in the wake of Donelson's fall, Campbell had no idea where he was headed next or what was apt to happen to him. Such things were out of his hands.

Monday, February 17,
Nashville and Fort Donelson
Fear and Misery

IN THE FRANTIC CAPITAL of Tennessee, Monday had dawned in more dismal rain.

Stores and shops were closed and all business halted, but more of the warehoused military supplies of food were beginning to be distributed, especially to needy women who had worked for the Confederate army and had not yet been paid. No news could be had from the *Nashville Union and American,* which abruptly closed its doors and ceased publication as of the day before. A Confederate major remembered that "the streets and walks were a complete jam of citizens and soldiers" wearing "downcast looks and muddy clothes." The flight of the previous day was continuing, with "people . . . vacating fine houses[,] leaving their contents within to the charge of a feeble door-lock." Looting spread. Government buildings were rifled, and clothing, blankets, meat, meal, and other goods were thrown out of fourth- and fifth-story windows to waiting crowds below. People staggered off under great loads.[1]

Around 7 a.m., a steamboat arrived from the direction of Fort Donelson. The vessel proved to be the *General Anderson,* from which Generals Floyd and Pillow got what Floyd remembered as an appalling view of the once-proud capital: "The rabble on the wharf were in possession of boats loaded with Government bacon, and were pitching it from these boats to the shore, and carrying what did not fall into the water by hand and carts away to various places in the city." The looters, Floyd soon wrote, claimed "that the meat had been given to them by the city council."[2]

Pillow had ridden overland on horseback from Donelson to Clarksville and got aboard the boat there. During the river journey he had begun justifying the surrender and seemingly endorsing Floyd and Buckner's reasoning. To some of Floyd's Virginia troops the Tennessean said that it would have been suicide for Donelson's garrison, which he numbered at thirteen thousand, to try to drive off the "upwards of 40,000" Federals. 3

Reaching Nashville, the fugitive generals reported to Johnston, who not only received them with "the greatest courtesy" but also took them into conference. Following the meeting, another disquieting rumor spread: that they and Johnston had decided to make a stand near Nashville. An alarmed Mayor Richard Cheatham, brother of General Frank Cheatham of Belmont note, went to confront Johnston about it, and then addressed a crowd in the public square. He announced that the Johnston-Floyd-Pillow council of war had agreed that *no* stand would be made in or near Nashville, that Johnston's army would depart the city before the arrival of the Federals and leave it to Buell undamaged. The mayor also said that the supplies would be distributed fairly among the poor.

This announcement was of great interest because the very opposite appeared to be happening. Floyd, whom Johnston immediately placed in charge of evacuating Nashville's storehouses of military-related materiel, had halted the distribution of supplies to the needy. Instead he had begun pressing civilian men and wagons into service to haul as many of the cached items as possible to the railroad. There the civilians were to load the goods onto southbound cars to preserve them from capture in the expected Federal onrush.4

Toward the afternoon's end, a handbill advertised a Pillow speech in the public square at 7 p.m. The event was disappointing. The usually garrulous brigadier spoke for not much more than five minutes, assuring the crowd that no battle would be fought in Nashville or its surrounding area and that residents were in no danger of harm from Federal officers, "who are gentlemen and of course will behave as such toward you.

"The Federals will be with you only for a time," he proclaimed, "and I pledge you my honor that this war will not end until they are driven across the Ohio River."

With that, he took his honor from the podium and rushed it aboard a train for his Maury County estate sixty miles south, his rapid departure leaving many Nashvillians understandably unconvinced that they remained safe where they were. Later that evening, a crowd gathered across the river in front of Johnston's headquarters, and a man "seeming to be half drunk" reeled up the steps. "We have come to demand of our generals whether they intend to fight for us or not," he shouted. Turning to the crowd, he added: "Yes, fellow citizens, we have a right to know whether our generals are going to fight for us or intend abandoning us and our wives and children to the enemy. We will force them to tell us!"

Floyd, Hardee, and Munford all had to make speeches to the "mob," Munford later remembered, "before they could be induced to disperse." Floyd explained to the crowd that the Donelson troops had given up only when they reached "the end of human endurance" and that, for the moment, retreat by Johnston's remaining force was wise. Floyd, a southeast Virginia mountaineer, added that the Confederates "would be sure to whip the Federals when they got them back into the mountain gorges, away from their gunboats." The erstwhile Donelson commander seemed to have forgotten his garrison's smashing victory over Foote's armada.[5]

The effort to deny the coming Federals anything militarily valuable quickened. That night the *General Anderson,* along with a couple of craft that had been undergoing conversion into Confederate gunboats, were burned at the Nashville wharf by military authorities, prompting a ringing of the city's firebell. Seeing the flames, many Nashvillians were surprised that the two Cumberland River bridges, the railroad and suspension spans, had not also been burned.[6]

*   *   *

Eighty miles northwest, northern-bound steamboats filled with captured Confederates were leaving Fort Donelson regularly. Jack Campbell was not allowed to look for his regiment among the other transports until late that evening, by which time he found that the vessel carrying the Forty-eighth already had shoved off. He returned to the *Neptune* barely in time to go with the Third Tennessee as it was transferred to another vessel, the *Tecumseh.*

Captivity became steadily more unsettling and demeaning. Just prior to *Tecumseh*'s cast-off from the Dover landing, the Union guards claimed they thought they saw a man swimming ashore to try to escape, and they started firing in that direction, giving the prisoners an idea of what they faced if they tried it. After the boat had got under steam, two Federal officers and a party of enlisted men came around relieving Confederate officers of their side-arms, "rudely thrusting their hands" into Jack Campbell's pockets while he was asleep. That night, Campbell slept in a chair on the *Tecumseh* deck "until I got so cold I had to go inside, where it was so crowded I could get barely enough room to sit down."[7]

Colonel McGavock had stayed close to his Dover hotel room for much of the day, "wishing to avoid as much as possible the supercilious stare of the Yankees, who hold their heads aloft . . . as if they had accomplished something by their valor—not thinking for a moment that they were badly whipped at every point on Saturday, and that our surrender was for . . . bad

Generalship on our side—and not bravery or great deeds on theirs. They outnumbered us at least four to one and really deserve no credit."[8]

The tension between captives and captors was heightened by a sudden rumor that in the Dover jail some dead Federals had been found with battle wounds and tied hand and foot. The rumors prompted "the highest excitement amongst" the Donelson victors and spawned dark threats against Confederates, as Buckner soon informed Grant. The Kentuckian said he already had investigated the rumor and found it "absurd." He asked that Grant investigate the rumors for himself in the interest of Confederate honor and in order to prevent Union acts of retribution. Grant's headquarters complied by sending a party of officers with some of Buckner's Confederates to investigate. General Bushrod Johnson, who had had the jail keys prior to the surrender, was asked about it and strangely replied to Buckner on February 17 by letter, instead of face-to-face. In the letter, Johnson confirmed that to the best of his knowledge no prisoners had been confined to the jail.

Another Confederate officer, Major Alexander Casseday, reported hearing the rumor of the dead Federals in the jail from some of his captors. Accompanied by Federal officers, Casseday investigated and found three Federal corpses along with a Confederate "laid out for decent burial," "cotton being placed on the mouths of two of them to absorb the froth." They had received medical attention; bandages placed on some of their wounds were visible without removing their clothes. Casseday wrote that Union officers escorting him agreed that charges of inhumanity were unfounded and that the corpses had been placed in the jail by Federals.[9]

A number of the blankets the Confederates complained of having had taken from them were Federal issue, captured in the overrunning of McClernand's camps on Saturday. Grant wrote General George Cullum at Paducah that he was "trying to have these collected and returned." Describing them ("grey with the letters US in the center"), Grant recommended that "all such found upon the prisoners" whom he was now sending north "should be taken from them and returned here." This same day, the 17th, he wrote Cullum again to ask that five thousand blankets and a thousand overcoats be sent to Donelson "as soon as possible," explaining that "many were lost on the battlefield and the men are now without."[10]

The final number of Confederate deportees, as well as that of the entire Donelson force during the battles, would be matters of dispute. Twenty thousand in the garrison and at least fourteen thousand captured appear to be the most reasonable estimates.[11]

Confederate Colonel McGavock kept to himself, brooding about "the sad disaster to our army and our cause" and its consequences: "Some 12,000 of our best troops are to be incarcerated in northern prisons, the Capital of

Ten to be attacked in a few days and properly destroyed, if not evacuated, the heart of the Confederacy penetrated, and a blow stricken that will cost much blood and treasure to retrieve, if ever."

That evening McGavock, Tenth Tennessee commander Adolphus Heiman, and some other Tenth officers were among the last of a group of "six or eight hundred rebel prisoners"—including Jack Campbell of the Forty-eighth Tennessee and Chaplain Deavenport of the Third—who filed onto the *Tecumseh* under guard of "two companies of Yankees." McGavock soon would find the craft "very much crowded and very disagreeable." It would not depart the Dover dock until the middle of the night, and Deavenport reported that the Third Tennessee had been aboard since around noon. Its members then had to endure sitting at the Dover wharf until 2 a.m.[12]

Not all the steamboat passengers on this day were captives or guards. One of these was the runaway slave who had come into Union lines shortly before the arrival of Buckner's first truce party early Sunday morning. According to reporter Coffin, Grant ("like a sensible man") in this case ignored Halleck's order excluding blacks from Federal lines and allowed the fugitive to board one of the transports bound for Cairo. When the boat soon stopped at a landing for wood and the black was recognized by locals, they claimed that he was the property of a Union man. This was an artifice beginning to be adopted by many slaveholders in the path of the Federal armies, because "property" could not legally be confiscated from persons espousing the National cause. People at the landing demanded that the slave be put off the boat and remanded to his master.

". . . [B]ut the officers on board," Coffin wrote, "knowing what service he had rendered . . . kept the negro under their protection and gave him his liberty."[13]

February 18–21, Union and Confederate

Consequences

Many men whose health survived Donelson's frigid privations saw it quickly deteriorate.

In writing of the Confederates' journey north, Jack Campbell wrote that abundant "suffering was caused among the prisoners by the boat being so crowded and so many being sick from exposure and bad diet and water. A good many had their feet frostbitten in the trenches at the fort." Similarly, Federal Sergeant F. F. Kiner of the Fourteenth Iowa, in addition to his frostbitten great toes on either foot, came down with "a bilious attack" and affliction with "rheumatism through my limbs" so debilitating that he had to be helped in and out of bed.

"Our exposure during the siege was so severe, and our diet so unwholesome, that for several weeks after the surrender, a great many men of the brigade were sick," he wrote.[1]

February 18, the day that Campbell noted the Confederate sickness and Kiner was prostrated by illness, prisoner Buckner penned a letter to Mary Kingsbury Buckner—and mailed it with the assistance of Grant, whom Buckner had asked the day before whether officers were permitted to write "private letters (open) to their friends in the Confederate states." Mary Buckner was in Columbus, Kentucky, during the Donelson fighting and may have been staying at the home of its Confederate-sympathizing mayor, B. W. Sharp.[2]

DOVER, TENN., Febry 18, 1862

MY DEAR MARY:

I am a prisoner of war. Gen. Floyd left with a few of his own troops and Gen. Pillow deserted his troops for his own safety. You know me well enough, my little wife, to be assured that whatever the fate of my soldiers, my sense of honor compels me to share it whether it be in their glory or their captivity. They won the

*victory the day before the surrender and had fairly cut their way through the ene-
my's line; but after the whole object of the fight had been attained and the retreat
of the army secured, I was ordered back to the lines by Gen. Pillow and subsequently by Gen. Floyd; and at the last moment I am left to bear the blunder of
my superiors.*

*I will leave here today or tomorrow for Cairo, from that point I do not know my
destination. As soon however, as it may be determined I will write to you . . .
Please say to Gen. Johnston that I hope he will endeavor to effect my exchange at
the earliest possible day.*

*I hardly know whether to be thankful for my escape. I was much exposed during
the different battles but escaped unhurt. Our losses were heavy, but much lighter
than that of the Federals who suffered severely . . .*

*Kiss my sweet little girl for me, and be assured of my undying love. Remember
me most kindly to Col. and Mrs. Sharp. Should you be in need of funds, Col.
Sharp will supply. Should you join me [in the North] ask Col. Sharp to furnish
you with gold in exchange for your southern money.*[3]

Buckner's rigid code of honor doubtless would not have allowed him to
avail himself of the opportunity to escape even had it come along, and in the
short run that was his good fortune. Unionists in his native state had already
despised him and indicted him for treason for his Confederate sympathies
while commanding the Kentucky State Guard, and, in the wake of his surrender, feelings toward him across the rest of the South were just as harsh.
The day after Buckner wrote to Mary, the assistant U.S. secretary of war
warned Halleck that care and a circuitous route must be taken in moving
Buckner northward because he was in danger of being lynched "if he is
brought into Kentucky."[4]

*   *   *

Buckner's safety was just one of myriad considerations that had to be taken
into account. Grant had found that processing the horde of Confederate
captives was an enormous task. He wrote to Halleck's chief of staff on
February 17: "It is a much less job to take (prisoners) than to keep them."
Apparently, throughout the day of the surrender and afterward, significant
numbers of the captured continued to slip away. "It appears that during the
night a large number of captured animals have been run off and many prisoners escaped," Grant wrote McClernand on February 17. He repeatedly
ordered the taking of measures by cavalry patrols and others to prevent

BUSHROD RUST JOHNSON

further attrition, but it kept occurring. The day Buckner wrote his letter to Mary, no less than a general got away.[5]

Bushrod Johnson's habitual tendency to blend into the background served him well in the Donelson aftermath. Johnson had seen his men sent off down the river on steamers. Claiming to have had no part in the surrender or been so much as taken notice of by his Federal counterparts, he later would report that he walked out for a late afternoon stroll with another Confederate officer, Captain J. H. Anderson of the Tenth Tennessee. "With no purpose or plan of escape," the pair meandered "toward the rifle pits on the hill formerly occupied by Colonel Heiman, and[,] finding no sentinel to obstruct me, I passed on and was soon beyond the Federal encampments." He would officially add in a report filed March 4: "If my escape involves any question of military law, duty, or honor, I desire it may be thoroughly investigated, and I shall submit with pleasure to any decision of the proper authorities."

The fact that Johnson made such an offer suggests that he knew very well that his action did involve a military or ethical question. He *had* taken part in surrendering—had, in fact, led a Union general, Lew Wallace, to Buckner's headquarters after accompanying a flag of truce into Federal lines. But then he apparently made himself as unobtrusive as possible among the Confederate prisoners (even avoiding Buckner) before taking his February 18 stroll. A general could not have simply and unpremeditatedly wandered off as Johnson claimed he did. He and Anderson would have had to secrete horses and at least a few provisions to make the seventy-five-mile trek to Nashville in forbidding weather. Johnson plainly was not eager for the kind of scrutiny that one of the war's first two surrendered generals might attract—especially the one who was a Northerner and a former abolitionist. That could be disastrous to any future he might have left on either side of the Mason-Dixon Line.[6]

*   *   *

Grant's post-surrender task, meanwhile, was a nightmare of personnel management and logistical snarl. He had to tally and arrange for the transport of a staggering number of prisoners, wounded, and supplies to prisons, hospitals, and depots at Cairo and other locations across the North. He eventually would estimate that just the food supplies that had been captured at Fort Donelson would be able to sustain his men in most of their wants for three weeks; he reported that it included enough rice to feed them for the rest of what he still assumed would be a short war. On the 17th, the second day after the close of fighting, he still was trying to get all the wounded aboard hospital boats, to obtain blankets and overcoats for soldiers still suffering from exposure in the rain and cold, to organize guarding of all roads and other entryways into the Donelson entrenchments from the river south of Dover to its banks north of Fort Donelson, and to quell the persistent looting of captured property by individual soldiers. On February 18, he ordered newly arrived General Stephen A. Hurlbut to post one or two whole regiments of fresh troops in and around Dover to prevent "plundering generally" by Federal soldiers, suggesting that "patrols, and strong ones at that, be sent out at once."[7]

The next day the *Allen Collier*, a steamboat chartered by the Cincinnati branch of the Sanitary Commission, arrived with surgeons, nurses, and hospital stores. Grant issued the Cincinnatians passes through all lines at will, but red tape prevented these volunteers from seeing patients until nine-thirty at night. The scene they then witnessed was daunting. According to the physician in charge of the mission, the patients included men still "arriving from the various places where they had been taken from the field of battle.

Our examination showed that the individual condition of the wounded was deplorable. Some were just as they had been left by the fortune of war [four days earlier]; their wounds . . . yet undressed, smeared with filth and blood, and all their wants unsupplied. Others had had their wounds dressed one, two, or three days before. Others, still, were under the surgeon's hands, receiving such care as could be given them by men overburdened by the number of their patients, worn out by excessive and long-continued labor, without an article of clothing to give to any for a change, or an extra blanket, without bandages or dressings . . . with few medicines and no stimulants, and with nothing but corn meal gruel, hard bread, and bacon to dispense as food.[8]

The wounded had to really want to stay alive.

*   *   *

Despite the enormous number of details he had to oversee, Grant's eyes never left the southern horizon for long. With this huge, exhilarating victory to his unquestionable credit, he itched to push the Union advantage and—in the homely phrase of his opponent Forrest—"keep the skeer on" the retreating Confederates. On the 16th, he wrote Halleck's chief of staff, George Cullum at Cairo, that he hoped to take Clarksville, the next step toward Nashville, by the 18th, acknowledging meanwhile that to do so he would need the gunboats and that they probably would not be ready by then. On February 17, Grant wrote again, saying he expected to "take and garrison Clarkesville in a few days." On the 19th, he wrote Cullum that he would enter Clarksville on the 20th and could "have Nashville" a few days later. Flag Officer Foote, who had arrived back at the front, was again eager to move forward in concert with him, as at Cairo in late January.

Foote and Grant's chief of staff, Colonel Webster, reached Clarksville on the 19th. They found, Foote reported, that "two-thirds of the citizens had fled from the place, panic-stricken . . . the city was in a state of the wildest commotion from rumors that we would not respect the citizens either in their persons or their property." Foote added, in this communication written apparently to Halleck, that he planned to "proceed with all possible dispatch up the Cumberland River . . . and in conjunction with the army make an attack on Nashville. The Rebels have great terror of the GunBoats." Foote and Webster quickly learned that the Confederates were abandoning the Tennessee capital. At Grant's suggestion, Webster wrote to Halleck's headquarters that the Foote party had been told that "Gen Johns[t]on had left Nashville for Columbia. Another gentleman in town told me that Nashville had made offers to capitulate to some Federal army which was near them.

He said he has seen a man from N. who told him this." Webster added that they were begged "to push on to Nashville as fast as possible."9

Grant visited Clarksville on February 20 with a military band and a couple of companies from the Illinois brigade commanded by Colonel W. H. L. Wallace. The soldiers marched down the streets but met no welcome except from the slaves—"Most of the white inhabitants had left," Wallace wrote his wife. On Foote's visit of the day before, the flag officer had found that the railroad bridge had been burned by the fleeing Confederates, and now Grant found white flags waving from Dover to Clarkesville and rumor saying they were to be seen all the way to Nashville. He wrote Cullum of his "impression that by following up our success Nashville would be an easy conquest." Then, perhaps remembering Halleck's contemptuous initial reaction to his recommendation to attack Fort Henry, he added: "I only (throw) this out as a suggestion based simply upon information from people who have no sympathy with us." He made his proposal on February 21. The same day Foote telegraphed that "Genl Grant and myself consider this a good time to move on Nashville . . . The Cumberland is in a good stage of water, and Genl Grant and I believe we can take Nashville."10

*   *   *

Once again, as when the pair were kept chafing at Cairo for weeks before being loosed on Fort Henry, the Union brain trust was playing individual ego games and forgetting the primary goal. Its dawdling let Albert Sidney Johnston hurry remnants of the Confederacy's primary western army past Nashville.

On February 18, Halleck outraged Foote. He wired Grant, rather than Foote, to prevent the terror-spreading gunboats from going up the Cumberland past Clarksville. Foote apparently complained to his fellow New Englander, reporter Coffin. Coffin soon wrote that the flag officer had "intended to push up the river to Nashville and intercept General Albert Sidney Johnston, who he knew must be falling back from Bowling Green, but he was stayed by a dispatch from General Halleck to General Grant. 'Don't let Foote go up the river.'" The old sea dog was infuriated by more than Halleck's affront to him personally. He was bitter at his army superiors' refusal to capitalize on the momentum of the Donelson capture. "The gunboats could have reached Nashville in eight hours," he told Coffin.11

Halleck's decision was prompted by not only his characteristic caution but also his recognition that McClellan was reserving the capture of Nashville and Middle Tennessee for Buell. That was fine with Halleck, who had such contempt for civilian political influence on the military that he

did not realize the huge potential impact of the first recapturing of a seceded state's capital. The St. Louis commander was fixated on the line of the
Tennessee River and achieving what he assumed were the more important
military rewards: the flanking of Columbus and the Confederacy's other
Mississippi River fortifications all the way to Memphis—as well as threatening the hub of the all-important Memphis & Charleston Railroad at
Corinth, Mississippi.[12]

Halleck was indulging his ambition, too. On first receiving Grant's telegram imparting news of the victory, Halleck became momentarily giddy, but
he quickly recovered his sense of direction. The day after the Donelson surrender, he telegraphed McClellan in Washington, demanding command of
all the western Union armies "in return for Forts Henry and Donelson." He
rightly reasoned that the Federal western effort needed centralized direction
instead of separate fiefdoms at St. Louis, Louisville, and elsewhere, and he
seemed even more disturbed that this accident of history was bringing the
un-soldierly Grant to the fore. Still waiting for the Hitchcock appointment to
be finalized, Halleck proposed to take charge of Grant's army in person and
retain its general as a subordinate. He further tried to minimize Grant's suddenly swelling image and to bolster his own plans to replace the Donelson
victor by asking that two other western brigadiers—Lincoln family friend
John Pope in Missouri and the vaunted but highly inactive Buell—be promoted to major general simultaneously with Grant.[13]

Meanwhile Grant, whose ego was far less evident than that of his superiors, must have reflected on how lucky he had been. Lucky that the Confederates had not come out and attacked him on the 12th, when his Federals
were strung out along the two Henry-Donelson roads. Lucky in the same respect again on the 13th, when his troops were sidling southward trying to extend their lines to the river in front of Dover. Implausibly lucky in initially
being able to coop up the Confederates within the fort with fewer troops
outside than were on the inside. Luckier still that on the 15th McClernand's
thin and heavily outnumbered line of Illinoisans on the right held long
enough against their attackers to allow a galloping return from Foote's gunboat and the organization of the counterattacks. And lucky beyond all measure that Pillow had ordered his and Buckner's men back into the trenches
after driving McClernand two miles across the Donelson front. These were
all godsends that could only have been conferred by a fate turned, after thirty-nine years, suddenly bounteous.

But Grant could reflect, too, that he had made some of his own luck. He
had known that Pillow, whether present or absent, would not attack on the
12th. On the 15th, instead of doing what virtually all of his peers would have
done and either retreated or at the very least dug in to await nightfall at the

point to which he had been pushed, he had—by immediately launching the crucial counterattacks—acted as if he had the forty or fifty thousand men that the Confederate high command feared he had. His own pugnacity had produced their surrender.

Grant's habitual mindset was on whatever job was at hand, and he now must have begun to get his first intimations that doors to greater achievement and acclaim might be opening. Maybe he also began to perceive that the initials erroneously conferred on him at West Point (to which he had gone as H. U.—for Hiram Ulysses, rather than U. S.—Grant) could suggest to the public mind not only the words he so memorably borrowed from General Smith in the reply to Buckner's surrender note but also, perhaps, ultimately those of the name of the republic itself.

The newspapers and the public, so often mistaken about the significance of public events as they happen, were getting this one right; they understood that Grant's victory at Fort Donelson was gigantic in the life of the Union. Donelson's fall had prompted joy across the North almost as manic as the fear and trembling it prompted across the South. The celebrating at Cairo was so loud that Confederates could hear it ten miles downriver at Columbus, and a journalist there telegraphed that the Confederacy's backbone had been broken on the Donelson ridges. Governor Yates of Illinois quickly headed for Dover to oversee medical care for the battle's host of wounded Illinoisans, and on his way he wired Chicago that his route was lined with "thousands on the road and at the stations, with shoutings and with flags. Thank God that our Union is now safe . . . forever." The *Chicago Tribune*, no Grant admirer, approved the pandemonium and explained itself: "Such events happen but once in a lifetime." Correspondents praised Grant's coolness in the face of the crisis of February 15 and vied with each other to capture his habitual dogged fixation on the work at hand. They employed his initials to dub him Unconditional Surrender Grant.

Cairo was only hours away by boat, so Grant knew most of all this nearly as soon as it happened.

Within the week, he would write a few atypical giddy lines to Julia:

I see from the papers, and also from a dispatch sent me by Mr. [Illinois congressman] Washburn[e], that the Administration have thought well enough of my administration of affairs to make me a Maj. General. Is father afraid yet that I will not be able to sustain myself? He expressed apprehensions on that point when I was made a Brigadier.

Someone higher up, too, was perhaps getting his first dim intimation of the potential in Grant's nerve and determination. Very late in the evening of the victory day, February 16, before receiving any recommendation from Halleck, Secretary of War Edwin Stanton had brought to Lincoln a nomination of Grant to major general, and the President had signed it. It was an emphatic reward to Grant for the victory he won; it was not one handed out with simultaneous promotions for Pope and Buell.

That same day, reflecting on the momentous news from Tennessee, the President had added a prophetic observation regarding the Confederacy and the Federal volunteers whose sufferings, at bottom, had staked Grant to his triumph.

"If the Southerners think that man for man they are better than our Illinois men, or western men generally," Lincoln said, "they will discover themselves in a grievous mistake."[14]

35

February 18–23, Forrest in Nashville
"Ruin at Every Step"

By THE TIME FORREST arrived in the Tennessee capital—around 10 a.m. on February 18—he was aware of the chaos awaiting him. He had seen it all around him on the frigid two-day trek from Fort Donelson.

He and his band of escapees had found the roads crawling with sick and furloughed Confederates who had been at home or recuperating in various hospitals and were now hurrying southward to avoid capture. Their frantic passage down roads and lanes spread panic through the rural population. Many people left their houses behind to join the martial disorder.

Forrest and his soldiers had camped at the end of the first day about two-thirds of the way to the village of Charlotte, which they had reached the next morning. There Forrest had been forced to confront rampant civilian terror head-on in the person of a state senator on a horse that had been ridden so hard from Nashville that it had turned "white with sweat-foam," according to Forrest's authorized biography. The senator apparently had been among a handful of legislators called together by Governor Harris to formally adjourn their body to Memphis—just before Harris and much of the state's executive branch piled aboard Memphis-bound train-cars. The legislator cried that Nashville had surely been captured by now by Federals who had also sent a column of ten thousand troops toward Charlotte to cut off and capture the Donelson fugitives. Forrest threatened the senator with "summary punishment" for disseminating "false intelligence," his authorized biographers assert. To try to calm Charlotte's residents, he had publicly belittled the legislator's story and underscored his own contempt for it by delaying in Charlotte to have some of his regiment's horses re-shod.

But when his little force took up its march again, he had indicated he would take no chances, just in case the politician had not been exaggerating. Only a mile out of the village, he had ordered his men to discharge their weapons to ready them for any action that might lie ahead. These shots had promptly stampeded another Confederate cavalry regiment that

347

had been in the vicinity and had already heard the senator's wild tale. In the wake of this unintended rout of their fellow Confederates, Forrest's men had gathered up the tents, food, cookware, other supplies, even wagons wrecked along the roadside. It was nearly enough goods and equipment to replace those the regiment had been unable to transport out of Fort Donelson.[1]

Arriving in Nashville at 10 a.m. on February 18, Forrest found it virtually ruled by a "mob . . . composed of straggling soldiers and citizens of all grades. [They] had taken possession of the city to that extent that every species of property was unsafe. Houses were closed, carriages and wagons were concealed to prevent the mob from taking possession of them. Houses were being seized everywhere."[2]

He reported to Johnston, just leaving for Murfreesboro. The Confederate western commander told him that Floyd had been placed in command of the effort to save whatever Nashville supplies could be salvaged. Forrest's attitude toward being again assigned to the man who had presided over the debacle of the Donelson surrender council appears nowhere in the records. What does appear is that although ordered that day, Tuesday, to establish patrols to guard the city from its own inhabitants and soldiers, he complied relatively minimally. He confined his exhausted troopers to specifically ordered guard duties while allowing them a rest until Thursday morning. Their aid was nevertheless significant. Floyd's report indicates that Forrest's regiment, along with other cavalry under Captain John Hunt Morgan, "rendered signal and efficient service in dispersing the mobs which gathered in the vicinity of the warehouses containing Government property, and which often had to be scattered at the point of the saber." Forrest's men quelled the throngs with saber charges, water from a fire-hose, and in at least one case, a blow from a pistol-butt. When one looter tried to pull Forrest himself off his horse, the Memphis lieutenant colonel promptly administered the heel of his side arm to the man, sending the assailant away howling.

A Morgan subordinate's account praises the salvage efforts initiated by Floyd, but Forrest—who at Donelson had gotten to know Floyd far better than Morgan's men did—confined his report to his own work. Two days later, he had the command of Nashville to himself. On Thursday, February 20, Floyd left for Murfreesboro and handed over the military supervision of the city. Floyd instructed Forrest to save whatever else he could but to evacuate by Friday.[3]

With full responsibility now on his shoulders, Forrest sprang into action. He reported saving seven hundred boxes of clothes, several hundred bales of military overcoats and other military items, more than seven hundred wagonloads of meat, and thirty wagonloads of ammunition. He only partially complied with Floyd's order to withdraw to Murfreesboro on Friday,

February 21; he did send most of his unit to Murfreesboro on that day but personally remained in Nashville with a forty-man detachment for forty-eight more hours. He wanted to haul away the rest of the ammunition.

Forrest would later complain to Richmond that the trains employed in such work as the private evacuation of the family, furniture, and friends of Quartermaster V. K. Stevenson could have saved many more and maybe all of the supplies. As it was, he added, when he departed on Sunday, February 23, he was forced to leave behind some of the materiel and many sick and wounded soldiers. Federals later reported recovering five thirty-two-pounder cannons and seven twenty-four-pounders, as well as other guns at an ordnance depot.

"The panic was entirely useless and not at all justified," Forrest wrote of the rioting and civic disorder that turned the Tennessee capital into a mammoth seeming mad-house. He was manifestly correct. An entire week passed between the fall of Donelson and the first appearance of Federal soldiers in its environs—and even these were on the opposite side of the Cumberland. 4

*   *   *

News of the initial visit of Foote and his gunboats to Clarksville on February 19 had fired another Nashville rumor: the dreaded ironclads were on their way for certain this time. The hearsay doomed the suspension and railroad bridges across the Cumberland. They had to come down to delay and hamper the Federal invaders. Mayor Cheatham and others beseeched Floyd to spare the structures, noting that many of the city's market supplies had to be gotten from Edgefield via the suspension span. The pleas earned the bridges only a few more hours. Floyd permitted a final crossing by a lot of local traffic, a large herd of cattle, and as much military transportation as could get across on that day. Then, about 10 p.m., the floor of the highway conduit—built in 1850 and designed by the Tenth Tennessee's Colonel Adolphus Heiman, a Nashville architect in civilian life—was torched and its cables severed, sending the flaming structure plummeting into the Cumberland. Afterward the railway trestle, which had allowed crossing of the river by the Louisville & Nashville and the Edgefield & Kentucky lines, was similarly torched. Prominent physician John Berrien Lindsley, who was working that night, saw the burning of both bridges and in awe confided to his diary that he had "never witnessed a more strikingly beautiful scene . . . The wire bridge was a line of flooring of fire, the railroad bridge a perfect framework of flame; the whole lit up brilliantly the quiet sleeping city and suburbs."5

The dismal winter rains continued almost nonstop. They flooded the Cumberland and its feeder creeks and inundated some tracks and bridges

on the Nashville & Chattanooga line. Forrest had had to haul part of the
supplies he saved, including large amounts of meat, by wagon several miles
south of Nashville to get them onto rail cars of the Tennessee & Alabama
Railroad. On February 23, two days after Floyd had ordered him to evacuate,
he and his forty-man rearguard detachment closed out their Nashville
labors. They were moving a last shipment of ammunition and loading a final
procession of wagons for departure southward to Columbia when some concerned Nashvillians approached. That morning, a large crowd on the
Nashville wharf had watched Mayor Cheatham cross to Edgefield in a small
boat to confer with Federals beginning to appear on the far side of the Cumberland. Now, fearing reprisal by the invaders, the mayor had delegated this
group of local citizens to ask Forrest to leave.

He agreed to comply, then punctuated his departure with an explosion
and arson. The cavalryman and his little band of troopers blew up an arsenal, set its undestroyed contents afire, and spurred their horses toward
Murfreesboro. Despite the Forrest detachment's four days of hard work, the
Confederate army lost half its Nashville stockpiles and supplies. The estimated value was five million dollars.[6]

Behind them, Mayor Cheatham remained busy, seeking a Federal officer
with enough rank to accept the city's surrender. Twice that day, Cheatham
visited Edgefield. The first time he found only a cavalry captain; the second,
a colonel. Following each visit, he addressed crowds in the public square to
report his findings. He had been assured that their rights and property
would be protected, he said, adding that they should go about their usual
business.

"Property" was of especial concern. On that harrowing Stampede Sunday
of a week earlier, members of one church heard their pastor advise them "to
quietly retire from the city for fear of an insurrection" by "the servile population." Now, on Cheatham's second trip across the Cumberland, the city's
chief executive asked for the specific policy the conquerors would follow in
regard to "the negro question." He "received for reply that the Federals
came to re-establish the Union and to offer the protection guaranteed by
the Constitution of the United States, and that, in this spirit, the property of
every citizen, of whatever description, would be protected."[7]

Federal protection took its time arriving, though. Forrest and his forty
men had remained in the city so long that when Buell, ponderous and ob-
sessed with the defensive, arrived with nine thousand footsore Federals at
Edgefield on the night of February 24, a report that a small contingent of
Confederate cavalry was still in the city delayed him further. He did not want
to cross the Cumberland "until I could do so in sufficient force as to run no

great hazard," Buell reported. Nine thousand men against forty (who in ac-
tuality had retreated the day before) would seem "sufficient force" to most
officers, but not Buell.

Nashville, albeit undefended, was nevertheless a gift that Buell had to be
forced to accept. His close friend McClellan had fended off Halleck's demands for ascendancy in the West; Halleck, in turn, kept Grant and Foote at
arm's length as they pleaded to continue pushing the retreating Confederates southward. The blood and other suffering of Grant's men had made
Nashville's fall inevitable, but McClellan had designated Buell for the acclaim of capturing it. Grant captured it anyway, by proxy. Buell woke up in
Edgefield on February 25 to learn with embarrassment that his own subordinate, Brigadier General William (Bull) Nelson, had arrived at dawn on a
dozen steamboats and landed seven thousand men across the Cumberland.
He had done so on orders from Grant.

Even then, Buell considered bringing Nelson's men back across the Cumberland. On February 26, Buell wrote that he "deemed it unadvisable" to
withdraw Nelson's troops, "lest it should embolden the enemy and have a
bad effect on the people." It was a veiled condemnation of Grant, whose new
major general's stars made him senior to Buell. Buell complained that Nelson's disembarking on the Nashville side of the river left him with little
choice but "to cross with all the force at hand . . . Our force is too small, and
offers a strong inducement to the enemy, only 30 miles distant, with some
30,000 men, to assume the offensive; but I have deemed it necessary to run
the risk."[8]

The day before, February 25, Mayor Cheatham had crossed the river yet
again and practically pushed the keys to the city into Buell's timorous
hands in a formal presentation. A journalist for a St. Louis paper described
the surrendered western mini-metropolis as "a deserted city . . . streets
silent, market places empty, stores closed. Ruin appears at every step . . .
Union feeling—there is none, and people do not pretend to show any."[9]

*   *   *

The Confederates Grant had captured were seeing a different part of America from theirs, and the sight was distasteful in the extreme. Captain Jack
Campbell of the Forty-eighth Tennessee, bound for Camp Chase in Ohio, recalled that the boat trip was made in "cold and disagreeable" weather.

At night we had to pile up like hogs, scarcely room enough for all on the floor,
which was covered over with mud, slop, and tobacco spittle . . . This night

[February 19] we lay over at Cairo, having passed Paducah early in the evening, where the Federal soldiers stationed there gathered on the wharf as we passed by and seemed to rejoice very much at our misfortune. Our boys, determined not to be outdone, cheered lustily for Jeff Davis. [On February 20] our boat proceeded up the Mississippi River, which was very full of ice . . . At two points the boats were fired into from the shore and several prisoners were wounded. All the railroad bridges on the Missouri side were guarded.

At some stops, though, they were gratified to discover many Southern sympathizers. "[A]t St. Louis late in the evening . . . a crowd of citizens . . . on top of a boat . . . made a great to-do over us[,] somewhat surprising us at seeing such a strong Southern sentiment there. They gave us baskets of apples, cake, and tobacco."

At St. Louis, the officers and enlisted men were separated. Campbell was put aboard the *Hiawatha*, which then was towed out into the middle of the river "to prevent, I suppose, us seeing the Southern sentiment manifested by the fair daughters of St. Louis." If that was indeed the purpose of the towing, it was in vain. Secession sympathizers approached on ferries to throw edibles onto the *Hiawatha* and to help the prisoners exchange Confederate money for Federal, "dollar for dollar." Soon the guards "were particular to keep us at a respectful distance . . . Boys were frequently arrested and ladies insulted for buying apples and having them thrown into the [*Hiawatha*]."

After a couple of days, Federal guards transferred Campbell and his fellow officers to the *Nebraska*, but the Confederate-sympathizing boys and women continued to come out "in the cold and wind . . . Saw two small boys arrested for throwing apples on the boat and a Federal officer shake his fist in a lady's face (for the same offense). A Confederate officer cut a button off his uniform and threw it to a lady . . . She stooped forward to get it[,] when the guard thrust his bayonet in front to push her back. She pushed it out of the way and secured the button." On February 26, a Confederate-sympathizing acquaintance brought Campbell the first change of clothes he had had since his frantic straggle from Fort Henry. The next day, thanks to some of the St. Louis ladies, the prisoners also received the first soap they had seen since boarding the transports.

But St. Louis was soon behind them. That same day, the 27th, they were ordered to "get up our bundles" and made to march a mile to railroad cars bound for Columbus, Ohio. That night was "very disagreeable—so crowded—great many sick"—as they traveled with no heat, no light, and no drinking water. When they paid people at stops to bring them water, the payees frequently took their money and disappeared.

"When we arrived [at Xenia, Ohio,] some abolitionists came to the window and commenced talking to Frank J. McClain's (negro) boy, Wilse, telling him that he was now as free as any one and that he ought to leave his master."[10]

Chaplain Deavenport and enlisted men of the Third Tennessee endured jeers and taunts from "great crowds . . . at all landings" until their steamboat brought them to Alton, Illinois, where a quarter-century earlier abolitionist newspaper editor Elijah Lovejoy had been assassinated. There they found a few "sympathizers . . . among the ladies, but generally speaking we met only with insults."

At Alton, Deavenport and the Third Tennessee also were made to board a train, as Jack Campbell and the Forty-eighth had been, but Deavenport's was bound for Chicago. He and his fellow prisoners arrived there about 1 p.m. on February 23, the Sunday on which Forrest departed Nashville. The experience was horrifically unforgettable. According to Deavenport:

> It was a gloomy day, the rain had thawed the ground some two or three inches deep. The [railroad] cars ran near the prison, but we were carried some two miles beyond into the heart of the city that the citizens might see us. It was a day that can never fade from memory. The streets were muddy, we were placed in the center, a strong guard on each side with orders to bayonet us if we did not keep the middle of the street . . . And now came a scene that . . . I pray to God never to see again. On every hand crowds of men, women and children. Every door, window, fence and every foot of ground was occupied . . . . All were there and seemed to vie with each other to see who could insult us the most . . . They seemed at a loss to determine what we were, whether men or animals . . . Children were heard to exclaim, "Ma, they are white like us." All were wild with joy . . . The milk of human kindness seemed turned into gall in their breasts. In that vast crowd no friendly, pitying eye was seen . . . Women walked through the mud by our side at least a mile, not to comfort, but laugh at us.

There was, though, a heartening feature. An orderly of Deavenport's company had kept a pet rooster named Jake, a mascot who had managed not to be eaten by the soldiers during Donelson's privations and with them had braved its battles. As his comrades slogged drearily along amid the hoots of the Illinois civilians, Jake rode his master's knapsack, and the fowl seemed "to possess something of the unconquerable spirit" of its fellow Confederates. "Every few steps," Deavenport wrote, Jake would throw back his head and crow.

The doleful procession finally neared the prison, Camp Douglas, a wind-lashed sixty acres that had been laid out beside Lake Michigan for the training of Illinois volunteers. The captives saw the Stars and Stripes hanging across the middle of the street "for us to walk under." When they reached it, though, the double file of prisoners disdained their guards' bayonets and parted in the middle, avoiding their erstwhile country's flag. Half of them took one side of the street, half the other.[11]

February 16–March 13, Grant-Halleck

"Enemys Between You and Myself"

ALL TOO SOON, Grant learned that his Fort Donelson joys would not be unalloyed. Although the victory dramatically infused his shaky reputation with an aura of power, it also prompted his Union foes to try even harder to break him. None would try harder than his superior, Machiavellian Henry Halleck. Early on, though, the Donelson victory seemed to solve all problems in that quarter.

About the time of Nashville's formal surrender, Grant got what had to have been a very welcome letter from Lieutenant Colonel James B. McPherson of Halleck's staff.

McPherson, like so many other unwounded officers and men who had undergone the ghastly privations at Henry and Donelson, had become dangerously sick in the wake of the fighting. Unlike most, he was able to return to St. Louis for medical attention. Writing on February 21, he told Grant he hoped "to join you next week" and, in a substantial and chatty letter, confided that "the joy and excitement which pervaded this community" because of the fall of the forts was impossible to describe.

> *Genl. Halleck is exceedingly gratified and says you could not have done better—Immediately upon receipt of the news he telegraphed to the President to nominate you for a Major General. You will not be troubled anymore by Kountz. His character is found out and I think he will be dismissed.*

McPherson was not alone among Grant's assigned monitors who became admirers. Two other men sent or self-appointed to check up on his drinking before and during the Henry and Donelson campaigns—John Rawlins, and Lieutenant William Rowley, who was close to Grant congressional sponsor Washburne—had ended up being defenders. This was despite, or maybe because of, the fact that Grant, while not abrasive, had never gone out of his way to impress them. Sherman recalled barely noticing him at West Point, although they were there for a year together. But the closer many people got to this man whose reserve kept him from getting too close to almost anyone, the more they seemed to like him. Possibly it was the laconic perseverance with which he tackled both war and life. In any case, it usually did not take Grant long to inspire devotion in subordinates. He seems to have gained McPherson's loyalty between the time when he was temporarily assigned by Halleck to Grant on January 31, and the Donelson surrender two and a half weeks later.

What McPherson told Halleck on the subject of drinking when he returned to St. Louis is not known. McPherson may have been too socially correct a man to volunteer that kind of information, but he unquestionably had come to like Grant. They were fellow Ohioans: McPherson the son of a poor blacksmith who became mentally incompetent while his son was growing up. The boy worked in a store until a benefactor befriended him and helped get him an education, first at an academy, and then at West Point, where he graduated at the top of his class. He shared with Grant a firm grounding in life's vicissitudes that was perhaps their common bond.

McPherson's letter from St. Louis, in addition to disclosing Halleck's reaction to the Donelson victory, imparted other information on Halleck's affairs that had to have been burningly interesting to Grant:

> *Genl. Halleck says Genl. Hunter* [commander of the Department of Kansas] *behaved nobly, but Buel acted like a dog in the manger—The former transferred nearly all his troops to Missouri and placed them at Hallecks disposal* [during the Henry-Donelson campaign] *—while the latter would not cooperate at all—Genl. Halleck telegraphed to him his position, and told him the rebels were reinforcing Donelson from Bowling Green and asking him to advance, and he replied he could not on account of the mud—the Genl. then telegraphed him to make a demonstration & he replied that he never made demonstrations, now I suppose he will claim all the credit of having forced the rebels to evacuate Bowling Green—for the life of me in times like this I cannot see why men are not willing to act for the good of the cause and not self—My hand is not very steady as I have been taking medicine & I don't know whether you can make this out— Give my regards to all the members of your staff & hoping soon to be with you I am . . .*[1]

McPherson *was* soon back with Grant. On February 16, from Donelson, Grant had requested that Halleck permanently assign McPherson to his staff. The next week, Grant similarly appointed Rowley of the Forty-fifth Illinois Infantry. Grant likely did not know for certain the initial missions of either man, but their connections to powerful people interested in his habits had to have been fairly obvious. Why they might have been placed in his vicinity must have occurred to him. McPherson, for example, was an engineer, and Grant's own chief of staff, Webster, not only was an engineer but also a highly accomplished one, having helped design the raising of the level of land in downtown Chicago above that of the adjacent waters of Lake Michigan. Grant's request to have both McPherson and Rowley permanently assigned to his staff may have been meant as a signal that he was sober and intended to stay that way. He also ended up immensely liking the two, possibly because of the manner in which they seemed to approach the work at hand. He highly valued men who kept their mouths shut and did their jobs. In the Henry-Donelson campaign, McPherson turned out to be one of the finest of those people, and Grant would never forget it.

A few days before getting the McPherson letter, Grant received one from another willing co-worker, the onetime upperclassman who had hardly noticed him at West Point. William T. Sherman was now giving Grant his undivided attention. Sherman, another Ohio native, had been sent in mid-February by Halleck to Paducah, Kentucky, at the mouth of the Tennessee River, to facilitate movement of men and materiel to Grant at Fort Donelson. He had written Grant on February 15: "I . . . will do everything in my power to hurry forward to you reinforcements and supplies, and if I could be of service to you myself would gladly come, without making any question of rank." Sherman's brigadier general's commission predated Grant's—he also was, unknown to Grant, one of the people whom Halleck was trying to draft to replace the Donelson commander. Yet in another letter the same day Sherman was, if anything, more emphatic in asserting that in his mind rank distinctions were far subordinate to the job at hand. "Command me in any way," he wrote.[2]

The respect and sensitivity in such communications were not lost on Grant. To the contrary, on the occasion of his promotion two years later to lieutenant general, in 1864, Grant would write to Sherman to inform him of the fact and add: "I want to express my thanks to you and to McPherson, as the men to whom, above all others, I feel indebted for whatever I have had of success."[3]

*   *   *

Some of the contents of McPherson's February 21 letter had to have been highly intriguing to Grant. The Donelson victor already knew that he had been promoted to major general, but he had heard no personal congratulatory word from Halleck—who, along with the rest of the St. Louis loyalists, went all but out of control in exultation over Donelson.

Throughout Grant's day of triumph, Halleck still knew nothing of it, although on that date he did get word that a Federal assault had managed to penetrate some of the fort's trenches. He did not know the ultimate outcome, though, until late the next morning, February 17. A wire came from Cairo, where Henry Walke's *Carondelet* had arrived a little earlier, whistle blowing, with Grant's telegram. Halleck put a bulletin of the Donelson victory on the wall outside the posh Planter's House and then, smoking a cigar, called for a clerk to bring two baskets of champagne and open it for the cheering throng. "I want you to give public notice," Halleck giddily told the clerk, "that I shall suspect the loyalty of any male resident of St. Louis who can be found sober enough to walk or speak within the next half-hour." Fifteen hundred people gathered in front of his headquarters to give three cheers each for Foote and him, according to the *Chicago Tribune*, which neglected to mention any cheers for Grant, the former St. Louis resident. (The *Tribune*, of course, was no Grant admirer, its editors having repeatedly expressed private worry that he possessed an unseemly thirst.) When the St. Louis crowd demanded a speech, Halleck obliged—and neglected to mention that he had never ordered Grant to take Fort Donelson and had instead ordered him to entrench and try to hang on at Fort Henry. Now, though, Halleck nimbly appropriated the credit for the smashing triumph.

"I promised when I came here that with your aid I would drive the enemies of our flag from your state," he declaimed to wild applause. "This has been done, and they are virtually out of Kentucky and will soon be out of Tennessee!"[4]

He quickly tried to capitalize on Grant's victory by grasping for more authority to deal with the increasingly fluid front. There was evidence of Confederate movement from now-flanked Columbus and Halleck loudly professed to fear an attack on Paducah, Cairo, or Fort Henry; a fourth, and more realistic, option for the Columbus Confederates was simply to retreat, which was what Polk actually was doing. Halleck also insisted that Johnston was about to make a stand at Clarksville—at a moment when Johnston's army was in the process of moving beyond Murfreesboro seventy miles south of Clarksville. This "is the crisis of the war in the west," Halleck shrilled in one of several wires to McClellan on February 17. That same day, learning of Grant's victory, he demanded supreme command in the West "in return for Forts Henry and Donelson." But he forbade Grant and Foote from following up the Donelson victory while he immersed himself in military politics. Spreading hearsay that "fifteen steamers loaded with troops have reached Columbus" from New Orleans, he continued to shamelessly importune, beg, and wheedle McClellan for authority over Buell. A more objective observer would have understood that McClellan was far too friendly with Buell to confer any such thing.5

As Halleck held his impatient subordinate back, he continued to try to replace him—with almost anybody. On February 17, in the first flush of the victory news, he had wired McClellan of his intention to go down and take over Grant's army himself. The next day, he tried for the third time to give Grant's job to Buell, who refused to take it. On February 19, Halleck indicated to McClellan that he was considering assigning Major General David Hunter, the Department of Kansas commander, to take over Grant's army. Almost manically, he appeared to give the credit for Grant's victory to anybody but Grant. He informed Hunter that, "more than to any other man out of this department," Hunter was due recognition for the Donelson victory because he sent reinforcements when Halleck was desperately trying to swell Grant's army between the rivers. That same day, February 19, he sent McClellan another wire, this time saying that General Smith deserved the praise for the Donelson victory and should be honored for it; "the whole country will applaud." He continued in a similar vein with McClellan, Assistant Secretary of War Thomas A. Scott, and others in authority, always at Grant's obvious expense. McClellan, for his part, kept these strident entreaties at arm's length while trying to prod the balky Buell to get on down to Nashville and pick up the laurels there. At the same time, the Union army's overall commander berated both Buell and Halleck for not keeping him supplied with frequent updates of the changing situations in their departments.6

Now was no time for Grant to give Halleck another opening to criticize him directly, but on February 26, with no such intention, he did. Increasingly restless and inquisitive in dispatches to his superiors as to "what the next move will be," Donelson's eager victor announced in a February 25 letter to Halleck chief of staff Cullum that he intended to go to Nashville "immediately after the arrival of the next mail should there be no orders [in the mail] to prevent it." The purpose of a Nashville visit was to "have an interview with the comdg. officer and learn what I can of the movements of the enemy," Grant wrote to Julia on his proposed date of departure.7

He received no contradictory order, and on February 26 he headed up the Cumberland toward Nashville. At Clarksville, he was surprised to find the same steamboats that, on his orders, had taken General Nelson's troops to Nashville a couple of days earlier. Now they were back at Clarksville taking on more troops. Grant disembarked from his own steamboat and called on Smith, whom he had put in command at Clarksville, to find out what was happening. Smith showed him a panicked-sounding order that had just arrived from Buell in Nashville. Buell claimed that Nelson's landing in the Tennessee capital, rather than across the river in Edgefield, "has compelled me to hold this side [of the Cumberland] at every hazard." If Johnston attacked, "and I am assured by reliable persons that, in view of my position, such is his intention," the Buell force of fifteen thousand was "altogether inadequate," Buell scolded. He therefore was ordering Smith—Grant's subordinate, not Buell's—up from Clarksville to Nashville as fast as the steamboats could bring him. Grant, with his seemingly touchy insecurity regarding the prerogatives of rank, had to be especially conscious that his new major general's commission made him Buell's senior.

Grant had to feel wronged in many ways. In sending Nelson down in the first place, Grant had thought he was doing Buell and the Union's Tennessee campaign a favor. Nelson had been released, tardily, by Buell to reinforce Grant at Donelson, but Donelson had fallen before Nelson got there. So Grant had sent Nelson back to Buell, assuming Buell needed Nelson's troops more in Nashville. He also thought that when they arrived Buell could use the steamboats carrying them to ferry the rest of his men across the Cumberland from Edgefield. In doing this presumed favor, Grant of course had no idea that Buell did not *want* to be on the other side of the Cumberland, the same side that Albert Sidney Johnston's Confederates were on. Grant surgeon Brinton later voiced a sentiment doubtless felt by many Grant men. Brinton wrote in a letter home that by ordering Nelson to Nashville, Grant had "captured Nashville with Buell's men, Buell himself being an unwilling spectator from the . . . wrong side of the river."

Buell, a distinguished prewar career soldier whose rank nevertheless was brigadier general, seemed to want to tell the new Major General Grant, as he had told Major General Halleck, that he—General-in-Chief McClellan's friend and mentor—would do what he liked, rank be damned. Emphasizing his disdain for Grant's promotion, Buell had sent the steamboats back to Clarksville, ordered up Smith out of Grant's command, and by inference sneered at Grant's instruction to Nelson to go to Nashville. Smith remarked to Grant that the order he had received from Buell was "nonsense." Grant, prudent in dealing with military peers, said it nonetheless had to be obeyed, and Smith agreed. He continued putting his men aboard the steamers as fast as possible, and Grant re-boarded his own steamer and went on to the state capital he had captured with Buell's army.

He had written Julia that he was going to Nashville to see the "cmdg officer" there—Buell—to learn his views on Confederate movements, and after the Clarksville stop he had even more reason to see Buell. Buell, at the same time, had reason not to want to face Grant. So Grant spent most of his Nashville day waiting for Buell, who remained in Edgefield, to cross the Cumberland.

In contrast to the almost incessant rainy ones since the onset of the Fort Henry fighting, this day was "beautiful," the trip "pleasant," and Nashville "a most beautiful city, with a magnificent capitol building, & better than all, the old flag waving over it," according to W. H. L. Wallace, who was along. Writing his wife the day he returned, Wallace reported that he and McClernand visited presidential widow Mrs. James K. Polk and found her "'secesh' but a very lady like person." They also discovered about eighty-five Union prisoners taken at Fort Donelson, including approximately forty (likely captured by Forrest) from Wallace's home regiment, the Eleventh Illinois.

Late in the day, still having seen nothing of Buell, Grant sent a note across to Edgefield saying that the hour was getting so late that he was going to have to return to Fort Donelson. Only then did Buell cross the river, and the two generals met on the Nashville wharf. The encounter was brusque. Grant told Buell that all his information indicated that the Confederates were withdrawing as fast as they could. Buell dismissed Grant's opinion, saying fighting had been reported as close as ten miles away.

"Quite probably," Grant replied. "Nashville contained valuable stores of arms, ammunition, and provisions, and the enemy is probably trying to carry away all he can." He added that any fighting had to be skirmishing between Union scouts and Confederates guarding the rear of the supply-trains they were trying to save from Union capture. In other words, Buell should have been thinking more of pursuing and hindering the Confederate salvage effort than worrying about being attacked. Perhaps offended by Grant's recitation of realities which should have been obvious, Buell stoutly differed, maintaining that Nashville was in real danger of being assailed. The normally mild Grant protested that he believed his own information was correct. Buell said he "knew" his information was.

"Well, I do not 'know,'" Grant acknowledged, implying that Buell did not either. With a verbal shrug and sigh, Grant added that Smith was loading his troops at Clarksville and would soon arrive, as Buell had ordered. Rest easy, Grant might as well have told him; Smith will defend you and Nashville from the Confederate phantoms.[8]

Grant was, of course, correct that the main body of Johnston's army was long gone. He was wrong, though, about the direction in which most of the Confederates were heading. That Johnston had gone southeast to Murfreesboro indicated to Grant that the Confederate commander's destination was Chattanooga, which was possibly what Johnston wanted the Federals to think. And, perhaps indicating the quality of Grant's sources of information, Johnston *had* sent Floyd with twenty-five hundred men to Chattanooga on February 25, the day before Grant's trip to Nashville. But after initially putting the rest of his troops on southeast-bound trains out of Murfreesboro on February 26, Johnston debarked them and headed due south to strike the Memphis & Charleston tracks in northern Alabama. There—rather than farther southeast at Stevenson, Alabama, which he had first considered his fallback point—he would be much nearer Corinth, Mississippi, where he could link up with the Beauregard-Polk army retreating from Columbus. At Corinth he would concentrate all the Confederate troops that could be had and mount an offensive to try to retake all the ground lost by the fall of forts Henry and Donelson.

From Nashville, Grant went back to Clarksville and then to Fort Donelson to try to ready his troops for the next advance. He spent several days trying to get the wagons left behind at Cairo when he left there for Fort Henry. He also had lost significant numbers of soldiers in the Donelson battle and from sickness afterward. On March 2, Halleck ordered him to return to Fort Henry to prepare for a two-pronged expedition down the Tennessee River. The two targets were to be Paris, a northern Tennessee town on the Memphis, Clarksville & Louisville Railroad, and, much farther south, a bridge at Eastport, Mississippi, on the Memphis & Charleston. Halleck's aim was to prevent Johnston from reuniting his own army with the Polk-Beauregard wing, which on March 1 burned and evacuated its fortress on the Mississippi River bluffs at Columbus, Kentucky.

Grant was eagerly anticipating moving forward again. He seemed to feel that on the Donelson ridges he had vanquished and left behind his career's old demons and was ready to get on with the war. In the letter to Julia the day before he left for Nashville on February 26, Grant had written that "in spite of enemies"—and he obviously did not mean Confederates—"I have so far progressed satisfactorily to myself and the country and in reviewing the past can see but few changes that could have bettered the result."

When he arrived back at Fort Henry, though, he found that he had been mistaken. His Federal foes proved more powerful than he had assumed. McPherson's cheery assessment of the Kountz situation, and by implication all continued linking of Grant and whisky, was premature.9

*   *   *

Halleck now proceeded to show how unfair, mean-spirited, and maliciously dishonest he could be. His behavior toward Grant in early March of 1862 indicated why fellow attorney Edwin Stanton, after investigating Halleck's financial dealings in California, could brand him "destitute of principle." Wanting to fire a subordinate you sincerely believe is unqualified is one thing; smearing him with lies is another. Halleck showed most of these qualities only to history, however. He was a master at covering his tracks.

Grant, of course, knew none of these things. Since leaving Cairo a month earlier, he had found his communications with St. Louis erratic. Although a telegraph line was being pushed toward Tennessee following the Fort Henry and Fort Donelson battles, communications to Grant had to be brought southward from Cairo by boat. Similarly, Grant's dispatches to Halleck's headquarters had to go by boat to Cairo (where Halleck's very close friend and chief of staff, George Cullum, had been installed closer to the action) and then be telegraphed on to St. Louis. Most of Halleck's communications to Grant during and following the campaign had been arriving late or not at all. This was apparently because a telegrapher on the Union line was a Confederate spy who eventually decamped, taking some unsent messages to Grant with him.

So Grant had no prior warning that, in the wake of his great victory, he remained in deep trouble with his commander. He only learned it, out of the blue, in a cryptic, crushing Halleck wire dated March 4: "You will place Major Genl Smith in command of expedition, & remain yourself at Fort Henry. Why do you not obey my orders to report strength and positions of your command?"[10]

Twenty-three years later Grant would write, with his usual understatement, that he was "surprised" by the message. Thunderstruck would have been a better word, although not one the outwardly unexcitable Grant would have ever used. He had had no congratulation from Halleck, but at least he had received McPherson's private assurance that Halleck thought the performance at Donelson "couldn't have been better." Now suddenly Halleck had berated him for not complying with Halleck orders he had never received—when actually he had fastidiously written to headquarters regarding his every move. He turned for advice and solace to his mentor, Smith, who soon wrote a friend: "Fancy his surprise when he received no communication from the General for two weeks after the fall of Donelson, and then a telegram of bitterest rebuke! He showed it to me in utter amazement, wondering at the cause, as well he might."[11]

Grant had received no previous inquiry from Halleck about his troop numbers, quite possibly for reasons having nothing to do with the secession-sympathizing telegrapher. According to available records of correspondence sent out from his office, Halleck had made no such inquiry. He had, however, been busy making queries elsewhere, undermining Grant in every important quarter. On March 3, Halleck wrote McClellan that he had "had no communication with General Grant for more than a week" and then launched a shameful character assassination behind Grant's back:

> *He left his command without my authority and went to Nashville. His army seems to be as much demoralized by the victory of Fort Donelson as was that of the Potomac by the defeat of Bull Run. It is hard to censure a successful general after a victory, but I think he richly deserves it. I can get no returns, no reports, no information of any kind from him. Satisfied with his victory, he sits down and enjoys it without any regard to the future. I am worn-out and tired with this neglect and inefficiency. C. F. Smith is almost the only officer equal to the emergency.*

McClellan almost certainly now recalled his own infuriating old-army encounter with a drunken Grant in the Northwest. The same day, he wired back a strong suggestion approved by Secretary of War Stanton: that Halleck put his unkempt subordinate under arrest "if the good of the service requires it." McClellan added a line indicating that he was all too familiar with Grant's best-known failing. In this wire of which every previous sentence had to do with Grant, McClellan assured Halleck: "I appreciate the difficulties you have to encounter." With that encouragement, Halleck, the next day, March 4, added the note that he surely knew could consign Grant to military oblivion once and for all. "A rumor has just reached me that since the taking of Fort Donelson General Grant has resumed his former bad habits. If so, it will account for his neglect of my oft-repeated orders. I do not deem it advisable to arrest him at present, but have placed General Smith in command of the expedition up the Tennessee. I think Smith will restore order and discipline."[12]

Halleck's citation of "a rumor" was almost certainly untrue. Given the tone and substance of McPherson's February 21 letter to Grant, it seems obvious that no rumor of "bad habits" was carried by McPherson; if anything, McPherson apparently told Halleck just the opposite. Lew Wallace had been sent back to Fort Henry the day of the surrender. McClernand and other officers and staff members were along on the February 28 trip to Nashville, which undoubtedly would have discouraged Grant from doing any drinking then even had he considered it.

Halleck's use of the equivocal term "rumor" makes it seem very possible that there was no such thing. His foundation for bringing up the subject, besides McClellan's veiled reference, may well have been no "rumor" but, rather, the very official and still-fresh Kountz material. A copy of it surely remained somewhere on his desk, and he likely assumed McClellan had seen or at least heard about the one forwarded to Secretary Stanton.

By again bringing up the bottle, the St. Louis chief obviously sought to tarnish Unconditional Surrender Grant in the estimation of the White House and keep viable his own plan to replace the Donelson victor.[13]

Halleck's short wire ordering Grant to turn over the Tennessee River expedition to Smith evoked an immediate and stunned response. On March 5, Grant wrote back that he was complying with Halleck's instructions and added: "I am not aware of ever having disobeyed any order from Head Quarters, certainly never intended such a thing. I have reported almost daily the condition of my command and reported every position occupied."[14]

Dismayed by Halleck's wire, Grant wrote a short note to Julia that night and explained that he was "in a very poor humor for writing. I was ordered to command a very important expedition up the Tennessee river and now an order comes directing one of my juniors to take the command whilst I am left behind here with a small garrison. It may be all right but I dont now see it."[15]

The next day he received a fuller, stiffer, and even less merited reprimand from Halleck. Claiming that McClellan had asked for daily reports of "the numbers and positions of the forces under your command," Halleck added that Grant's "neglect of repeated orders" to supply that information "has created great dissatisfaction & seriously interfered with military plans. Your going to Nashville without authority & when your presence with your troops was of the utmost importance was a matter of very serious complaint at Washington, so much so that I was advised to arrest you on your return."[16]

Halleck, of course, had not been "advised" to do that; he had been told to if he thought it was necessary to the welfare of the army. McClellan also had *not* asked for daily reports from Grant; he had, on February 21, chided *Halleck*, as well as Buell, for not keeping him abreast of matters in *their* headquarters.

Grant had no way of knowing any of this, but he had had enough.

When he received the second Halleck message he had had twenty-four hours to digest the first, and he now counterattacked with the same aggressive spirit with which he had grabbed Paducah, assailed Belmont, and launched the Donelson countercharges of February 15. He wrote Halleck from Fort Henry on March 7:

Your dispatch of yesterday just received. I did all I could to get you returns of the strength of my command. Evry move I made was reported daily to your Chief of Staff, who must have failed to keep you properly posted. I have done my very best to obey orders and to carry out the interests of the service. If my course is not satisfactory, remove me at once. I do not wish to impede in any way the success of our arms. I have averaged writing more than once a day, since leaving Cairo, to keep you informed of my position; and it is no fault of mine if you have not received my letters. My going to Nashville was strictly intended for the good of the service and not to gratify any wish of my own.

Believeing sincerely that I must have enemys [sic] *between you and myself who are trying to impair my usefulness, I respectfully ask to be relieved from further duty in the Dept.*

U. S. Grant
Maj. Gen.[17]

The man ordered to relieve him, his mentor/subordinate Smith, empathized. A visit to Nashville by Grant was "perfectly proper if he thought fit to go," Smith said in a letter to a friend. Grant was, Smith wrote, "a very modest person," but he was not a stupid one. He surely knew that as the conqueror at forts Henry and Donelson, the most important Union triumphs of the war, he could put heavy pressure on Halleck by asking for transfer.

He, or aide John Rawlins, went farther than that—all the way to Washington. Copies of both letters, Halleck's and Grant's, were sent to Illinois congressman Washburne, who promptly took them to the White House. Halleck then swiftly learned that McClellan's permission to remove Grant was not the final word. On March 10 Halleck received a telegram from U.S. Adjutant General Lorenzo Thomas. Speaking for Lincoln and Stanton, Thomas sounded almost as curt as Halleck had in the wires he sent Grant: "By direction of the President[,] the Secretary of War desires you to ascertain and report whether General Grant left his command at any time without proper authority, and, if so, for how long; whether he has made to you proper reports and returns of his force; whether he has committed any acts which were unauthorized or not in accordance with military subordination or propriety, and, if so, what."

Halleck must have been taken aback—if not, indeed, frightened. He was being challenged by no less than the president and the secretary of war to produce proof of what he had written McClellan about Grant. A copy of the Kountz charges was on Stanton's desk as well as Halleck's, and still Stanton, Halleck's old enemy from California days, demanded that he produce details on just what Grant had done that was "unauthorized or not in accordance with military propriety." Halleck's malicious and duplicitous campaign against the winner of the war's most resounding Union victories was suddenly being threatened with high-profile exposure.

Halleck, though, was the only major Union commander whose department—thanks hugely to Grant—was producing results. Lincoln and Stanton had tired of McClellan's arrogant refusal to fight. "Little Mac," sensitive about having won no battles of his own since becoming commander of all the Federal armies, had now taken, and in some quarters had been given, credit for managing by telegraph Grant's victory at Fort Donelson—although there *was* no telegraph line to Donelson.

Stanton asserted that victories could be won only by participants. He had feared disaster at Fort Donelson following the repulse of Foote's gunboats on February 14. But when news arrived of Buckner's capitulation, the usually forbidding secretary read Grant's "unconditional surrender" ultimatum to a Washington crowd at the War Department, then actually leapt in the air and called for three cheers for Grant. And when the *Washington Star* published a story the next day saying the tremendous victory was all due to the magisterial management of McClellan, Stanton took it upon himself to personally write *New York Tribune* editor Charles A. Dana that, rather than the godlike performance described by the *Star*, McClellan's actions in the telegraph office during the battle had been worthy of a cartoon. McClellan, Stanton wrote, had energetically gone through the motions of "by sublime military combinations capturing Fort Donelson six hours after Grant and Smith had taken it sword in hand."[18]

So in their collision over Grant, both Halleck and the White House were walking on eggs; each had to have the support of the other. The day after Lincoln and Stanton pointedly asked for full particulars, rather than innuendo, regarding Grant's behavior, the president gave command of the West to Halleck, and Halleck backed away from firing Grant.

Halleck was not confident of his position with Stanton, who had led that probe of California land swindling and accused Halleck's firm of cheating Mexicans out of the title to the world's largest mercury mine; that case, embarrassingly enough, was now finally coming before the Supreme Court.

So Halleck swiftly wriggled backward. He wrote to Lorenzo Thomas—and, thereby, to Stanton—that he had made the requested investigation into Grant's purported shortcomings and that the subordinate's assumed offenses had been adequately explained. Halleck told Thomas he "respectfully recommend[ed] that no further notice be taken," as "all . . . irregularities have now been remedied."[19]

The blunt Lincoln-Stanton query to Halleck likely had not been intended as a strong personal endorsement of Grant or a stiff warning that he henceforth would be protected property. Instead, its forbidding sound was in the interest of the administration's conduct of the war, a warning to Halleck not to tarnish its first smashing victories, rather than a defense of Grant himself.

Without Donelson, of course, there would have been no White House defense, and Halleck would have been free to relieve him. Notwithstanding

Congressman Washburne's dedicated lobbying on Grant's behalf, Lincoln had congratulated McClernand, not Grant, following the Belmont fight, and the White House for many more months remained much more interested in the influential Illinois ex-congressman. The oft-quoted Lincoln endorsement of Grant that supposedly occurred only a few weeks later—"I can't spare this man; he fights"—may very well be apocryphal, and Stanton, even after his jump for joy at learning of Grant's surrender ultimatum, *had* endorsed McClellan's suggestion to Halleck to arrest Grant if Halleck thought it necessary. A lot more time had yet to pass before Lincoln and Stanton would become decided Grant adherents. James Harrison Wilson would say that, before he came west from Washington to join Grant's staff nine months after Donelson, he had become "satisfied that the chief honors" won by Grant's army "would be given to McClernand, if the president and secretary of war could manage it without a public scandal." Wilson also wrote that "there is no doubt that the administration lent ear" to the many charges against the Donelson victor.[20]

So the administration saved him—because after Fort Donelson it would cause a public scandal to do otherwise. And Halleck, doubtless with sighs of both relief and frustration, hurried off another wire to Grant, who by now had asked again to be "relieved from further duty until I can be placed right in the estimation of those higher in authority." To cool the brewing controversy and keep Grant from sending his resignation further up the chain of command, Halleck unceremoniously reversed his position of a week earlier. He wrote Grant that he could not "be relieved from command. There is no good reason for it . . . Instead of relieving you, I wish you, as soon as your new army is in the field, to assume the immediate command & lead it on to new victories."[21]

37

Mid-March, Harvest of Donelson

A Military Governor

BY NOW, THE TWIN VICTORIES at forts Henry and Donelson were reaping far-reaching political, as well as military, harvests. Tennessee had become the first seceded state to be reclaimed, even though only partially, and Lincoln needed to reinstate it in the Union as swiftly as possible to signify that secession's national gulf was just temporary and was being steadily bridged. How to accomplish the reinstatement was the question.

Buell, almost as soon as he could be pushed into Nashville, began counseling that the makeup of a new civilian administration should be as close to the antebellum one as possible. On February 28 he advised McClellan to "use all the means you have to induce the President to pursue a lenient course, and as far as possible to reconstruct the machinery of the General Government out of material here, of which an abundance can be found that is truly loyal, though for some time overpowered and silenced."

But Tennessee was complicated. Even before the war the state had been deeply divided several ways: between Democrats and old-line Whigs, the eastern mountains and the western cotton delta, slaveholders and non-slaveholders, comparatively poor mountaineers and plantation-tilling aristocrats. It was all but impossible for such a recent newcomer as Buell to *know* who was "truly loyal," especially with throngs of slaveholders claiming to be, in order to evade the Confiscation Law and retain their "property." So Lincoln took some, but markedly not all, of Buell's advice. He decided to reconstruct Tennessee out of Tennessee material, all right, but the Tennessean he chose to head it, although the owner of a handful of slaves, was a lightning rod, not an olive branch. U.S. Senator Andrew Johnson, whose six-year term was near its end with no hope of another under his state's partially recaptured circumstances, had made powerful secession-decrying speeches in late 1860 and throughout 1861 while many other national leaders wrung their hands. On March 3, against Buell's specific advice, Lincoln chose Johnson to become Tennessee's military governor. The most obvious problem with it

was that, because of Buell's stolid resistance against Lincoln's repeated be-
seeching, the eastern mountains that were Johnson's home area and political base remained in Confederate hands. Lincoln had assigned this Tennessee maverick to govern territory historically controlled by his enemies.

Nonetheless, it was Johnson who on March 7 boarded a Washington train
on a necessarily roundabout trek to Tennessee. Crossing Pennsylvania and
southern Ohio, he and a small party of colleagues—including loyalist Tennessee congressmen Horace Maynard and Emerson Etheridge—then took a
steamboat from Cincinnati to Louisville. By March 12, Louisville & Nashville
Railroad president James Guthrie had managed to assemble a two-car train
"patched up from odds and ends" that had been left in the wake of the Confederate withdrawal from Bowling Green. The engine resembled "a snorting
wreck on wheels" that barely managed to pull a boxcar.

Just by agreeing to come to Nashville, Johnson had demonstrated that he
was brave. Despised by his state's secessionists (the Memphis *Avalanche* had
described him a year earlier as "Embalmed in hate and canonized in
scorn"), he already was reported to be the object of assassination plots. He
had been warned by Buell that his arrival back in Tennessee should be "without any display," and he and his companions complied. Coming late on the
night of March 12 to a municipality still under the pall of its Federal shock,
the Johnson party found just a single light visible in the whole city from their
rickety conveyance. They were hurried to the gloomy St. Cloud Hotel under
cover of the sheltering darkness.

The following evening Johnson must have been cheered, at least somewhat, by a serenade from a military band. He responded with an hour-long
speech briefly excerpted by the Cincinnati *Commercial.* Claiming to have returned "with no hostile purpose," Johnson nonetheless briefly and porten-
tously referred to suffering that he said was still being endured by his own
family a couple of hundred miles to the east. The Johnsons, and men who
had married them, had personally participated in the November bridge-
burnings and other reprisals against what they regarded as Confederate oppression of unionist East Tennessee. Now they and countless other East Tennesseans continued to pay high prices for their loyalism, forced to hide out
and see many of their houses—including the senator's own—confiscated under a Confederate sequestration law. The new military governor could hardly help coming home resentful.

". . . I come to aid you in the upholding and defending of this the best
Government that God ever spoke into existence!" Johnson declaimed that
evening, employing a phrase he had used on the Senate floor many times in
describing the broken Union. "I have never deserted that Government. How
could I? The exiled—my wife driven hither and thither, her servants stolen,

my home a rebel hospital—how could I desert the glorious Government under which I had been so richly and abundantly blessed . . . ?"

He decried the "wicked deception that had been practiced upon the people" in the election of 1860, when Southern leaders of the Breckinridge, Douglas, and Bell factions all quit the Union as soon as their candidates lost. He said that he himself had been tricked into campaigning in 1860 for Breckinridge, who turned out to be a "disunionist at the time." He said the war had been caused not by slavery, which was "but a pretext," but rather by the "disappointed ambition" of Southern leaders.

Such a contention is explicable only by Johnson's prejudices and the realities of the era. America was overwhelmingly and virulently racist, and white Southerners had been taught for generations to desperately fear emancipation. Even across the North only a minority of whites wanted the war to be about slavery, because most dreaded the bloodbaths and societal upheaval that seemed certain to follow wholesale liberation of the slaves. Johnson's view of the war's cause was influenced not only by his own slave-ownership but also by his unabashed hatred of the rich Gideon Pillows and Jefferson Davises of the world. Like many who pull themselves onto society's upper rungs by their bootstraps, Johnson, a former tailor, took personally any disparaging reference to working people. Fifteen years earlier, when they were both congressmen, Davis had made such a remark in debate, and Johnson had quickly risen to deride the South's "illegitimate, swaggering, bastard, scrub aristocracy." He had despised Davis ever since.

Now, in his first speech as Tennessee's military governor, Johnson soon returned to his earlier theme of personal loss. "Why all this persecution against me and mine?" he asked. "Why am I exiled, driven from my home, and my hard-earnings taken from me? Simply because I adhere to my Government and yours, my flag and your flag, the Government and the flag of your fathers. Because I loved them too well. Because, having been born and bred under them, I have determined to die under them."

The *Commercial* reporter wrote that Johnson's "voice rang out like a clarion through the silent city" as he recounted the bitter harvest that secession was now reaping: "bridges, crops, dwellings destroyed; brother arrayed against brother in deadly conflict; families torn asunder; widows brokenhearted and orphans crying for bread . . . He pointed the eyes of secessionists present to this scene and asked, had they not suffered enough . . . ? Had they not been duped and deceived by such as [Confederate president Jefferson Davis] . . . ?"

That his voice was reported to have rung out over a silent city, with "secessionists present," indicates Johnson's effort produced little applause, but he pushed on. He made a few remarks that were generally pacific in tone, but then referred again to "East Tennessee, where his desolate home was." He beseeched his fellow countrymen to come forward now to its defense and declared "his willingness to share with them any and all dangers for the rescue of Tennessee from the jaws of the infernal monster" of secession. He concluded on a note that he had repeatedly struck on the Senate floor—and that Tennesseans were destined to hear a lot more.

"Traitors should be punished," he said, "and treason crushed."[1]

For Confederate oppression of East Tennessee, retribution was in the wind.

38

February 23–Onward

Forrest: "Come On, Boys"

IN THE WAKE of their flight from Fort Donelson, Floyd and Pillow were disgraced across the South.

An appalled Jefferson Davis ordered them relieved of duty. More than two weeks after the surrender, neither had yet filed a report of his role in the disaster, and on March 4 Confederate Secretary of War Judah Benjamin badgered Johnston for an official account, writing that the Confederate Congress was "very impatient for it." In the same dispatch, Benjamin complained that although Pillow had sent nothing of the kind to Richmond, he "has committed the offense of publishing his report" in newspapers. On March 11, Davis fired Floyd outright. Pillow, though, was a more delicate matter. His fellow Confederate Tennesseans, feeling betrayed by the Richmond government, were as angry at Davis as Davis was at Pillow and Floyd. Davis ended up consigning Pillow to limbo for six months and then tossing him paltry duties from then on.

Forrest shared some of their disrepute, without the official censure. His behavior, of course, had differed from Floyd's and Pillow's in important respects. Unlike his Donelson superiors, he had made several efforts to take away with him as many men as possible. Rather than scurry off on commandeered boats, he had departed on horseback ready to cut his way out with his saber. And he had left none of his responsibilities to be borne by others. Nevertheless, according to a fellow Memphis-rooted Confederate, Forrest was regarded along with the two generals "in certain high quarters"—of the military and the government, apparently—"as guilty of little less than insubordination in getting away from Fort Donelson as [he] did."[1]

In most Confederate quarters, though, Forrest had instantly and widely become a hero, which doubtless influenced Davis. Unlike Floyd and Pillow, the cavalryman had shown himself to be their virtual opposite: the quintessential combatant. How was the Confederacy's president going to convince a shaken Southern populace that an officer wearing an overcoat torn by fifteen bullets and splashed with the blood of his own horses deserved censure? Especially censure for insubordination to generals unworthy of his servitude, when his leaving was out of disgust at their refusal to keep fighting? And after Donelson, two weeks before Davis began taking action in the matter by dismissing Floyd, Forrest had gone well past the extra mile in saving as many supplies as possible at Nashville.

Like Floyd and Pillow, Forrest received no hint of disapproval from Albert Sidney Johnston. The commander of the Confederate West, almost universally held responsible for losing two-thirds of Tennessee, was enduring the hottest popular condemnation of anyone, but he endured it without trying to shift blame.

After Donelson, Forrest needed more men—and soon got them. When he reported to Johnston in Murfreesboro on February 23, the western chief ordered him southward to Huntsville, Alabama. There Forrest gave his riders two-week furloughs and orders to return by March 10. They all did—and many came back with fresh recruits. In addition, whole new companies were brought in from Memphis and other areas of West Tennessee, enlisted by Forrest's brother Jesse and the unit's erstwhile adjutant, C. A. Schuyler. Suddenly regiment-sized, "Forrest's Cavalry" was authorized to elect new officers, and its namesake was declared its colonel by acclamation.

Resting and recruiting at Huntsville, the new colonel doubtless reflected on his war so far. The experience could only push him further along the controversially individual path he had taken all his life. On Dixie's streets, split-second decisiveness in crises had made him more effective than the educated patricians who were viewed as his social superiors. On two military battlefields, he had seen the same hold true.

The contrast between his command decisions and others' seemed night-and-day. At Sacramento, left to his own devices, he had triumphed so spectacularly that the outnumbering of his foe appeared not to matter. At Fort Donelson, serving commanders who in military and civilian life were regarded as his betters, he had seen each prove, when the fire was hottest, to possess faults he did not. Of his two fellow citizen-soldiers among Donelson's four generals, former Secretary of War Floyd had seemed afraid to make a decision, and Pillow had been all too ready to make a wrong one. The two West Pointers, Buckner and Bushrod Johnson, had seemed, if anything, more frightened than Floyd. Buckner, Floyd, and Johnson all had been too timid to reach for victory when it hung in the balance, while the feistier Pillow had suffered lapses of nerve or brain. Going in, the four had been viewed as among the West's better generals. Coming out, they inspired no respect at all.

So Nathan Bedford Forrest, never very deferential to start with, became less so. The Donelson fight had shown him that all the superficial niceties of civilian and military high rank were just window-dressing. War came down to the same thing that counted most in civilian life: the core of the individual, whether that individual had the will to command men and to kill them. Forrest had known long since that he could do both, and with his own hands when necessary. Fort Donelson had shown him that most of his fellow officers, though, were not so sure.

His military manner began to change after that. Previously, his recruiting posters had used genteel terms imitative of the aristocratic class he had scratched and clawed for a quarter-century to join. Doubtless written by newspaper friends whose sheets had advertised his slave-yards, his initial enlistment solicitations had trumpeted an "excellent opportunity" to "those desiring to engage in the cavalry service" to embrace their responsibilities as "freemen" and "rally to the defense of your liberties, your homes and your firesides!" But over the several weeks following the Donelson escape and his extraordinary effort to save the Nashville supplies, the ads reflected less of the labored pretense at refinement and more of the man behind them. Two months after Donelson, the transformation would be complete, and an item would appear in the Memphis *Appeal* inviting two hundred new troopers to arrive at his headquarters "with good horse and gun" and only if they wished "to be actively engaged." It would add:

"Come on, boys, if you want a heap of fun and to kill some Yankees."[2]

Early March 1862, Grant

"Hope to Make a New Subject Soon"

GRANT HAD LEARNED large lessons. Like Forrest, at Donelson he had gotten strong intimations that his pugnacious talents were extraordinary; *un*like Forrest, he had the rank to use them more fully. Always a hard worker, an inveterate attacker in war and in life, Grant had seen his inner essence united at last with good fortune, and the result was a stunning, life-changing victory.

This triumph built confidence, which he almost immediately needed. The Halleck controversy and the Kountz affair made him more prudent in dealing with his own. In the enigmatic episode with Halleck, he found himself thrown from heights he had stormed into a chasm of prospective oblivion. Once more, though, he attacked, sending—or allowing an aide to send—copies of the Halleck correspondence to Congressman Washburne. Halleck's created crisis then vanished, while Kountz's document began yellowing in piles of bureaucratic paper. Grant thus hauled himself out of another valley of despair. Two such all-or-nothing victories in the space of a month pooled inside him the beginnings of an increasing sense of personal power. But he had a personality on which it was not wasted. He would not brandish it.

Now ninety miles west of Nashville, camped on the east bank of the Tennessee River at Fort Henry, he had to have been mystified but happy that the "enemys" between himself and Halleck, whoever they were, had retreated. He had no idea that the greatest of them had been his commander. Halleck had doused that fire by telling Grant that he had been his savior, not the instigator of the affair, and Grant, deeply grateful, was none the wiser.

Grant now realized, though, that he and his commander were oil and water. In a letter to Julia during this period, Grant wrote that he would like to be transferred to a "more independent" position—but added his assessment of Halleck as "one of the greatest men of the age." Sounding suddenly conscious that the letter might become published somewhere, he added that "there are not two men in the United States who I would prefer serving under" than McClellan and the St. Louis commander. "They would be my own chois for the positions they fill if left to me to make."[1]

His brief suspension from command had two personal bright spots. In early March, he was surprised and unquestionably gratified to receive a formal declaration of wholehearted support signed by McClernand, W. H. L. Wallace, and several members of McClernand's staff. The document's language, sounding like McClernand prose, is so strong as to suggest that the drinking rumor Halleck claimed to have heard may have been real after all and that McClernand was trying to bury tracks he might have left.

Soon afterward, aboard the steamboat *Tigress*, Grant was plainly moved to receive an ornamental sword specially ordered by steamboat superintendent George W. Graham and three of Grant's subordinates. One of them, Colonel C. Carroll Marsh of the Twentieth Illinois, said in presenting the item commemorating the Donelson victory that its arrival had "fortunately" been delayed—"fortunately, I say, because at this moment when the jealousy caused by your brilliant success has raised up hidden enemies who are endeavoring to strike you in the dark, it affords us an opportunity to express our renewed confidence in your ability as a commander." Unable to express himself publicly even in front of his own officers and friends, Grant confessed this incapacity, and staff member Hillyer did the honors for him. Surgeon Brinton, who was aboard the *Tigress* that day, later remembered that Grant, "unable to answer and overcome by his emotions," fled through the door of the cabin onto the deck outside. There Brinton, who had been unaware of the sword presentation ceremony, stumbled across him and was surprised at his appearance . . .

"[T]ears were on his face, unmistakably."[2]

*　　*　　*

He had one more hard lesson coming—soon. Restored to command, he would get surprised again at Shiloh in early April, before learning not to take an enemy for granted as he had done with Pillow at Donelson.

In military politics, though, he had graduated. The Kountz arrest was the last incident in which he would act too quickly and too harshly toward enemies in his own ranks. With McClernand and other problematic subordinates, he would wait until he had the high ground and overwhelming ammunition. With McClernand, that would not come until May 1863, after McClernand—similar to Pillow after Donelson—published one of his orders in newspapers before ever sending it to Grant. Grant was besieging Vicksburg at the time and, believing that a misleading McClernand call for reinforcements had cost many needless casualties, finally sent the politician home to Illinois. Grant's forbearance with McClernand was characteristic, but it may also have had roots in the Donelson aftermath. Grant's suspicion during the Halleck intrigue, because of complaints that had been lodged against him from Illinois friends of Lincoln, was that his "enemy" was the president himself—and McClernand was a longtime Lincoln associate.

Grant staff member James Harrison Wilson, who would deliver to McClernand the Grant order removing him, marveled at his chief's "patience and forbearance" in dealing with the scheming ex-congressman. Despite being "inexorable and unrelenting towards one who he thought had intended to do him official and personal injury" (as with Kountz), Grant took care to make no charge against McClernand that would reach Lincoln or the War Department until Grant himself had such military success that his position with the Union public at large "was unassailable," Wilson wrote. Grant did not gladly suffer criticism even from friends, Wilson went on, but he added that Grant refused to quarrel with deficient subordinates, preferring to patiently bear their shortcomings until they could be "quietly but surely eliminated." But any of them foolish enough to criticize his generalship were "more summarily disposed of" the more assured he became of the security of his position.[3]

In crucial ways, Grant remained very much himself. In his post-Donelson letters to Julia, he was pretty much the unassuming and sometimes wryly humorous correspondent he had been before. Six days after the surrender he reported himself "ready for anything even to chasing Floyd & Pillow. There is but little hope however of ever overhawling them . . . I have no doubt but you have read enough of Fort Donelson until you have grown tired of the name so I shall write you no more on the subject. Hope to make a new subject soon. Give my love to all at home. Kiss the children for me and write me all the news." In another letter:

"I hope this war will not continue long and when it does end I want to have a few hundred dollars at least independent of everybody. My pay now is over $6000 per year and I can live off of one thousand even as a Maj. Gen. Keeping my horses is necessarily somewhat expensive but in other particulars I spend but very little."[4]

Again at the head of an army as of mid-March, he was still fighting the bad cold with which he had left Cairo at the beginning of February, but he was eager to go in quest of the "new victories" Halleck requested. On March 15, he wrote another short note to Julia that, before ending with the customary "Kiss the children for me and give my love to all at home—Ulys.," described his new situation. He had been ordered to proceed up the Tennessee, he said, " in command of the whole force." Unknowingly headed

toward Shiloh, he added two sentences that encapsulate the casual fearlessness of this man who in boyhood had swung on horses' tails.

"What you may look for is hard to say, possibly a big fight," he wrote.
"I have already been in so many that it begins to feel like home to me."[5]

Understated as usual, the words hardly sound like those of a Napoleon.
They were from a man in a habitually rumpled jacket who liked to ride horses fast, a man with a superstitious aversion to backing up and retaking steps
he had already taken. So he did not back up. He would go from Donelson to
make another bad mistake at Shiloh but would again hang on and refuse to
lose. And after Shiloh he would endure another, more public drinking furor,
but his Donelson acclaim again would sustain him. He would go on to capture Vicksburg and his career's second army, opening the Mississippi from
Minnesota to the Gulf. Then he would unleash Sherman on Georgia, saving
Lincoln's presidency and thereby winning the war that forever changed
America. Appomattox, where he accepted the surrender of a third Confederate army, was by then a foregone conclusion.

But even in the celebrated 1885 autobiography hailed as the greatest by a
general since Julius Caesar, Grant never sounded like a Napoleon. And he
wasn't one. Unlike Bonaparte, once he got going—at Fort Donelson—
Ulysses Grant was never beaten.

PART V

AFTERMATHS

Aftermaths

The Campaign

The bloodletting at Forts Henry and Donelson turned into a four-year hemorrhage that bled white one nation trying to be born and another trying not to perish. The lucky and yet deserved victories of Foote and Grant shook the slave states to their foundations. The capture of thousands of Confederates at Donelson, coupled with nearly as many who became casualties at Shiloh, forced the Jefferson Davis government, a year before Lincoln's, to institute South-wide conscription to keep armies in the field. It was the first draft in American history.

The Henry-Donelson campaign slashed an ever-widening, mortal wound that split the Confederacy asunder. It also saved and launched the career of Grant, and Grant's victories kept the Abraham Lincoln administration from being swept aside in 1864 by Peace Democrat George McClellan, who pledged to quit the fight and cede victory to Dixie. Unconditional Surrender Grant reunited the United States and rid it of the brutal and damning institution of slavery, permitting it to become a beacon of freedom and the world's most powerful nation.

The War

The Federal high command laxly followed up the captures of Fort Henry, Fort Donelson, and Nashville. Despite Lincoln's urging, his government's decisions were neither astute nor energetic until it finally handed most of the military decision-making to Grant in March 1864.

He never admitted it, but Grant was surprise-attacked by the Confederates again at Shiloh. Unentrenched, his army of about forty thousand was assailed by about the same number of Confederates and nearly pushed into the Tennessee River by the end of the first day. The overnight arrival of Buell's army from Nashville helped Grant launch a counterattack the next day and retake the field from the Confederates. Afterward, it was popularly alleged, with no foundation, that he was drunk when the Confederate attack came. He had to endure a more public scandal that cast him as a sot.

But thanks in great part to renown he already had achieved at Fort Donelson, Grant survived—and eventually returned to field command to capture another army at Vicksburg and, at long last, despite the fabled powers of Robert E. Lee, Lee's Army of Northern Virginia.

The various Confederate surrenders of 1865—from Lee's at Appomattox to Forrest's in Alabama to Kirby Smith's in Texas—followed the filling of untold acres of military cemeteries, innumerable unmarked graves, and all-but-infinite ranks of surviving men, women, and children whose lives were altered forever by the American holocaust.

William J. Kountz

According to his business biography, which seems to have been more of a thinly disguised autobiography, Kountz resigned his military commission shortly after the Donelson battle; his resignation was accepted April 1, 1862. The thumbnail account neglected to explain why Kountz took this step. Nor did it mention that Kountz pulled strings trying to obtain another position supervising army river transportation several months later. Apparently Kountz came close to securing another commission, until Grant found out what was happening; Kountz's attempt immediately collapsed. His biographical sketch, first printed in the late 1880s, would maintain "he has built, owned and controlled more steamboats than any other man on Western and Southern rivers." Surviving into the twentieth century, he outlived Grant—whose name appears nowhere in Kountz's admiring sketch—by two decades.

Albert Sidney Johnston

The Confederacy's western commander would die seven weeks after Fort Donelson at Shiloh. He bled to death from a leg wound that he seems to have had no idea he had suffered until too late, possibly because of the old Texas dueling injury that left him with reduced sensation in that part of his body. Johnston went on to become a demigod in Southern memory, spared widespread, long-term blame for his Donelson indecision. He became regarded in legend as the one man the Confederacy's hopes could not afford to lose.

Henry Halleck

Grant's commander in the Henry-Donelson campaign shelved his unloved subordinate again after Shiloh. Halleck personally took charge of the Union's primary western army for a forgettable three months from April to

July 1862 that brought it to a virtual halt. Having gathered one hundred thousand men, he progressed less than a mile a day because he insisted on entrenching every night on a laborious crawl to the railroad center of Corinth, Mississippi, where the Confederates had retreated from Shiloh. Before he got there Corinth was abandoned, and the Confederate army there stole off and invaded Kentucky.

Mostly on victories won by his subordinate Grant, Halleck became regarded (despite his Corinth campaign) as the most capable of the Union generals, and by mid-1862 Lincoln had placed him in command all the Federal armies. But Halleck was so afflicted with hemorrhoids that he sometimes could do no more than lie on couches, and he shrank from decisions required of him.

Grant was promoted past him in the spring of 1864. Because Grant preferred duty at the front, Halleck became in effect his Washington secretary. Sometime during Halleck's 1862–1865 Washington stint, the underhanded communications he sent McClellan about Grant in early 1862 disappeared from government files. Grant never saw them until after the war.

Halleck died in 1872 following an apparent stroke.

Bushrod Johnson

The haunting of Bushrod Rust Johnson by his youthful slave-aiding and his forced exit from the U. S. Army apparently ended only with his death. After Donelson, he went on to fight at Shiloh, Perryville, Stones River, and Chickamauga, as well as at the Crater and other engagements on the Virginia front. He performed with real distinction at Chickamauga. But three days before Appomattox, when he found his position overrun, he and two other generals deserted with their troops and hid in the woods. He then was relieved of command and, unlike the other fugitives, treated with open disrespect by Robert E. Lee.

After the war, Johnson struggled, ending up on a rundown farm in Macoupin County, Illinois, which he somehow had managed to buy and pay off during the war. There he lived with his mentally challenged son, who had spent the war with in-laws in the North who told him that his father was in the Union army. In 1880, a few days before his sixty-third birthday, the general suffered a paralyzing and soon fatal cerebral hemorrhage.

Johnson's nephew, Robert U. Johnson, became one of the two editors of the landmark four-volume series *Battles and Leaders of the Civil War*. But for nearly a century the uncle's headstone in an unkempt cemetery near Brighton, Illinois, identified him simply as "Gen. Bushrod R. Johnson," neglecting to specify the army he had served. His body was exhumed and reburied in 1977 in Nashville, in a family plot he had purchased before the war.[1]

James Churchill

Lieutenant Churchill of the Eleventh Illinois survived, returned to his unit, and was promoted to captain on May 10, 1862. Following the war, he was discharged at the brevet rank of lieutenant colonel.[2]

John B. Floyd

The self-deposed commander of Fort Donelson was cashiered from Confederate service by Jefferson Davis soon after the evacuation of Nashville. After returning home to southwest Virginia, he got himself appointed major general in the state's militia, raised a band of guerrillas, scourged his mountainous area's many Union loyalists, and was considered a nuisance by Confederate authorities trying to recruit regular troops from the same region. His health soon failed, and he died in August 1863 at his home near Abingdon. Never accounted one of the South's better commanders, Floyd has been described by at least one modern historian as "arguably the worst."[3]

John A. McClernand

Probably because of his fearlessness in combat and his tendency to hold nothing back when attacking, as well as his strong connections to Lincoln and other political powers, McClernand continued to be tolerated by Grant for more than a year following the capture of Donelson. During that time, Grant's power grew, and his patience apparently reached its final straw in the face of McClernand's attribution to his division the feats of others in the Vicksburg campaign. A markedly verbose "order" not sent through headquarters but instead published in several Midwestern newspapers glorified McClernand's troops and, by unmistakable inference, their commander himself.

On June 18, 1863, Grant issued (unfairly and without authority, some have contended) an order of his own: for McClernand's removal. Grant's real reason for dismissing him seems to have been McClernand's battlefield dispatch exaggerating the position of his Thirteenth Corps in a call for support from the rest of the army at Vicksburg on May 22, 1863. Because of McClernand's claim that his men already had possession of two Confederate redans, Grant threw in the rest of his troops and saw many of them slaughtered.

Kountz may have been involved in at least a small way in Grant's decision to finally rid himself of the ex-congressman. Evidence of a McClernand-Kountz collusion continued up to a couple of months before McClernand was sacked. The two were together in Springfield in the fall of 1862. The following January Kountz, by then a Pittsburgh banker, apparently offered his services to Secretary of War Stanton and was told to report to McClernand. On March 15, McClernand wrote Kountz an introduction to Abraham Lincoln, on the back of which Kountz wrote: "On the 13th of March 1863 Genl. Grant I am informed was Gloriously drunk and in bed sick all next day If you are averse to drunken Genls I can furnish the Name of officers of high standing to substantiate the above."

Grant learned Kountz was back on the scene, and on March 16, 1863, Grant aide John Rawlins wrote McClernand about it. Rawlins asked "by what authority" Kountz was with a McClernand unit "and on what business and report the same to these Headquarters." McClernand answered vaguely that Kountz had left the day before, and that was that.

After being dismissed by Grant in June, McClernand loudly protested and resorted to every tactic and friend he could, but to no avail. He retreated to Illinois civilian life, and never again attained a level commensurate with his prewar political influence. He did serve as chairman of the Democratic national convention in 1876. Nearly a quarter-century after that, he died of dysentery.[4]

Gideon Pillow

After his skiff-borne skedaddle across the Cumberland, Pillow never received another chance at high Confederate command. Like McClernand, however, Pillow refused to go quietly. He pestered his superiors for more than a year with long epistles endlessly attempting to justify his passing of the Donelson command to a man determined to capitulate. At one point, Pillow said he would have to resign if his arguments were not sustained, but when the Confederate secretary of war said his resignation was accepted, Pillow had to clarify that he had not actually resigned but only threatened to.

He complained bitterly to the Confederate government. Among his litany of misfortunes he included the burning of his cotton by Confederates to keep it out of Union hands. He also mentioned the uncertain fates of six unmarried daughters depending on his support. He wrote Jefferson Davis protesting that Confederate Secretary of War Randolph was his enemy because Randolph was related to a witness against him in the fateful military inquiry a decade and a half earlier in Mexico. But his efforts at resurrection to his former prominence (and, in fact, promotion above it)

were doomed—most immediately by his McClernand-like decision to pub-
lish his official Donelson report in newspapers before sending it on to
Richmond.

Suspended from any command for the first six months following Donelson, he eventually was allowed on a spur of the moment to lead a brigade at
Stone's River on January 2, 1863. There Confederate General John C. Breckinridge would privately allege (not altogether convincingly, given Pillow's
customary battlefield demeanor) that during a charge he saw Pillow cowering behind a tree. After that, Pillow held mostly administrative recruiting
and conscripting positions, illegally but skillfully rounding up many men
who previously had been exempted. In so doing, he turned some Southerners against the Confederacy while adding indispensable manpower to Joseph
E. Johnston's army in 1864.

Following the war, he and Isham G. Harris formed a law partnership in
Memphis and associated themselves with suspected Ku Klux Klansmen during Grant's term in the White House. Pillow also unsuccessfully sought the
return of 235 mules taken from his estate for Union use during the war and
offered Grant his political support in trade for the return of the animals.
Eventually, he descended into bankruptcy, with two of his formal creditors
being Isham G. Harris and Bushrod Johnson. In 1878, a year after Harris was
elected to the U.S. Senate from Tennessee, Pillow would die hideously of yellow fever near Helena, Arkansas.

Because both Floyd and Johnston died so soon after Donelson, Pillow has
been unfairly saddled by history with the full weight and shame of an unnec-
essary surrender to which, at least, he never agreed. Unfortunately for his
memory, his nearly total lack of character has inspired only two dedicated
co-biographers to do him perfect justice.[5]

Lew Wallace

Lew Wallace got lost at Shiloh seven weeks after Fort Donelson. At least that
was the contention of Grant and Grant's aides after that epic battle. Stationed four miles away at Crump's Landing on the morning of April 6, Wallace was ordered by Grant to march to a position on the Union right when it
became obvious that the Confederate assault was not just pickets pot-shot-
ting. Wallace took his division on a road that would have led him to the original Union right, but by then the furious Confederate onslaught had forced
Grant's right to retreat. While the battle raged, Wallace's men marched and
countermarched for seven hours over fifteen miles of rugged terrain. Although aided by three separate couriers from an increasingly displeased

Grant, Wallace's troops took until sundown to find the relocated right. By that time the battle's disastrous first day was done, and Grant's army had been all but driven into the Tennessee River.

Wallace's military career got lost along with his army. Under heavy public fire for getting surprised by the Confederates that day, Grant never forgave his politically powerful Indiana lieutenant who could have provided vital aid. Some observers say Grant used Wallace as a scapegoat. In any case, Wallace held only comparatively inconsequential commands after that, and none was under Grant.

In addition to writing the celebrated novel *Ben Hur: A Tale of the Christ*, Lew Wallace went on to become two things Grant never was: an appointed politician (governor of New Mexico Territory and ambassador to Turkey) and an after-dinner speaker. He died in Crawfordsville in his native Indiana in 1905.[6]

Simon Bolivar Buckner

Buckner was kept in solitary confinement for five months at Fort Warren Prison, in Boston Harbor. After his exchange on July 31, 1862, he returned to duty and served the Confederacy through the end of the war. He commanded a division at Perryville and a corps at Chickamauga and rose to the rank of lieutenant general.

Later in his career, Buckner was elected governor of Kentucky in 1887 and was the vice presidential nominee on the unsuccessful national "Gold Democrats" ticket in 1896. For a time, he also edited the *Louisville Courier*. To the end of his life, he retained an ability to produce the precise and, if need be, biting prose with which he had pilloried Pillow in 1857.

Buckner's Fort Donelson surrender was often mentioned by political antagonists, but he defended himself against it publicly only once—at age eighty, in an open letter to Kentucky Governor J. C. W. Beckham that displayed his talent for verbose sarcastic invective. After recounting his role at Donelson, he added: "The Confederate government, which, it might be thought, was an interested party in these transactions, saw fit to retire my two seniors from all active duty and to promote me to a higher grade for what, they supposed, was my proper action on that occasion. You evidently dissent from their judgment. If your infantile prattlings could have reached the ears of the Confederate authorities, they might, perhaps, have saved them from the commission of this error. But, unfortunately, you were not then born; nor had flaming comet or other miraculous messages informed the world of your approaching advent and the wisdom which would then enlighten it."[7]

Andrew H. Foote

Flag-officer Foote, for all practical purposes, received his deathblow at Fort Donelson. The wounds to his body and psyche never healed from the bludgeoning they took at the hands of Donelson's Confederate cannoneers. "I was touching the pilot with my clothes when he was killed," he wrote his wife of the ordeal aboard the *St. Louis* on February 14. "I won't run into the fire again, as a burnt child dreads it." He kept that pledge. He would not draw his final breath for more than a year, and when he did his death would be attributed to Bright's Disease, a kidney affliction. But by then, in behavior vastly different from that exhibited in his memorable cooperation with Grant, he delayed long enough at the Mississippi River battle of Island No. 10 to let General John Pope's army, rather than his own gunboats, take the laurels.

Despite a lengthy leave for recuperation and then a desk assignment in Washington, the damage to his foot never healed. He was headed, nonetheless, for an important new assignment commanding the navy's blockade of Confederate ports along the Atlantic when he was stricken ill en route. He died on June 26, 1863, at the Astor House in New York.[8]

Nathan Bedford Forrest

For Forrest, Fort Donelson was the first course in a dismaying Confederate military education. It drove one of the South's most adept, courageous, and ruthless leaders out of the mainstream of the Confederate officer corps and onto the backroads of the western theatre.

Soon after the Confederate humiliation at Donelson, Forrest would witness the same sort of command failure at Shiloh. There he spent much of the night after the first day's Confederate victory unsuccessfully warning his superiors that Buell had arrived on the opposite bank of the Tennessee and was being ferried across. Forrest accurately forecast that if the Confederates did not do something immediately they would be "whipped like hell" the next morning; superiors told him to go back to his camp and remain vigilant. He would follow Shiloh with another victory of troops over whom he had sole command. That was at Murfreesboro on July 21, where he captured a Union force the size of his own and shook the Federal occupation of central Tennessee to its boot heels.

Eventually, the disparity between victories he crafted himself and sour disappointments suffered under the leadership of others, or perhaps just disgust, led him to all but quit the Confederate chain of command. He did that in memorable fashion, too, threatening to kill his commander, General

Braxton Bragg, if Bragg ever again crossed his path. Forrest spent most of the balance of the war operating quasi-independently, accepting orders from higher up to make raids, including ones on Grant's supply lines, but directing these operations on his own. These included the infamous Fort Pillow Massacre of April 1864, in which Forrest troops stormed a Union fort and killed many members of the garrison—especially ex-slaves who had joined the Union army—as they were trying to surrender.

Jefferson Davis disregarded Forrest's rustic genius and mostly let elitist friendships decide who commanded the South's armies. Forrest *was* a difficult, chip-on-shoulder subordinate to deal with, although he seems to have been less so when working with qualified and cultivated superiors such as Richard Taylor and Dabney Maury. By much of the Confederacy's martial leadership, however, Forrest appears to have been unofficially marginalized for his ill-educated ungentlemanliness. There was also his unsavory antebellum commercial enterprise. Southern society waxed squeamish about the business of buying and selling members of the race whose sweat staked it to many of its grandiose refinements.

Like Grant, Forrest was a little too plebeian, too warlike, and too western for the taste of most of his elitist superiors. Had he been more welcomed into the Confederacy's military chain of command instead of being tolerated by it—had he therefore become a leader of armies rather than of backwater cavalry units—some of the decisions and laurels of Southern soldiery in the West might have been brighter, the war longer, and the eventual outcome less certain. It was not to be.

His surrender in 1865 turned out to be a token gesture. Surely influenced by aristocratic exclusion that had made him an outsider, he lunged beyond the pale of mere marginalization. According to believable legend, for the Ku Klux Klan's shadowy two or three formative years, he accepted leadership of this supreme scourge of President Grant and Reconstruction.

But he had to make a living. The war had destroyed his fortune. Like Grant before the conflict, Forrest after it battled titanically and unsuccessfully against the whims of economic fate. He tried to build a Memphis-to-Selma railroad and was ruined by a financial panic in 1873. He and Mary Ann ended up on a leased plantation that he operated on an island in the Mississippi River, renting county prisoners for labor. Two years before he died frail and used-up at fifty-six, a minister's sermon on the folly of building a house on a bad foundation caused the specter of his failed enterprises to pass before his eyes. Outside the church door, he tearfully confessed to the cleric that his extraordinary life had been built not on a rock of heavenly assurance but, rather, on shifting sands of struggle for earthly eminence.

Much of what he attained of the latter has long faded. After the 1960s, when the centennial of his war was overshadowed by a long-delayed new American conflict for minority rights, his fame as a brilliant warrior never regained ascendance in the public mind over the appetite for injustice implicit in his direction of the KKK.

Ulysses S. Grant

Grant never was able to quite shake his drunkard's reputation, nor could anything else quite shake the nation's faith in him. This man who had sold firewood on the streets of St. Louis to keep his family from hunger proceeded just a decade later to become president of the Union he was universally credited with having saved. Elected chief executive in 1868, he headed an administration wracked by scandals bred of his inability to recognize that others were not necessarily as honest as he was.

For nearly a century most historians, reflecting the prejudices of an America that remained aggressively racist, savaged his presidency. More recent writers have been kinder, and they should be.

Displaying the sort of courage that sustained him through the war, Grant refused to abandon the freed slaves to the unjust intentions of their former owners. But their equality under the Constitution was an ideal for which few Civil War–era whites, South or North, had had much stomach. Grant's noble effort was nationally abandoned with his exit from office, and before the 1960s his reputation, like Forrest's *after* the 1960s, foundered.

His trust in untrustworthy men ruined him financially in 1884, eight years after leaving office, but he remained a tower of personal heroism into his last days. He wrote his *Personal Memoirs* in a final dogged struggle with throat cancer that apparently was brought on by the plethora of cigars that well-wishers started sending him after the Donelson surrender. In his last and perhaps greatest act of quiet courage, he finished the *Memoirs* and assured the financial well-being of Julia and their children just weeks before his death.

In those last days, old friends came to pay their respects. The one permitted by Julia to stay longest was one whom her husband had not seen since Donelson—Simon Buckner.

Grant could no longer speak. Lying on a couch and propped with pillows, he had to write down what he wished to contribute to the conversation. When the reunion ended Mrs. Grant gave several of the pieces of paper to Mrs. Buckner. Later Buckner's widow recalled that Grant indicated in that final interview that if he had known Buckner was in command at Donelson, not merely acting as a secretary for Pillow, the reply to Buckner's request for surrender terms on February 16, 1862, "would have been different."

Less than a week later, Grant died. At the family's request, pallbearers at his funeral included four Civil War generals. Sherman and Sheridan represented the Union army. The Confederates were Joseph E. Johnston and Buckner.9

NOTES

PART I
CHAPTER 1

1. Graham, *Nashville*, 29; Connelly, *Army of the Heartland*, 3–9; *Nashville Republican Banner*, October 15, 1861. As for the railroads, Nashville—like the rest of the agriculturally based Confederacy—was better equipped with lines than it was with trains to use them. The Louisville & Nashville company had just forty cars and no locomotives in the Tennessee capital in mid-1861 because management elected to hold most of its rolling stock in Louisville, a fact that could seriously influence Union and Confederate planning and movement in coming months. (Stonesifer, *The Forts Henry-Heiman and Fort Donelson Campaigns*, 52–53; Black, *The Railroads of the Confederacy*, 71, 72, 141; *Nashville Republican Banner*, July 5, 1861.)

2. Johnson and Buel, *Battles and Leaders of the Civil War*, volume 1, hereafter referred to as *B & L* 1. 347; Tucker, *Andrew Foote*, 42–44, 55, 59, 75–76, 111, and 118.

3. *B & L* 1, 360; Tucker, 73, 89–94, 122.

4. Anderson, *By Sea and By River*, 85–86.

5. U.S. Service Schools, *Fort Henry and Fort Donelson Campaign* (hereafter referred to as "Source Book") 136; Tucker, 122, 134.

6. Grant, *Personal Memoirs*, 152; Feis, *Grant's Secret Service*, 60–63.

7. Marszalek, *Commander of All Lincoln's Armies*, 105–106. Halleck's longtime best friend, George W. Cullum, had been serving as aide to McClellan's venerable, aging predecessor, Winfield Scott, and Scott preferred Halleck as his successor. President Lincoln did not want to make that ultimate appointment so quickly, but he did consent to making Halleck a major general, then the army's highest rank.

8. Simon, *The Papers of Ulysses S. Grant*, volume 3, 202, 202n., 228, 316–318n. In writing his father that he feared losing his command, Grant added that although "I believe my administration has given general satisfaction not only to those over me but to all concerned . . . This is the most important command within the department . . . and will probably be given to the senior officer next to General Halleck himself. There are not so many brigadier generals in the army as there are brigades, and as to divisions they are nearly all commanded by brigadiers" (p. 228).

9. Richardson, *A Personal History of Ulysses S. Grant*, vi, 207; Warner, *Generals in Blue* (1964), 455; Eicher and Eicher, *Civil War High Command*, 493, says Smith was in the Utah Territory in January 1861, was at Fort Washington, Maryland, April 6–9, Department of Washington, April 9–19, and Fort Columbus, New York, April 27, where he apparently remained assigned until being promoted to brigadier general just prior to his transfer to western Kentucky in early September. Grant's commission as brigadier was dated in May.

10. Lew Wallace, *An Autobiography*, volume 1, 149–150; Catton, *Grant Moves South*, 87–89.

11. Kiper, *Major General John Alexander McClernand*, 56, 60.

12. Gould, *Fifty Years on the Mississippi*, 646–650.

13. Simon *3*, 289, 320–321, 324–328.

14. Simon *4*, 53–55n; Parker, "William J. Kountz, Superintendent of River Transportation Under McClellan, 1861–1862," 237–254.

15. Wallace, 1, 353.

16. Simon *4*, 114–118n. Regarding the *Tribune*, the Chicago newspaper likely had some of its own axes to grind. Avowedly abolitionist, the *Tribune* was one of the earliest and strongest publications supporting Lincoln. It included with Bross's complaint an anonymous letter saying: "Until we can secure pure men in habits and men without their own little slaves to wait upon them, which is a fact here in this camp with Mrs. Grant, our country is lost." Simon *4*, 119. The paper's ire also may have been raised by Grant's apparent naiveté in journalistic matters. Richardson, p. 209, says Grant had Rawlins strike from a *Tribune* story a reference to the expulsion of three slaves from Union lines at Bird's Point, Missouri, in obedience to a Halleck order, because Grant did not think it was true. Immediately afterward, when a reporter from the *Chicago Times* filed a report of the same incident (which said the slaves had come into the lines at risk to their lives to provide valuable military information) and convinced Grant it *was* true, the general allowed it to go through and casually asked the *Times* reporter to inform the *Tribune* reporter that he, too, could go ahead and report the incident. The *Times* man, apparently preferring to have an exclusive, did not tell his *Tribune* colleague, after which the *Tribune* "denounced Grant bitterly for suppressing news and carrying out Halleck's infamous order." It perhaps should be added that the Bird's Point commander, Chicagoan Richard Oglesby, technically complied with Halleck's order to put the slaves out of the lines but then had men waiting just outside town to help them get to a boat to deliver them to safety across the river in Illinois. As to Bross's emphatic abstemiousness, it is referred to in J. Cutler Andrews's *The North Reports The Civil War*, 679.

CHAPTER 2

1. Egerton, *Nashville*, 113.

2. The prewar biographical material on Buckner is from Stickles, *Simon Bolivar Buckner*. Buckner's early secessionist activities and Lincoln's reaction are found in Stonesifer, 43–44; Johnston, *The Life of Albert Sidney Johnston*, 302–303; Nicolay and Hay, *Abraham Lincoln*, vol. 4, 235.

3. Hughes and Stonesifer, *The Life and Wars of Gideon J. Pillow*, 166–167.

4. Cummings, *Yankee Quaker, Confederate General*, 21–34, 57, 170–171.

5. Faust, *Historical Times Encyclopedia of the Civil War*, 24, 382; Connelly, 63.

6. *B & L* 1, 545–546.

7. Roland, *Albert Sidney Johnston*, 10, 59–60, 117, 151, 163, 251–252.

8. Ibid., 31–46, 81–102, 166, 168–184, 281.

CHAPTER 3

1. Lewis, *Captain Sam Grant*, 22; Porter, *Campaigning With Grant*, 342; Simpson, *Ulysses S. Grant*, 3, 4, 16.

2. Grant, 13, 20; Perret, *Ulysses S. Grant*, 33, 78–88.

3. Grant, 132.

4. Feis, 14; Lewis, 14; Smith, *Grant*, 26; Grant, 131.

5. Simpson, 44; Smith, 52, 56.

6. Smith, 54, 40.

7. Grant, 125.

8. Perret, 121; Grant, 114; Smith, 30, 92, 94; Simpson, 1, 6, 67, 71, 72; Simon *1*, 344, 347. For Grant's schooling in Ripley and Maysville, see Grant, 10. For a superb picture of the pro- and antislavery struggle in the area and time in which he was growing up, see Hagedorn, *Beyond The River*, 59–184. Hagedorn's book documents that the pros and cons of slavery and its fugitives were continual and highly volatile topics in Ripley, Ohio, Maysville, Kentucky, and in Georgetown, Ohio, during his growing-up years in the area. The abolitionist-leaning journalist Reid says in his book *Ohio In The War*, 357, that Grant "detested the Abolitionists," but this is doubtless an abolitionist sympathizer's overreaction having to do with Grant's wish to distance himself from a movement that seemed oblivious to the need to keep the various sections of the nation together under one flag. Many abolitionists were so repelled by the monstrous moral wrong of the institution that they believed the North's antislavery states should secede to escape participation in a grave national sin. In his *Personal Memoirs*, 112, Grant recalls having grown up a Whig and having stayed one in the prewar army; in an 1859 letter, Simon *1*, 352, Grant recalls never having voted an "out and out Democratic ticket in my life" and that his one friend on the five-man county commission in St. Louis, when he was trying for an appointment as county engineer, was a Free Soiler. On the other hand, he voted for the Democrat James Buchanan for president against Free Soiler/Republican John C. Fremont in 1856 because he feared the election of a Republican "meant the secession of all the Slave States, and rebellion" (Grant, 113).

9. Brinton, *Personal Memoirs*, 37; Simpson, 74.

10. Smith, 93.

11. Simpson, 58, 281; Smith, 86, 87.

12. Ibid., 90–93.

13. Ibid., 83, 96–97; McFeely, *Grant*, 132–135.

14. Grant, 127; Smith, 83.

15. Lewis, 313; McFeely, 133.

CHAPTER 4

1. Rainey, *W.H. Rainey & Co.'s Memphis City Directory and General Business Advertiser for 1855–1856*, 251.

2. Henry, *As They Saw Forrest*, 287–288.

3. Coahoma County, Chancery Clerk's records, 559; Wyeth, *That Devil Forrest*, 15; Lytle, *Bedford Forrest and His Critter Company*, 19–20.

4. *American Eagle*, 2; Jordan and Pryor, *The Campaigns of Lieutenant Gen. N. B. Forrest and of Forrest's Cavalry*, 23–24; Wyeth, 18; Mathes, *General Forrest*, 11–12; Henry, *"First with the Most" Forrest*, 24, 25; Curlee, "The Phenix," 103; *DeSoto County Times*, August 14, 1986, sect. D., 3.

5. Memphis *Daily Appeal*, June 27 and 28, 1857; April 7, 1857; July 21, 1858; March 23, 1859; August 11, 23, September 11, 1860.

6. Memphis *Daily Avalanche*, August 6, 1860, 3, August 15, 1860, 2; Coahoma County, Book 6, 559; Clarksdale *Press Register*, July 21, 1984.

7. Wyeth, 14–15; Goodloe, *Confederate Echoes*, 179; Morton, *The Artillery of Nathan Bedford Forrest's Cavalry*, 181.

8. *The War of the Rebellion: Official Records of the Union and Confederate Armies* (hereafter referred to as *O.R.*) (1) 4, 513.

CHAPTER 5

1. Simon 2, 3–4.
2. Lewis, 420.
3. Smith, 107, 113–117, 118.
4. Grant, 140, 141; Smith, 118–119; Simon 2, 194–195; O.R. (1) 4, 189.
5. O.R. (1) 4, 188–189; ibid., 180; *Philadelphia Inquirer*, September 6, 1861, 1.
6. O.R. (1) 3, 267–269; 4 (1), 517, 554; Catton, 70–73; Smith, 124–126; Feis, 44–52; as will be seen in these references, several Grant and Belmont scholars have concluded that at least some of the orders that Grant cited as causing him to attack Belmont may have been manufactured later on; Feis, though, also says that Grant's action could have been seen as inspired by Fremont's strategy. Also see Hughes, *The Battle of Belmont*, 45, 47; the term "Gibraltar of the West" was later used to denote Vicksburg, Mississippi.
7. Smith, 646n.; Schutz and Trenerry, *Abandoned by Lincoln*, 62; Simon 3, 228; Catton, 69.
8. Williams, *Lincoln Finds a General*, 76–78; Grant, 143; Hughes, *Battle of Belmont*, 50, 65, 68, 74–77, 104, 125, 127–128, 166–171.
9. Grant, 148.
10. *Official Records of the Union and Confederate Navies in the War of the Rebellion* (hereafter abbreviated *ORN*), series 1, volume 22, 399; Hughes, *Battle of Belmont*, 184–185; Grant, 149.
11. *ORN* (1) 22, 355, 397, 399–400.

CHAPTER 6

1. Fisher, *War at Every Door*, 58.
2. O.R. (1) 4, 250; ibid., 7, 701.

CHAPTER 7

1. Jordan and Pryor, 42–43.
2. Ibid., 45–46.
3. O.R. (1) 7, 65–66; Jordan and Pryor, 53.
4. O.R. (1) 7, 66.

5. Ibid., 64.

6. Wyeth, 35; Jordan and Pryor, 53–54.

CHAPTER 8

1. White, *Messages of the Governors of Tennessee*, vol. 5, 304; *B & L* 1, 377–378.

2. Bircher, *A Drummer Boy's Diary*, 15–16; *B & L* 1, 386.

3. Engle, *Don Carlos Buell*, 138–142; O.R. (1) 7, 530–531, 450–51.

4. O.R. (1) 4, 487–488; O.R. (1) 7, 927.

5. O.R. (1) 7, 98.

6. Ibid., 90; McKinney, *Education In Violence*, 127; Temple, *East Tennessee and the Civil War*, 445.

7. Johnston, 396.

8. Ibid., 399; O.R. (1) 7, 103, 104, 105, 764. Crittenden's official report says he did not learn about Thomas's lagging "re-enforcement" or the flooding of Fishing Creek until January 18, but he also says he called the council of war on Friday night, the 17th, with that knowledge.

9. Ibid., 105; Humes, *The Loyal Mountaineers of Tennessee*, 163–164; Worsham, *The Old Nineteenth Tennessee Regiment*, 20; O.R. (1) 7, 106.

10. Ibid., 111; Temple, 446; O.R. (1) 7, 106, 114.

11. Ibid., 90, 106.

12. O.R. (1) 7, 87; *B & L* 1, 388; O.R. (1) 7, 87.

13. Worsham, 22; Johnston, 401.

14. *B & L* 1, 388–389.

15. Worsham, 23; O.R. 7 (1), 91, 93, 105.

16. Ibid., 113–114.

17. Worsham, 22; McMurray, *History of the 20th Tennessee Volunteer Regiment*, 124.

18. O.R. (1) 7, 108.

19. McMurray, 202; Worsham, 23–24.

20. *B & L* 1, 390.

21. Worsham, 202; McMurray, 29; Worsham, 202.

22. McKinney, 131.

CHAPTER 9

1. Grant, 152; Andrews, 159–160; Smith, 120.

2. Andrews, 159–160.

3. O.R. (1) 7, 572–574.

4. Ibid., 572, 574.

5. Ibid., 574, 576.

6. Ibid., 121.

PART II

CHAPTER 10

1. Cooling, *Forts Henry and Donelson*, 89–91; O.R. (1) 7, 575, 579; Kiper, 68; Stonesifer, 121–123; Catton, 134–135.

2. Isabel Wallace, *The Life and Letters of General W. H. L. Wallace*, 153–154.

3. O.R. (1) 7, 58, 577, 579; Stonesifer, 125; Avery, *History of the Fourth Illinois Cavalry Regiment*, 52.

4. Lew Wallace, 1, 366.

5. O.R. (1) 7, 561; Simon *4*, 123n.

6. *ORN*, 528.

7. O.R. (1) 7, 125.

8. Grant, 153–54; Tucker, 140.

9. Isabel Wallace, 154.

10. Simon *4*, 149, 153; O.R. (1) 7, 128, 137–138.

11. Stonesifer, 141; Richardson, 214; Slagle, *Ironclad Captain*, 157–158.

12. O.R. (1) 7, 124, 586; Grant, 154; Abbott, *The History of the Civil War in America*, 451–452; Williams, vol. 3, 200; Gosnell, *Guns on the Western Waters*, 47–48; Cooling, 100.

13. Tucker, 122; *ORN*, 365, 376, 391, 394, 400.

14. Ibid., 399–400.

15. Ibid., 442, 461–462, 468.

16. Ibid., 444, 473. For Halleck's opinion of gunboats as well as mortar boats, see O.R. 7, 571–572, 578.

17. Williams, 200; Gosnell, 47–48.

CHAPTER 11

1. Reed, *Combined Operations in the Civil War*, 85.

2. *Confederate Military History*, 63; Robert Erwin Johnson, *Rear Admiral John Rodgers*, 166; *ORN*, 318–320.

3. Anderson, 87.

4. Ibid., 281.

5. Gould, 649; Sears, *The Civil War Papers of George B. McClellan*, 22; Simon *4*, 115n.–116n.

6. *ORN*, 281–82, 283, 286.

7. Ibid., 284–285; Gould, 649.

8. Parker, 242; Johnson, 165–166.

9. Gould, 649; Simon *4*, 116.

10. Marszalek, 44; Simon *3*, 324, 325–328n.; Parker, 243–248.

11. Ibid.; Simon *3*, 324, 360n., 361, 361n.; Simon *4*, 22–23, 114, 116; *ORN*, 477; The Rawlins quotation is from Kiper, citing Helen Todd, 29–30.

12. Simon *4*, 54; Ibid., 95; Parker, 250. In charging that Kountz wanted to get one of his boats into government service, Grant indicated that he may have been ignorant of the true extent of things. According to Parker (238, 251), Kountz had eight steamboats and already had most of them in government service by autumn of 1861—and they would continue to serve through the end of the war.

13. Simon *4*, 111–113n.

14. Parker, 245–248; Simon *4*, 111–113n., 115n.; Simon *3*, p. 271n.; Parker, 251; Kiper, 56.

CHAPTER 12

1. Grant, 152. Preeminent Grant scholar John Y. Simon has written that Grant's memory may have "exaggerated" the unpleasantness of the Halleck interview, since (1) it did not dissuade Grant from almost immediately trying again to convince Halleck to attack Fort Henry, and (2) Halleck quickly complied. There seems little question, however, that Halleck could be a very unpleasant man. Halleck's quotation comes from Catton, 124, citing Emerson, "Grant's Life in the West," *Midland Monthly*, May 1898.

2. McFeely, 48; Marszalek, 98, 122, 134, 248; Simon *4*, 306; Ambrose, *Halleck*, 5–7.

3. Sherman, *Memoirs*, 220; Marszalek, 114.

4. For the Buell-McClellan communications on a diversion on the Tennessee and Cumberland and Halleck's eventual knowledge of it, see, for instance, O.R. (1) 7, 451, 473, 487, 521, 524, 526, 527, 528. For the first communication to Halleck re: Halleck's request for the commissioning of Hitchcock, see O.R. (1) 7, 930. It is dated January 29, 1862.

5. Weigley, *The American Way of War*, 84; Isabel Wallace, 143; O.R. (1) 8, 509–511; Engle, 152.

6. Simon *3*, 278, 317n., 370; McClernand and Brigadier General Cullum, Halleck's chief of staff, were acquainted and apparently on good terms. Simon *4*, 105n.

7. O.R. (7), 120, 121.

8. Engle, 150–161.

9. Ibid., op. cit., 115n.; *ORN*, 525; O.R. (1) 7, 121.

10. Brinton, 131.

11. Catton, 506, n. 11; Simon *4*, 313; O.R. (1) 7 , 944; Smith, 141.

CHAPTER 13

1. O.R. (1) 7 , 137; Tucker, 139.

2. O.R.(1) 7 , 144; Cooling, 13–14, 127.

3. Stonesifer, 26–27; Johnston, 423–424; O.R. (1) 7, 132.

4. Warner, 74; Creighton, "Wilbur Fisk Foster: Soldier and Engineer," 265; Tucker, 136; Cooling, 46, 47; Van West, *Tennessee Encyclopedia of History & Culture*, 416–417; Stonesifer, 2, 16–28; O.R. (1) 7, 144–145. Johnston had put Tilghman in command of the forts (O.R. [1] 4, 560) because of perceived negligence in discipline, training, and construction by McGavock (Johnston, 415). Tilghman quickly recommended that a strong fort with "heavy guns" be established on the hill across the Tennessee from Fort Henry (O.R. [1] 7, 723), but when Chief Engineer Jeremy Gilmer on Johnston's staff differed with him on the need for "heavy guns" he apparently lost interest (Johnston, 423–424).

5. *B & L* 1, 368–369.

6. O.R. 7 (1), 132; Johnston, 416, 423–424. Despite Johnston's pleas to Southern governors and prominent citizens, these supplied slaves in nowhere near the numbers needed. One thousand each were required at both Fort Donelson and Forts Henry-Heiman, with Nashville and Clarksville each needing 1,500; but

fewer than 500, less than one-tenth the necessary total, were sent (Johnston, 416), and even these, most of whom arrived escorted by the Twenty-seventh Alabama Infantry in early January (O.R. [1] 7, 132, 817–818), apparently were not used on the fortifications because of bickering between Tilghman and engineers Joseph Dixon, a newly promoted captain in the Confederate Army, and Charles Hayden of the Tennessee Corps of Engineers. The hill on which Fort Heiman was located rose 90 feet above the river, which at normal stage was 1,260 feet wide at that point (O.R. 4 [1], 460). Heiman itself had four walls and covered an acre (O.R. [1] 7, 74); it contained two pieces of light artillery (Stonesifer, 35). Fort Henry proper took in about three acres. According to the map drawn by engineer Lieutenant Colonel James B. McPherson after the battle [*Official Military Atlas of the Civil War*, Plate 11, number 1], it was surrounded by a moat twenty feet wide and nine feet deep, a belt of marshy land, and rifle pits where the ground rose eighty to one hundred feet above the marsh. Northward along the river bank, trees had been cut to afford visibility and abatis formed. Along the fort's north-facing wall (downriver) the Confederates had placed a ten-inch columbiad, three thirty-two-pounders, and two forty-two-pounders for which there was no ammunition. The wall facing northwest (and the river) mounted a twenty-four-pounder rifle gun and three more thirty-two-pounders. On the northeast wall facing landward, the Confederates placed four thirty-two-pounders, while on the wall facing the southeast they put a twenty-four-pounder and two twelve-pounders.

7. O.R. (1) 7, 132, 133, 149. Visibility downriver from Fort Henry's walls was good. Trees had been cut and fashioned into abatis for two and a half miles along the riverbank to the north (Stonesifer, 35).

8. O.R. (1) 7, 149–150; Stonesifer, 137.

9. Garrett, *Andrew Jackson Campbell Diary*, 2–4, 9–11.

10. O.R. (1) 7, 138, 150.

11. O.R. 7 (1), 137, 138, 140, 141; Garrett, 11; Gower and Allen, *Pen and Sword*, 584.

12. O.R. (1) 7, 151.

CHAPTER 14

1. O.R. (1) 7, 127–129; Stonesifer, 154–155; Crummer, *With Grant at Fort Donelson, Shiloh, and Vicksburg*, 19.

2. *B & L* 1, 362; O.R. (1) 7, 149.

3. Cooling, 103; Simon 4, 147, Tucker, 140; *B & L* 1, 362; Tucker, 141.

4. Ibid., 116, 117; Slagle, 159.

5. *ORN* (1) 22, 538; Slagle, 159; Cooling, 103. Foote's starting time is used here because he wrote it in a letter to his wife that day. Tilghman estimated it forty-five minutes earlier in reports written the next day and a week later, when the battle may have understandably seemed longer in his mind or he perhaps wanted, for equally understandable reasons, to exaggerate the fort's resistance. Tilghman's version was that Foote fired his first shot at 11:45 a.m.

6. Tucker, 142; *B & L* 1, 363.

7. Stonesifer, 157; undated *Boston Journal* account in Frank Moore, Rebellion Record, 75–76; *B & L* 1, 364.

8. Ibid., 365; Tucker, 143; *ORN* 22, 541; Slagle, 160–161.

9. Lew Wallace, 1, 370.

CHAPTER 15

1. *B & L* 1, 365, 370, 372; O.R. 7 (1), 141; *B & L* 1, 363; O.R. 7 (1), 134, 152.

2. Garrett, 11; Gower and Allen, 585.

3. O.R. (1) 7, 141–142, 151–152.

4. Ibid., 142, 146–147.

5. *B & L* 1, 371.

6. O.R. (1) 7, 146–147, 152.

7. Slagle, 161–162; *B & L* 1, 371; *ORN* (1) 22, 538; O.R. (1) 7, 147.

8. Stonesifer, 162; Hoppin, *Life of Andrew H. Foote*, 203.

9. Ibid.; Andrews, 163.

10. Lew Wallace, 370–371.

11. Garrett, 12.

12. Gower and Allen, 585; Garrett, 12.

13. O.R. (1) 7, 152; Gower and Allen, 585–586.

14. O. R. (1) 7, 129.

CHAPTER 16

1. *B & L* 1, 367; Walke's memory—decades later—of the circumstances of his entering the fort were incorrect. Contrary to Foote's report at the time, Walke recalled that he, instead of Stembel and Phelps, took possession of the fort to hold it for Grant (but he does not say Foote sent him, so he possibly went on his own); *Source Book*, 327, 404; Cooling, 100; Brinton, 114; Isabel Wallace, 154.

2. O.R. (1) 7, 142; Porter, 7.

3. Simon *4*, 157, 158n.; *ORN* 22, 485.

4. Gower and Allen, 587.

5. Garrett, 13–14.

6. *Source Book*, 454; O.R. 7 (1), 152.

CHAPTER 17

1. *B & L* 1, 372; Simon *4*, 163.

2. Slagle, 176; Tucker, 152.

3. O.R. (1) 7, 142–143.

CHAPTER 18

1. Warner, 51–52.

2. Jordan and Pryor, 41; Henry, 39, 43; Johnson, *The Partisan Rangers of the Confederate States Army*, 40.

3. Jordan and Pryor, 25; Wyeth, 18–19; *Memphis Daily Appeal*, July 4, 1854.

4. *Chicago Tribune* (which copied the New York newspaper account), May 4, 1864; Shelby County, Tennessee, Register's Records, Book 16, 125.

5. Maury, *Recollections of a Virginian*, 215; Wyeth, 628, 630.

CHAPTER 19

1. Smith, 147, 650 n.

2. Simon *4*, 163, 164, 165; *Philadelphia Inquirer*, Feb. 8, 1862, 1; Cooling, 109; *Source Book*, 391.

3. O.R. (1) 7, 121, 574, 575; Ibid., vol. 8, 509; Simpson, 41.

4. O.R. (1) 7, 583–589.

CHAPTER 20

1. O.R. (1) 7, 153–154.

2. Ibid., 154–155; Hardin County, on the Tennessee-Alabama border, voted 1,051 to 498, to remain in the Union, as did Decatur County, just north of it, by 550 to 310; White, 305.

3. O.R. (1) 7, 155–156.

4. Cooling, 108; *Nashville Weekly Patriot*, February 16, 1862, 4.

CHAPTER 21

1. Richardson, 217; *ORN* (1) 22, 427, 428.

2. Simon *4*, 164, 165, 104n.

3. Ibid., 168–169, 169n.; O.R. (1) 7, 595.

4. Simon *4*, 171–172, 166n.; O.R. (1) 7, 595.

5. Feis, 59–62, 66.

6. Simon *4*, 171–72, 175, 176–177n.

7. Ibid., 177, 188, 189no; O.R. (1) 7, 599.

8. O.R. (1) 7, 130. As to the changing relationship between Grant and Mc-Clernand, see Grant's comment regarding McClernand's report of the Fort Donelson battles, ibid., 170.

9. Ibid., 594.

10. Ibid., 595, 598, 600, 605.

11. Thomas and Hyman, *Stanton*, 127–138; Simon *4*, 113n.

CHAPTER 22

1. Garrett, *Campbell*, 14.

2. Gower and Allen, 586.

3. Johnston, 428–429, 432–433.

4. Ibid., 429; O.R. (1) 7, 762, 788, 811; Johnston, 417, 491; O.R. (1) 7, 845.

5. Williams, *P.G.T. Beauregard*, 116.

6. Ibid., 118; O.R. (1) 7, 861–862; Johnston, 489, 491.

7. Williams, 118; Johnston, 487.

8. Grant, 173.

9. Catton, 125, quotes the *Cincinnati Enquirer* as saying in December that "The movement will not go down the Mississippi but up the Tennessee, where Gen. Halleck's forces, 75,000 strong, will leave the river and march to the rear of

Columbus, Hickman and other points toward Memphis. This will compel the Rebels at Columbus and other points to fall back on Memphis, thus leaving the river clear for the gunboats and transportation vessels to pass up and down un-molested"; Parks, *General Leonidas Polk*, 205, 206.

10. Johnston, 433–434, 437.

11. O.R. (1) 7, 272. As for Floyd's temper and vacillation, he had resigned from the Buchanan administration at the end of December 1860 as the cabinet wrangled over how to react to South Carolina's challenge to the re-supply of Fort Sumter and other installations in Charleston harbor. Floyd contended that Buchanan had promised South Carolinians that he would only take action in the harbor in the face of a hostile act; in resigning, Floyd said he would not be part of an administration that broke solemn promises. According to Thomas and Hyman, 97 and 103, when Buchanan became outraged and took personal offense at the wording of the resignation, Floyd then wrote him an apology and offered to soften the letter. Within a week, meanwhile, Attorney General Edwin Stanton found that Floyd verbally ordered transfer of 124 cannon from Allegheny Arsenal in Pennsylvania to Southern destinations, 103–104, and Stanton got the order rescinded in time to prevent the weapons' removal.

12. Parks, 186–187; Grant, 133–134; Roland, 170–173: O.R. (1) 7, 865.

13. O.R. (1) 7, 863; Rowena Reed, 87.

14. Marszalek, 163–169; O.R. (1) 7, 752, 844–845; Johnston, 433.

15. O.R. (1) 7, 863, 865.

16. Ibid., 259, 260, 261, 270, 272.

17. *B & L* 1, 145–146; Faust, 113–114.

18. For Johnston's view of Buell as the main danger, see Johnston's letter to Confederate Secretary of War Judah Benjamin, O.R. (1) 7, 792–794; nowhere in this long letter, in which he first recites his work at Bowling Green and then lists various other dispositions of troops across his line, does Johnston so much as mention the forts on the rivers. Theoretically, Johnston would have been right in assuming Grant was not entrusted with the main Federal attack. As Rowena Reed observes in *Combined Operations*, 68, McClellan meant for the main Federal attack to be Buell's move against Nashville. The problem was that Buell could not be persuaded to move, let alone fight, leaving a vacuum for Grant, with the grudging permission of Halleck, to jump into.

19. *B & L* 1, 372.

CHAPTER 23

1. O.R. (1) 7, 595, 600.

2. Ibid., 600, 601.

3. Simon *4*, 179–180.

4. O.R. (1) 7, 600.

5. Ibid., 600, 601, 603, 604; Reed, 85; *ORN* (1) 22, 550.

6. Lew Wallace, 375–377; Kiper, 72; Simon *4*, 183, 184–185n. John Y. Simon, editor of the Grant Papers, notes that Wallace's autobiography recalled the meeting as being at 2 p.m., Feb. 10, on the steamboat *Tigress*, whereas the account Wallace wrote for *B & L* 1, 404–406, puts it at 10 a.m., February 11,

aboard the *New Uncle Sam*. But Grant's written request for a "conference" with McClernand "and your brigade commanders" was on the *New Uncle Sam* at 3 p.m., February 10. For Grant on councils of war, see Smith, p. 388n.

7. Grant, 157, 158.

8. O.R. (1) 7, 600, 601; Kiper, 74; Grant, 158.

PART III
CHAPTER 24

1. Kiner, *One Year's Soldiering*, 23.

2. Simon 4, 191n., 192n.; Lew Wallace, 378; *B & L* 1, 410; Grant, 160; O.R. (1) 7, 674; Badeau, *The Military History of Ulysses S. Grant*, 36.

3. Ramage, *Rebel Raider*, 82–83; O.R. (1) 7, 170–171, 183–184, 329, 383–384.

4. Hagedorn's *Beyond The River* memorably traces the uneasy and often violent Maysville-Ripley axis for decades prior to 1861.

5. Grant, 10.

6. Bordewich, *Bound for Canaan*, 135–136.

7. *Memphis Weekly Appeal*, April 7, 1858; *Memphis Daily Appeal*, May 24, 1858; *Memphis Eagle & Enquirer*, April 11, 1858.

8. Bancroft, *Slave Trading in the Old South*, 255–256; *Memphis Daily Appeal*, June 25, 1858.

9. Jordan and Pryor, 20, 23–24, 25; Henry, 25.

10. *B & L* 1, 406; O.R. (1) 7, 171–172.

11. *B & L* 1, 431.

12. Slagle, 175–177.

13. O.R. (1) 7, 278; Cooling, 136; *B & L* 1, 430–431.

14. Cooling, 135; Coffin, *The Boys of '61, or Four Years of Fighting*, 81; *B & L* 1, 398.

15. O.R. (1) 7, 162.

16. Ibid., 191, 211.

17. Kiner, 23, 24.

CHAPTER 25

1. Jordan and Pryor, 55–56; O. R. (1) 4, 551; O.R. (1) 7, 383. The personally reviewed manuscript of his biography written by Jordan and Pryor five years later, on p. 56, decreases the estimated number of this enemy force and describes it simply as "evidently the escort of staff officers making a reconnaissance. This detachment, dismounted as the Confederates appeared, quickly springing to their horses, made off precipitately to the rear, eagerly pursued by Forrest to the immediate vicinity of Fort Henry, with a running discharge of fire-arms all the way, resulting in the loss to the Federals of several killed and wounded, a prisoner, some twenty stand of arms, and a lot of overcoats and cavalry equipments." The biography adds that on the way back toward Donelson "another Federal cavalry detachment was observed, and an ambush laid to entrap it; but . . . a premature discharge of fire-arms from some over-eager men upon the advance warned the enemy in time to withdraw by rapid flight."

2. Ibid.; Cooling, 109; Jordan and Pryor, 56.

3. Hughes and Stonesifer, 206–209.

4. O.R. (1)7, 758; Hughes and Stonesifer, 210–211.

5. Ibid., 211.

6. O.R. (1) 7, 278–279.

7. Ibid., 869.

8. Ibid., 864, 867; Stickles, 132, 137.

9. Ibid., 107–120, 151, 233; *The Republican Banner & Nashville Whig*, Oct. 28, 1857, 2; Oct. 31, 1857, 2; Feb. 23, 1858, 2; Stickles, 40–41, 121, 132–133; McGavock, 438, 455. Hughes and Stonesifer say Pillow's Camargo ditch became "perhaps the most celebrated in American military history," 47. He dug it on the inside of his parapet rather than the outside, where it was customarily used to raise the scaling height of the rampart. Pillow's was the laughing stock of regular officers after that.

10. O.R. (1) 7, 272, 328–329.

11. Ibid., 347, 351.

12. O.R. (1) 7, 276, 359.

13. O.R. (1) 7, 342, 347.

14. Ibid., 383–384.

15. Ibid., 870.

16. O.R. (1) 7, 329, 359, 384; Stonesifer, 204.

17. Ibid., 32–34; and McFeely, 56.

18. Stickles, 22–24.

19. Ibid., 10, 14, 24, 34–35, 39.

20. O.R. (1) 7, 271–272, 329; Stonesifer, 204; *Life of Johnston*, 437, 481–482.

21. O.R. (1) 7, 868; Cooling, 131; Stickles, 134–135.

CHAPTER 26

1. Ibid.; O.R. (1) 7, 592, 595, 600; Ambrose, 29, 30.

2. O.R. 7 (1), 267, 407. Captain Jack Davis estimates the Confederate trenches extended three miles, while Lieutenant Colonel Jeremy Gilmer says "nearly two"; Gilmer, as the engineer, would seem the more authoritative.

3. Ibid., 162, 601.

4. Ibid., 163, 609.

5. Wilson, "Reminiscences of General Grant" in Cozzens, *B & L* 5, 120–21; Simon *4*, 193n. Wilson, 119, says that when urged a year later by Wilson and other staff members to get rid of McClernand because he was such an intensely political double-dealer, Grant refused "saying, quietly but firmly: "I can't afford to quarrel with a man whom I have to command."

6. O.R. (1) 7, 172.

7. *B & L* 1, 431.

8. Ibid.; *ORN* (1) 22, 588. Oddly, Walke's initial report to Foote and his later account for *B & L* 1, differ in the matter of the wounded.

9. *Source Book*, 932; O.R. (1) 7, 227.

10. Ibid., 231–232.; Kiner, 24.

11. Ibid., 220, 223.

12. Morton, *The Artillery of Nathan Bedford Forrest's Cavalry*, 27.

13. Davis, *The Orphan Brigade: The Kentucky Confederates Who Couldn't Go Home,* 65.

14. O. R. (1) 7, 343; Morton, 26–28.

15. Kiner, 28; O.R. (1) 7, 227–228.

16. *Source Book,* 932.

17. Ibid., 202, 204 (Colonel Smith's battle report incorrectly dates these events as occurring on the 15th, but it is obvious from a reading of his entire document that they occurred on the 13th); Ibid., 368; Cooling, 145.

18. O.R. (1) 7, 206, 213; *Source Book,* 858.

19. Ibid., 679; *Military Annals of Tennessee,* 516.

20. Cummings, 194–195.

21. *B & L* 1, 431, *ORN* (1) 22, 588.

22. O.R. (1) 7, 394, 398; Stonesifer, 227.

23. Garrett, 15.

24. O.R. (1) 7, 174, 185, etc.

25. Kiner, 28, 29.

26. O.R. (1) 7, 163, 601.

CHAPTER 27

1. Cooling, 148; Kiner, 29.

2. J. L. Scott, *36th Virginia Infantry* (H. E. Howard, Inc., Lynchburg, Virginia, 1987), (1) 7, 330.

3. Ibid., 399.

4. Lew Wallace, 380–383.

5. Cooling, 153; Tucker, 155; Grant, 161,

6. Lew Wallace, op. cit., 387–388.

7. O.R. (1) 7, 338.

8. O.R. (1) 7, 330, 379; Hughes and Stonesifer, 222; Cooling, 149–151.

9. Tucker, 155; *B & L* 1, 433.

10. O.R. (1) 7, 399.

11. Ibid.; *B & L* 1, 433.

12. Wyeth, 47.

13. *B & L* 1, 433; Badeau, 42; Garrett, 14; *Spotwood Fountain (Spot) Terrell Diary,* Tennessee State Library and Archives, 3.

14. *B & L* 1, 433.

15. Ibid., 433–434.

16. Ibid., 435; Tucker, 155–156; O.R. (1) 7, 391, 393, 395, 399–400, 401.

17. *Terrell Diary,* 3–4; O.R. (1) 7, 166.

18. *B & L* 1, 434; Tucker, 156; Stonesifer, 253; O.R. (1) 7, 166.

19. *Source Book,* 663, 859; O.R. (1) 7, 393, 400.

20. Ibid., 255.

21. *ORN* (1) 22, 611, 612.

22. O.R. (1) 7, 268.

23. Ibid., 270–271, 330–331.

24. Ibid., 268. But in the minds of most of the other commanders present, Pillow's pipedream seems to have been regarded as pretty much that, although several mention in their reports that the subject was discussed. See,

for example, Gilmer, 263. Colonel Baldwin of the Fourteenth Mississippi reported on p. 338 of O.R. (1) 7 that the "regiments composing our left wing were to form at 4 a.m. on the same ground and in the same order as on the previous evening, and to advance, under command of General Pillow, to attack the extreme right of the enemy . . . This movement was to be supported by our right wing, under General Buckner, who was to move from the lines at a later period, follow up the first blow, and, *should the combined movement not prove successful in creating a panic in the enemy's ranks, a way might at least be opened, by turning his right, for the egress of our whole force. In anticipation of thus attempting our escape, the men were directed to take knapsacks, blankets, and all the rations that could immediately be provided.*" Notably, the last sentence does not specifically say that Floyd ordered "the men" to take their knapsacks, etc., which suggests that Baldwin and some of the other unit commanders did it on their own "anticipation" that an escape was to be made. It also suggests that they did not regard an enemy "panic" as a probability. Colonel Heiman of the 10th Tennessee, ibid., 369, reported his understanding was that the Confederates would make their assault and then act—retreat or, apparently, pursue a "panic"-stricken enemy—"according to circumstances."

25. Gower and Allen, 591.

CHAPTER 28

1. O.R. (1) 7, 199, 214, 215.
2. O.R. (1) 7, 237.
3. Grant, 162.
4. O.R. (1) 7, 163, 175.
5. Ibid., 384.
6. O.R. (1) 7, 339, 385; Jordan and Pryor, 71, 90n.
7. O.R. (1) 7, 221, 185.
8. Ibid., 216, 217, 218, 339.
9. Ibid., 361, 385.
10. Ibid., 277, 339, 356.
11. Ibid., 216, 277, 340, 385; Stonesifer, 277.
12. Grant, 163; O.R. (1) 7, 159, 163; Simon *4*, 211; Kenneth Williams, 502n.; Smith, 157.
13. O.R. (1) 7, 176.
14. Ibid., 176, 177.
15. Ibid., 190.
16. Cummings, 198–199; Jordan and Pryor, 74–75, 81, 74n.
17. Grant, 163.
18. O.R. (1) 7, 331, 367. For Floyd's inconspicuousness, see Cooling, 174.
19. *William Lewis McKay Diary*, Tennessee State Library and Archives, 37–38; O.R. (1) 7, 331.
20. Ibid., 331, 344–345; Diary of the Rev. Thomas Hopkins Deavenport, Chaplain, Third Tennessee, Tennessee State Library and Archives, 8.
21. *McKay Diary*, 38.
22. O.R. (1) 7, 343.

23. Ibid., 189.

24. Ibid., 201, 343–344.

25. Ibid., 186; Stonesifer, 290; Wyeth, 52. Forrest's report is not clear on which road he took here, and accounts differ, but an examination of the map indicates that this route, remaining a little closer to the flank than is generally assumed in his move to the right, most probably takes him directly from the Gumbart position to that of his next target.

26. Ibid., 196, 199.

27. Faust, 443; Warner, *Generals In Blue*, 282; Grant, 129–130.

28. Stonesifer, 294; O.R. (1) 7, 200. See Bearss-Cooling map, "February 15, 10:30 a.m."; for the "confusion" of the Eighth Illinois, see O.R. (1) 7, 186; for the moving up of the Eleventh to relieve the Thirty-first Illinois, see O.R. (1) 7, 187.

29. Ibid., 196, 199–200; Churchill, "Wounded At Fort Donelson," page first [they are unnumbered].

30. Cooling, 173–174.

31. O.R. (1) 7, 201, 242; *B & L* 1, 402.

32. Brinton, 91.

33. Churchill, page second.

34. Jordan and Pryor, 77.

35. O.R. (1) 7, 282.

36. *Deavenport Diary*, 8.

37. Jordan and Pryor, 81; O.R. (1) 7, 343.

38. Ibid., 343.

39. O.R. (1) 7, 208, 385.

40. Ibid., 208.

41. Jordan and Pryor, 83–84.

42. *B & L* 1, 417.

43. O.R. (1) 7, 236, 243, 251.

44. Ibid., 243–244.

45. Ibid., 282; *B & L* 1, 419–420.

46. *Harper's Pictorial History of the Great Rebellion*, 240.

CHAPTER 29

1. Kiner, 35; Brinton, 118; Simon 3, 10; Sandburg, *Abraham Lincoln*, 466.

2. Grant, 163. Some eminent historians charge Grant with underestimating Pillow and the Confederate command by going to see Foote aboard the gunboat and leaving no one in charge in his stead, but this contention seems arguable. He did misjudge Pillow in assuming Pillow would stay within the Confederate lines, but the fact that Grant would go so far in person to see Foote could as easily indicate how indispensable he regarded the gunboats in any attempt to capture the fort. He was sure that the facility contained more men than he had outside it and knew that it appeared likely to be reinforced at any time. Halleck and the rest of the Union high commanders were terribly afraid that Johnston was falling back from Bowling Green to strike Grant and, as Halleck would anxiously wire McClellan early on February 16 [O.R. (1) 7, 625]: "Unless we can take Fort Donelson very soon we shall have the whole force of the enemy on us.

Fort Donelson is the turning point of the war." Grant almost always exuded confidence, even when doing so sounded hollow, but he also usually tended to be
methodical, and his leaving of no one in command seems as likely to have resulted from an oversight as an immoderate underestimation of his opponents.

3. Richardson, 221; Grant, 163–164; Smith, 157.

4. O.R. (1) 7, 237–238.

5. Isabel Wallace, 160; *B & L* 1, 420.

6. O.R. (1) 7, 237–238.

7. Ibid., 350, 352, 353, 355.

8. Ibid., 348.

9. *Deavenport Diary*, 9.

10. O.R. (1) 7, 253, 238, 332, 348.

11. Ibid., 269, 327, 332–333, 348; Cooling, 181–182.

12. O.R. (1) 7, 287.

13. Simon *4*, 214.

14. *B & L* 1, 421–422; Grant, 164.

15. *B & L* 1, 422; Grant, 164–165; Richardson, 221; Richardson and other
contemporary sources use the "whip" quote, rather than the "be victorious" that
Grant uses in *Personal Memoirs,* and the homelier quote seems more likely to
have been used on the battlefield and is therefore the one used here.

16. Grant, 164–165; Cooling, 185.

17. Ibid., 185; O.R. (1) 7, 223; and *B & L* 1, 423.

18. Kiner, 34, 35; Stonesifer, 313; Brinton, 121; Source Book, 933, 34.

19. *Source Book,* 705; *Magazine of American History,* January 1886, 40; O.R. (1)
7, 230, 378.

20. O.R. (1) 7, 378, 344; Stonesifer, 313.

21. *Deavenport Diary,* 9; O.R. (1) 7, 333, 334, 344.

22. Ibid., 361.

23. *ORN* (1) 22, 588; Cooling, 195; Simon, 224–225; *B & L,* 424; O.R. (1) 7,
233, 238, 245, 361–362.

24. *Source Book,* 935, 937.

25. Brinton, 145.

26. O.R. (1) 7, 160, 164, 283, 294, 334, 386; Morton, 34; Edwin C. Bearss,
Unconditional Surrender: The Fall of Fort Donelson, 3 [Bearss's highly plausible rec-
onciliation of the many conflicting facts and timelines in the accounts of eyewit-
nesses to the surrender is tremendously helpful to an understanding of this con-
voluted event]; Cooling, p. 204.

27. O.R. (1) 7, 255–256; Gower and Allen, 592.

28. O.R. (1) 7, 269, 287, 293, 349.

29. *Deavenport Diary,* 9.

30. Bearss, 4; O.R. (1) 7, 230, 232; Kiner, 34–35.

31. O.R. (1) 7, 222, 234, 239.

32. Churchill, third page.

CHAPTER 30

1. O.R. (1) 7, 287, 293; Bearss, *Unconditional Surrender,* 4–6.

2. Jordan and Pryor, 84, 88, 83n. The number of bullet marks on Forrest's overcoat has been disputed by some as having no evidential basis, but it appears in a footnote in Forrest's authorized biography, which he took responsibility for [viii n.]. Since it involved four days of the fighting, in which he habitually sought the hottest points, it does not seem implausible to this writer.

3. O. R. (1) 7, 287; Bearss, 5–6.

4. O. R. (1) 7, 296; Bearss, 8.

5. O. R. (1) 7, 287; Wyeth, 64; Bearss, 8–9.

6. O. R. (1) 7, 334.

7. Ibid., 295; Bearss, 9.

8. O.R. (1) 7, 283, 296, 334.

9. Ibid.

10. Jordan and Pryor, 88, 91; O.R. (1) 7, 295.

11. Ibid., 269, 298.

12. Ibid., 298, 334.

13. Ibid., 297.

14. Ibid., 294, 298, 300.

15. Ibid., 349, 362, 369–370; Gower and Allen, 592.

16. *Deavenport Diary*, 10; Kegley, "Bushrod Johnson: Soldier and Teacher," 255; O.R. (1) 7, 362; Gower and Allen, 592–593.

17. O. R. (1) 7, 295, 386; Jordan and Pryor, 94n.

18. Hughes and Stonesifer, 237.

19. O.R. (1) 7, 256, 274.

20. Gower and Allen, 593.

21. O.R. (1) 7, 381.

22. Kiner, 36; Cooling, 208.

23. Richardson, 225.

24. Kiner, 36.

25. *Deavenport Diary*, 10; Cooling, 209.

26. Richardson, 223.

27. Ibid., 225, 226.

28. Brinton, 129.

29. O.R. (1) 7, 160, 161; Brinton, 129–130; Cooling, 209.

30. O.R. (1) 7, 381–382; Bearss, 18–19.

31. O. R. (1) 7, 381–382; Bearss, 18.

32. Gower and Allen, 593; Cooling, 204.

33. Wyeth, 60–61; O.R. (1) 7, 378–379.

34. Ibid., 161.

35. Ibid.; Stickles, 168.

36. Lew Wallace, 1, 430.

37. Bearss, 33.

38. Lew Wallace, 1, 430–431.

39. Coffin, 80, 81; Isabel Wallace, 162, 164.

40. Grant, 168; Coffin, 80; Stickles, 171.

41. Gower and Allen, 593.

42. Stickles, 174; Coffin, 83.

43. Simon 4, 221; O.R. (1) 7, 335.

44. Bearss, 38, 45; Simon 4, 229, 226n.; Coffin, 83; O.R. (1) 7, 270, 291, 625, 628.

45. Bearss, 38; Gower and Allen, 594; Coffin, 81–82; Cooling, 212.

46. Ibid., 220, 220n., 221–222n.

47. Bearss, 39; Stickles, 173.

48. Simon 4, 219–220, 224–225, 228.

49. Churchill, third and fourth pages.

50. Morton, 34; Gower and Allen, 594.

51. Simon, *Memoirs of Julia Dent Grant*, 95–96; Simon, *Grant Papers 4*, 226.

PART IV
CHAPTER 31

1. Jordan and Pryor, 92; *Confederate Veteran*, "First Battle Experience—Fort Donelson," vol. xiv, November 1906, 501.

2. Jordan and Pryor, 88–89, 92–93, 89n. Latter-day dissenters as familiar with the ground as Forrest have rested their arguments on the fact that Forrest's men did not ride all the way to Forge Road. Lew Wallace maintained after the war (*B & L* 1, 424) that following his attack to retake the McClernand ground lost the previous morning "the road to Charlotte was again effectually shut, and the battle-field of the morning, . . . was in possession of the Third Division." But not strongly. Wallace's right flank reached only the west side of Forge Road, and mostly with cavalry; master plan map of Fort Donelson by Edwin C. Bearss, April 17, 1959.

3. Jordan and Pryor, 92–93.

CHAPTER 32

1. McKee, *The Great Panic*, 5–8; *Harper's Pictorial History of the Civil War*, 240n.

2. Ibid., 240; Johnston, 493, 495.

3. McKee, 8; Johnston, 499; Cooling, 234; Durham, *Nashville*, 13.

4. Schroeder-Lein, *Confederate Hospitals on the Move*, 47, 53.

5. McKee, 8, 9; Durham, 7, 8, 14.

6. Horn, *The Army of Tennessee*, 99; Womack, *Call Forth The Mighty Men*, 88.

7. B. F. Bunting letter from Murfreesboro, Tennessee, February 26, 1862, fourth page, Tennessee State Library and Archives.

8. Durham, 8, 16; Bunting, op. cit., said that the Rangers followed the exodus out of Bowling Green with about 1,500 troopers after firing the fairgrounds, which contained 50,000 bushels of corn, "pork-houses" containing 250,000 pounds of meat, saddles, tents, etc., that could not be moved and a house in town where their "things" had been stored—"this . . . to prevent their falling into the hands of the enemy," Bunting wrote; "he will get nothing belonging to the Rangers . . . This was the only burning done by military authority," but "fine houses were burning all around the city."

9. Ibid., fifth page; McKee, 20.

10. Cooling, 45; Durham, 16.

11. Ibid., 15; Womack, 92.

12. Durham, 15, 17; *Confederate Veteran*, September 1896, 290; McKee, 11, 14.
13. Durham, 9, 10, 20.
14. Bunting, op. cit., fifth and sixth pages.
15. *Deavenport Diary*, 11.
16. Garrett, 20.

CHAPTER 33

1. Horn, *Tennessee's War*, 63; Durham, 22; Duke, *Morgan's Cavalry*, 58.
2. O.R. (1) 7, 428.
3. Hughes and Stonesifer, 238.
4. O.R. (1) 7, 428; Horn, 63.
5. Johnston, 496; McKee, 19–20. (Floyd's words here may or may not have come at the same time as his appearance with Hardee and Munford. Johnston's biographer describes the mob in the later view of Munford. McKee says that after hearing so little from Pillow, the public square crowd went to the home of S. D. Morgan, where Floyd was staying, and prevailed on him for more details.)
6. Horn, 63–64.
7. Garrett, 20–21.
8. Gower and Allen, 595–596. His recitation of numbers indicates the common Confederate conception rather than the truth. Grant had arrived at Donelson with about fifteen thousand and, by the battle's final day, had about twenty-seven thousand.
9. Simon *4*, 478, 479.
10. Ibid., 233–234, 235.
11. *New York Tribune* reporter Albert D. Richardson, who was with Grant at Donelson, puts the number at 14,620 in *A Personal History of Ulysses S. Grant*, 236. Rations for a few more than fourteen thousand prisoners were reported issued at Cairo, and these may not have included those for the wounded. General Cullum, commanding at Cairo in Grant's absence, wrote General Halleck on February 19 that more than eleven thousand prisoners would have been sent "up the Missisippi" by the following morning and that another 1,400 wounded or sick had been sent to Paducah, Kentucky, and another 1,200 to Mound City, Illinois. McGavock's diary rounded off the figure at twelve thousand and did not seem to be referring to wounded. As for the total in the garrison, the apparently large number who seem to have just walked out over the first couple of days—added to the estimated three thousand who left in organized units with Floyd and Forrest—plausibly indicate that there were at least twenty thousand present during the fighting.
12. Gower and Allen, 595–596; *Deavenport Diary*, 11.
13. Coffin, 85.

CHAPTER 34

1. Garrett, 21; Kiner, 42.
2. Simon *4*, 233n.; Stickles, 175–176.
3. Ibid.

4. O.R. (1) 7, 942.

5. Simon *4*, 233, 237.

6. Cummings, 207–209; O.R. (1) 7, 364, 365. Grant and Johnson were acquainted. Johnson had been in his fourth year at West Point when Grant was a plebe, and both had served in the Mexican War, Grant gloriously and Johnson disastrously.

7. Simon *4*, 233, 235, 236, 238, 241, 245.

8. Newberry, *A Visit To Fort Donelson*, 4, 5.

9. Simon *4*, 227, 235, 245, 246n., 258n.

10. Ibid., 246n., 253n., 257, 258.

11. Ibid., 258n., 260n.; Coffin, 84.

12. Reed, 68. Halleck *had* suggested a combined movement on Nashville to Halleck on January 20, O.R. (1) 8, 508–509, but he only regarded the Tennessee capital as "the first objective point" on the "line of the Cumberland or Tennessee" rivers, "the great central line of the Western theater of war." By now he had to have been all too aware that McClellan was reserving Nashville for Buell.

13. O.R. (1) 7, 628. It frequently has been written or implied that Halleck had become jealous of Grant, but, while it is probable that Halleck had become sensitive to seeing any credit go to Grant while planning to replace Grant with a more qualified officer, to say that Halleck was jealous of Grant resembles saying that a duck hunter has become jealous of his golden retriever because the dog gets to bring back the slain duck. The two men were on such different levels, both militarily and egotistically, that it never would have occurred to Halleck, who regarded himself as author of the Donelson victory, to be jealous of Ulysses Grant, the recipient of his orders—even though, in reality, Halleck had never ordered Grant to do what he did.

14. Thomas and Hyman, 173; Catton, 179; Smith, 166; Simon *4*, 271, 272n.

CHAPTER 35

1. Jordan and Pryor, 99–101.

2. O.R. (1) 7, 429, 430.

3. Ibid., 102; O. R. (1) 7, 429–431; Duke, 58–59.

4. Jordan and Pryor, 103, 104; Wyeth, *Forrest*, 73; O.R. (1) 7, 425–426, 431.

5. Durham, pp. 33, 34.

6. Jordan and Pryor, 104; Durham, 43–45; McKee, 27, 28; O.R. (1) 7, 430; Cooling, 237.

7. McKee, 28. Buell, like McClellan a proslavery Democrat, would often be accused by Northerners, including Northern soldiers, of being more concerned about the rights and welfare of slave-owners than of his own forces. Buell believed that sort of policy was the only kind that would neutralize an insurrection-minded local population; his Northern critics claimed to believe no policy could.

8. Ibid., 425, 659.

9. O.R. (1) 7, 424; Durham, 47.

10. Garrett, *Campbell*, 21–25.

11. *Deavenport Diary*, 12, 13.

Chapter 36

1. Simon 4, 222n., 223n.

2. Ibid., 215n., 216n.

3. Whitelaw Reid, *Ohio In The War*, 446.

4. Ambrose, *Halleck*, 33; O.R. (1) 7, 624; Williams, 260; Smith (from *New York Tribune*, Feb. 18, 1862), 164; exactly why the habitually sober Halleck would be encouraging a St. Louis crowd to be otherwise is hinted at by apparently the same writer who wrote the *New York Tribune* article. That was Albert D. Richardson, one of the earliest Grant biographers, who says in *A Personal History of U. S. Grant*, 235, that after Halleck pasted his own hand-written account of the Donelson victory on the hotel bulletin board, he "growled" to an "excited crowd" but "with unusual humor": "Humph! If Grant's a drunkard and can win such victories, I shall issue an order that any man found sober in St. Louis to-night be punished by fine and imprisonment."

5. O.R. (1), 627, 628, 632, 633.

6. Ibid., 632, 636, 637, 640, 645.

7. Simon 4, 286, 287.

8. Ibid, 298n.; Brinton, 143; Grant, 171–173.

9. O.R. (1) 7, 674, 675, 905; Simon 4, 292; Grant, 175.

10. Ibid., 174, 175.

11. Ibid., 175; Smith, 178; Simon 4, 344n.

12. O.R. (1) 7, 680; Simon 4, 320.

13. Ibid., 222n, 255n, 228n.

14. Ibid., 318, 319.

15. Ibid., 327.

16. Ibid., 331n.

17. O.R. (1) 7, 646; Simon 4, 331.

18. Smith, 177; O.R. (1) 7, 683; Thomas and Hyman, 173–174.

19. Simon 4, 344n.; Marszalek, 86–92, 120; O.R. (1) 7, 683, 684.

20. Hughes, *Belmont*, 195–96; Simpson, 136, 122; Wilson, "Reminiscences of General Grant," *B & L* 5, 119.

21. Simon 4, 353, 354n., 355n. Grant understandably deduced that one of his most decided and powerful "enemys" was McClellan. In his memoir *(McClellan's Own Story)*, 217, the onetime general-in-chief recalled that more than a year after this heated exchange of dispatches, one of his other subordinate generals, William B. Franklin, who had graduated first in the West Point class in which Grant stood twenty-first, "wrote to me that on meeting Grant at Memphis, or some such point on the Mississippi, Grant asked what had made me hostile to him. Franklin replied that he knew I was not hostile but very friendly to him. Grant then said that that could not be so for, without any reason, I had ordered Halleck to relieve him from command and arrest him soon after Fort Donelson, and that Halleck had interfered to save him. I took no steps to undeceive Grant, trusting to time to elucidate the question." Of seeming significance is that by the time Grant put the question to Franklin, McClellan was not only no longer general-in-chief but he also no longer had any command at all, having been sent home by a disgusted Lincoln administra-

tion. Franklin's reply to Grant's inquiry may be less reflective of the truth in March 1862 than it is of the fact that a year later an unemployed McClellan wanted to reconnect with a rising Grant—without antagonizing Halleck, the sitting general-in-chief.

CHAPTER 37

1. O.R. (1) 7, 671; Graf and Haskins, *The Papers of Andrew Johnson*, 197n., xxxv–xxxviii, 202, 203n.; William C. Davis, *Jefferson Davis*, 130–131.

CHAPTER 38

1. J. Harvey Mathes, *General Forrest*, 49. Mathes, a fellow Confederate, knew Forrest in Memphis and had the assistance of Forrest's son in writing his book.

2. *Memphis Avalanche*, Aug. 26, 1861, 2; Henry, *Forrest*, 82.

CHAPTER 39

1. Simon *4*, 306
2. Brinton, 149; Simon *4*, 338n., 376n.
3. Wilson, "Reminiscences of General Grant," *B & L 5*, 120–121.
4. Simon *4*, 271, 284, 305, 306.
5. Ibid., 375.

PART V

1. See Cummings, *Yankee Quaker, Confederate General.* The exhumation occurred with much help from the Sons of Confederate Veterans. Of various local newspaper articles that appeared during the two years that were required to bring the reburial to pass, only one—in *The Nashville Tennessean* of August 17, 1975, p. 8—mentioned Johnson's dismissal from the U.S. Army for attempted bribery. Even this article mentioned only that Johnson came from a Quaker, abolitionist family, not that he was once an active helper of runaway slaves.

2. Source Book, 1389.

3. Warner, *Generals In Gray*, 90; Faust, 265; Steven E. Woodworth, *Jefferson Davis and His Generals*, 80.

4. See Terence J. Winschel, "Fighting Politician: John A. McClernand" in Steven E. Woodworth, ed., *Grant's Lieutenants: From Cairo To Vicksburg*, 129–150; for the Kountz correspondence, see Simon, 275.

5. Hughes and Stonesifer, 241, 270–274, 307, 313, 319, 321; O.R. 7 (1), 320, 321, 325.

6. See Stacy D. Allen, "Lewis Wallace: If He Had Less Rank" in Woodworth, *Grant's Lieutenants*, 70–89; Warner, *Generals In Blue*, 536.

7. Stickles, 420.

8. Slagle, 185; Tucker, 203, 204.

9. Stickles, 172, 324–330.

BIBLIOGRAPHY

Abbott, John S. C. *The History of the Civil War in America.* New York: Henry Bill Publisher, 1864.

Ambrose, Stephen E. *Halleck: Lincoln's Chief of Staff.* Baton Rouge, Louisiana: State University Press, 1962.

American Eagle. Fort Pickering, Tennessee. March 21, 1845.

Anderson, Bern. *By Sea and By River: The Naval History of the Civil War.* New York: Alfred A. Knopf, 1962.

Andrews, J. Cutler. *The North Reports The Civil War.* Pittsburgh: University of Pittsburgh Press, 1955.

Avery, P. O. *History of the Fourth Illinois Cavalry Regiment.* Humboldt, Nebraska: The Enterprise: A Print Shop, 1903.

Badeau, Adam. *The Military History of Ulysses S. Grant.* New York: D. Appleton, 1885.

Bancroft, Frederic. *Slave Trading in the Old South.* Baltimore: J. H. Furst Company, 1931.

Bearss, Edwin. "Unconditional Surrender: The Fall of Fort Donelson." *Tennessee Historical Quarterly*, March–June, 1962.

Bircher, William. *A Drummer Boy's Diary.* St. Paul, Minnesota, 1889.

Black, Robert C., III. *The Railroads of the Confederacy.* Chapel Hill: University of North Carolina Press, 1952.

Bordewich, Fergus M. *Bound for Canaan: The Underground Railroad and the War for the Soul of America.* New York: Harper Collins, 2005.

Brinton, John H. *Personal Memoirs.* New York: Neale Publishing Company, 1914.

Bunting, B. F. *Letter.* Tennessee State Library and Archives, February 26, 1862.

Catton, Bruce. *Grant Moves South.* Boston: Little, Brown and Company, 1960.

Chancery Clerk's Records. Coahoma County, Mississippi.

Chicago Tribune, May 4, 1864.

Churchill, James. "Wounded At Fort Donelson," in *The Campaign for Fort Donelson.* Harrisburg, Pennsylvania: Historical Times, Inc, 1966.

Clarksdale, Mississippi, *Press Register*, July 21, 1984.

Coffin, Charles Carleton. *The Boys of '61 or Four Years of Fighting.* Boston: Estes & Lauriat, 1883.

Confederate Military History. Atlanta: Confederate Publishing Company, 1899.

Confederate Veteran. Nashville: S. A. Cunningham, 1893–1932. Reissue Wilmington, North Carolina: Broadfoot Publishing Company, September 1986.

Connelly, Thomas Lawrence. *Army of the Heartland: The Army of Tennessee, 1861–1862.* Baton Rouge: Louisiana State University Press, 1967.

Cooling, Benjamin Franklin. *Forts Henry and Donelson: The Key to the Confederate Heartland.* Knoxville: University of Tennessee Press, 1987.

Creighton, Wilbur F. Jr. "Wilbur Fisk Foster: Soldier and Engineer," in *Tennessee Historical Quarterly.* Nashville, Fall 1972.

Crummer, Wilbur F. *With Grant at Fort Donelson, Shiloh, and Vicksburg*. Oak Park, Illinois: E. C. Crummer and Company, 1915.

Cummings, Charles M. *Yankee Quaker, Confederate General: The Curious Career of Bushrod Rust Johnson*. Rutherford, New Jersey: Associated University Presses, 1971.

Curlee, Elizabeth M. "The Phenix: Hernando, Mississippi, 1841–46." M.A. thesis, Oxford, University of Mississippi, 1970.

Davis, William C. *The Orphan Brigade: The Kentucky Confederates Who Couldn't Go Home*. New York: Doubleday and Company, 1980.

———. *Jefferson Davis: The Man and His Hour*. New York: Harper Collins, 1991.

Deavenport, The Rev. Thomas H., Chaplain, Third Tennessee Infantry. *Diary*. Tennessee State Library and Archives.

DeSoto County (Mississippi) Times. Hernando, August 14, 1986.

Duke, Basil W. *Morgan's Cavalry*. New York: The Neale Publishing Company, 1906.

Durham, Walter T. *Nashville, The Occupied City: The First Seventeen Months—February 16, 1862, to June 30, 1863*. Nashville: Tennessee Historical Society, 1985.

Egerton, John, ed. *Nashville: The Faces of Two Centuries, 1780–1980*, Nashville: PlusMedia, 1979.

Eicher, John H., and David J. Eicher. *Civil War High Command*. Stanford, California: Stanford University Press, 2001.

Engle, Stephen D. *Don Carlos Buell: Most Promising of All*. Chapel Hill: University of North Carolina Press, 1999.

Faust, Patricia L., ed. *Historical Times Illustrated Encyclopedia of the Civil War*. New York: Harper & Row Publishers, 1986.

Feis, William B. *Grant's Secret Service*. Lincoln, Nebraska: University of Nebraska Press, 2002.

Fisher, Noel C. *War at Every Door: Partisan Politics and Guerrilla Violence in East Tennessee, 1860–1869*. Chapel Hill: University of North Carolina Press, 1997.

Garrett, Jill Knight. *Andrew Jackson Campbell Diary*. Columbia, Tennessee: Jill K. Garrett, 1965.

Goodloe, Albert T. *Confederate Echoes*. Nashville: Smith & Lamar, 1907.

Gosnell, H. Allen. *Guns on the Western Waters*. Baton Rouge: Louisiana State University Press, 1949.

Gould, E. W. *Fifty Years on The Mississippi, or Gould's History of River Navigation*. St. Louis, 1889; reissue, Columbus, Ohio: Long's College Book Company, 1951.

Gower, Herschel, and Allen, Jack, eds. *Pen and Sword: The Life and Journals of Randal W. McGavock*. Nashville: Tennessee Historical Commission, 1959.

Graf, Leroy, and Ralph W. Haskins. *The Papers of Andrew Johnson*, Vol. 5, 1861–1862. Knoxville: University of Tennessee Press, 1979.

Graham, Eleanor, ed. *Nashville: A Short History and Selected Buildings*. Nashville: Historical Commission of Nashville–Davidson County, 1974.

Grant, Ulysses S. *Personal Memoirs*. New York: Penguin Books, reissue, 1999. Charles L. Webster & Company, 1885.

Hagedorn, Ann. *Beyond The River: The Untold Story of the Heroes of the Underground Railroad*. New York: Simon & Schuster, 2002.

Harper's Pictorial History of the Great Rebellion. Chicago: McDonnell Brothers, 1866–1868.

Henry, Robert S. *As They Saw Forrest.* Jackson, Tennessee: McCowat–Mercer Press, 1956.

———. *"First With The Most" Forrest.* Indianapolis: Bobbs–Merrill Company, 1944.

Hoppin, James M.. *Life of Andrew H. Foote.* New York, 1874.

Horn, Stanley F. *Tennessee's War, 1861–1865, described by participants.* Nashville: Tennessee Civil War Centennial Commission, 1965.

———. *The Army of Tennessee: A Military History.* Indianapolis: Bobbs-Merrill Company, 1941.

Hughes, Nathaniel Cheairs Jr. *The Battle of Belmont.* Chapel Hill: University of North Carolina Press, 2002.

———. *General William J. Hardee: Old Reliable.* Baton Rouge: Louisiana State University Press, 1965.

Hughes, Nathaniel Cheairs Jr., and Roy P. Stonesifer Jr. *The Life and Wars of Gideon J. Pillow.* Chapel Hill: University of North Carolina Press, 1993.

Humes, Thomas W. *The Loyal Mountaineers of East Tennessee.* Knoxville: Ogden Brothers & Company, 1888.

Johnson, Adam. *The Partisan Rangers of the Confederate States Army.* Louisville, Kentucky: G. G. Fetter, 1904.

Johnson, Robert Erwin. *Rear Admiral John Rodgers.* Annapolis: Naval Institute Press, 1967.

Johnson, Robert U., and Clarence C. Buel. *Battles and Leaders of the Civil War,* vol. 1. New York, 1887.

Johnston, William Preston. *The Life of General Albert Sidney Johnston.* New York: DaCapo Press reissue, 1997.

Jordan, Thomas, and J. P. Pryor. *The Campaigns of Lieut.-Gen. N. B. Forrest and of Forrest's Cavalry.* New Orleans, 1868; New York: Morningside Press reissue, 1977.

Kegley, Tracy M. "Bushrod Johnson: Soldier and Teacher," in *Tennessee Historical Quarterly,* September 1948.

Kiner, F. F. *One Year's Soldiering.* Lancaster, Pennsylvania, 1863.

Kiper, Richard L. *Major General John Alexander McClernand: Politician in Uniform.* Kent, Ohio: Kent State University Press, 1999.

Lewis, Lloyd. *Captain Sam Grant.* Boston: Little Brown and Company, 1950.

Lytle, Andrew. *Bedford Forrest and His Critter Company.* Seminole, Florida: Green Key Press, 1984, reissue.

Magazine of American History. New York and Chicago, A. S. Barnes & Company, January 1886.

Marszalek, John F. *Commander of All Lincoln's Armies: A Life of General Henry W. Halleck.* Cambridge, Massachusetts: The Belknap Press of Harvard University Press, 2004.

Mathes, J. Harvey. *General Forrest.* New York: D. Appleton and Company, 1902.

Maury, Dabney H. *Recollections of a Virginian.* New York, 1894.

McClellan, George B. *McClellan's Own Story.* New York, 1887.

McFeely, William S. *Grant: A Biography.* New York: W. W. Norton & Company, 1981.

McKay, William Lewis. *Diary.* Tennessee State Library & Archives.

McKee, John Miller. *The Great Panic.* Nashville: Johnson & Whiting, 1862. Reissue, Elder–Sherbourne, 1977.

McKinney, Francis F. *Education in Violence: The Life of George H. Thomas and the History of the Army of the Cumberland.* Detroit: Wayne State University Press, 1961.

McMurray, W. J. *History of the Twentieth Tennessee Volunteer Regiment, C.S.A.* Nashville: Publication Committee (W. I. McMurry, Deering I. Roberts, and Ralph J. Neal), 1904.

Memphis *Daily Appeal.* April 7, 1857; June 27 and 28, 1857; May 24, 1858; June 25, 1858; July 21, 1858; March 23, 1859; August 11 and 23, 1860; September 11, 1860.

Memphis *Eagle & Enquirer.* April 11, 1858.

Memphis *Weekly Appeal.* April 7, 1858.

Memphis *Daily Avalanche.* August 6 and 15, 1860.

Military Annals of Tennessee. Nashville, 1886.

Morton, John Watson. *The Artillery of Nathan Bedford Forrest's Cavalry.* Nashville: Publishing House of the Methodist Episcopal Church South, 1909.

Nashville *Republican Banner.* July 5, 1861; October 15, 1861.

Nashville *Weekly Patriot.* February 16, 1862.

Newberry, Dr. J. S. "A Visit To Fort Donelson, Tenn., for the Relief of the Wounded of Feb'y 15, 1862; a Letter." Tennessee State Library and Archives.

Nicolay, John G., and John Hay. *Abraham Lincoln: A History.* New York: Century, 1904.

Official Records of the Union and Confederate Navies in the War of the Rebellion. Washington: U.S. Government Printing Office, 1894–1914.

Parks, Joseph H. *General Leonidas Polk, C.S.A.: The Fighting Bishop.* Baton Rouge: Louisiana State University Press, 1962.

Moore, Frank. *Rebellion Record.* New York, 1862–1868.

Parker, Theodore R. "William J. Kountz, Superintendent of River Transportation Under McClellan, 1861–1862," in *Western Pennsylvania Historical Magazine,* Vol. 21, No. 4, December 1938.

Philadelphia Inquirer. September 6, 1861; February 8, 1862.

Perret, Geoffrey. *Ulysses S. Grant: Soldier and President.* New York: Random House, 1997.

Porter, Horace D. *Campaigning With Grant.* Secaucus, New Jersey: Blue and Gray Press, 1984, reissue.

Rainey, W. H. *W. H. Rainey's Memphis City Directory and General Business Advertiser for 1855–56.* Memphis, 1855.

Ramage, James A. *Rebel Raider: The Life of General John Hunt Morgan.* Lexington, Kentucky: University of Kentucky Press, 1986.

Reed, Rowena. *Combined Operations in the Civil War.* Annapolis, Maryland: Naval Institute Press, 1978.

Reid, Whitelaw. *Ohio In The War.* Columbus, Ohio: Eclectic Publishing Company, 1893.

Republican Banner and Nashville Whig. October 28, 1857; February 23, 1858; October 31, 1858.

Richardson, Albert D. *A Personal History of Ulysses S. Grant.* Hartford, Connecticut, 1868.

Roland, Charles P. *Albert Sidney Johnston: Soldier of Three Republics.* Austin: University of Texas Press, 1964.

Sandburg, Carl. *Abraham Lincoln: The War Years,* vol. 1. New York: Harcourt, Brace and Company, 1939.

Schroeder-Lein, Glenna R. *Confederate Hospitals on the Move: Samuel H. Stout and the Army of Tennessee.* Columbia: University of South Carolina Press, 1994.

Schutz, Wallace J., and Walter N. Trenerry. *Abandoned by Lincoln: A Military Biography of John Pope.* Chicago: University of Illinois Press, 1990.

Scott, J. L. 36th Virginia Infantry. Lynchburg, Virginia: H. E. Howard, Inc., 1987.

Sears, Stephen W. Ed. *The Civil War Papers of George B. McClellan.* New York: Perseus Books, 1992.

Sherman, William T. *Memoirs.* Westport, Connecticut: Greenwood Press, 1972, reissue.

Simon, John Y. *Personal Memoirs of Julia Dent Grant.* New York: G. P. Putnam's Sons, 1975.

Simon, John Y. Ed. *The Papers of Ulysses S. Grant.* Carbondale: Southern Illinois University Press, 1972.

Simpson, Brooks D. *Ulysses S. Grant, Triumph Over Adversity: 1822–1865.* New York: Houghton-Mifflin Company, 2000.

Slagle, Jay. *Ironclad Captain: Seth Ledyard Phelps and the U.S. Navy, 1841–1864.* Kent, Ohio: Kent State University Press, 1996.

Smith, Jean Edward. *Grant.* New York: Simon and Schuster, 2001.

Stickles, Arndt. *Simon Bolivar Buckner: Borderland Knight.* Chapel Hill: University of North Carolina Press, 1940.

Stonesifer, Roy P. Jr. *The Forts Henry-Heiman and Fort Donelson Campaigns: A Study of Confederate Command.* Ph.D. dissertation. Ann Arbor, Michigan: University Microfilms, Inc., 1980.

Temple, O. P. *East Tennessee and the Civil War.* Cincinnati: R. Clarke Company, 1899.

Terrell, Spotwood Fountain. *Diary.* Tennessee State Library & Archives.

Thomas, Benjamin P., and Harold M. Hyman. *Stanton: The Life and Times of Lincoln's Secretary of War.* New York: Alfred A. Knopf, 1962.

Tucker, Spencer C. *Andrew Foote: Civil War Admiral on Western Waters.* Annapolis: Naval Institute Press, 2000.

U.S. *The Fort Henry and Fort Donelson Campaigns.* Fort Leavenworth, Kansas: The General Service Schools, 1923.

Van West, Carroll, ed. *Tennessee Encyclopedia of History and Culture.* Nashville: Rutledge Hill Press, 1998.

Walke, Henry. *Naval Scenes and Reminiscences of the Civil War in the United States on the Southern and Western Waters.* New York, 1877.

Wallace, Isabel. *Life and Letters of General W.H.L. Wallace.* Chicago: Lakeside Press, 1909.

Wallace, Lew. *An Autobiography*. New York: Harper & Brothers, 1906.

War of the Rebellion, A Compilation of the Official Records of the Union and Confederate Armies. Washington: Government Printing Office, 1880–1901.

Warner, Ezra J. *Generals In Gray*. Baton Rouge: Louisiana State University Press, 1959.

———. *Generals In Blue*, Baton Rouge: Louisiana State University Press, 1964.

Weigley, Russell F. *The American Way of War*. New York: MacMillan Publishing Company, 1973

Western Pennsylvania Historical Magazine. December 1938.

White, Robert H. *Messages of the Governors of Tennessee, 1857–1869*, vol. 5. Nashville: Tennessee Historical Commission, 1959.

Williams, Kenneth P. *Lincoln Finds A General*, vol. 3. New York: The MacMillan Company, 1952.

Williams, T. Harry. *P.G.T. Beauregard, Napoleon in Gray*. Baton Rouge: Louisiana State University Press, 1955.

Wilson, James Harrison. "Reminiscences of General Grant," in Peter Cozzens, *Battles & Leaders of the Civil War*, Volume Five. Chicago: University of Illinois Press, 2002.

Womack, Bob. *Call Forth The Mighty Men*. Bessemer, Alabama: Colonial Press, 1987.

Woodworth, Steven E. *Jefferson Davis and His Generals*. Lawrence: University of Kansas Press, 1990.

Woodworth, Steven E., ed. *Grant's Lieutenants: From Cairo to Vicksburg*. Lawrence: University of Kansas Press, 2001.

Worsham, W. J. *The Old Nineteenth Tennessee Regiment, C.S.A.* Knoxville: Paragon Printing Company, 1902.

Wyeth, John Allan. *That Devil Forrest: The Life of General Nathan Bedford Forrest*. New York: Dayton, Ohio: Morningside Bookshop, 1975, reissue.

ACKNOWLEDGMENTS

Many deserve thanks for aid and inspiration in the development of this book.

First, immeasurable gratitude must go to my incomparable wife, who repeatedly forgave her husband for his habit of being AWOL upstairs, snowbound in February 1862.

Attorney Daniel Merriman of Knoxville and Maryville, Tennessee, an extraordinarily dedicated devotee of history, lent invaluable early insight and encouragement (when they were most needed) after kindly consenting to be the manuscript's first reader.

My sister, former English teacher Carol Carlson of Sneads Ferry, North Carolina, provided much early assistance in line editing for inconsistencies and typographical mistakes.

Historian John Y. Simon of Southern Illinois University, who as longtime editor of the *The Papers of Ulysses S. Grant* is the preeminent authority on Grant, most graciously imparted not only analysis but also enormously appreciated encouragement.

Historian John F. Marszalek, professor emeritus at Mississippi State University and eminent authority on Henry Halleck, despite deep disagreement with a lifelong journalist's non-academic approach, nevertheless volunteered with incredible generosity to line edit the manuscript (which I never would have presumed to request) and to volunteer a host of detailed suggestions that materially improved the final draft.

Jim Jobe and the staff of the Fort Donelson National Military Park graciously responded to many questions and other demands on their time.

One-of-a-kind literary agent Deborah Grosvenor, a former book editor, deserves huge credit for going many extra miles and devoting countless hours of thought and preparation to introducing the project to publishers in a commanding form.

Longtime journalistic colleague and onetime roommate Rudy Abramson, a distinguished author and editor, has my deep gratitude for introducing me to Deborah—as well as for his treasured friendship of more than forty years.

The executive editor at Basic Books, Lara Heimert, excellence-driven and brilliant, has been a wonder to work with in making the manuscript as palatable as a final product can be, given the limitations of the author.

Lori Hobkirk of The Book Factory, Brandon Proia of Perseus Books, and Cynthia Young of Sagecraft Desktop Publishing and Design, have contributed much extra effort in trying to make the maps, pictures, and type as attractive and reader-friendly as possible.

Media design professor Ray Wong of Middle Tennessee State University selflessly contributed his time and expertise to carefully partition and copy parts of the Bearss-Cooling maps of the Fort Donelson battle's final day.

Journalism professor and author David Badger of Middle Tennessee State University provided the great favor of helping find and check out many useful books from the MTSU library.

The staffs of a number of other libraries have been similarly helpful. These include the Jean and Alexander Heard Library at Vanderbilt University; the Tennessee State Library and Archives, which most notably is to be credited for the extraordinary Bearss-Cooling maps of the final battle at Fort Donelson, which were done under the auspices of the National Park Service—drawn by Edwin Bearss, compiled by B. F. Cooling, and drafted by L. S. Wall—and then donated to the TSLA; and my hometown facility, the Justin Potter Library in Smithville, Tennessee, where staff members have acquired books through interlibrary loan, made copies of book excerpts and maps, and provided other much-needed services. Thanks also are due the St. Louis County Library in St. Louis, the Senator John Heinz Pittsburgh Regional History Center, and the Public Library of Cincinnati and Hamilton County.

Valeisha Kelly of Visions Photography was very helpful in speedily getting pictures taken and ready for publication.

Any mistakes herein are the fault of the author and in no way connected to any of the kind people above.

Finally, respectful thanks are extended to the historians who have labored over nearly a century and a half—from Albert Richardson, Thomas Jordan, and J. P. Pryor to Edwin Bearss, B. F. Cooling, and John Y. Simon—to research, write, and illuminate this subject. Even more gratitude must go to the soldiers and sailors at Fort Henry and Fort Donelson and to two extraordinary men for their courageous roles in an epic drama: Ulysses Grant and Nathan Bedford Forrest, quintessentially American warriors.

INDEX